GREEK GODS, HUMAN LIVES

GREEK

What We Can Learn from Myths

GODS,

MARY LEFKOWITZ

HUMAN

YALE UNIVERSITY PRESS New Haven & London

LIVES

Designed by Richard Hendel
Set in Quadraat type by The Composing Room of Michigan, Inc.
Printed in the United States of America by R. R. Donnelley & Sons

The Library of Congress has cataloged the hardcover edition as follows:

Lefkowitz, Mary R., 1935–
Greek gods, human lives : what we can learn from myths / Mary
Lefkowitz.
p.   cm.
Includes bibliographical references and index.
ISBN 0-300-10145-7 (alk. paper)
1. Mythology, Greek.   I. Title.
BL790 .L44 2003
292.1'3—dc21   2003010659

A catalogue record for this book is available from the British Library.

The paper in this book meets the guidelines for permanence and durability
of the Committee on Production Guidelines for Book Longevity of the
Council on Library Resources.

ISBN 0-300-10769-2 (pbk. : alk. paper)

10 9 8 7 6 5 4 3

Front-matter illustrations: frontispiece, detail from p. 42; p. vi, detail from
p. 22; p. viii, detail from p. 121.

FOR AMALIA MEGAPANOU

CONTENTS

PREFACE

The Greek gods are still part of our lives, even though we do not literally believe in them. They survive in our imagination through classical mythology, because myths are in essence stories about the supernatural in human life. But sometimes how we read the myths makes it difficult for us to see that they are essentially stories about religious experience. We first learn about Jason and the Argonauts or the Trojan War as the stories are told in narratives by modern writers. We concentrate on the fate of the heroes. But the ancient writers who originally told these stories never failed to take note of the actions of the gods.

This book describes the central role played by the gods in narratives by Greek and Roman writers. Rather than talk about individual myths in isolation, I shall examine the role played by the gods, retelling the stories in outline. I shall keep close to the shape and emphasis of the original narratives so that readers can follow the discussion even if they have never read the texts before. But I hope that even people who have read the texts many times will discover that they can better understand the ancient narratives if they concentrate on the gods. Many of the problems we encounter when reading ancient texts disappear if we do not forget about the gods or dismiss them as irrelevant.

I have written this book because in recent years most popular writers about Greek mythology treat the gods as if they were another species of human being. Even classical scholars still write about the gods with some condescension, as if they were simply extensions of the human psyche or mere literary conventions. Hugh Lloyd-Jones in *The Justice of Zeus* (1983) and Jasper Griffin in *Homer on Life and Death* (1980) have shown why these approaches are mistaken. This book offers detailed evidence from a variety of sources that supports their point of view. My own understanding of Greek piety also owes much to Jon Mikalson's *Honor Thy Gods: Popular Religion in Greek Tragedy* (1991).

This book seeks to explore in great detail and in a wide range of literature the importance of the gods' role in the *Iliad*, to which Giulia Sissa and Marcel Detienne briefly call attention in *The Daily Life of the Gods* (1989). In *The Gods in Epic* (1991), D. C. Feeney raises for a scholarly audience many stimulating questions about the function of the gods in the fictional worlds created by Hellenistic poets.

But whereas Feeney describes how poets comment on one another's works through their characterization of the gods, this book asks different questions of a broader range of the materials. I concentrate on descriptions of divine action in order to show how ancient writers call attention both to the power and to the limitations of the traditional religion.

In this book I have followed wherever possible the conventions of spelling and abbreviation used in the third edition of *The Oxford Classical Dictionary* (1996). The letters with macrons, *ē* and *ō*, indicate the Greek letters *eta* and *omega*, but I have not included them in familiar names, such as Athena, that are not susceptible to misreading in the way that names like Dikē and Demophoōn might be. Unless otherwise noted, citations of the original Greek sources refer to line numbers (such as *Theogony* 22), or, for longer works, to book and line numbers (that is, *Odyssey* 6.42 means book 6, line 42). Translations, unless otherwise noted, are my own.

ACKNOWLEDGMENTS

My thanks first of all to the gods, without whose aid no human achievement is possible, for helping me to understand why and how they sometimes choose to take an interest in the lives of mortal beings.

I might never have written this book if friends and colleagues had not urged me to do so and provided me with moral support and much helpful criticism over the course of many years. Here thanks are due especially to Hugh Lloyd-Jones, Glen Hartley, and Lynn Chu. I am particularly grateful to Larisa Heimert of Yale University Press, whose astute comments have improved every chapter; to Elizabeth Johnson, for her close and patient scrutiny; and to Corinne Gentilesco for helping me track down appropriate illustrations. I also acknowledge the generous support of Wellesley College in the form of a sabbatical research grant and additional grants for research assistance.

I am grateful to the University of California Press for permission to use quotations from Aeschylus, *Oresteia*, edited and translated by Hugh Lloyd-Jones (© 1979, Hugh Lloyd-Jones), and to the publishers and the Trustees of the Loeb Classical Library to use quotations from Sophocles, volumes 20 and 21, translated by Hugh Lloyd-Jones (Cambridge: Harvard University Press, copyright © 1944 by the President and Fellows of Harvard College; The Loeb Classical Library is a registered trademark of the President and Fellows of Harvard College).

Introduction

Nothing, or virtually nothing, happens without the gods. That is the message of most ancient Greek myths, at least as the Greeks themselves tell the stories. This message may seem surprising to us today, because the gods depart so much from our notion of divinity. We find it hard to imagine that even the Greeks took their gods seriously, or that they supposed that such gods as theirs might control the course of events and intervene in their personal lives. But in the great narratives of myths, such as the *Iliad* and the *Odyssey*, and in Athenian drama, the gods are always there, working in the background, even if not directly before our eyes. The myths are not frivolous, although they are often told in ways that entertain or delight us. And even gods who do not conform to our notions of what a god is can nonetheless be considered divine and worthy of our attention and respect.

In this book I want to take you back in time, so you can see what the myths meant to audiences in the ancient world, and how they helped ancient people understand and come to terms with the world around them. Although I believe that the myths still have much to teach us today, I am not going to suggest that these ancient narratives can begin to answer all the serious questions we are confronted with about the nature of human life and the meaning of our existence. Ancient life was in many ways simpler than ours, and more continuously dangerous. Ancient people could not avoid seeing death all around them. They could not put it aside, sanitize it, or distance themselves from it as easily as many of us can today. The animals they ate they killed themselves; death came to families sooner and with greater frequency, for men, women, and children alike. Life was short and hard, even for those who possessed great wealth and had gained some limited control over their environment. In such conditions, beings like the gods who are supposed to be undying, ageless, and powerful command special respect and admiration.

Seeing the myths in this way, as the ancients saw them, shows why we do the Greeks an injustice if we assume that their religion was frivolous or immoral. The stories of heroes, such as the *Odyssey*, not only describe suffering and conquest but also, and more importantly, help us understand what it is to be human, with all the limitations of the human condition. The gods care deeply about those human beings who are related to them by blood. They will also support exceptional people who pay them particular honor and display qualities that the gods respect. But they are not, in general, particularly concerned with the lot or hardships of humans as a whole.

The gods' partisanship for particular mortals has often been understood as mere favoritism, and it is certainly true that having divine connections gives some mortals a distinct advantage over others. Ultimately, however, even favoritism does not succeed unless it is bestowed with justice. Because the mortal man Paris, when given the choice, judged Aphrodite more lovely than the goddesses Hera and Athena, she promised him the most beautiful woman in the world. But the most beautiful woman in the world, Helen, was a gift that could not be given without violating the laws of marriage and hospitality. As soon as Paris took Helen away from Menelaus, her husband in Sparta, and brought her across the sea to his home in Troy, he called upon himself the enmity of Zeus, the god who had a particular interest in the laws of hospitality, and Hera, the goddess of marriage.

Paris also made the mistake of angering the powerful goddesses Hera and Athena by not deciding the beauty contest in their favor. Hera and Athena turned against the Trojans when they let Paris keep Helen in Troy and refused to return her to Menelaus. The two goddesses used their considerable powers to aid Menelaus and his allies from Greece when they came to fight against Troy, and Zeus, although he cared for the Trojans and their allies, ultimately allowed the Greeks to conquer Troy. Justice is done in the end, but the process is neither neat nor swift, thanks to the conflicts between the different gods. Because some gods are more powerful than others or more responsive to individual human needs, mortals can never be confident of their support, or know for sure that pleasing one god will not result in offending another. Zeus is the most powerful god, but unlike God in the Old Testament he does not have absolute control. So mortals can never be certain that they have done the right thing, and there is no one set of divine laws that they can follow. Nonetheless, the notion of conflict among the gods offers a realistic but unsentimental means of explaining why things do not always turn out the way we expect them to.

Why do mortals find it so difficult to understand that the gods are ultimately concerned with justice? One important reason is that the gods work on a different timetable. Because they do not grow old or die, they have little sense of urgency. The gods do not need to work to survive; they are supplied with nectar and ambrosia and a secure home on Mount Olympus. Homer does not fail to remind his audience of the contrast between the lives of gods and those of men. As he describes it in the *Odyssey*, "They say that there [Mount Olympus] is the seat of the gods, ever secure: it is not shaken by winds or drenched with rain nor do snow-

Aphrodite, Athena, and Hera (holding an apple) approach Paris, who sits playing his lyre at right. (Red-figure hydria, 500–450 B.C., by the Painter of the Oinoche in Yale. British Museum, London, E 178.)

storms assail it, but always brightness is spread about it, without clouds, and a clear light plays about it. There the blessed gods take pleasure every day" (*Odyssey* 6.42–46).

The gods are not only "blessed"; they are often described by the phrase "they who live at their ease" *(rheia zōontes)*. That is why (as mortals often fail to understand) gods do not always take the time or trouble to become involved in the affairs of humans. Despite their occasional interest in mortal matters, they regard humanity as an inferior species, vastly different from themselves. The gods who "live at their ease" on Mount Olympus with Zeus did not create mortals in their present form, although they are prepared to show gratitude for the honors humans give them. They did not make human beings in the likeness of gods to rule all the creatures on earth, or bless them and tell them to be fruitful and multiply, as God does in the Old Testament (Genesis 1.26–29). Before any women existed on earth, men were the special concern of Prometheus, a minor god from an earlier generation of deities. The present condition of humanity depends heavily on how Zeus chooses to deal with Prometheus. According to the epic poet Hesiod, Zeus hid the means of life from men, so that they need to work long and hard to survive. He took fire away from them, because Prometheus deceived him. When Prometheus persisted in his defiance by bringing the fire back, Zeus sent them women as a punishment, not to be their helpmeets and companions. In the end, he gave them justice, though only in return for a favor that Prometheus granted him.

If human characters in the myths express doubts about the intentions of the gods and their involvement in human life, it is because they cannot appreciate or do not want to understand how different the gods are from themselves. Some of the confusion stems from the ways gods choose to manifest themselves to mortals.[1] Often a god will assume the form of some mortal familiar to the person he or she wishes to address, or take on the aspect of some person one might expect to meet in the course of an ordinary day, a young girl or an old woman. When gods speak to mortals, or mortals describe them speaking to each other, they speak Greek and talk like human beings. In art, they appear in human dress, though in larger size than the mortals they accompany. When the craftsman god Hephaestus depicts an army attacking a city on the shield he makes for Achilles, he shows how "they went forward, and Ares and Pallas Athena led them, both worked in gold, and they were clad in golden clothing, beautiful and large with their weapons, like gods, both standing out clearly, and the mortals were smaller" (Iliad 18.516–19).

The similarity of the gods' appearance to that of humans causes confusion and allows mortals to suppose that gods are more like themselves than they really are. So the myths show over and over again that the resemblance between god and mortal is superficial, and the difference in power and intelligence insuperable. As the poet Pindar wrote, "The race of men and that of gods is one; from a single mother [Earth] we both draw breath, but every separate power keeps us apart, so that man is nothing, and for the other the brilliant heaven eternally remains a safe dwelling place" (Nemean Odes 6.1–4). He says in another poem, "Man is a dream of a shadow" (Pythian Odes 8.95–96). The most one can hope for is a moment of excellence or success in which one might appear to resemble a god, however fleetingly: "Whenever the Zeus-given glory comes, a bright light falls upon men and life is sweet" (8.96–97).[2] Humans will inevitably strive to obtain more, but it is dangerous to forget one's limitations as a mortal, and we mortals do so at our peril. Many myths address this tendency on the part of human beings to forget who they are. It is an underlying theme in the most influential works of Greek literature, the Iliad and the Odyssey, and it is important in virtually every extant Greek drama.

How can we begin to understand what ancient writers wanted to tell us about the gods if we cannot interview them or talk with any members of their audiences? We can begin to get an impression of their assumptions about the nature of the gods by examining what they had to say about another religious tradition, Christianity, when it first became necessary for them to deal with it, in the second century A.D. How would they, as non-believers in one god, have described the story of creation in the Hebrew Bible, or the New Testament story of Jesus' death and resurrection? Why did they find it hard to accept the notion that Jesus was divine when they themselves addressed their emperors as gods?

Around A.D. 178, an educated pagan named Celsus composed a treatise, *True Doctrine*, attacking Jewish and Christian beliefs. We know nothing about Celsus's life and background, but it is clear that he found many biblical narratives hard to believe and was rather shocked by the Christian notion of divinity. Celsus could understand why a mortal would want to become a god. But reversing the process, as Jesus was said to have done, seemed to him irrational and unworthy of belief. Christianity's early Greek defender Origen, in *Against Celsus*, summarized Celsus's argument like this: "The god is good and beautiful and happy, and lives in what is most beautiful and excellent. If he comes down to men, he must be transformed, and the transformation will be from good to evil and from beautiful to ugly and from happiness to misery and from the best to the worst. Who would choose to be transformed in this way?" (*Against Celsus* 4.14).[3]

Celsus did not believe that a god would want to take the form of an ordinary person without power or refuse to defend himself against attack. In his view, a real god would be someone like the Roman emperor, with unlimited power and authority, not like Jesus, who lived in poverty and hired himself out as a workman (1.28, 29). Why would a god care about "sinners, poor people, and refuse" and associate with them (6.53)? A real god would not eat mortal food instead of nectar and ambrosia (1.69, 70). He considered the narrative of Jesus' birth absurd. Why would God have singled out an obscure woman who was neither wealthy nor of royal birth (1.39)? Nor could Celsus believe in the story of the death and resurrection of Jesus. A god would have behaved with dignity when confronted with human mockery and disaster (2.33). Ichor, not blood, would have flowed from the wounds of a god (2.36). Celsus could not understand how dead human beings could be restored to life and join the immortals (2.77, 5.14). In his religion the dead were kept apart both from the living and from the gods of Olympus. In Greek stories men who disappeared and then returned many generations later always returned as themselves in human form, never as gods (3.26).

Celsus was astonished that Christians were expected to rely on faith rather than proof (1.12). Why be asked to accept without questioning fantastic tales like the stories of Jesus' birth and resurrection (6.8)? In the religious tradition to which he belonged, asking questions of the gods was not considered impious; interrogation of the gods was an accepted means of trying to discover what the gods wanted humans to do or to know. Celsus asked, not unreasonably, how Christians could object to people who worshiped more than one god when they themselves worshiped both Jesus and his father (8.12). And he wondered why the Christians attacked people for making statues of their gods when they themselves worshiped a mere mortal: "Won't everyone think you ridiculous, when you attack other gods who have made themselves manifest as idols, and worship not an idol but an actual corpse who is more miserable than the real idols themselves, and seek for a father similar to him?" (7.40).

If we are to see the ancient gods from the point of view Celsus had, we need to assume that the universe was not designed for human beings, and that gods exist primarily for their own benefit rather than for ours. We must assume that they take an interest in human beings only when their own interests are involved, such as their own honor and the maintenance of justice. We need to understand that gods favor only those human beings who can further their interests, and that these will tend to be leaders, heroes, and aristocrats rather than followers. It is a different way of looking at the world, although it nonetheless has some influence on us because of the importance the myths have always had in Western literature. Many of the ideas we still hold sacred today have their origins in Greek myth and in the ancient Greeks' tragic notion of human experience.

The aim of this book is to show how important the gods are in human life. There is a need for such a book, because in the most popular treatments of Greek myth the role of the gods is often misrepresented and almost never sufficiently emphasized. The ancient Greek notion of divinity is very different from that of the modern monotheistic religions. Most of us have been raised to think (however vaguely) that there can be only one god, a god who is essentially good and who is interested in the welfare of humankind. The God of the Old Testament hands down laws for his worshipers to follow. The Greek gods provide no one authoritative source of written guidance, and in their dealings with human beings they can often appear capricious, petty, and self-indulgent. They choose human beings as sexual partners, in most cases only to abandon them. Such sexual involvement can appear to us both cruel and inappropriate because sexuality is irrelevant, and even foreign, to both the Hebrew and Christian notions of divinity.

Modern writers and readers often find it hard to imagine that the ancient Greeks could have believed in their own very different gods. They are sympathetic to the ancient thinkers and writers who themselves were critical of how the gods were portrayed in epic, and they are comfortable with the portrayal of the gods in the works of later poets, where they appear to behave more like human beings than like deities, without concern for the common good or for justice. But today more people learn about Greek mythology from modern summaries of the stories than from any ancient writers. Some of the most popular English-language mythology books offer accounts of the gods that are at best misleading, as is easily illustrated by a few examples of how the role of the gods is characterized in books that can be found on the shelves of bookstores and public libraries.

In *The Age of Fable; or, the Beauties of Mythology*, first published in 1855, Thomas Bulfinch (1796–1867) began his account of the "romantic poem of the Odyssey" with the departure of Odysseus from Troy. The *Odyssey* itself begins with the goddess Calypso holding Odysseus in her power, and Athena approaching her father

Zeus to seek his release; for seven years Odysseus has wanted to return home to his wife and son, but Calypso will not let him. It is only after Athena intervenes on his behalf that he is able to begin his voyage home. Zeus allows Odysseus to return because he has always honored the gods, and he admires the man's intelligence. Bulfinch's telling of the story in chronological order immediately diverts the emphasis of the original poem away from the gods. Similarly, Bulfinch ends his account of the *Odyssey* with Odysseus defeating the suitors who have been courting his wife, Penelope.[4] But Homer's narrative continues after Odysseus has killed all the suitors and been reunited with her. In the last book of the *Odyssey* the suitors' relatives seek vengeance, and there is war between them and the family of Odysseus. Here again the gods have a crucial role. At the very end of the poem Zeus and Athena make sure that Odysseus does not carry his revenge too far; the last speech in the poem is given to Athena.

The gods are more in evidence in Edith Hamilton's *Mythology*, a book first published in 1940 and still widely available. Hamilton (1867–1963) often quotes from the ancient sources, but she makes her gods more approachable, more humane, and more closely involved in human life than they actually were in the tales Greeks told. She speaks of them as "human gods," which is misleading in the extreme. The gods were ageless, immortal, and powerful. They took the form of human beings only as a disguise when it suited their purpose, to approach or communicate with human beings. Homer's Mount Olympus, the home of the gods, is inaccessible to humankind. But Hamilton supposes that "human gods naturally made heaven a pleasantly familiar place. The Greeks felt at home in it." Celsus clearly would have been horrified to learn that many centuries after his death he would be represented as a believer in "human gods," since he considered gods to be in every respect superior to mortals. His gods would not be concerned with ordinary human beings or involved in anything that was mundane or insignificant. The gods that Celsus believed in, the gods of mythology, were in our terms elitist, and they associated mainly with members of the aristocracy.

For the most part, the Greek gods kept away from humans and their world, since they were so much happier and more comfortable in their own home. If they came to earth it was for a specific reason, to intervene on behalf of a particular person, or to abduct a mortal man or woman. But even when gods took mortals as sexual partners, the liaison was brief, because mortals soon grew old and died. Zeus did not have "endless love affairs," as Hamilton claims.[5] The number was large, but finite, and none of his liaisons with mortal women offered them anything like a close, continuing intimacy.

A similar sentimentality may have kept Hamilton from referring to the battle with the suitors' families in the last book of the *Odyssey*. As she tells it, the story ends on a happy note, with Odysseus and Penelope reunited after twenty years. But the ancient Greeks would not have supposed that the *Odyssey* could end there, since they knew that vengeance would be demanded for the suitors' deaths. The end of the *Odyssey* provides a vivid illustration of the Homeric gods' concern for justice in human life, yet Hamilton says nothing about it.[6] The gods are prepared to help Odysseus, but only when he acts in ways that ensure that the will of Zeus will be accomplished, and his justice enforced.

Robert Graves (1895–1985) is often consulted as an authority on myth, and *The Greek Myths*, his two-volume work first published in 1955, is still in print. But Graves takes the myths out of their ancient contexts, telling each story in its chronological order, from beginning to end, relying on a variety of sources, blending them all together into a lively narrative. His account of the adventures of Odysseus begins when the hero leaves Troy and continues after the *Odyssey* ends, through to the story of the death of Odysseus at the hands of Telegonus, Odysseus's son by Circe. Graves clearly disapproves of the way the *Odyssey* concludes, with the bloody battle against the suitors' relatives. He notes disapprovingly: "So the *Odyssey* breaks off with Laertes, Odysseus, and Telemachus, a patriarchal male triad of heroes, supported by Zeus-born Athene and triumphing over their foes."[7] Graves seems not to be comfortable with the Greek notion of revenge, and he is ready to blame Athena for allowing Odysseus to win, on the grounds that this violent behavior is "patriarchal." But Homer never raises the issue of patriarchy or refers to the remarkable story of Athena's birth. Athena appears at the end of the *Odyssey* not to grant victory to Odysseus or to reinforce the values of patriarchal society, but to settle and draw up a treaty "without bloodshed" (*Odyssey* 24.532). The *Odyssey* ends not with a "triumph" but with a peaceful settlement. By emphasizing male-female conflict in his account of the *Odyssey*, Graves makes Athena seem to be less concerned with justice than she is in Homer.

Joseph Campbell (1904–1987) in his various books about myth did more perhaps than any of his predecessors to make mythologies and fairy tales of many cultures accessible and immediate, and his books and teaching enjoyed wide popular success. Campbell believed, with some reason, that myths of all peoples are full of wisdom and can enrich our lives, if only we are ready to listen to them. But he also proceeded on the basis of the rather questionable assumption that all myths, from all cultures, conveyed the same basic messages and followed virtually the same narrative patterns. In his view, all founders of religions have gone on a quest that included departure, fulfillment, and return; Moses ascends the mountain, Jesus goes into the desert. To Campbell, this journey and its personal goals are more important than the hero's public accomplishments.

Campbell is interested in what human beings do in the stories, not in the actions of the gods. He is so concerned with making the myths relevant to the life of modern human beings that in his mythology he seeks to turn everyone into a hero. As he wrote in 1949 in *The Hero with a Thousand Faces*: "In the absence of an effective general mythology, each of us has his private unrecognized, rudimentary, yet secretly potent pantheon of dream. The latest incarnation of Oedipus, the continued romance of Beauty and the Beast, stand this afternoon on the corner of Forty-second Street and Fifth Avenue, waiting for the traffic light to change." In Campbell every man is a hero, and the gods act just like ordinary men. "Mt. Olympus became a Riviera of trite scandals and affairs," he explained.[8] Campbell is at his most anachronistic when he seeks to make the gods and heroes approachable and similar to ourselves. The ancients regarded the myths from a distance. They took place in a time long past, indefinitely distant from the present. The great heroes were not like us; their experiences were both more significant and more terrible.

Campbell also changes the emphasis of stories to give them modern psychological meanings. He believes that Circe sends Odysseus to the land of the dead to attain a deeper knowledge of human sexuality. But as Homer tells the story, the reason Odysseus journeys to the underworld is to find out about his return home. Only the prophet Tiresias—who is now dead—can tell him about the dangers he will face and how best to deal with them. Tiresias says nothing about sexuality. Only a hero in the twentieth century (like Tiresias in T. S. Eliot's *The Waste Land*) would set off on a journey with the goal of discovering himself, and spend so much time reflecting on what it was like to have been at different times in his life both male and female.[9]

Campbell also inserts an element of spirituality into the travels of Odysseus that is entirely absent in Homer. The Island of the Sun is "the island of highest illumination," where Odysseus might have achieved full enlightenment.[10] Campbell's Odysseus, like a yogi, is searching for self-knowledge and seeking to renounce worldly values. In the *Odyssey*, however, Odysseus recognizes where he is not by what he sees but by what he hears: the lowing of the sun god's cattle. Tiresias has warned him not to let his men touch the cattle if they are to survive and make it back home. When in spite of this advice they do eat them, the gods immediately send terrifying portents (12.394). Zeus promises the sun that he will strike their ship with a lightning bolt in the middle of the sea. The episode of the Island of the Sun is not the moment of highest illumination, in fact, but the nadir of the hero's journey, the beginning of seven years of lonely isolation from other human beings on the goddess Calypso's island, and of intensified desire on his part to return to his wife and native land.

By adapting the myths to modern ways of understanding, Campbell deprives them of their original meaning. No ancient Greek accounts fail to recognize the presence of the gods in every aspect of human life, or to demonstrate the power of the gods over humankind. The ancients themselves always wished to mention the gods, if only in passing. Even Socrates, who was condemned to death for his alleged impiety, assures his supporters that the gods have not neglected him. The gods, he says, have allowed him to be condemned because departure from life would be what is best for him (Plato, *Apology* 41c–d).

Why do the authors of these popular versions of the myths ignore or misrepresent the important role the gods play in human life? Perhaps Campbell fails to notice the gods' presence because he does not always refer directly to the original sources. But Bulfinch, Hamilton, and Graves frequently cite the ancient texts, and Hamilton often quotes from them directly. The problem is, I think, that these writers present their own summary accounts of the myths rather than show how particular ancient writers might have approached them. They do not mention the role of the ancient gods if they appear to be in any way peripheral to the authors' accounts of the actions of the mortal characters in their stories. In their different ways, each of these popular writers leaves readers with the impression that in Greek mythology the actions and wishes of human beings are more important than those of the gods, even though in the original literature the opposite is much more likely to be true. The Greek gods do not live up to modern expectations because they are not primarily concerned with the welfare of the vast majority of human beings. It is no wonder, then, that modern readers tend either to disregard them or to try to discover in them only those qualities that accord with modern notions of divinity, and to emphasize these. We prefer Athena as a loving goddess, as she is in Hamilton's account of the *Odyssey*, to Homer's Athena, who although fond of Odysseus is even more concerned with maintaining the gods' own laws about justice and piety.

In this book I will try to offer a more accurate picture of the role of the gods in ancient mythological narratives, by giving an account of the actions of the gods in the ways that ancient writers described them. Instead of summaries of myths compiled from many different sources, readers will see the narratives in the forms that ancient writers gave them, not in chronological order from start to finish, but with the emphasis and structure of the originals. In that way readers will be able to see the gods in the roles that the ancients assigned to them, without the intervention of modern notions of causality and motivation. I realize that it will be impossible for me, or for anyone, to be entirely objective. But I have tried hard to question my own assumptions, and to ask myself and other modern writers the kinds of questions that someone who believed in the ancient gods would have posed. I have concentrated primarily on longer narratives that provide us with an opportunity to understand the gods' plans in some detail *and* to examine mortal responses to what the gods have done to them.

Since this is a book about religion as it is described in myth, I shall concentrate on traditional myths, like the story of Odysseus or Orestes, and on narratives in epic and drama, because these genres remained popular throughout antiquity. I make an exception to include a brief discussion of the *Golden Ass*, or *Metamorphoses*, of Apuleius because his narrative uses many traditional motifs, such as the journey, and his story deals specifically with the central theme of this book, the attempt of mortal beings to understand and come to terms with forces beyond their control. But I have deliberately chosen not to discuss works by other writers who drew on elements of the traditional mythology in constructing their narratives, because that influence is more remote than it is in Apuleius and would require more extensive commentary and additional background material. So in this book I do not discuss the treatment of the gods by historical writers, or the myths invented by the comic poet Aristophanes or the philosopher Plato, even though they ask interesting and important questions about the action of the gods in human life.

Relying on existing ancient narratives as a guide to ancient mythology means that I shall not try to offer accounts of many important myths because they are not narrated in detail in any surviving work of literature. To reconstruct those myths, I would need to use narratives from many different ancient sources, written in a variety of time periods, and in the process I would run the risk of importing modern taste and values into my accounts of those myths. I have also chosen not to discuss shorter narratives and allusions to myths because they too would require more extensive commentary and be less accessible to a modern audience. My hope is that a discussion of the mythic narratives represented here will serve as a guide to understanding the meaning of other myths, even when the stories survive only in summary or in scattered allusions in ancient authors.

The advantage of this approach is that the prima facie explanations offered by the ancient Greek authors themselves may offer more effective interpretations of most myths than the rationales we can construct today. In the myths each crime, each refusal to do what a god commands, each failure to give due honor to a divinity, has consequences. Wrong actions can cause problems for succeeding generations in a family, or for a whole city or army. In the case of Greek mythology, and Roman adaptations of it, there is less need for decipherment and complex interpretation than in the case of the mythologies of other cultures, because they are preserved in a highly developed literature. We do not need to sift out the stories from sets of oral narratives by living speakers who use different narrative conventions from our own. The story of Odysseus is told to us by a master poet whose works were read throughout antiquity, and many of whose narrative strategies are still in use today.

Although I believe that the myths as narrated in the original sources still have much to teach us about the nature of human life, even though the universe they describe is not centered on human beings, I do not mean to say that ancient Greek religion had no deficiencies, or that it has the answers to all the questions we might ask today about the meaning of divinity. This book is not intended to promote "the glory that was Greece and the grandeur that was Rome," or to offer unqualified praise of everything the Greeks and Romans did.[11] The ancient Greeks practiced slavery, like virtually every other ancient society that we know about. And it is certainly true that in most cases they did not allow women rights equal to those of men. These deficiencies have encouraged some modern critics to suppose that the Greeks are directly responsible for the problems our societies face today. But nothing in Greek myth, not even the story of the fall of Troy or the founding of Rome, suggests that the ancient Greeks favored war over peace or slavery over freedom, or thought that women were incapable of high moral reasoning. On the contrary, the myths place consistent emphasis on the value of individual lives and the importance of taking action against injustice.

Although this is a book about the gods in Greek mythology, and for that reason concentrates on Greek and Latin literature, I do not wish to imply in any way that the Greeks and Romans were not influenced by other cultures in the Mediterranean. On the contrary, they continued to learn about other religions so long as they continued to worship the gods their mythology described. In my last chapter I shall discuss a particularly interesting example of a conversion from the traditional religion to the cult of the Egyptian goddess Isis. This conversion takes the form of a physical journey, in which the hero, like Odysseus, learns through suffering and danger. It is a story not about self-realization but about understanding what it is to be human, and how humans can best exist in a world controlled by a benevolent deity.

The basic plan of this book is straightforward: it offers an overview of the actions of the gods in some influential works of Greek and Latin literature, including a linear account of what the gods do. I start from the assumption that the narrators of these works of literature composed them primarily for audiences that believed those gods existed, and that the myths conveyed, however literally or figuratively, essential truths, even though those truths are often harsh. That is not to say that ancient writers did not allow the characters in their stories to question the motives and even the existence of the gods. I simply make the observation that they wrote about the world as if it were controlled by the gods, and as if action on the part of gods was normal and not in any way artificial. The illustrations that appear throughout this book show how the gods change the course of mortal lives, even when they appear to mortals in human form or stand outside or on the periphery of the action. Although artists often tell the stories differently from or more concisely than writers, they never forget that in the traditional myths gods always play dominant roles.

Unlike some modern writers, I am also going to suggest that there is much we still can learn from the religion depicted in the myths, because it describes the world as it is, not as we would like it to be. The gods of traditional Greek and Roman religion do not exist for the benefit of humankind, and they do not always take an interest in what mortals are doing. The gods do not always agree with one another about what should happen in the future, and innocent human beings who are caught up in the conflict suffer or die and are not always avenged. Justice is done in the long run, but often not to the satisfaction of the mortals who are directly involved. It is a religion from which it is possible to derive little comfort, other than the satisfaction that comes from understanding what it is to be human.

CHAPTER 1

Origins

The ancient Greeks did not have a sacred text like the Bible. No one decided what versions of the myths were authoritative. Authors were free to tell the stories as they chose, with their own emphasis, provided they preserved the principal characters and basic plots. The Greeks learned about the gods from poetry written in the eighth and seventh centuries B.C., the most important and influential of which, Hesiod's *Theogony* and *Works and Days*, and the great epics attributed to Homer, the *Iliad* and the *Odyssey*, still survive. Hesiod's poem *Theogony* offers an account of the beginnings of the world and a genealogy of the gods, detailing their names and how they are related to one another. At the same time, it explains why, in a world with so many different gods, the lives of humankind are dominated by a particular family of gods on Mount Olympus, the head of which is Zeus. Hesiod describes how Zeus came to be the most important god and shows why it is better for the world as a whole that Zeus (rather than his predecessors) is in charge. Hesiod's *Works and Days* tells myths that explain why Zeus has made life hard for humans and why they must work to survive while the gods live at their ease, free from cares.

Hesiod wrote his epic poems in roughly the same era as Homer, probably in the eighth–seventh centuries B.C., although no one knows exactly when, or even whether he came before or after Homer. But unlike Homer, Hesiod does tell us something about himself in the course of his two poems, as the information becomes relevant to his theme. He says in the *Works and Days* that his father came from Cyme in Asia Minor, "fleeing from cruel poverty, which Zeus gives to men, and he settled near Mount Helicon in a miserable village, Ascra, cruel in winter, harsh in summer, no good at any time" (*Works and Days* 638–40). But even though Zeus made his father's life hard and drove him away from his home, Hesiod tells us in the *Theogony* how Zeus's daughters the Muses gave him the gift of song. The gods give both bad and good, and no mortal can accomplish anything extraordinary without the help of the gods.

Zeus became the most important god because he used intelligence as well as power, and he used his intelligence to ensure that he would not be replaced by an even stronger successor. He cared about justice, and he gave the other gods rights and privileges in return for their allegiance to him. But even though Zeus, a male god, is the ruler, he works in conjunction with other gods, including many goddesses, who encourage, discourage, and even direct the actions of the male gods. Sexual attraction allows females to get their way without force, by a deception so potent that Zeus can use it as a means of punishing humankind. In *Works and Days*, Hesiod explains how Zeus took the "means of life" away from mortals, but another god, Zeus's cousin Prometheus, stole fire from the gods to help humans. In reprisal Zeus ordered the god Hephaestus to create the first woman, who was sent to punish men, not, like Eve in Genesis, to be a helper and a comfort. So Zeus has made life hard, like God in Genesis after Adam and Eve disobeyed him. But, as Hesiod shows in other myths, mortals have made it even harder for themselves by refusing to honor justice.

ZEUS AND HIS ANCESTORS

Hesiod's *Theogony* begins with an invocation to the Muses of Mount Helicon. He describes how the nine Muses, the daughters of Zeus, wash in one of the nearby springs and then go to dance on the peaks of the mountain. From there, wrapped in thick mist, they walk at night singing of Zeus and Hera of Argos, Athena, Apollo, Artemis, Poseidon, Themis, Aphrodite, Hebe, Dione, Dawn, the Sun, the Moon, Leto, Iapetus, Cronus, Earth, Oceanus, Night, and all the other immortal gods. After mentioning the names of all these gods Hesiod relates what the Muses once said to him:

> They once taught Hesiod beautiful song, as he was pasturing his lambs beneath holy Helicon. First the goddesses, the Muses of Mount Olympus, the daughters of aegis-bearing Zeus, addressed this speech to me: "Shepherds of the wilderness, evil disgraces, mere bellies, we know how to tell many lies that are like the truth, and we know, when we wish, to speak the truth." So spoke the daughters of great Zeus, ready of speech, and they gave me a staff, a branch of live laurel to pluck, a wonderful thing, and they breathed divine song into me, so that I might sing of what will be and what was before, and they told me to sing of the race of blessed ones that live forever, but always to sing first and last of themselves. (*Theogony* 22–34)

These lines tell us that Hesiod has learned his song from the Muses, but when they gave him the staff that marked him as a poet, they offered him a sharp reminder of the difference between themselves and mortals like himself. He is a miserable creature, a slave to his stomach who lives in ignorance of what is really true and what is not. The Muses know the difference, because they are gods. The branch of laurel wood marks him as someone to whom they have given a precious gift, but it means that his duty as a singer is to praise the gods, beginning and ending with themselves.

So Hesiod stops talking about himself and begins to speak of the Muses, "who with their singing gladden the great mind of Zeus on Olympus, telling of what is and what will be and what was before, each taking up the song" (36–39). The Muses sing and dance, so that the peaks of Olympus resound with their song. They sing of Earth and Heaven and their children, and then of Zeus, the greatest of the gods, and finally of men and of the giants. Then the poet tells the story of the Muses' birth, how Zeus lay with their mother, Memory, for nine nights, and how they now live a short distance from Olympus, with the Graces and Desire. They go to Olympus, singing of how their father overcame his father Cronus, and how he assigned the gods each a place and awarded them honors.

Once he has described the Muses' song, Hesiod gives all their names: Clio, Euterpe, Thalia, Melpomene, Terpsichore, Erato, Polymnia, Urania, and Calliope. Each has powers of her own, but Calliope is the head of them all, because she accompanies kings. A king whom the Muses love can speak sweetly, and his people can see that he rules justly and is able to stop quarrels; they honor him as if he were a god, and he stands out from the others in the assembly: "Such is the sacred gift of the Muses to humankind" (93).

Song is not only a means of conveying information: it gives pleasure and takes away pain (96–103). In that way it is an even greater gift for mortals than it is for the gods, who have no real sorrows to forget, since death and disease cannot affect them. Hesiod now asks the Muses to help him sing about the genealogy of the gods (104–5). He requests that they sing of the gods who were born from Earth and Heaven, and Night, and the children of the Sea, and their children, who divided the wealth and distributed the honors among them, and who first occupied Mount Olympus: "Tell me all this, Muses who dwell in Olympus, from the beginning, and tell me who were the first among the gods" (114–15). Even before Hesiod begins his main narrative he indicates that a central theme of his poem will be the division of power and the distribution of honors among the gods, and that Zeus and his family, the dwellers on Mount Olympus, are the most important gods.

From the Void (Chaos) was born the goddess Earth, "who is the seat, fixed forever, of the gods who hold the peaks of Mount Olympus" (117–18); other gods came from the Void as well, and Earth gave birth to Heaven, who became her husband, "equal to herself [in size], so that he might form a complete boundary for her, and that he might be a seat for the blessed gods, fixed forever" (127–28). Then she bore the Mountains, the Nymphs, and the Sea. With Heaven as father, she gave birth to more children, including Oceanus, Hyperion, Iapetus, Theia,

Rhea, Themis, Mnemosyne, Phoebe, Tethys, and Cronus the crooked-minded, who hated his father, and the one-eyed Cyclopes, who later gave Zeus the thunderbolt and made the lightning for him. Heaven hated all his children, and he put them back again inside their mother so they could not come into the light. "Heaven was pleased with his evil work, but great Earth moaned as she was constrained within, and she thought of a deceitful plan" (158–60).

Earth got Heaven to stop hiding his children inside her by taking the moral initiative against the injustice. She asks her children to avenge the "evil outrage of your father, for he was the first to plan disgraceful deeds" (165–66). All the others are afraid, but Cronus the crooked-minded agrees to help her, echoing her words, "I do not care about our accursed father, for he was the first to plan disgraceful deeds" (171–72). Earth hides Cronus in ambush, then creates and gives him a great sharp sickle of gray stone. When Heaven comes to make love to Earth, Cronus uses the sickle to cut off his father's genitals. The avenging deities called Erinyes are born from the drops of blood, and Aphrodite, the goddess of love and desire, grows out of the genitals themselves, which Cronus throws into the sea. Heaven in his anger calls his children Titans, a name that reflects what has happened: his children "had strained [titainontas] in deception to punish him, for which in time there would be vengeance" (209–10).

Only after cataloguing the children of the other Titan gods, such as the monsters and rivers of the world, does Hesiod relate the story of the Titans Cronus and Rhea, who are the parents of Zeus and his brothers and sisters Hestia, Demeter, Hera, Hades, and Poseidon.[1] Cronus swallows Zeus's five siblings as soon as they are born, because he had learned from his parents that it was fated for him, strong as he was, to be overcome by his son (461–65). Rhea, like her mother Earth before her, takes the initiative against her husband to save her children. Before Zeus is born, Rhea asks her parents, Earth and Heaven, to think of a plan to save him and to make Cronus pay for the crime he committed against his father. They tell her to go to Crete when the child is about to be born, so she brings him there at night and hides him in a deep cave, where Earth takes care of him. Rhea then wraps a great stone in swaddling clothes and gives it to Cronus: "He picked it up and put it into his stomach, the wretch; he did not realize in his heart that thereafter instead of the stone his son remained invincible and untroubled; he soon would conquer him and drive him by force from his power and would rule among the immortals" (487–91). Hesiod emphasizes the unthinking and violent behavior of Cronus, which contrasts with how Zeus later uses his intelligence to see to it that he will not be replaced by a successor.

Zeus grows up rapidly, as only a god can. A year after swallowing them, Cronus vomits up his children, tricked by Earth and overpowered by his son Zeus; the stone ends up in Delphi, later a principal shrine of Zeus's son Apollo.[2] Zeus's first act is to release Heaven's sons the Cyclopes, and in gratitude they give him thunder, lightning, and the thunderbolt: "Trusting in these he rules over mortals and

Rhea gives a stone wrapped in swaddling clothes to Cronus.
(Red-figure column krater, 500–450 B.C. Louvre, Paris, G 366. Réunion
des Musées Nationaux/Art Resource, New York. Photo: Hervé Landowski.)

immortals" (506). Then he reckons with the Titan gods who have not been loyal to him, first confronting the children of his uncle Iapetus: Atlas, Menoetius, Prometheus, and Epimetheus. Zeus subdues Menoetius with a thunderbolt and sends him into the darkness; he compels Atlas to stand at the ends of the earth holding up the broad sky with his head and hands. He binds Prometheus to a rock and sends an eagle to feed every day on his immortal liver, which always grows back again.

The reason Prometheus must be punished is because he tried to outwit Zeus. The story of Prometheus, curiously, involves mortals, although Hesiod makes no attempt in this poem to explain why they were created or by whom. Mortals and immortals had gathered for a feast at Mekone (later known as Sicyon), in the northern Peloponnesus, many years earlier. Prometheus sacrificed an ox, and after the meat was cooked he tricked Zeus by wrapping the bones in fat so that they, rather than the meat, would appear to be the more appetizing portion. Zeus saw what Prometheus had done, but he took the bones anyway, and since that time people have offered the gods the bones of the animals they sacrifice and kept the meat for themselves. This trick with the bones made Zeus angry, so in requital he took fire away from the mortals; Prometheus then deceived Zeus by stealing fire in a hollow reed and giving it back to them.

So Zeus retaliated against men for the theft of fire. He had his son Hephaestus create a maiden from earth and give her a golden diadem, and caused his daughter Athena to dress her. "When he had made this beautiful evil in return for good, Zeus took her where the other gods and men were" (585–86). Both gods and men were amazed when they saw this "headlong deception, which men cannot manage; from her come generations of women, a great pain for mortal men on earth; women are no help in times of cruel poverty, but only in times of plenty" (589–93). Hesiod compares women to the drones in a hive whom the other bees must work hard to feed; "so Zeus who thunders on high made women as an evil for mortals, companions in harsh suffering" (600–602). In addition, Zeus gave another evil in recompense for good: if a man should escape marriage, he will have no children to look after him when he is old or to inherit his property. A man is fortunate if he gets a sensible wife; "for him bad fights against good throughout his life" (609–10). But a man who gets an evil wife has unending sorrow. "So it is not possible to deceive or evade the mind of Zeus" (613).

The cunning and intelligence of Zeus are made to stand out in this telling of the story, but Hesiod does not explain why Zeus should punish men for the deception Prometheus practiced on him, or why Prometheus is willing to run the risk of incurring the wrath of Zeus by stealing fire back again. Hesiod's audience must have understood that there was some special connection between Prometheus and humanity; according to a later story, it was Prometheus who created man, possibly in the hope of having allies in the struggle against Zeus.[3] In any event, men are punished for the trickery of Prometheus, not for their own transgressions, as was Adam in the Hebrew Bible. God made Eve as a helper and companion for Adam, but Zeus sends woman to increase man's suffering. The best women can offer their husbands only a mixture of good and evil, and the worst can bring only sorrow. Zeus did not create humankind, and he is not primarily concerned with their welfare. (The story appears again in Hesiod's *Works and*

Atlas holds up the world, while Zeus's eagle tears out Prometheus's liver.
(Laconian cup, 565–550 B.C. Museo Gregoriano Etrusco, Vatican, no. 16592.)

Days, where he calls the woman Pandora and places specific emphasis on the folly of Epimetheus, brother of Prometheus, and the diseases and trouble the woman brings to mankind. Here again the story brings out the great discrepancy between human ignorance and the wisdom of Zeus, concentrating on how he outwits Prometheus with even more clever forms of deception.)

Hesiod now returns to the story of how Zeus established his hegemony over the other gods. He fights against the Titans for ten years, but then Earth advises him to release Heaven's sons Obriareus, Cottus, and Gyges from their fetters and bring them back from the ends of the earth; each of them has fifty heads and a hundred arms. With their help, and by using his own weapons of thunder and lightning, Zeus and his allies are able to confine the Titan gods to Tartarus: in a war where the combatants cannot be killed, victory can be achieved only when one side is imprisoned or somehow repressed by the other. Tartarus is as far below earth as heaven is above it, and a bronze barrier covers it. It is guarded by the monsters Obriareus, Cottus, and Gyges—known as the Hundred-handers—and Atlas stands there as well. Next to it Night and Day have their house, as do Night's sons Sleep and Death. The house of Hades, guarded by the terrifying fifty-headed dog Cerberus, is nearby, and so is the home of the goddess Styx, by whom the gods swear their most solemn oath.

After conquering the Titans, Zeus must face one more enemy, the monster Typhoeus (or Typhon), son of Earth and Tartarus (821–22). With his great strength and his hundred snake-heads, breathing fire and uttering terrible sounds, Typhoeus would have become king of the gods "if the father of gods and men had not thought keenly" (838). Zeus thunders until the whole world is shaken: Olympus, the earth, the sea, Hades, and the Titans in Tartarus. He leaps from Olympus with the thunder and lightning and strikes Typhoeus down; the earth burns and melts, and Zeus throws the monster into Tartarus. Even so, Typhoeus still causes trouble: he is the source of the sudden storm winds, or typhoons, that attack sailors and destroy the work of farmers. The gods, following the advice of Earth, urge Zeus to be their king and ruler, "and he divided their privileges among them" (883–85). Unlike his predecessors, Zeus takes special care to give the gods who have sided with him rewards and privileges.

At this point Zeus has conquered his last enemy and become king of all the gods, so it seems likely that Hesiod's epic poem in its original form would have ended at this point, although he might also have added a final formal reference to the Muses, since they told him "to sing first and last of themselves." As the poem has come down to us, however, it continues with a catalogue of Zeus's consorts and the children who were born from these unions. Marriage, coupling, and childbirth are critically important matters, because so much depends on the question of succession.

Zeus's father and grandfather were both overcome by their sons. How will Zeus avoid begetting a son who is even more powerful and clever than he is? His wife, Metis (Intelligence), one of the daughters of Oceanus, is said to be "the wisest of gods and of men," and Earth and Heaven warn that from her "very wise children would be born" (887, 894). The first of these children who were to be born to Zeus was Athena, "whose courage and wisdom were equal to her father's"; after Athena, Metis was fated to bear a son with a mighty heart who would be king of gods and men (896–98). So Zeus, in his wisdom, heeds the warning of Earth and Heaven by swallowing Metis before she can give birth to Athena. Athena is then born by springing from his head; in this way Zeus ensures that she will be closer to him than to her mother, and she will perhaps even become the most important and powerful of all his children. He also makes it impossible for Metis ever to conceive the son who could replace him. And he is able to keep her within himself, "so that the goddess might give him advice about what was good and bad" (900). After his triumph over the Titan gods, no relative of Metis dares come to her defense because they know that Zeus has the thunder and lightning.

Metis is followed by numerous other consorts of Zeus. His second wife is Themis (Divine Justice), and she gives birth to Eunomia (Orderly Government), Dikē (Justice), Peace, and the Seasons, all of whom bring order to the lives of hu-

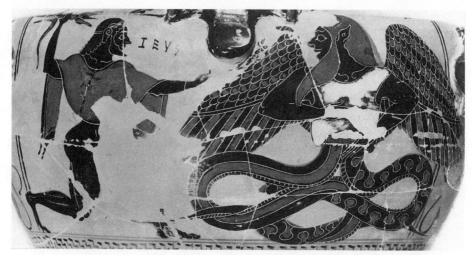

Zeus prepares to throw a thunderbolt at the winged monster Typhoeus. (Black-figured Chalcidian hydria, 540–530 B.C., by the Unsigned Amphora Painter. Staatliche Antikensammlungen und Glyptothek, Munich, no. 596. Photo: Koppermann.)

mans. Themis is also the mother of Clotho, Lachesis, and Atropos, the three Fates who control mortals' fortunes and the length of their lives. Zeus has still other wives after Themis: Eurynome, mother of the Graces; Demeter, mother of Persephone; Leto, mother of Apollo and Artemis; and finally Hera, mother of Hebe, Ares, and the birth goddess Eileithyia. After he has enumerated the wives of Zeus, Hesiod provides a list of other marriages made by the Olympian gods. This is followed by a catalogue of unions between goddesses and mortal men, and the names of the children so produced who become great heroes, like Thetis's son Achilles and Aphrodite's son Aeneas. The poem as we have it ends with this account of goddesses and their children without much description of their characters or actions.

The treatment of goddesses in these concluding lines differs strikingly from the main narrative of the *Theogony*, where goddesses play a more active role. Earth and Rhea take the initiative in seeing that justice is done, and Earth advises Zeus on a course of action that ensures his domination. Although the mother goddesses do not have physical powers equal to those of the male gods, they do not hesitate to speak out and to use persuasion and deception whenever necessary.[4] Motherhood, too, gives them singular influence over their children, who owe them special respect for having given them life and nurturing them. Particular goddesses acquire distinctive authority because of their relation to Zeus, as do his daughters the Muses and Athena. Others are rewarded because they sided with him against the Titans, and these favorites include Styx, who is welcome on Olympus with Zeus, and Hecate. Earlier Hesiod has mentioned that Styx, daugh-

The gods look on while a fully armed Athena is born from the head of Zeus, who holds a thunderbolt. (Red-figure kylix, ca. 500–490 B.C. British Museum, London, E 15.)

ter of Oceanus, was the first to go to Zeus, and "he honored her, and gave her great gifts; he determined that she would be the great oath of the gods, and that her children would live near him always" (399–401).

Hecate, the granddaughter of Cronus's sister Phoebe, also receives particular honor from Zeus (411–15, 423–25). Hecate's cult had special meaning for

Athena emerges from the head of Zeus, as Hephaestus, holding his ax,
looks on at left. (Red-figure pelike, ca. 460 B.C., by the Painter of the
Birth of Athena. British Museum, London, E 410.)

Hesiod's family, which may be why he devoted a good deal of space to her; Hecate was worshiped in Asia Minor, where his father came from, and Hecate's father is called Perses, which was also the name of Hesiod's brother (*Works and Days* 10).[5] But the main reason why Hesiod singles her out for special praise is because of the honors Zeus bestows on her. Hecate's privileges include wide influence over almost every important aspect of human life; she is the goddess humankind should call on in matters of government, war, athletics, horsemanship, sailing, hunting, animal husbandry, and the nurturing of children. Hesiod makes it clear, however, that one can never count on her support but must always strive to deserve and encourage it; he repeatedly says that Hecate can help if she chooses to do so (*Theogony* 439, for example).

Mortals make only a brief appearance in the *Theogony*. There are the shepherds, "evil disgraces, mere bellies," like Hesiod himself, who graze their flocks on Mount Helicon and worship the Muses. There are the men Zeus punished for the deception of Prometheus with the destructive gift of women, and the mortals who may be helped by Hecate "if she is so inclined" (443). Only a few exceptional men and women have intercourse with gods and produce sons who become heroes. On balance, the gods take only a sporadic interest in mortals, more often to harm than to help them.

↦ ZEUS AND HUMANKIND ↤

In Hesiod's other epic poem, *Works and Days*, the gods' relationship to humans remains the same. The poet asks the Muses to sing of their father Zeus, and begins by describing the power Zeus has over mortals and asking for his assistance: "Through him mortals are famous or unknown, mentioned or unmentioned, on account of great Zeus. For easily he makes a man great, and easily strikes the great down, easily he makes the conspicuous man small and makes the inconspicuous grow, easily he straightens the crooked man and blasts the proud, Zeus who thunders on high, who lives in the highest dwelling. Now you listen, look and hear, and make your laws straight with justice!" (*Works and Days* 3–10). Zeus has complete control over human life, and accomplishes easily what mortals can do to one another only with considerable effort, if at all. Since Hesiod knows that Zeus cares about justice in human life, he calls on the god to intervene on his behalf in a dispute with his brother Perses. The brothers had earlier agreed on the division of their inherited property, but Perses bribed the officials and took away a larger share.

There are not one but two goddesses called Eris (Strife), Hesiod says, and this explains why human life is so hard. One causes war and arguments; mortals hate her, but they honor her because they must, since that is the will of the immortals. The other is the older daughter of Night. Zeus has placed her at the roots of the earth, and she is much better for humans because she gets lazy people to work and encourages competition. Hesiod urges his brother not to let the evil-hearted Eris keep him from working, suggesting in his way that everyone would be better advised to work for a living.

Why do human beings need to work? Because "the gods have hidden men's sustenance. Otherwise you might easily work for a day and have enough for a year even if you sat idle" (42–44). In other words, men would be like the gods who live at their ease. Hesiod now tells the same basic story he told in the *Theogony* about how Zeus gave woman to man as a punishment for the crimes of Prometheus (*Theogony* 570–612). But in *Works and Days* he gives it a different emphasis: woman is not only an evil in herself; she also brings diseases and suffering with her. In this version of the story Zeus hid men's sustenance because he was angry with Prometheus: "Zeus devised miserable sorrows for mankind; he hid fire" (*Works and Days* 49–50). (Again Hesiod does not explain why there is a connection between Prometheus and humankind.) When Prometheus then gave the fire back to them, Zeus became angry and said he would give "a huge burden" to Prometheus and men of the future (56). There is no need for Zeus to use his special weapons of lightning and thunder, or call up the Hundred-handers against them. Because human beings have only limited understanding and grow old and die, they are relatively easy to deceive and punish.

Zeus laughs with pleasure at the scheme he has devised for punishing mortal men. He tells Hephaestus to mix earth with water and create a maiden as beautiful as a goddess. Athena teaches her to weave, and Aphrodite, the goddess of love, pours grace around her head, as well as desire and longing. Zeus tells his son Hermes, who acts as his messenger, to give her a bitch's mind and a thieving nature. Athena dresses her; the Graces and Persuasion arrange her jewelry, and the Seasons bind flowers in her hair. Hermes, in keeping with Zeus's plan, gives her lies and deceptive speeches and a thief's character; he also gives her a voice, and he calls the woman Pandora, since all (*pantes*) of the gods have given her a gift (82). Zeus gets Hermes to take the woman not to man but to Epimetheus as a gift. Epimetheus (Afterthought) forgets that his brother Prometheus (Forethought) has warned him not to accept a gift from Zeus, but rather to send it back again, "so that nothing bad might happen to mortals; but he took it, and then understood only when he had the evil creature" (88–89).

Before that time, Hesiod explains, men had "lived without misery and hard suffering and cruel diseases, which give men over to the fates, for men grow old quickly in misery" (90–92). But the woman, plotting evil destruction for mankind, takes the lid off the storage jar she has been carrying and scatters the good things that were in it abroad, and they are all lost to men. Only hope remains in the jar, because the woman puts the lid back before it can escape, in keeping with the plans of Zeus.[6] "But in addition thousands of sorrows wander about among men; the earth is full of evils and the sea is full. Diseases come upon men by day, and at night they travel about, uncontrolled, and bring suffering to mortals in silence, since wise Zeus took away their voices" (100–105). Unlike the Old Testament, in which God makes woman for man as a gift rather than a curse, and punishes Adam and Eve only after they have disobeyed his explicit orders not to eat from the Tree of Knowledge, in Hesiod's world human beings are innocent victims of a quarrel between gods.

Zeus is responsible for the conditions of human life, and this is the point that Hesiod wants to emphasize. He now tells another story, which he says will explain "that gods and mortals came from the same source," although in fact the stories show only that the gods have allowed life to become progressively harder for men (108). First, during the reign of Cronus, the gods made a Golden Generation of men who "lived like gods with untroubled hearts, without pain and sorrow, and no dreadful old age came upon them" (112–14). They spent their days in feasting, and when their time came they died in their sleep. The earth brought forth two harvests a year, and no farming was needed to produce it. They lived in peace with their many blessings. But after their deaths, "according to the will of great Zeus" they became good spirits who guard mankind; shrouded in mist, they travel over the earth to oversee judgments and crime, and bring wealth to mortals (122–26).

The Golden Generation eventually disappeared, however, although Hesiod does not explain why the gods allowed this to happen. Nor does he say why the gods replaced it with a second generation of men, the Silver Generation—far worse than the Gold, unlike them in both body and mind. Childhood for them lasted a hundred years, and when men did grow up they lived only a short time because of the misery brought on them by their folly: "They could not stop committing crimes against each other, and they did not serve the immortals or offer sacrifices on their altars, as is right for men in their dwelling places. Zeus became angry and hid them, because they did not give due honor to the blessed gods who hold Olympus" (134–39). These men are called "blessed mortals of the underworld" and still are honored. Hesiod seems to assume that it was sometime during this generation that Zeus overthrew Cronus as king of the gods, because he alone creates the next generations.

The first of these was the Bronze Generation, which Zeus made from ash trees. These men did not resemble the Silver Generation: they were fearful and threatening, and they cared about war and violence. Their limbs were powerful, although they ate no bread, and their armor, weapons, and houses were made of bronze. They perished because they slaughtered one another, and they died unmemorialized. After they were gone, Zeus made a fourth generation, "more just and more noble, a godlike race of heroes who are called demigods" (158–60). They too were involved in wars, which were fought over the flocks of Oedipus at Thebes and over Helen at Troy. Zeus settled this generation at the ends of the earth, "and they live with hearts free from care in the islands of the blessed beside deep-swirling Oceanus, happy heroes, for whom the life-giving fields bring forth a sweet harvest three times in a year" (170–73).

But Zeus replaced this hero generation as well, this time with the present generation, which appears to be worse than any of its predecessors: "I wish that I had never been in the Fifth Generation of men, but that I had died before or been born afterward. For this is now truly an Iron Generation: for by day they will not cease from struggle and at night from misery, for the gods will give them harsh cares; still even for them good will be mixed with evil" (174–79). Hesiod predicts that Zeus will destroy this generation also when its people become even more morally corrupt than they are at present. Children will be born with gray hair on their temples, fathers will not be like their children, hosts will not be like their guests, and comrades will not be like their comrades. A brother will not be a friend as in former times, and people will not honor their parents when they grow old. Might will be right, the evil and violent will be rewarded, and oaths will be foresworn (189–94). Perhaps Hesiod is thinking here of his own case, of his brother who is not a friend but who has treated him unjustly; he sees what happened to him as part of a general pattern and predicts that this behavior will lead to destruction. Zelos, the god of contention, will live among men; Shame and Vengeance, wrapped in their white robes, will leave the earth for Mount Olympus; and "miserable humans will be left with their cruel sorrows, and there will be no respite from evil" (200–201).

In spite of this bleak future, however, Zeus still offers the men of the Iron Age an opportunity to be prosperous and just, for they still have the ability to settle quarrels by means other than violence. The rules of the animal world do not apply to humans (276–79). If a hawk carries off a nightingale, the nightingale must go where the hawk takes her (207–11). Hesiod's brother Perses, like the hawk, now has power over him. But unlike the nightingale, Hesiod can appeal to Zeus and can use his power of speech to describe the benefits of heeding the goddess Justice (Dikē). If men who take bribes and make unfair decisions drag her away (as they appear to have done in Hesiod's case), Justice cries out and follows them wrapped in mist, bringing harm to them and their households. Zeus sends vengeance to the city of the unlawful; often he destroys the whole city because of one man, and sends suffering to them, and famine and plague, and the people waste away. The women do not bear children and their families decrease, "through the plans of Olympian Zeus; sometimes a whole army is lost or a wall or the son of Cronus takes vengeance on their ships in the sea" (245–47). But if men choose instead to make honest judgments, their cities flourish, and Peace protects their young: "Zeus of the broad brows does not allot to them the portion of war" (229). Famine and Ruin never come there, their crops thrive, and the women bear children who are like their fathers.

How does Zeus know about the wrong that men do on earth? He has thirty thousand immortal informants who live among the mortals on earth, wrapped in mist so no one can see them. They tell the goddess Justice about wrongdoers, and she tells Zeus "about the mind of unjust men, so that the people pay the penalty for the folly of their rulers who with evil intentions divert judgments from the right path and make crooked arguments" (249–62). "The eye of Zeus sees all and knows all and if he is so inclined sees even this affair, and he does not forget what sort of justice our city contains within itself" (267–69). Hesiod would not want himself or his son to be righteous if he thought that the unjust man might triumph over the just; "but I do not suppose that wise Zeus is yet allowing that to happen" (273).

Hesiod explains to Perses how men can prosper even though the gods have hidden their sustenance under the earth. They must work for their living: "Work, Perses, descendant of Zeus, so that Hunger will hate you, and revered Demeter of the beautiful crown will love you, and fill your basket with sustenance" (299–301); "possessions should not be stolen; those given by the gods are much better" (320). If a man commits adultery or hurts orphan children or abuses his aged parents, Zeus will take vengeance on him. Perses should offer sacrifices to the gods and pray to them with burnt offerings, when he goes to bed and when he rises in the morning, "so that they may have a heart and mind friendly toward you, so that you may derive benefit from another man's portion, and another man not benefit from yours" (340–41).

The world as Hesiod describes it is full of gods, and every man must be vigilant and pious if he is to prosper. The gods can help the farmer in numerous ways. The rising and setting of the Pleiades, the daughters of Atlas, provides the framework of the growing season (383–84). A man should pray to Hades, the ruler of the lower world, and to Demeter, the goddess of grain, for the crop to come out of the earth and ripen (465–66); Zeus sends the autumn rain and also has the power to grant a successful harvest (415–16, 474). But it is never easy for mortals to ascertain what Zeus is planning, Hesiod warns: "The mind of aegis-bearing Zeus is different at different times, and it is hard for mortal men to know it" (483–84).

Because the Muses have taught him, the poet can give instructions about every aspect of human life.[7] A man should not pour a libation to Zeus and the other gods in the morning with unwashed hands, "for they do not hear you, and spit out your prayers" (726).[8] He should know which days of the month Zeus favors: the first, fourth, seventh, eighth, and ninth days are holy; the seventh was the day on which Zeus's son Apollo was born. It is important to know and to practice such specific pieties, because they help one to win the favor of the gods: "Fortunate and happy is the man who knows all of the days and works without wronging the gods, judging birds of omen, and avoiding transgression" (826–28).

Through his reflective and reiterative narratives, *Theogony* and *Works and Days*, Hesiod explains how the Olympian gods took control of the world and how they have affected the lives of humankind, a species that they did not create but nonetheless have continued to allow to exist. Zeus made life hard for men and sent them woman, but he gave them justice, which enables them to live in communities so long as they are prepared to observe it. Even though Zeus cannot be everywhere and watch everyone at all times, there are many other gods who observe what men do and report to him about their actions. The farmer's life, as he sees it, demands constant reverence for the gods and constant effort to learn the plan of Zeus, despite the difficulty involved. The responsibility for doing what is right rests with the human being, and humans are obliged to remember that their actions will affect the fate of others around them. Someone who commits injustice risks not only his own life but also the lives of others, since Zeus has no qualms about destroying the innocent along with the guilty. Justice is what enables all of them to live with their fellow men, since it requires people to think about the welfare of others.

This is the great lesson that humans can learn from Hesiod's tales. Hesiod begins the *Works and Days* by describing the justice of Zeus. Without it, humans would live like beasts, and the weak would be in the hands of the strong, like the nightingale clutched in the hawk's talons. But he refers to Zeus without the continual expressions of gratitude and affection that he has for a divinity who is prepared to be more compassionate and generous to humankind in general, like Hecate in the *Theogony*. Hesiod never forgets, and never lets his audience forget, that it is Zeus who has made it necessary for humans to work hard to survive, and that Zeus is the god who saw to it that men must live with the added burden of women. In both poems there is a clear message for mortals: Zeus did not create the world for them, but only tolerates them within it. Human beings must struggle to survive and to understand; only Zeus has abiding strength and knowledge, and the power to use it for good or for evil.

CHAPTER 2

Gods Among Mortals

In the world that Hesiod describes, the gods intervene in human life to show mortals why they should be worshiped and to tell them how to maintain their cults and honor them. In the *Theogony*, Hesiod makes it clear that the gods can help mortals if they are so inclined. The goddess Hecate can make a man a distinguished orator or athlete; she helps kings, horsemen, fishermen, and farmers—if she wants to. Hesiod's *Works and Days* shows that mortals can try to get the gods' active assistance in three ways: by prayer, by sacrifice, and by just actions. But his narrative gives far more attention to how Zeus has punished humans, for their own wrongdoing or for that of Prometheus. Zeus takes fire away from man, and when Prometheus brings it back, he sends woman to man, to be a burden to him. In the *Works and Days* the woman brings diseases and suffering into men's lives, whereas before she came they had been free of them. So Hesiod leaves his audience with an overall impression that the Olympian gods are not ordinarily inclined to become involved with humankind, with one important exception: both male and female gods are interested in having intercourse with mortals and producing mortal children. Only the third generation of gods is involved with mortals in this way; there are no myths about the earlier generations of gods mating with mortals.

⊹ᵗ THE GODS AS ANCESTORS ⊹

Why did the Olympian gods take mortal partners, and why did they wish to have mortal children who, like all mortals, would suffer and die? Certainly desire is a factor, since both male and female gods choose to mate with beautiful mortals. But the gods had unlimited opportunities to have sexual relations with other gods, so they must have had other motives as well. The most important of these was control. By mating with mortals, the Olympian gods could produce children who would be loyal to themselves, as opposed to Prometheus or some other god. These children would be stronger and better than ordinary mortals. As Hesiod tells us in *Works and Days*, the mortal children of the gods were known as demi-gods (in Greek, *hemitheoi*, or half-gods), and they belonged to the fourth generation of humankind. These were the heroes of myth, the ones who fought at Troy and who lived some time before Hesiod's own generation.

The *Theogony* as it has come down to us concludes with a brief catalogue of some of these unions between gods and mortals, beginning with the children thus produced who were born mortal but later became immortal. The mortal Cadmus, the king of Thebes, had a daughter named Semele, and she bore Zeus's son Dionysus; "a mortal bore an immortal, and now they are both gods" (*Theogony* 942). Then there is Heracles, son of Zeus and the mortal woman Alcmena; Heracles became immortal and took the goddess Hebe, daughter of Zeus and Hera, as his wife. Dionysus married Ariadne, the daughter of the mortal Minos, himself a son of Zeus, and Zeus made Ariadne immortal. The list also includes Aeētes and Circe, the immortal son and daughter of Helios, the sun god, and Medea, the immortal daughter of Aeētes and a daughter of Oceanus. Next comes a list of the goddesses who mated with mortal men and bore children "like the gods in appearance" (968). These include Ploutos (Wealth), the son of Demeter and Iasion, who travels across land and sea bringing prosperity to whoever encounters him; Achilles, the "courageous destroyer of men," son of the sea goddess Thetis by the mortal Peleus (1007); Aeneas, son of Aphrodite and the Trojan Anchises; and the sons of Odysseus who were born to the goddesses Circe and Calypso.

Ancient readers evidently enjoyed hearing lists of names, and of course they could learn their mythology this way; Hesiod's *Theogony* lists the names of fifty daughters of Nereus, twenty-six rivers, and forty-two daughters of Oceanus.[1] The lists of the children of gods and mortals provide a basic who's who of heroes and their family trees. Many Greeks traced their own families back to a god or a hero. Hesiod apparently was one of them, for he addressed his brother Perses as a "descendant of Zeus" as a way of reminding him that he should live up to a certain standard of behavior. The poet Tyrtaeus, to get the Spartan troops ready for battle, says to them: "Come now, you should be courageous, for you are descended from unconquerable Heracles."[2]

The lists give us no real idea, however, of what the audience might have learned from the stories of unions of gods and mortals other than genealogy. To get an impression of what additional meanings a poet might attach to the stories we need to look at what remains of an epic poem that in antiquity was joined to the end of the *Theogony*. This narrative was known as the *Catalogue of Women*, or simply as the "like-her's" (*Eoeae*), because each new story was introduced by the phrase "and like her was . . ." Most ancient writers thought that Hesiod wrote this poem, but modern scholars believe that it was almost certainly written by another author some generations later. The poem also included the names of the grandchildren of the gods, for they were the ancestors of all the great families in the Greek world.

Only fragments of the *Catalogue* survive, but we know from a piece of papyrus that it began with an invocation to the Muses: "Sing now of the tribe of women, Olympian Muses with your sweet voices, daughters of Zeus who holds the aegis, who were the best, . . . who loosened their girdles, . . . joining in love with gods . . . , for then banquets were shared, and sitting-places were shared between the immortal gods and mortal men, but their lives were not equal in length" (*Catalogue* frag. 1.1–10). Hesiod also speaks of a time when gods and men took their meals together, as at Mekone or Sicyon, when Prometheus cut up the portions of a sacrifice, and when Zeus took Pandora to the place "where the other gods and men were." It becomes clear as the *Theogony* continues that men and gods were regularly in such close communion until the time of the Trojan War.

A few lines later the poet of the *Catalogue* asks the Muse to tell him "the women in whom Olympian Zeus of the wide brows first sowed his seed, the generation of famous kings . . . and Poseidon . . . and Ares . . . and Hermes . . . and Heracles" (frag. 1.14–22). It would have been possible for him to arrange the *Catalogue* by listing the children of each god, but instead the poet concentrates on the genealogies of the human families who had the most important descendants, the founders of cities and the famous heroes of Greek myth and legend. First were the descendants of Aeolus, which included Tydeus, the father of Diomedes, one of the important heroes of the *Iliad*. Then come the descendants of the river god Inachus in Argos. These included Io, another consort of Zeus, whose descendants included Heracles and Europa (the mother of Minos and Rhadamanthys) and Cadmus, the founder of Thebes. Then came the descendants of Pelasgus in Argos, and finally those of Atlas, such as Pelops, the ancestor of Agamemnon and Menelaus. Virtually all the famous names in mythology can be accounted for in one or more of these family trees. In genealogical terms what Hesiod tells Perses is literally true, that "gods and mortals came from the same source" (*Works and Days* 108).

In the surviving fragments of the narratives, the gods descend to earth to beget children and grant favors to the women they have chosen.[3] The poet occasionally describes how the god contrived to seduce the mortal. Apparently he tells us that Zeus tricked Europa by turning himself into a bull, which "breathed the scent of saffron" and carried her off to Crete (*Catalogue* frag. 140). But most of the poem is about the children that were born from these unions and their many descendants. The women are not chosen at random; they are part of Zeus's larger plan. Zeus chose Alcmena to be the mother of his son Heracles because she "surpassed other women in looks and height, and in intelligence, no woman could compete with her of all those whom mortal women bore to mortal men" (frag. 195).

Europa bends down to stroke Zeus, who has taken the form of a bull, while the god Eros flies overhead. (Red-figure Apulian amphora, ca. 330 B.C. Vatican Museum X 7, inv. 18106.)

Europa running alongside Zeus as a bull. (Red-figure bell krater, ca. 480 B.C., by the Berlin Painter. Museo Nazionale, Tarquinia, Italy, RC 7456.)

The gods also intervene to determine the destiny of their descendants. Poseidon, the god of the sea, desired Tyro because she "surpassed all mortal women in beauty," and by him she became the mother of Pelias and Neleus (frag. 30.33–34). Neleus was the father of twelve sons, eleven of whom were killed by "Zeus's mighty son" Heracles (frag. 35.5–8). Poseidon gave one of these eleven sons, Periclymenus, the power to transform himself into animals, yet he was deceived by Athena and tried to fight against Heracles: "The fool, he was not afraid of Zeus's son with his enduring heart, not of him nor his terrible bow, which Apollo had given him" (frag. 33a.28–29). Still, the gods appear to have seen to it that the twelfth son, Nestor, "avoided death and dark destruction" (frag. 35.9). The poet also tells how Zeus kept a close watch on Sarpedon, his son by Europa, when he was fighting at Troy (frag. 141.21, 26, 28).[4]

The close relationship between gods and men came to an end, however, at the time of the Trojan War. The Hebrew Bible preserves a similar tradition. The immortal giants known as the Nephelim "saw that the daughters of humans were attractive, and they took wives from whomever they chose," but God saw that men had done much evil on earth and decided to destroy them (Genesis 6.4–8).[5] Ancient commentators on Homer relate that in the epic *Cypria* (now lost), when Zeus was angry at men and wanted to destroy them, the god Mōmos (Blame) advised Zeus to save himself the trouble of producing a flood by begetting a beautiful daughter, so that many men would die fighting over her at Troy.[6] But in the *Catalogue of Women*, the blame is put on the behavior of Helen and her two sisters rather than on Zeus. According to the poet of the *Catalogue*, Aphrodite saw the daughters of Tyndareus and was jealous of their beauty, so "she gave them bad reputations" (frag. 176.2). Timandra left her husband Echemus, Clytemnestra left Agamemnon for Aegisthus, and "Helen disgraced the bed of Menelaus" (frag. 176.7).[7] When Helen leaves her husband for Paris, the gods disagree about what to do: "Zeus who thunders on high planned remarkable deeds, to wreak havoc on earth and annihilate the race of mortal men. . . . He had reason to destroy the souls of the demigods" (frag. 204.96–100).

From the surviving fragments of the papyrus it appears that Zeus at this point wanted to send "sorrow upon sorrow" and separate the gods from mankind (frag. 204.105). When Apollo saw men suffer as they tried to ward off death from their children, he "took pleasure in the force of the intelligence of his mighty father, as he devised great sorrows for man: many beautiful leaves were scattered as they fell to the ground from the tall trees, and the fruit kept tumbling earthward, as the North Wind blew piercingly because of Zeus's plan, and the sea . . . and everything kept shaking from it, and the strength of men was becoming weakened, and their harvest was decreasing in the season of spring" (frag. 204.122–29).[8] The conduct of the daughters of Tyndareus (one of whom, Helen, is really Zeus's own daughter) had something to do with why Zeus decided to change the relationship between gods and men, and to keep the gods from begetting or bearing any more mortal children. As in the biblical story of Adam and Eve, man cannot remain in paradise without the moral cooperation of women.

From a modern point of view it is remarkable that so little appears to be said in the *Catalogue* about the sexual aspects of the unions between gods and mortals. Intercourse is alluded to in a brief phrase, "with Aphrodite's help she lay with . . . and bore" (frag. 23a.35); "Poseidon lay with her . . . and she bore" (frag. 43a.55, 58). The poet will say why a male god is interested in a particular woman, and describe how he managed to seduce her. His main interest is in the pursuit, and the children that resulted from it; also, clearly, he wished to explain why in later times, including his own time, the gods had stopped taking human partners. In the surviving fragments there is no detailed account of what the women themselves thought about their encounters with the gods.

But other writers tried to describe the emotional aspects of such unions. The *Homeric Hymns*, a collection of thirty-three epic poems addressed to various gods and goddesses, were thought in antiquity to have been written by Homer, although scholars now believe they were the work of different bards sometime after the *Iliad* and the *Odyssey* were composed. One of these, the Homeric Hymn to Aphrodite, tells the story of the liaison between the Trojan Anchises and the goddess Aphrodite in a carefully constructed and polished narrative; the structure of the verse emphasizes the contrast between gods and mortals.

The poet of this work begins by asking the Muse to sing of Aphrodite, the goddess who arouses sweet desire in both gods and men, as well as in all the animals in the world. Athena, Artemis, and Hestia, the three maiden goddesses, are the only beings whom Aphrodite "cannot persuade the hearts of or deceive" (*Homeric Hymns* 5.7). By mentioning these three important goddesses first, before saying anything about Aphrodite's powers, the poet gives his audience the impression that the more civilized and productive aspects of human existence lie outside Aphrodite's purview, and that her gifts might have a destructive effect that the maiden goddesses choose to avoid. Athena, daughter of Zeus, cares about wars and construction and weaving. Artemis, Zeus's daughter by Leto, cares about hunting, the cities of just men, and music and song. Hestia, sister of Zeus, is the oldest of the children of Cronus—and the youngest, too, since she was the last to emerge from her father's stomach. Even though Poseidon and Apollo wanted to marry her, she refused and asked her brother Zeus to support her oath to remain a maiden always. Instead of marriage, Zeus gave her the privilege of being the goddess of the hearth, and as such she receives a portion of the sacrifices offered both in homes and in all the temples of the gods: "Among mortals she is the most revered of the goddesses" (5.32).

The goddess of love and desire may not be able to exercise her wiles over Athena, Artemis, and Hestia, but "there is no way to escape Aphrodite for any of the others, either blessed gods or mortal men" (5.34–35). Aphrodite has the power to affect judgment for the worse, and "she even led astray the mind of Zeus" (5.36). She made him mate with mortal women, deceiving his wife and sister Hera, the greatest of goddesses: "Zeus, whose wisdom is imperishable, made her his respected wife with her good understanding" (5.43–44). Good sense and marriage, the poet implies, have nothing to do with Aphrodite.

Zeus also wants Aphrodite to mate with a man so she cannot boast that she has made all the other gods and goddesses have love affairs with mortals. To effect his plan and make her like all the rest, he "put sweet passion into [Aphrodite's] heart to be joined in love with a mortal man," and particularly so she would desire Anchises, "who resembled in form an immortal god" (5.45–46, 55). It is clear that from the point of view of the gods there is something undesirable about mating with a mortal and producing mortal children, but the poet waits till later in the hymn to explain what it is. First he describes how Aphrodite goes to her shrine in Paphos, on Cyprus, to wash and dress herself (5.58–65). Once dressed, Aphrodite goes to Mount Ida near Troy to find Anchises; as she goes through the forest wild animals follow her, and she puts sweet desire in their hearts, and they all go off in pairs into the shadowy groves.

Aphrodite finds Anchises in his sheepfold, playing the lyre. Anchises is frightened when he sees "her beauty and height and shining clothes" and her radiant jewelry (5.85). He concludes rightly that she is a goddess, "either Artemis or Leto or golden Aphrodite, or noble Themis or blue-eyed Athena," or one of the Graces or the nymphs of the mountain (5.93–94). He promises to build an altar to her and offer her sacrifices in every season. Then he prays that in return she may bestow on him particular blessing, so that he will have a long and happy life and children who survive: "Regard me with favor, and make me a man distinguished among the Trojans, and later grant that I may have flourishing offspring, and that I live long and well and see the light of the sun, happy among my people, and come to the threshold of old age" (5.102–6).

Anchises is behaving as a mortal should when he suddenly encounters a particularly beautiful and well-dressed stranger, but Aphrodite now deceives him. She tells him that she is not a goddess but the daughter of the king of Phrygia, explaining that she can speak his language because she had a Trojan nurse, and that Hermes brought her to him to be his wife and bear his children. She asks him to take her to meet his father and mother and brothers, and to send a message to her parents to send him bridal gifts: "Do these things and prepare the lovely wedding feast that is honorable both among mortals and the immortal gods" (5.141–42). Then she puts sweet desire in his heart, so that he is unwilling to wait. He says: "Once I have gone into your bed, you who are like the immortal goddesses, I would be willing to go down to the house of Hades" (5.153–54). He swiftly removes all the elaborate clothing and jewelry that the Graces had adorned her with in Paphos. The poet does not describe the sexual act but merely records that it happened. Instead, his emphasis is on the difference between divine and mortal understanding: "And then by the will of the gods and destiny he slept with the goddess, a mortal man, not knowing clearly what he did" (5.166–67).

Aphrodite pours sleep on Anchises, then dresses herself and stands beside the bed. No longer assuming the guise of a maiden, she appears in her own form, her head now touching the rafters, and "an immortal beauty shone from her face, such as is that of Cytherea [another name for Aphrodite] with her golden crown" (5.174–75).[9] The goddess awakens her mortal lover abruptly and mocks him, since she knows the answers to all the questions that she asks: "Get up, son of Dardanus, why do you enjoy unbroken sleep? And tell me if I seem to you to be the same as the woman you first saw with your eyes" (5.177–79). Anchises is afraid and covers his head with his cloak: "Goddess, as soon as I first saw you with my eyes I knew that you were a goddess, but you did not tell me the truth; I beg you, by Zeus who holds the aegis, do not let me live without strength among men, but have pity on me, for a man who sleeps with the immortal goddesses does not

Zeus pulls Ganymede toward him; Ganymede is holding a cock
that Zeus gave him as a gift. (Red-figure kylix, 460–450 B.C.,
by the Penthesilea Painter. Museo Nazionale, Ferrara, Italy, 9351.)

flourish in life" (5.185–90). Anchises does not explain why he is afraid of being
made strengthless and too weak to live, but in other myths the lover of a goddess
dies as a result: Artemis killed Aphrodite's lover Adonis, and Zeus killed Demeter's lover Iasion. Aphrodite, however, reassures him: he has nothing to fear because he is dear to the gods, and she will bear a son who will rule among the Trojans and have generations of descendants. He will be called Aeneas, "because I
had painful [ainon] sorrow, because I fell into a mortal's bed" (5.198–99). It is the
mortality of Anchises, rather than the act of intercourse, that causes her sorrow,
for he will die, and her son will die, and so will all his descendants.

Aphrodite now explains that the Trojans were always most like the immortals
in appearance. Zeus carried off one of them, Ganymede, and made him immortal, and gave immortal horses to his father, Tros, to compensate for the loss of his
son. Eos, the goddess of dawn, carried off the Trojan prince Tithonus, and although she asked Zeus to grant him immortality she forgot to ask also for eternal
youth—so when he began to turn gray she left his bed, and when he grew old she

closed him off in a chamber. Gods, who are forever young and beautiful, are particularly averse to old age, as Aphrodite makes clear to Anchises: "I would not choose to have you be immortal and live all your days like [Tithonus]; if you could live as you are now in looks and in stature, you might be called my husband; then grief would not cover my heart. But soon savage old age will surround you, ruthless old age that afterward accompanies mortals, dreadful, wearying, which the gods despise" (5.239–46).

Aphrodite is also angry because she can no longer boast that she has caused the other gods to mate with mortals, now that she has done so as well. She is also ashamed because she too has committed an act of folly, "since I was greatly deluded, miserably, unutterably, I have wandered in my mind and placed a child under my girdle by sleeping with a mortal" (5.253–55). She tells him that mountain nymphs will look after her son until he is five years old; then they will bring him to Anchises. Anchises must say that the boy is a child of one of the nymphs and not boast that his mother is Aphrodite, lest Zeus strike him with a thunderbolt: "'I have told you all; do you put it into your mind, hold it there and remember, and respect the wrath of the gods.' Thus having spoken she rushed away to windy heaven" (5.289–91). Anchises is left alone, with his life forever changed. But Aphrodite too is unhappy, because of the wound to her pride and the contact with the pain and decay of mortality.

If this poet had written the Catalogue, he might have placed more emphasis on how unions with mortals can bring sorrow even to the gods, who ordinarily live free from care. Certainly divine mothers suffer when their sons are in danger. In the Iliad, Aphrodite is wounded at Troy by Diomedes when she comes to rescue her son Aeneas, and Thetis mourns for her son Achilles even before he is dead (Iliad 5.334–40, 24.84–86). The dawn goddess Eos carrying the body of her dead son Memnon was a favorite subject in ancient art; perhaps it offered some comfort to mothers who had also lost their sons in war.[10] But the male gods also mourn the loss of their sons. Zeus sheds tears of blood when his son Sarpedon is about to be killed by Patroclus, and Ares strikes his thighs in grief and anger when he discovers that his son Ascalaphus has been killed in battle (16.459–61, 15.110–14). Involvement with mortals can bring sorrow even to gods who are not bound to them by ties of blood. In the Odyssey, Calypso is reluctant to let Odysseus leave her. In later versions of the myths, Aphrodite mourns for her lover Adonis; Artemis is enraged by the death of her hunting companion Hippolytus. Relationships with mortals have disadvantages even for the gods, because they bring them into contact with the pain and death they could otherwise have kept at a distance from their eternal lives.

For mortals also contact with the gods is at best a mixed blessing. Anchises gets a son who becomes a great hero. But the princess he thought he had been given as a bride disappears from his life; Aphrodite never returns to him, even to bring him their child. He never married a mortal wife. Since everyone at Troy

Zeus pursues Ganymede on one side of a vase; on the other side (facing page) he chases a mortal woman. (Red-figure kantharos, 490–480 B.C., by the Brygos Painter. © 2002 Museum of Fine Arts, Boston. Catharine Page Perkins Fund, no. 95.36.)

knows who the mother of Aeneas is, it seems that Anchises in time did reveal the secret and was punished for it. Tithonus enjoyed some years as the consort of Eos, but immortality without agelessness brought him only misery. The goddess abandoned his bed when his hair turned gray, and later she shut him up in a room: "His voice flows endlessly, but he does not have the strength that he once had in his bent limbs" (*Homeric Hymns* 5.237–38).

For mortal women, union with a god invariably brings the benefit of a child, "for the beds of the gods are not unproductive" (*Catalogue* frag. 31.2–3). The children, unlike ordinary children, are not only certain to survive; they invariably become important in some way, either as a hero or as the founder of a city. But usually the god abandons the mortal woman immediately after he has intercourse with her and does not help to raise his children. The woman will be left on her

own and may even lead a miserable life for some time before the god or their children can come to rescue her from her troubles.[11] The conditions of divinity make it impossible for gods to share their lives with mortals. They are repelled by human old age and decay, and they seek to avoid the sorrow and loss that is inextricably bound up with the human condition.

⊁⁞ CULTS ESTABLISHED BY GODS ⁞⊀

Gods also intervene in human life to ensure that mortals pay them sufficient honor. According to Hesiod, the custom of sacrifice originated at one of the meals that gods and men took together in the days before the gods broke off their close association. The practice stemmed from the feast at which Prometheus tricked Zeus into choosing the bones rather than the meat, which also became the

Eos, goddess of the dawn (left), prepares to take Tithonus off to her home at the end of the earth. (Red-figure kylix, 470–460 B.C., by the Telephos Painter. © 2002 Museum of Fine Arts, Boston, Catharine Page Perkins Fund, no. 95.28.)

occasion for Zeus to punish Prometheus and mankind. In any case, the gods had no need of meat, since they lived on nectar and ambrosia; they derived pleasure from the scent and the smoke from the cooking meat, because it told them that the men had given up something valuable to honor them. Other poets tell stories about how the gods saw to it that humans honored them also through ritual and by building shrines. In these myths, the gods came to earth in disguise to establish their cults there, selected the places where they would be worshiped, and chose the people who would serve as their priests or priestesses.

The main source for this kind of lore is the Homeric Hymns. One of these, the

Homeric Hymn to Demeter, tells the story of how the goddess of grain came to have a cult at Eleusis, near Athens. As the tale begins, Demeter's daughter, Persephone, is out with her friends picking flowers when suddenly the earth opens up and Hades, the god of the underworld, carries her off in his chariot. It turns out that Zeus, who is Persephone's father, had given his brother Hades permission to take her as his wife. Persephone cries out in anguish as she is carried off, but as long as she can see the earth, heaven, and the sea she still has hope that she may see her mother and the other gods again. The mountains and the sea resound with her voice, and her mother hears her. She covers her head and wanders across the earth looking for her daughter, without eating or sleeping, until finally she learns where Persephone is from the sun god, Helios. Avoiding Olympus, Demeter disguises herself as an old woman, "destroying her appearance for a long time," and goes to Eleusis (Homeric Hymns 2.90–94).

There Demeter waits by the well until the four daughters of Celeus, the king of Eleusis, come to get water. Callidice, the oldest of these, asks her who she is and assures her that she would be welcome in any of the houses of the city. Demeter replies by giving them an account of herself that is calculated to be exactly what they most want to hear—the same tactic Aphrodite used when she came to Mount Ida to seduce Anchises. Demeter tells the young women that she is called Doso ("the giver"), and that she was brought by pirates to Thoricus on the east coast of Attica, whereupon she fled across country. She claims not to know where she is and hopes that "all the gods who dwell on Olympus give you husbands and grant that you bear children" (2.135–36). She asks where she can find work as a nurse for a child or as a housekeeper. Callidice offers her sympathy for what she has suffered: "Mother, mortals must accept what the gods give them, even when they bring grief, because the gods are much stronger" (2.147–48). She offers to go ask her parents if they would like to hire her as nurse for their newborn only son. The girls soon come back to lead her to their home, and the goddess follows them wrapped in a dark cloak.

When the goddess steps on the threshold her head touches the roof beam, and the doorway is filled with a divine brilliance (2.188–89). Metaneira, the baby's mother, is filled with "shame and reverence and pale fear," and she offers the old nurse a seat on the bed, but neither she nor any of the others suspect that she is a goddess (2.190–91). "Doso" refuses the bed, instead sitting on a stool brought to her by a woman called Iambe, and does not eat or drink until Iambe tells her jokes. She refuses wine "because it is not lawful," but eats a mixture of barley, water, and mint known as a kykeon. Even this she takes "for the sake of the rite" (2.207–11). By referring in this way to the rituals that will be practiced in the future, the poet suggests that everything the goddess says and does while in Eleusis is to be remembered. Metaneira addresses her with sympathy, using almost the same words that her daughter had used earlier, saying that she looks like the daughter of a king, "but mortals must accept what the gods give them, even when they bring grief, for the yoke lies upon their necks" (2.216–17). She offers to reward her handsomely if she can see to it that her son survives childhood. Demeter again says what a mother would most want to hear, that she can nurse him and utter the incantations that will protect him from the attacks of witchcraft and evil (2.227–30).[12]

Under Demeter's care the baby, Demophoōn, "grows like a divinity"; "Demeter would anoint him with ambrosia as if he were the son of a god and breathe sweetly on him and hold him in her lap, and at night she would hide him in the fire, like a coal," to bestow immortality on him (2.235–40). But one night Metaneira sees her putting Demophoōn into the fire and becomes afraid, crying out and striking both her thighs (2.245–46). This foolish behavior angers Demeter, so she takes the child out of the fire and puts him on the ground, and she refuses to try to appease Metaneira. The mother's concern for the child's life has made it impossible for him to become immortal.

Demeter stops pretending that she is a mortal. Like Aphrodite with Anchises, she begins by reflecting on the limitations of human understanding: "Mortals are ignorant and thoughtless and cannot predict whether the fate that comes on them is good or evil, and you in your thoughtlessness have made a mistake that cannot be remedied. For I swear by the bitter water of the Styx that I would have made him immortal and ageless for all of his days, and made him my son and have given him boundless honor. But now there is no way for him to escape death and the fates" (2.256–62). Nonetheless she promises that he will have undying honor because she has nursed him, and the young men of Eleusis will always hold a mock battle in honor of Demophoōn. Finally the goddess reveals who she is: "It is I, Demeter the honored, who is the greatest blessing and joy for immortals and mortals" (2.268–69). She tells the family to build a temple to her above the well where she met the girls: "I myself will teach my rites, so that in the future you can appease my heart by performing them with due reverence" (2.273–74).

Once Demeter has made her identity known, she gives orders and no longer shows any interest in the mortals' feelings. Like Aphrodite did with Anchises, she suddenly throws off old age when she reveals her true self: "Beauty wafted about her, and a lovely scent was shed from her fragrant clothes, and a light shone far away from the immortal skin of the goddess; her bright hair spread over her shoulders and the whole house was filled with brilliance, as if from a thunderbolt" (2.276–80). Metaneira faints as Demeter leaves the house. The baby's sisters pick him up off the ground where he has been left lying, but they cannot make him happy: "Inferior helpers and nurses were holding him; throughout the night they tried to appease the renowned goddess, shaking with fear" (2.291–93). In the morning they tell their father, Celeus, what has happened, and the king calls the people of Eleusis together and tells them to build the temple.

And so they do. The temple is duly built, but still Demeter stays away from Olympus and sends a year of famine to the earth. Humankind would have perished altogether, and the gods would have received no gifts or sacrifices, if Zeus had not understood what was happening and sent the goddess of the rainbow, Iris, to Demeter, who was inside her temple at Eleusis. Iris tells Demeter to return to Olympus, but she refuses; other gods come to offer her gifts, but she swears that she will not return or let the grain grow until she is able to see her daughter again. She expresses no concern for the human beings who are suffering from the famine. It becomes clear that she is angry with Zeus, not because he allowed his (and Demeter's) brother Hades to marry Persephone, or because she thought her brother was an unworthy husband. The problem is that Hades took Persephone away from where all the other gods lived to his dwelling place under the earth. If Persephone had married one of the gods on Olympus, Demeter would still have been able to see her every day, and Persephone would not have been so unhappy, because she would have been able to see her mother.

So Zeus sends Hermes to bid Hades to allow Persephone's return to the light and the company of the other gods. He finds Hades sitting on a bed with Persephone, "who was most reluctant because she longed for her mother" (2.344). Hades obeys the will of Zeus and tells Persephone to go to her mother, but without her knowing it, he gives her some pomegranate seeds, knowing that if she eats anything in the underworld she must return to him (2.392–400). His chariot carries her swiftly back to Eleusis, where Demeter waits in her temple, and when they arrive she rushes to embrace her daughter. Demeter asks Persephone if she has eaten anything while she was with Hades, for if she has, she will have to return to him for a third of the year. Persephone tells her that she ate a pomegranate seed; had she eaten nothing, she would not have had to go back to the underworld, but as it is at least she will be able to spend two-thirds of the year with her mother and father on Olympus. Hecate joins Demeter and Persephone, and then Zeus sends Rhea to ask them to return to Olympus. This time Demeter obeys, and she also makes the fields send up their crops again, "and all the wide earth flourished with leaves and flowers" (2.472–73). Demeter did not hesitate to send a famine to the world when it served her purpose, but now that she has her daughter back with her for most of the year she is willing to let the crops grow again, for the benefit both of humankind and of the gods, who will once again receive their sacrifices. Even so, every year winter returns, and the trees and fields are barren while Demeter grieves during the time her daughter is apart from her in the underworld with Hades.

Before returning to Olympus, Demeter teaches the kings of Eleusis her holy rites, "which no one can transgress or learn about or speak of, for a great reverence for the gods keeps back their voice. Happy is the mortal who has seen these rites. But he who has not participated in the rites or who has no part in them does not have a share of the same things when he is dead in the misty darkness" (2.478–82). These rituals came to be known as the Eleusinian Mysteries, the exact details of which were kept secret. The rites honored Demeter and her daughter, but as the poet explains they also brought a distinct benefit to humankind, for those who were initiated into them had a better existence after death. Demeter and Persephone also bring rewards to the living: "Greatly happy is the mortal whom these goddesses willingly love; straightway to him they send to dwell near the hearth of his great house Wealth, who gives prosperity to mortal men" (2.486–89). The poet concludes by praying to Demeter and Persephone: "Willingly, in return for my song, grant me a living that brings comfort to the heart" (2.494). The hymn is an incomparable portrait of the deep affection shared by a mother and daughter. But the poet has also left a vivid impression of the damage Demeter can do to mortals when she is angry, and of the benefits she can bring to us all when she is not.

Another of the Homeric Hymns describes how Apollo, the god of prophecy, established his two most important cults. The Homeric Hymn to Apollo considers each cult separately; what has come down to us may have been, at least originally, two songs by different poets.[13] The hymn first describes how Apollo came to have a cult on the island of Delos. His mother, Leto, had traveled everywhere to find a place to bear her son by Zeus. But because of Hera's vengeful persecution, no place would receive her until she came to the rocky island of Delos. Leto told the island that men would gather there and bring rich sacrifices; this meant that the people of Delos would be fed by the hand of visitors, which would be a real benefit to the island because her own soil was not rich. Delos makes Leto swear by the Styx that Apollo will honor her and not despise her because of her rocky soil, and that he will build a great temple there. Leto, using another of Apollo's names, swears that "Phoebus will always have an altar and precinct here, and he will honor you above all others" (3.87–88).

With this promise, Leto finally can give birth—but her labor pains last for nine days, because Hera contrives to keep Eileithyia, the goddess of birth, from hearing that Leto needs her. Other goddesses who are assisting Leto, however, send Iris to bring the birth goddess. Leto throws her arms around a palm tree and kneels on a soft meadow; the ground beneath her smiles. The goddesses wash the baby, and Leto feeds him nectar and ambrosia. At that point the newborn god breaks out of his swaddling clothes and speaks: "May the lyre and curved bow always be dear to me, and I shall prophesy to mankind the unerring plan of Zeus!" (3.131–32). Apollo then begins to walk. The goddesses are amazed, and the island blossoms with gold and flowers. The god then travels to other places where he has many temples and groves of trees, but the poet insists that Delos is his favorite shrine, because its people are beautiful and numerous and prosperous, and they look as if "they were deathless and would live forever without growing old" (3.151–55). Also remarkable are the famous choruses of Delian girls, his servants who sing first of Apollo and Leto and Artemis and can imitate all the dialects and the music of the different people who gather at the festival.

The poet praises the Delian girls highly, but he is also eager to flatter his audience, for he wants it to believe that he is the same poet who wrote the *Iliad* and the *Odyssey* (3.173). Was he competing in a contest, or hoping that the audience would give him a generous reward for his song? His exact intentions are unknown, but he has left us with a sense of the excitement of a festival in honor of Apollo. Honoring the gods was not just a duty; it was a source of pleasure for the mortals involved. Such festivals provided an opportunity for them to meet and socialize and to compete in athletic contests. Festivals also gave poets and performers the chance to display their talents to people from all over the Greek world.

The second half of the hymn tells how Apollo established his sanctuary at Delphi. It begins by describing Apollo's journey from Pytho (another name for Delphi) to Olympus, and how once he arrives all the other gods become interested in song. The Muses sing of the immortal gifts of the gods and the sufferings of humans, "which they have from the gods because they live without understanding and helpless, and cannot find a cure for death or a respite from old age" (3.191–93). While Apollo plays the lyre, Harmonia, Hebe, Aphrodite, and the Graces dance as the Muses sing, joined by Ares, Hermes, and Apollo's sister Artemis. Zeus and Leto rejoice to see their son Apollo "playing among the immortal gods" (3.206).

In the next section of the hymn the poet concentrates on Apollo's actions in the world of mortals. He begins by asking whether he should sing of Apollo as a suitor and lover, as when he wooed Coronis alongside her mortal lovers or when he pursued Daphne. Each of these stories could have been expanded to illustrate the ignorance and helplessness of the mortals involved, but the poet rejects this course without explaining why. The audience would have known that neither tale ended happily. Coronis slept with another man while she was pregnant with Apollo's son Asclepius, so Artemis killed her with her arrows, although Apollo saved the child.[14] Daphne asked her father to turn her into a tree (her name means laurel) because she did not want Apollo to make love to her.

Instead of these myths the poet chooses to sing of Apollo's search for a place to establish his oracle. Apollo wants to help mortals as well as to receive honor from them, and he visits many locations to decide where this activity might best take place. Among these is Thebes, then uninhabited, without paths, and all forest. He comes to Onchestus, where there is a grove sacred to Poseidon; races are held there in which the horses, at least for part of the route, pull their chariots without the guidance of a driver, "for this was the rite from the beginning; the men pray to the god, and the god's apportioned power protects the chariot" (3.237–38).[15] Apollo visits still other sites in the area before he comes to the spring Telphusa, which he plans to use as the site for his temple and sacred grove. He tells Telphusa that he intends to build humans an oracle in the temple, where they will always offer him hecatombs, sacrifices of hundreds of animals. They will come from the Peloponnesus and from northern Greece and the islands, and Apollo will give them unfailing advice with his oracle in the rich temple.

Apollo then lays out foundations for the large temple he plans to build, but Telphusa is angry and urges him to build his temple elsewhere. She appears to be giving him sound advice: people will be distracted from his cult by her spring and the chariots it attracts. In reality, however, she does not wish to share the glory with another god. She suggests that instead he build his temple at Crisa on the slopes of Parnassus, although she doesn't tell him about the female snake that lives there. Apollo goes to Crisa and again predicts that men from all over the Greek world will come to visit his temple and oracle. He puts down the foundations, and the local people help him build the temple with polished stones.

Then Apollo fights and kills the female snake, which had been living in a nearby spring. The snake had done great harm to people and their flocks, and the poet keeps the audience in suspense while he explains that this was the snake that had guarded the monster Typhon. According to Hesiod, Typhon was the son of Earth and Tartarus, but the poet of this hymn says Hera gave birth to him without a father, because she was angry with Zeus for giving birth to Athena from his head.[16] As the hymn tells it: "She gave birth to Typhon, who was not like either the gods or mortals, dreadful, harsh, a plague to the gods. Queenly Hera the ox-eyed immediately took him and gave him [to the snake], an evil to an evil, and she took him in. He did much damage to the renowned tribes of men, and when any man met the snake she would bring him the day of his death, until the lord Apollo who shoots from afar shot a strong arrow into her" (3.351–57). As the snake writhes and roars in its death throes, Apollo tells it to rot (pythein) there—thus the place where the snake rots is called Pytho, and Apollo acquires the epithet Pythian. By killing the snake, Apollo has made his shrine safe for all the visitors who will come with their sacrificial offerings. Understanding now that Telphusa has tricked him, Apollo returns to her dwelling and hides her stream with rocky crags, and he builds an altar to himself in her grove. Now men pray to him also as the Telphusian.

Once Apollo has created a temple that gives oracles to human beings and made it safe for them to come there by killing the snake, he looks for men to serve as his priests. He sees a ship with many fine men, Minoans from Knossos, on the island of Crete, who are sailing to Pylos with their cargo. Apollo changes himself into a dolphin and jumps into their ship. None of the men understand that he is a god, and they try to throw him overboard, but he makes the ship shake. The men are frightened. A south wind drives the ship along, but when the men try to bring it into port at Taenarum it will not obey the helmsman. The ship is driven north, and then a west wind sent by Zeus propels it into the Gulf of Corinth and toward Parnassus, finally coming to land near Crisa.

There, Apollo leaps from the ship "like a star at midday," and sparks fly from him (3.441–42). He goes to his sanctuary and makes the fire flare up, striking fear into all the people of Crisa. Then he rushes back to the ship, this time in the form of a young man, and asks the men who they are and why they are so afraid, even though he knows what they will tell him. But he also gives them courage to answer. The Cretans' leader suggests that he must be a god and asks him to reveal where they are: "We have come here now with our ship by no means willingly; we are eager to return and find another road and other paths, for some one of the immortals has brought us here against our will" (3.471–73). Apollo replies that they will never return home to their city or their wives and families, because he has brought them there to keep his temple, which will have the greatest honor among mankind. He informs them that he is Apollo and that they will know the plans of the immortals, and because of this knowledge they will be honored continually for all time. He tells them to unload the ship and build an altar to him at the shore. The place is called Delphi, he explains, and they should pray to him as Delphinius, because he took the form of a dolphin (delphis) when he first came to their ship. The altar will also be called Delphinius and the Observer. They should pour a libation to the gods, eat their meal, and then come to his temple.

The men carry out his instructions, whereupon Apollo leads them to his temple, playing his lyre and singing, with the Cretans singing ie paion, a song of thanksgiving from their homeland. "Tirelessly they marched up the hill, and then came to Parnassus and its lovely land, where they were about to live honored by many men, and the god showed them the holy sanctuary and rich temple" (3.520–23). But the leader of the Cretans asks the god how they can live there, since the land is not fertile. Apollo smiles and explains, taking the opportunity to remind the mortals of their ignorance: "Foolish men, suffering hardships, who wish to have cares and harsh toil and adversity in your minds, I will tell you easily, and put it into your hearts. Each of you will hold a knife in his right hand and continually slaughter sheep. You will have in abundance all that the famous tribes of men bring to me" (3.532–37). The Cretans become the priests who "offer sacrifices to the god and relate the pronouncements of Phoebus Apollo of the golden sword, when the god speaks from his oracle in his laurel tree beneath the glens of Parnassus" (3.393–96). They will guard his temple and receive the men who visit, but he warns them to be righteous. "If there shall be a vain speech or deed and insolence, as is the custom among mortal men," he says, then other men will rule over them, and they will be subject to these rulers forever (3.540–41).

At this point the poet says his farewell to the god. By ending his narrative with a warning, he is reminding his audience once again of mortal limitations. He began the tale of Apollo at Pytho with the Muses singing of the gods' gifts and the sufferings of men, which are their lot because of their ignorance and helplessness. The Cretans have been slow to understand how generous Apollo has been to them, and in the future they may fail to follow the god's orders and suffer for it, simply because they are human.

Apollo builds his temple to receive honor from mortals, but he also gives them something in return: the oracles that give unfailing advice, if only humans have the intelligence to follow them. He also provides another real benefit by killing the snake that destroyed people as well as their flocks. He gives the Cretans the priesthood that entitles them to a share of the sacrifices in perpetuity, so that they no longer need to sail the seas to earn a living. The names of the sanctuary, Pytho and Delphi, remind mortals of what Apollo has done for them: he killed the snake, and he captured the Cretans by turning himself into a dolphin. The hymn shows the god intervening in mortals' lives first by coming to them in disguise as an animal, then appearing briefly as a god with flashes of light and fire, and then returning to speak to them in the form of a mortal man.

Like the mortals in the hymns to Demeter and Aphrodite, the Cretans are afraid and respectful. Although they do not completely understand what they have seen until he tells them who he is, they know that a god is near them, because their ship sails on without their guidance, and because of the sudden transformations they have witnessed. The god is generous to them, but at the same time he is indifferent to their pleas that they might return home to their wives and families. He watches over them closely and tells them precisely what to do, but when he is about to leave them he reminds them of their weakness and ignorance.

Because they have obeyed the god's orders, the Cretans will be well provided for in Delphi, even though they can never return home, just as Celeus and the Eleusinians prospered because they followed Demeter's instructions. But there is no such happy outcome for mortals who fail to respond when a god reveals to them that he is a divinity. Another story, told in the Homeric Hymn to Dionysus, the god of wine, provides a good example of what happens to mortals when they try to resist the power of a god.

In this poem, Dionysus disguises himself as a rich young man. Etruscan pirates seize the young man and take him aboard their ship, but when they try to bind him with pliant twigs, the bonds fall off. The helmsman warns the others that he must be a god, Zeus or Apollo or Poseidon. The ship's captain refuses to believe the helmsman and orders the crew to set sail, but when the wind comes up and fills the sails, "amazing things begin to happen to them" (7.34). Wine flows through the ship, and an immortal fragrance rises from it. A vine grows on top of the sail with bunches of grapes, dark ivy grows around the mast, and crowns of ivy appear on the oarlocks. The pirates ask the helmsman to put in to shore, when suddenly the god changes himself into a lion on the bow of the ship, and creates a bear in its middle. The bear stands up, eager for food, the lion roars, and the pirates rush toward the stern and gather around the wise helmsman. The lion seizes the captain, and the pirates all jump off the ship; they avoid death, however, when they are turned into dolphins. The god takes pity on the helmsman, holding him back and blessing him completely. He explains: "I am Dionysus; my mother is Cadmus's daughter Semele, who joined in love with Zeus" (7.56–57).

The point of the story is that Dionysus has deliberately set out to deceive the mortals and to test them. When the captain refuses to understand the truth, at

Dionysus turns the pirates into dolphins. (Black-figure kylix, ca. 530 B.C., by Exekias. Antikensammlungen und Glyptothek, Munich, no. 2044. Photo: Koppermann.)

first the god creates wonders that are beneficial, such as the wine and grapevine, or at least, in the case of the ivy, not harmful. It is only when the captain persists in his defiance that the god turns himself into a lion and puts a bear on the ship to frighten the men. Even then he seizes only the captain, and he does not kill the sailors. He spares the helmsman, the only one who recognized that the stranger was a god. Because he is the son of a mortal mother, Dionysus is always eager to show that he is nonetheless a divinity. He does not insist that a temple or an altar be built to him, or give the helmsman any specific instructions. The helmsman receives the protection of Dionysus simply because he has understood that the beautiful youth was really a god in disguise. Like Demeter and Apollo, Dionysus enters the lives of mortals for his own benefit, but he too, like them, is prepared to give gifts in return.

These poems show how the Olympian gods and goddesses bound themselves more closely to humankind by taking mortal consorts and producing the great families of the Greek world, and how they came to earth to establish their cults. In these tales the gods take an interest in their mortal descendants and are prepared to help other mortals who honor them. In return for the gods' favor, humans must seek to appease them and honor them by sacrificing their cattle and their crops. For mortals, the cults of the gods offer not so much solace as insurance, a protection against divine anger, as well as the prospect of gifts. Demeter and Dionysus can supply sustenance; Apollo can provide information about the future. But the poets never show gods talking, reasoning, and communicating with humans over a period of time, as God does with Adam and Eve in the Bible. In the *Homeric Hymns*, Aphrodite, Demeter, Apollo, and Dionysus tell mortals what they plan to do, but they are willing to lie to them or to deceive them by disguises. In their pursuit of due honor, they do not hesitate to frighten mortals, and they are prepared to destroy human beings if that suits their purposes, such as when Demeter causes a great famine on earth so that Zeus will allow her to be reunited with Persephone.

The gods have the power and the knowledge. To survive, humans must do what they can to appease them; they must know who the gods are and recognize the extent of their powers. These poems offer praise to the gods, but at the same time they provide mortals with the means of knowing how to understand the nature of the divinities who rule the world in which they find themselves.

CHAPTER 3

The Gods in the Iliad

The most important ancient Greek religious text was the Iliad. To us today it seems a surprising choice, because it is a long epic poem about the Trojan War and the deaths in battle caused by the wrath of one hero, Achilles. Nonetheless, even though its primary subject is killing and death, it describes the actions of the gods and their intervention in human affairs. Everything that happens in the Iliad is the result of the plan of Zeus. Other gods involve themselves in the war: Athena, Hera, and Poseidon on the side of the Greeks, and Apollo and Aphrodite on the side of the Trojans. The epic tells us what gods are prepared to do on behalf of mortals, but also about the limitations of their powers.

The Iliad was read wherever Greeks found themselves as long as ancient Greek continued to be spoken.[1] It is only by knowing what the gods do in the Iliad that we can understand the roles played by the gods in later Greek poetry, including Athenian drama. The Greeks learned from the Iliad about the characters of Zeus and his family. The Iliad explains how the gods communicate with humans, and what they are prepared to do for certain individuals whom they favor. It shows how gods can take many different forms when they make their interventions. It shows that, although they care about mortals, ultimately they care even more about satisfying their own desires. The exception to this rule is Zeus, who sees that justice is done in the end. But even he has his favorites, among the gods as well as among men; he has his own interests, and he follows his own timetable.

Most modern accounts of the Iliad concentrate on the actions of men, because the Iliad is primarily a poem about human life and death. The story of the Greek warrior Achilles and his anger, and the death and pain that it causes, provides an introduction to the tragic vision of human life and the nature of *atē*—the persistent delusion that keeps mortals from understanding the true consequences of their actions.[2] In this chapter I want to concentrate not on the heroes of the Iliad but on the gods, to show that they, and not human beings, direct the course of action of the epic. Mortals believe, rightly, that they have some power over life and death, but the events of the Iliad demonstrate that they do not have full awareness either of the causes or of the consequences of their actions. Ultimately, whether or not the mortals realize it, the gods are in control, though even they appear to be constrained in many respects by Destiny, or Fate (Moira). Some things cannot be changed, among them, most critically, human mortality and physical weakness.

No one knows exactly when the Iliad was composed, how exactly it was composed, or who composed it and for whom it was intended. It likely took the form we know about 700 B.C.; the basic narrative may have been compiled from numerous oral sources and recited many, many times before it was ever written down in its present form. Traditionally it has been ascribed to the work of a single poetic genius whose name was Homer, but nothing certain is known about who he was or where he came from. These issues have been debated since early antiquity, and we simply do not have the information we need to provide a definitive answer to any of these most pressing questions. But for our purposes it does not matter whether the Iliad was composed by a poet or poets who were able to use writing, or exactly when the poem took the form that it now has. Whoever wrote it, and however it was written, the gods are consistently characterized throughout the epic. To understand its theology, it is not so important to know when the poem was composed as to be able to understand when its action takes place relative to the chronology of events described in Hesiod's Theogony.

The Iliad takes place after Zeus and his family are firmly established on Mount Olympus, and after the gods had sought out mortal partners. Whoever composed the Iliad seems to be looking back in time to a heroic age when men were stronger and better than they were in his own era. Over and over again the poet of the Iliad reminds us that a hero, be it Diomedes or Ajax or Hector or Aeneas, is stronger than any man of his own time; old Nestor complains that no one today can fight the way he could when he was young. Specifically, the story is set at the end of the fourth generation of mortals, which Hesiod described in the Works and Days and looked back to with admiration, before the decadence of the Iron Age in which he lived.

For our purposes it is not necessary to engage in the complex debate over the authorship of the poem. Here I will assume (for it is only an assumption) that most of the epic as it has come down to us was designed and composed by a single author who deliberately planned the general direction his narrative would take. Certainly there is a reasonable consistency in how the gods and the age are described in the Iliad. For convenience I shall refer to this author as Homer, not because we are really sure that this was his name (since we know virtually nothing about him), but because that is what the ancients called him.[3] For my readers' convenience, I shall follow the order of events as they appear in the narrative, as if it had always been presented in the numbered books that have come down to us, although it may not have been divided up in that way by its original author. If we consider the narrative from the point of view of the gods, the Iliad appears to be divided into three sections: in the first (books 1–7), Zeus's two most powerful children, Apollo and Athena, dominate the action; in books 8–16, Zeus takes control in order to favor the Trojans; and in books 17–24 Zeus favors the Greeks.[4]

✦ APOLLO AND ATHENA INTERVENE (BOOKS 1–7) ✦

The subject of the Iliad is the anger of Achilles, the mightiest of all warriors of his time, but without the gods one man's anger would not have been so memorable, nor could it have caused the destruction that it did. Without the gods, there would have been no Iliad, and none of the suffering and death recorded in it. The gods are involved from the start. The poet begins by asking the Muse to tell the story: "Sing, goddess, of the anger of Achilles, which brought sorrow to many Achaeans, and sent many mighty souls of heroes to Hades, and turned them into food for dogs and all the birds, and the will of Zeus was accomplished" (Iliad 1.1–5). Homer refers to the army of besiegers from Greece collectively as Achaeans, Danaans, or Argives, names that refer to the people of Argos, the region near Mycenae, Agamemnon's home. Supporting him is his brother Menelaus, the king of Sparta, and his army, plus soldiers from twenty-seven other communities. In addition to Achilles, the most important Greek fighters are Diomedes from Argos, Odysseus of Ithaca, Ajax the son of Telamon, from Salamis, and Achilles' friend Patroclus.[5]

Even at the outset there is a terrifying demonstration of the gods' powers and mortals' vulnerability. Apollo, the son of Zeus, is angry because Agamemnon, the leader of the Greek military forces, has refused to show proper respect to his priest Chryses. The priest has offered to ransom his daughter Chryseis, whom Agamemnon had won as a war captive. But when Agamemnon refuses to return his child, the priest calls on Apollo, who comes down from Mount Olympus with his bow and arrows and sends a plague on the Greek army. "He went like night, and then sat apart from the ships, and sent forth an arrow, and the twanging of his silver bow was terrible" (1.47–49). The resulting plague first kills mules and dogs, and then the men themselves, and funeral pyres are always burning. Apollo's message is clear to everyone except Agamemnon. Mortals must first honor the gods, and only then consider their own desires. They must recognize that one wrong action on their part can harm others as well as themselves, because an angry god does not always take time to discriminate. Apollo kills many innocent men and animals, but not Agamemnon himself, even though it is Agamemnon who has insulted Apollo's priest and aroused the anger of the god.

Agamemnon discovers that his actions have caused the plague only when Achilles calls an assembly of the Greeks. The seer Calchas, himself a servant of Apollo, the god of prophecy, explains that the god will not stop the plague until

Chryseis is returned to her father. Agamemnon reluctantly agrees to give up the priest's daughter, but only in return for another war captive. When Achilles says that he must wait until more prisoners are taken, Agamemnon becomes angry and insists on taking Achilles' prize, the beautiful Briseis. Because he offends Achilles, Agamemnon helps to cause even more death and destruction. Achilles is so angry that he refuses to fight, and his withdrawal from battle leads to the deaths of many more Greek heroes, including his best friend, Patroclus. The Trojans suffer as well, because they mistakenly suppose that they, rather than the gods, are responsible for their own success, and their overconfidence leads to the death of their great leader Hector. The Iliad ends with Hector's funeral, and we know that Troy will soon be conquered by the Greeks.

Why did Zeus want his will to be accomplished in this way, with so much suffering and loss of life on both sides? That question is never answered directly. It is simply accepted as a fact that human beings must suffer and die, while the gods, for the most part, live removed from all care. But even though the gods are not troubled by hunger or illness or death, as mortals are, they do care about their children and about their own honor. Although the gods in the end all agree to do what Zeus wishes, Homer lets us see them disagreeing among themselves, and trying to act independently of Zeus. Even though Hera and Athena oppose him, Zeus is prepared to let many of the Greeks die because he owes a favor to another divinity, Achilles' mother Thetis, the daughter of the sea god Nereus. Thetis wants Zeus to make Agamemnon and the other Greeks realize that her son is the best fighter and the most worthy of honor.[6]

The war between the Greeks and the Trojans was itself a consequence of dissension among the gods. Hera and Athena were angry because they had been judged to be less beautiful than Aphrodite. The judge of the beauty contest among the goddesses was Paris, the son of Priam, king of Troy. Paris (who is also called Alexander) chose Aphrodite over Athena and Hera because Aphrodite offered to give him as his wife the most beautiful woman in the world. That woman was Helen, the daughter of Zeus by a mortal woman, Leda, the wife of Tyndareus, who was king of Sparta at the time of Helen's birth. But at the time when Paris made his fateful judgment, Helen had already been married to Agamemnon's brother Menelaus, the present king of Sparta.

When Paris, with Aphrodite's help, took Helen away from her home in Sparta, even though her husband Menelaus had welcomed him as a guest, he also aroused the enmity of Zeus by violating his law of hospitality. So when the Iliad begins, Zeus has already decided that the Greeks will take Troy. Homer mentions Paris's fateful decision in the course of a discussion among the gods in the last book of the Iliad. Even at the end of the epic, when it is clear that Troy will soon fall to the Greeks, Hera and Athena are still angry with the Trojans because of what Paris did. The two goddesses are joined in their continuing hostility toward the Trojans by Poseidon, who is still furious with Zeus for allowing the Greeks to

The three goddesses, led by Hermes, approach Paris, who reclines at far right: Hera (far left), bringing a lion and a scepter, Athena with a staff and her helmet, and Aphrodite carrying a crown and the god Eros. (Red-figure kylix, ca. 440 B.C., by the Berlin Painter. Staatliche Museen, Berlin, Antikensammlung, no. F 2536.)

be defeated by the Trojans in an earlier battle. The three gods "still hated the Trojans, as at first they had hated holy Troy and Priam and his people because of Alexander's [Paris's] *atē*; he had insulted the goddesses, when they came to his cattle yard, and praised the one who had given him sorrowful lust" (24.27–30).

Hera and Athena show their partiality for the Greeks at the beginning of the *Iliad*. When Agamemnon says that in place of Chryseis, the priest's daughter whom he must return, he will take away Achilles' prize, the young woman Briseis, Achilles considers whether or not he should kill Agamemnon on the spot. But suddenly Athena comes down from heaven to stop him. "The goddess whitearmed Hera had sent her, because she cared for both men in her heart and cherished them" (1.195–96). Gods usually visit mortals in disguise, so as not to alarm them. But Athena appears to Achilles as herself, although only he can see her. He turns around in amazement when she pulls him by the hair: "Her eyes flashed upon him fearfully" (1.200). But he is not afraid, and when the goddess asks him to restrain himself and to express his contempt for Agamemnon in words, Achilles agrees: "When a man obeys the gods, the gods listen to him" (1.218). Athena then returns to join the other gods on Mount Olympus. On a human level, her brief appearance provides a means of explaining why Achilles decides not to draw his sword against Agamemnon, but it has a larger meaning as well. It shows that Hera and Athena keep a close watch on the Greek leaders and look out for their welfare. It also shows that Achilles is more respectful of the gods than Agamemnon is, and he understands more clearly than Agamemnon what they can do to help or hinder human action.

It is not surprising that Achilles knows more about the gods than Agamemnon, because he is the son of a goddess. When Agamemnon's messengers come to take Briseis away from him, Achilles goes down to the edge of the sea and prays to his mother, Thetis, who comes to him from the depths. He asks her to go to Zeus and intervene on his behalf. He knows that Zeus will listen to her, because Thetis helped Zeus defeat Hera, Poseidon, Athena, and the other gods when at some point in the past they tried to bind him. Achilles wants Zeus to help the Trojans so that Agamemnon will realize that he has failed to pay sufficient honor to himself, "the best of the Achaeans" (1.412). The response Thetis makes to her son brings out the sharp contrast between the lives of gods and mortals. Thetis will live forever, but she weeps for her son, because his life is destined to be short and he is miserable. Meanwhile Zeus and the other Olympian gods have gone to feast with the Ethiopians, and she must wait for eleven more days before he returns. The Olympian gods keep to their own schedule, because for immortals there is no urgency.

When Zeus returns, Thetis comes to him and begs him to help her. Zeus says that if he does so he will anger Hera, his wife, and asks her to leave quickly so that Hera will not see her; nonetheless he swears that he will do as Thetis requests. He is reluctant to offend Hera; he too remembers how she, along with Poseidon and Athena, once tried to bind him. Zeus also knows how much Hera hates the Trojans: she is prepared to confront him every time he favors them. She argues with him now, because she knows that Thetis has come to see him. "You always like to be apart from me when you consider and make your secret decisions," she says (1.541–42). Zeus can silence her only by threatening her with violence, which makes the gods unhappy. Hera's son Hephaestus, the god of fire, knows how strong Zeus is, because Zeus once threw him from Olympus all the way to the island of Lemnos, where the people cared for him in his weakened state, and he now advises Hera to give in. He tells her, "I will not be able to help you, even though I am sorry for you, for it is hard to prevail against Olympian Zeus" (1.588–89). So Hera obeys Zeus and the gods continue with their feasting, and afterward they all return to the beautiful homes Hephaestus has made for them. Zeus lies down with Hera beside him. Dissension among the gods can have lasting consequences for mortals, but no disagreement can alter for long the lives of the immortals.

Human beings may think that they have control of their destinies and that they make the important decisions, but it is only the exceptional mortal who bears in mind that nothing can happen contrary to the will of Zeus. In Book 2 of the *Iliad*,

Zeus himself initiates the action. While the other gods sleep, Zeus remains awake, because he is thinking how he can honor Achilles and kill many of the Greeks (2.1–4). But unlike Apollo, Hera, or Athena, in Homer's telling Zeus does not intervene in human life directly; he always sends a messenger.[7] He tells Evil Dream to go to Agamemnon and tell him that Hera has persuaded all the other gods to support the Greeks, so that now at last he will be able to conquer Troy. Agamemnon calls an assembly, but he makes the mistake of testing his troops, telling them that he wants to return home. The army, instead of disagreeing with him, is only too eager to comply. "Then the Greeks would have returned home, contrary to their fate, had not Hera spoken to Athena" (2.155–56). Hera does not want the Greeks to "leave Helen behind as a triumph for Priam and the Trojans," so she sends Athena to the Greek army to persuade the men to stay (2.160–61).

Athena appears to Odysseus, the cleverest of the Greek warriors, and asks him to speak to the men. Odysseus brings the assembly back to order and addresses the army with Athena standing beside him in the form of a herald. He persuades them by reminding them that Calchas had predicted that they would take Troy during this year, the tenth of their siege. When the army had first gathered in Aulis to set sail for Troy, they saw a snake eat a sparrow's eight chicks and their mother, and then turn into stone (2.308–29). Then Nestor, the oldest and wisest of the Greeks, reminds them that when the ships set sail for Troy, Zeus sent another omen, lightning on the right-hand side (2.353). Since any event that happens without human intervention can be understood as a sign from the gods, even something so ordinary as a sneeze, the men do not doubt that these extraordinary events are divine messages. So everyone in the army offers a sacrifice to the gods, and the leaders offer a major sacrifice and prayer to Zeus. But "the son of Cronus did not yet answer their prayers; he accepted the sacrifice, but offered them unenviable hardship" (2.419–20). Agamemnon orders the heralds to marshal the army for battle, and Athena, holding the golden aegis, the sign of her authority, rushes through the troops, encouraging each of the fighters.[8]

Here again there can be no significant human accomplishment without the aid of the gods, and Homer reminds his audience of the fact by showing that he is more aware of it than Agamemnon or any of the other important figures in the Iliad. He asks the Muses to tell him who were the leaders of the Greek army. For the poet, this invocation is not just a formal convention; it is a serious act of piety, because the account he is about to give is a poetical tour de force, not only of memory but of skill in fitting proper names and place-names into a metrical pattern. He sings: "Now tell me, Muses who have your homes on Olympus, for you are goddesses and know everything, but we hear only what is said and know nothing, who were the leaders and captains of the Greeks. For I could not tell or give names to the multitude of men, not if I had ten tongues, or ten mouths, or a voice that could not break, or a heart made of bronze, if the Olympian Muses, the daughters of aegis-bearing Zeus, did not make mention of all those who went to

Troy" (2.484–92). And then he proceeds to recite a catalogue of all the Greeks who volunteered to help Agamemnon recover Helen for his brother Menelaus.[9] The army assembled at Troy was vast, perhaps as many as a hundred thousand men, in more than a thousand ships. There were twenty-nine contingents from all over the Greek world, and along with the names of the leaders of each, Homer gives the number of ships they came in, so that his audience has a sense of the relative size of each contingent.[10] Most came with thirty or forty ships, but the region of Mycenae, with Agamemnon as its leader, sent one hundred ships, and Sparta, with Menelaus, sent sixty. Diomedes came from Argos with eighty ships, but only twelve each accompanied the important heroes Ajax and Odysseus. When he has finished with his catalogue of the Greek ships, Homer provides a shorter list of the leaders of sixteen contingents from the communities of Asia Minor that came to help the Trojans.

The gods now intervene to keep the mortals from arranging an end to the war by means of a duel between Paris and Helen's former husband, Menelaus. Zeus is watching, but he refuses to grant the prayers for victory offered to him by both the Greeks and the Trojans (3.302). Just when Menelaus is about to kill Paris in the duel, Aphrodite comes to his rescue: "She snatched him away, with the greatest of ease, as a god can, and covered him in thick mist, and set him down in his fragrant bedchamber" (3.380–82). Aphrodite has not forgotten that Paris chose her, over Hera and Athena, when he was asked to judge which of them was the most beautiful.[11] On the battlefield, meanwhile, confusion over the sudden mysterious disappearance of Paris in the middle of his fight causes a temporary halt to the warring between the armies.

As soon as Aphrodite has brought Paris to Troy, she goes to fetch Helen for him. The goddess disguises herself as a slave who had come with her from Sparta. But Helen, like Achilles, is the child of a god and sees through her disguise, recognizing the goddess by her "beautiful neck and lovely breasts and flashing eyes" (3.396–97). At first Helen refuses to come, and it is clear from what she says that the goddess did not take Helen's feelings into consideration when she gave her to Paris; instead she treated her as the Greeks have treated the women they capture in war, as chattels, with no thought for their ties to their homes and families. "Where will you take me now?" Helen asks the goddess. "You go and sit beside him [Paris] yourself, and abandon the paths of the gods, and do not return and set foot on Olympus, but always take pity on him and guard him, until he makes you his wife or his slave! I will not go there to serve that man's bed; that would be disgraceful. Afterward all the women of Troy will blame me, and I have untold sorrows in my heart" (3.399–412). But Aphrodite is no more concerned with Helen's preferences now than she was when she led Paris to take her in the first place. The goddess does not punish Helen for her complaint, but she becomes angry and threatens to turn against her if she does not comply with her wishes: "Do not fight with me, wretch, lest I become angry with you and abandon you, and hate you violently as until now I have loved you. I will contrive cruel hatred for you among both the Trojans and the Danaans, and you will die a miserable death" (3.414–17).

At the beginning of Book 4 the gods themselves explain why they favor one mortal over another. What moves them more than anything is honor: what they want from mortals is respect, shown by acts of piety, such as the offering of sacrifices and the building of temples. Correspondingly, they resent neglect and insults to their honor. Zeus, of course, knows why Hera and Athena hate Paris, and he makes use of the goddesses' partisanship in his plan to help Achilles. He begins by taunting the two goddesses for staying away from the conflict between Menelaus and Paris, and suggests that they consider ending the war and returning Helen to Menelaus. But Hera refuses to accept a peaceful solution. Her desire to see Troy destroyed is so great that, as Zeus says to her, "if you could enter the gates and the long walls and eat Priam raw and Priam's children, and the other Trojans, then you might satisfy your anger" (4.34–36). It is only with an unwilling heart that Zeus will allow Troy to fall. The Trojans have always offered him due honor, and his altar has had its fair share of feasting, libations, and the smoke of sacrifice. In return for the destruction of Troy, Hera offers to let Zeus sack the three cities that are dearest to her, Argos, Sparta, and Mycenae. Hera's own honor matters to her far more than even her affection for her favorite cities, and she does not even stop to reflect on the damage that might be done or the innocent lives that might be lost. She asks Zeus to send Athena down to the scene of battle, to get the Trojans to break the truce.

Athena goes to the battlefield, assumes the form of the Trojan Laodocus, and persuades Pandarus, the leader of a contingent of Trojans, to shoot an arrow at Menelaus in violation of the truce—the bow Pandarus uses had been given to him by Apollo himself (2.827). But the gods do not forget Menelaus, and Athena intervenes to save his life, sweeping aside the arrow as a mother would brush away a fly, so that the arrow only wounds him (4.127–31). Then for some time the gods allow the men to fight among themselves. It is only when the Trojans begin to retreat that Apollo calls down from the citadel of Troy to rally them, and at the same time Athena goes along the ranks of the Greek army when she sees some men falling back (4.508–16).

In Achilles' absence, Diomedes emerges as an important fighter on the side of the Greeks. When he is wounded by another arrow, also shot by Pandarus, he prays to Athena to help him, and she responds by giving him strength and lifting the mist from his eyes so that he can recognize both gods and men; otherwise the gods would be invisible to him. She warns him not to fight with any of the gods except for Aphrodite (5.121–32). Diomedes kills so many men that Pandarus suspects that a god must be helping him: "He does not rage in this way without the

With Athena standing behind him, Diomedes thrusts his spear at
Aeneas, who falls backward as Aphrodite comes to help him.
(Red-figure calyx krater, 490–480 B.C., by the Tyszkiewicz Painter.
© 2002 Museum of Fine Arts, Boston, Catharine Page Perkins Fund, no. 97.368.)

help of a god, but one of the immortals stands beside him with his shoulders
wrapped in mist" (5.185–86). Diomedes confronts Pandarus and kills him because Athena guides his spear.

It is only because Aphrodite intervenes that Diomedes does not succeed in also
killing Aeneas, who tries to protect the body of Pandarus. Aeneas is one of the
most important heroes on the Trojan side, second only to Hector; Aphrodite herself is his mother, and she defends her son by throwing her arms around him.
Then Diomedes, who remembers Athena's instructions, goes after Aphrodite,
"because he knew that she was a cowardly god and not one of the goddesses who
have control of men's wars, such as Athena or Enyo, sacker of cities" (5.331–33).
Diomedes strikes Aphrodite with his spear, and from the wound pours "the goddess's immortal blood, ichor, which flows in the veins of the blessed gods, for
they do not eat food, and they do not drink bright wine, because they are without
blood and are called deathless" (5.339–42). Aphrodite cannot die but she can
feel pain, and she drops Aeneas, who is then taken away by Apollo in a dark mist.

Iris, a goddess who serves as Zeus's messenger, leads Aphrodite away from the
battle, and Ares, the god of war, takes her to Olympus. Here, as often in the Iliad,
a description of the life of the gods offers some respite from the long account of
human death and suffering. Aphrodite is soon cured and made comfortable. She
goes straight to her mother, Dione.[12] Athena taunts Aphrodite by referring to the
awful decision Paris made: "The Cyprian [Aphrodite] has been pursuing some
Achaean woman to make her follow the Trojans, since she is particularly fond of
them, and she has scratched her tender hand on a golden pin belonging to one of

the Achaean women" (5.422–25).[13] Zeus, who is also Aphrodite's father, advises her to stay away from war and concern herself with desire and marriage, the spheres of activity appropriate to her.

While Athena is absent, Apollo dominates the scene. As he takes Aeneas away, Diomedes tries to attack him, but Apollo pushes the hero's shield back three times. When in a fourth attempt Diomedes rushes at him "like a god," Apollo shouts: "Think, son of Tydeus, and fall back, and do not seek to believe that you are equal to the gods, because the races of immortal gods and of men who walk on the earth are not alike" (5.440–42). Apollo does not kill him, because the gods rarely kill mortals in single combat, although they will strike them down from afar, as Apollo did at the very beginning of the Iliad when he was punishing the Greeks for Agamemnon's insult to his priest. Rather than bringing Aeneas to his own home, Apollo takes him to the god's temple in Troy, because there Apollo's mother, Leto, and his sister Artemis will heal the warrior's wound and restore his glory. Apollo also creates an image of Aeneas and leaves that in his place, so that none of the mortals besides Diomedes are aware that the gods have rescued Aeneas.

While the Trojans and the Greeks fight around the image of Aeneas, Apollo calls on Ares to encourage the Trojans. Ares succeeds in rallying them, and Apollo brings Aeneas—now miraculously restored—back to the battle. But because Athena has lifted the mist from his eyes, Diomedes can see clearly why the Trojans have been so successful. He has learned a lesson from his attempt to fight against Apollo. Now he is terrified by the sight of the god Ares at the head of the Trojan army and does not attempt to confront him: "Comrades, how greatly we used to admire brilliant Hector for being a spearman and a brave warrior! But one of the gods is always beside him, to keep danger away from him, and now Ares stands beside him disguised as a mortal. Face toward the Trojans but meanwhile retreat, and do not seek to do battle with the immortal gods!" (5.601–6).

Athena does not become directly engaged in the fighting until Hera, angered by the Trojans' success, prepares to descend in her chariot. Now Athena puts on her armor and throws the terrifying tasseled aegis around her shoulders: "Terror is wreathed all around it; on it is Strife, and Strength, and chill Rout, and the head of the Gorgon, the dreadful beast, itself terrible and fearful, a portent of aegis-bearing Zeus" (5.738–42).[14] The two goddesses mount the chariot and obtain permission from Zeus to stop Ares. They leave their horses wrapped in mist near the river Scamander, and they step onto the battlefield; Hera takes the form of the herald Stentor and denounces the Greeks for cowardice. Athena goes to help Diomedes, who is still weakened from the wound Pandarus gave him earlier in the battle; she pushes his charioteer aside and gets into the chariot with him, and the axle creaks under their combined weight. Athena puts on the cap of Hades, which makes her invisible to Ares. She guides the spear of Diomedes so that he wounds Ares. The god of war runs off to Olympus, terrifying both armies with

Ajax fighting Hector: Athena stands behind Ajax at left as Hector, more vulnerable without his armor, falls back and Apollo comes to his rescue. (Red-figure kylix, 490–480 B.C., by Douris. Réunion des Musées Nationaux/Art Resource, New York, no. G 115. Photo: Chuzeville.)

his screams. He complains to his father, Zeus, who has little sympathy for him. In the meantime, Hera and Athena return to Olympus as well.

Without the actions of the gods, the outcome of the fighting would have been quite different: Aeneas would have died, and Diomedes would have withdrawn from battle because of the wound Pandarus inflicted on him. Many fewer men would have perished. Yet even the gods could not accomplish what they did without direct physical intervention: Apollo created a false image; Athena put on the cap of invisibility and rode with Diomedes. Diomedes alone is allowed to be fully aware of the extent of the gods' involvement in the mortals' lives; other men seem to be unconscious of it.

In Book 6 the seer Helenus advises the Trojan leader Hector to return to Troy and get the women to placate Athena so she will relent in her assault on their armies (6.86–92). The priestess Theano prays to Athena to stop Diomedes and offers her a sacrifice of a rich robe, but of course the goddess denies her request (6.311). When the sons of King Priam, Hector and Paris, return to the field of battle and the Trojans start to advance, Athena comes down from Olympus to Troy. Apollo suggests to Athena that they should cause the battle to stop, for one day at least, although he knows she and Hera will not rest until Troy is destroyed. So they agree to let Hector fight one of the Greek leaders, Ajax, in single combat. The two gods "sat, in the form of vultures, in the oak tree of father Zeus the bearer of the aegis, taking pleasure in the men" (7.59–61). Do they take the form of this particular bird because no one would think it remarkable to find vultures patiently waiting and watching near a scene of death?[15]

The duel between Hector and Ajax accomplishes nothing; Apollo comes to Hector's rescue, setting him back on his feet after Ajax has knocked him down, and the heralds at nightfall stop the fighting (7.272). Both sides agree to a truce so they can bury their dead. No effort on the part of humans can succeed in ending the war. The Greeks build a wall and a ditch to defend their ships, but the gods are watching them from Olympus, and Poseidon observes that they have neglected to offer a sacrifice to the gods (7.450). He complains to Zeus that their wall will rival the one he and Apollo had built at Troy for King Laomedon, Priam's father. But Zeus assures him that he can break down the wall as soon as the Greeks leave Troy and sail back to their homeland. Zeus thunders all night, and the Greeks, in terror, pour libations to him.

→| ZEUS TAKES CONTROL (BOOKS 8–16) |←

It is at this moment of apparent stalemate that Zeus takes control of the war. He calls the gods to an assembly and orders them not to intervene any further. He threatens to strike them down, or throw them into Tartarus, and reminds them of how much more powerful he is than any of them: if a golden cord were hung from heaven, and all the other gods pulled together on it, they could not bring Zeus to the ground. Then he drives his chariot to Mount Ida, near Troy, where he watches the battle from his sanctuary. Diomedes kills Hector's charioteer, and would have driven the Trojans back behind the walls had Zeus not thrown a thunderbolt in front of the chariot of Diomedes. As the Greek warrior leaves the battlefield, Hector boasts that Zeus has granted him victory and honor, and that the wall the Greeks have constructed will not hold him back (8.175–79). Hector's boastful words anger Hera, and she complains to Poseidon; but Poseidon, like her son Hephaestus in Book 1, advises her not to oppose Zeus. Nonetheless, Hera "puts it into Agamemnon's mind" to go himself to rouse the Greeks (8.218–19).

Zeus now gives new strength to the Trojans, who cross over the ditch and drive the Greeks back to their ships (8.335–36). The Greeks raise their hands to the gods in prayer, and Hera sees them and takes pity on them. She tells Athena that she is afraid the Greeks will all perish without their help, but Athena understands that Zeus will eventually intervene on their side. "Now he hates me," she says of Zeus, "and is carrying out the wishes of Thetis; she embraced his knees and touched his chin with her hand, and begged him to honor Achilles, sacker of cities. But the time will come when once again he will call me his dear bright-eyed one" (8.370–73).

When Athena and Hera leave Olympus to intervene directly in the battle, however, Zeus sends his messenger Iris to stop them by conveying his threats to lame their horses, throw them down, smash their chariot, and strike them with lightning. When they return to Olympus, Zeus comes back himself to confront them. He promises that on the next day Hera "will see the son of Cronus more fiercely destroying the great army of Argive fighters" (8.471–72). The Trojans are newly confident, and Hector has hope that they can finally defeat the enemy once and for all. Addressing his assembled troops, he says: "Would that I were immortal and ageless for all time, like Athena and Apollo, as surely as this day is bringing evil to the Greeks!" (8.539–41). Hector's words show that he does not realize his own limitations, and that he could never have been so successful without the support of Zeus.

In Book 9 the gods do not intervene in the affairs of mortals, because the men are not on the battlefield and issues of life and death are not immediately involved. Nonetheless, what the mortals decide to do without the intervention of the gods conforms to Zeus's plan. Agamemnon calls an assembly at which he blames Zeus for deceiving him: "Cruel Zeus the son of Cronus bound me fast with grave atē; he promised me and confirmed that I would sack well-built Troy and return home, but now he has planned a wicked deception and tells me to return to Argos in disgrace, after the loss of many men" (9.18–22). Agamemnon sees that Zeus has favored Achilles in his feud with Agamemnon by breaking the army of the Greeks. So he tries to appease Achilles by offering him many gifts and promising to return Briseis to him, swearing that he has not touched her, and says he will give him more gifts when they take Troy, and even let him have one of his daughters in marriage.

An embassy of high-ranking Greeks consisting of Odysseus, Ajax, and Achilles' old tutor Phoenix is sent to persuade Achilles to put aside his quarrel and rejoin the battle. Odysseus urges Achilles to control his anger, describing Agamemnon's generous offer; Phoenix reminds him of how the gods have affected his own life, telling him "even the gods, whose importance, honor, and power is greater than ours, can be persuaded" when men have done wrong and pray to them (9.497–501). He talks about Zeus's daughters the Prayers, who appear after a man has been visited by Atē (the goddess of delusion), and how they help men who respect them. But despite everything that Odysseus and Phoenix have said, Achilles refuses to accept Agamemnon's inducement and return to the Greek forces. Ajax observes that Achilles thinks only about himself and has abandoned his fellow soldiers in their time of need: "Achilles has made his proud heart savage, and he is not moved by friendship for his comrades, though we have honored him near our ships more than anyone, cruel man" (9.628–32). A god like Hera or Athena could get away with that kind of behavior, because they are powerful enough to have at least some independence. But (as Achilles fails to realize) human beings by necessity must depend on one another. His continued refusal to help his comrades will lead to terrible consequences, both for the Greeks and for himself.

In Book 10 Odysseus and Diomedes make a night attack on the Trojan army. Even in antiquity scholars suspected, and most modern critics agree, that this book was not written by whoever composed the main narrative but was added by a later writer. There are notable differences in style and vocabulary; also the actions of the gods seem inconsistent with those of the earlier books. At the end of Book 8, Zeus had threatened Athena, and she had withdrawn from the fray completely. But in Book 10, although the narrator does not explain why, Athena has been allowed to provide physical assistance to the two Greek leaders. We are told that Odysseus was chosen for the nighttime expedition because of Athena's partiality for him (10.242–45). Athena in this book sounds more like the Athena of the *Odyssey* than of the *Iliad*, because she takes a close personal interest in Odysseus, watches over him closely, and sends him frequent signs of encouragement. Nestor says to Odysseus and Diomedes: "Zeus loves you both, and so does bright-eyed Athena, daughter of aegis-bearing Zeus" (10.552–53). This confident remark seems out of keeping with the thoughtful anxiety expressed by Nestor at the beginning of Book 9, when he appears to believe that the Greeks cannot win unless Achilles can be persuaded to return to the fighting.

Book 11 takes up the story at the point where Book 9 left off: on a day when Zeus had promised to attack the Greek army more fiercely (8.471–72); the narrative of the deaths that occur as a result lasts until the end of Book 18. Zeus sends the goddess Strife, or Eris, to the Greek camp to rouse the army to battle. Hera and Athena do what they can from a distance to encourage the Greeks. They honor Agamemnon by thundering, something that elsewhere in the *Iliad* is done only by Zeus (11.45–46).

But just as the Greeks begin to advance, Zeus leads Hector aside, away from the battle; then, as the Trojans retreat, he comes down from Mount Ida holding a thunderbolt in his hands. He sends Iris to Hector to tell him to stay away from the battle until Agamemnon is wounded. After that Zeus promises to grant Hector the power to kill until he reaches the Greek ships and the sun sets. The poet emphasizes the role played by Zeus by asking the Muses who were the first and last to be killed by Hector, "when Zeus gave him the glory" (11.300). Odysseus is wounded, but Athena does not "allow the spear to reach his innards" (11.437–38).[16] Ajax holds the Trojans back while Odysseus is led off the field, but then Zeus himself drives Ajax back by making him afraid, and he slowly retreats.

Book 12 begins with another reminder of the gods' powers and the impermanence of human effort, especially when undertaken without divine support. The poet describes how, once Troy has fallen, Apollo will gather all the rivers and direct them toward the wall and ditch that the Greeks built without offering sacrifices to the gods; Zeus will send rain, and Poseidon will shake the earth with his trident and carry off into the sea the logs and stones with which the wall was made.

The Greeks are pinned down near their ships, "subdued by the scourge of Zeus," a term that reminds us of the god's terrifying strength (12.37).[17] Zeus is intent on giving the glory to Hector, but at the same time he makes sure that Hector does not go too far (2.173–74). He sends an omen: an eagle holds a snake, which bites the eagle, and the eagle drops it. When the Trojans see the snake writhing on the ground they are frightened, because they know the eagle is the bird of Zeus. Zeus supports Hector by sending a dust storm to confuse the Greeks, but Hector and the Trojans cannot break through the wall until Zeus helps them by getting his son Sarpedon, leader of the Trojan allies from Lycia, to attack (12.292–93). Zeus keeps Sarpedon from being killed by Ajax and his brother Teucer near the ships, and then he grants even greater glory to Hector (12.400–405). Hector is the first to leap inside the wall, and calling to the Trojans to follow him he picks up a great stone, which Zeus makes light for him (12.450). "No one other than a god could have confronted him or warded him off when he leapt inside the gates; his eyes blazed with fire" (12.465–66). No mortal could have achieved so much in the course of a single day without the support of the greatest of the gods.

But suddenly the Greeks begin to rally, because Poseidon decides to intervene. He is able to do so because Zeus, certain that no other god will dare interfere, has turned his eyes away from Troy. Poseidon has been watching the battle from the mountain on the island of Samothrace, and he has seen that the Greeks are losing. In four steps he arrives at his palace at the bottom of the sea, and then rides in his chariot to a cave near the island of Tenedos, across from Troy. Poseidon disguises himself as the seer Calchas, going through the Greek army encouraging commanders and soldiers alike. He becomes angry when Hector kills his grandson, so the god disguises himself as Thoas, the leader of the Aetolians, to encourage Idomeneus, leader of the Cretan contingent in the Greek army. "So speaking the god went back again in the midst of the suffering of men" (13.239).

In the battle that follows, Menelaus complains that Zeus has allowed the Trojans to be too successful on the battlefield: "Father Zeus, they say that you are the wisest of all men and gods, but all this comes from you, since you favor these insolent [hybristai] Trojans" (13.631–34). Zeus, however, keeps his own counsel and continues to urge the Trojans into battle (13.794); Ajax observes that they have been scourged by the lash of Zeus. Just then there is a favorable omen. An eagle, Zeus's own bird, flies down on the right-hand side, and the Greeks cheer. Hector wishes he were a god so that he could bring the war to an end. His words contrast sharply with the reality in which he finds himself. He and the other mortals are involved in an indecisive battle, and significant progress can be made only with the aid of divine intervention.

Poseidon now takes the form of an old man in order to encourage Agamemnon; he rushes across the plain and shouts "as loudly as nine or ten thousand men" to encourage the Greeks (14.148–49). Hera is happy to see what Poseidon is doing, because she is still angry with Zeus, and she decides to divert her husband's attention from the war by seducing him. She dresses beautifully, and asks Aphrodite to lend her the gods Love and Desire, concealing her true purpose. She also enlists the aid of the god Sleep, and when he objects that he is afraid of Zeus she promises to give him one of the Graces as a bride; as always, the powerful Olympian gods manipulate the lives of the lesser gods and of human beings to suit their own purposes.

When Zeus sees Hera, he is overcome by love and desire. He does not even notice that Hera, most uncharacteristically, does not complain when he reminds her of some of the other females he has slept with, even though in the past she has been violently jealous of some of them, such as Alcmena, whose son Heracles she has persecuted relentlessly as a result. Zeus creates a cloud to surround them, and while he is asleep the god Sleep goes to Poseidon, and Poseidon leads the Greeks into battle with his sword "like a thunderbolt" that holds men back in terror (14.386–87). The sea surges toward the Greek camp as Poseidon confronts Hector, and Ajax stuns Hector with a huge stone. The poet again invokes the Muses to tell him which of the Greeks was first to strip the armor from a Trojan, "after the renowned Earthshaker [Poseidon] had swayed the battle" (14.508–10).

When Zeus wakes up and sees Poseidon among the Greeks and Hector wounded, he realizes that Hera has deceived him. He reminds her that once, when he found that she had driven his son Heracles across the sea to the island of Cos, he hung her in the sky with anvils attached to her feet, and seized the gods that tried to help her and threw them down to earth. Zeus orders her to call Iris and Apollo; Iris will go tell Poseidon to return to his home in the sea, and Apollo will give Hector the strength he needs to return to the battle. Zeus then predicts what will happen: Achilles will send Patroclus into combat to help the Greeks, and after Patroclus has killed many men, including Zeus's own son Sarpedon, Hector will kill Patroclus. Then Achilles will kill Hector, and Zeus will favor the Greeks until they have taken Troy "through the plans of Athena" (15.71). Here he is alluding to the deadly scheme of the Trojan horse, which the Greeks will build with Athena's guidance (Odyssey 8.492–95). Thus Zeus will have accomplished his will, first by fulfilling his promise to Thetis, and then by destroying Troy.

Hera delivers the orders of Zeus to Iris and Apollo. Iris reminds Poseidon that Zeus is senior in birth, and stronger. Poseidon replies that each of the sons of Cronus has an equal share of the world: he has the sea, Hades the darkness below the earth, and Zeus the earth and the sky. But Iris replies that the goddesses who enforce justice, the Erinyes, always side with the older.[18] Poseidon takes her advice, but he promises that if Zeus does not allow Troy to be destroyed, his anger will be implacable. So he returns to the sea, and Zeus once again takes control of the battle.

Zeus now sends Apollo to help Hector, giving him the aegis that he customarily allows his daughter Athena to carry (Iliad 15.229–30). Hector realizes that it is a god who has addressed him, and the god does not try to deceive him: "Such a helper has been sent to defend and protect you, Phoebus Apollo of the golden sword; I have saved you before, both you yourself and your high city" (15.254–57). Apollo breathes strength into Hector, and then joins him in leading the Trojan army into battle. Apollo easily breaks down the ditch the Greeks have dug and makes a path across it, destroying the earthworks they had labored hard to make as easily as a child destroys a sand castle: "And so you, noble Phoebus, smashed the Greeks' great labor and anguish, and drove them to panic" (15.365–66).

When Zeus thunders in response to Nestor's prayer on behalf of the Greeks, the Trojans suppose that the god is sending them a favorable sign, and they push forward. As they rush at the ships like savage lions, "Zeus was waiting to see the blaze of burning fire from a ship, and from then on he would make the Trojans retreat from the ships, and give glory to the Greeks" (15.599–602). Zeus is still acting as Hector's ally, and among the multitude of men gives glory to him alone, "but he was not to live long; for already Pallas Athena was planning the day of his death at the hands of Achilles" (15.612–14). As Hector advances, Nestor rouses the Greeks, and Athena drives away the god-sent cloud of mist from the Greeks' eyes, so that light shines on both the Greeks and the Trojans (15.668–69). Zeus pushes Hector on from behind with his great hand, while Ajax tries to rouse the Greeks and keep the Trojans from setting fire to the ships.

It is at this point in the battle that Patroclus goes to his friend Achilles and asks to borrow his renowned armor before joining the fighting, as Ajax retreats in the face of "the proud Trojans hurling their weapons" (16.103–4). Since fire has come to the Greek ships, threatening their ability to return to their homes, Achilles lets Patroclus put on his armor and tells his troops, the Myrmidons, to prepare for battle, although he warns his friend not to try to attack Troy itself. He prays to Zeus to give Patroclus glory, and to let him return to the ships unharmed; but "Zeus granted one part of the prayer and refused the other" (16.250). When the Trojans see Patroclus in the shining armor of Achilles, they think that Achilles has returned to the battle and they begin to retreat.

Patroclus and the other Greeks now advance, killing so many Trojans that Sarpedon, leader of the Lycians and son of Zeus, gets down from his chariot to confront him. Zeus is greatly tempted to rescue his son from certain death, but Hera warns him that Sarpedon is fated to die, and if he spares him then all the other gods would want to save their own children too. So Zeus sheds tears of blood to honor his son (16.459–60). Sarpedon's comrade Glaucus, who is also wounded in the battle, complains that Zeus "does not defend his own son," without realizing that the god indeed tried to save him (16.522). Even the greatest of gods must yield to the impersonal and inexorable goddess Moira (Fate), who determines the allotted span of human life.

Flanked by two Greek warriors, the gods Sleep and Death lift up Sarpedon's body;
Hermes stands behind, ready to escort Sarpedon's soul to the underworld.
(Calyx krater, 550–500 B.C., by Euphronius. The Metropolitan Museum of Art,
New York, no. 1972.11.10, Purchase, Bequest of Joseph H. Durkee, Gift of
Darius Ogden Mills and Gift of C. Ruxton Love, by Exchange, 1972.)

Apollo heals Glaucus and strengthens him so that he can defend Sarpedon's body, and Zeus spreads darkness over the battlefield so that the struggle over the corpse will be difficult (16.567–68). Zeus then considers whether Patroclus should be killed in the fighting over Sarpedon, but he decides to let him go on driving the Trojans back. He makes Hector fearful and, while the Trojans retreat, sends Apollo to carry Sarpedon's body away, wash it in the river, and turn it over to Sleep and Death to take back to his home in Lycia.

Zeus then makes Patroclus forget the instructions Achilles gave him, not to try to storm the walls of Troy, for "Zeus's mind is always stronger than that of a man; he makes even a brave man fearful and easily takes victory away from him, but at another time he encourages him to fight" (16.688–90). Patroclus kills nine men in each of three assaults upon the Trojans, but on his fourth attempt he is confronted by Apollo. Patroclus does not see Apollo coming because the god is wrapped in a thick mist. Apollo strikes him from behind with the palm of his hand, knocks off his helmet, and stuns him. It is only after the Trojan Euphorbus has struck Patroclus with his spear that Hector attacks him, and claims to have killed him. Patroclus tells Hector that Apollo and Euphorbus struck him first, and with his dying words he predicts that Hector will soon die at the hands of Achilles. Hector does not heed the warning; like the other mortals in the book he cannot foretell what will happen, and he hopes for the best.[19] He does not realize that Zeus has already made plans for his death and the subsequent destruction of Troy.

ZEUS FAVORS THE GREEKS (BOOKS 17–24)

The gods keep close watch on the battlefield. Apollo takes the form of Mentes, a Trojan ally, and advises Hector not to try to capture Achilles' immortal horses, since he could not control them. Zeus watches Hector take Achilles' armor from the body of Patroclus and observes that it was wrong for him to have done so, because the armor was immortal, given by the gods to Peleus, father of Achilles. "Now I shall grant you great power," Zeus vows, "in recompense for this: that you shall not come back from the fighting, and [your wife] Andromache will never receive Achilles' armor from you" (17.206–8). Ares the war god enters Hector and fills him with strength, and the Trojans advance. When Ajax drives them back, Apollo takes the form of a herald and assures Aeneas that Zeus is supporting the Trojans. Aeneas recognizes the god, and tells Hector and the other Trojans that one of the gods has told him that Zeus is on their side (17.338–39).

But Zeus has not forgotten Achilles, even while he is granting the Trojans temporary success. He takes pity on the Greek hero's immortal horses, who are standing still, weeping for Patroclus (17.438–39). "Poor things," the god says to them, "why did we give you to lord Peleus, a mortal man, when you are ageless and immortal? Was it so that you could share the sufferings of miserable mortals? For there is nothing more pitiable than a human being, of all the creatures that breathe and walk upon the earth" (17.443–47). Zeus gives the horses the strength to return to the ships with Automedon, their charioteer, so that Hector cannot take them, and Ares takes away the force of Hector's spear so that Automedon escapes unharmed.

Continuing to pity the Greeks, Zeus sends Athena to help them (17.545–46). She comes wrapped in a cloud and speaks to each man, then takes the form of Achilles' tutor Phoenix to advise Menelaus, and is pleased when Menelaus (who does not realize who she is) prays that she may come to help him (17.555–68). While she gives strength to Menelaus, Apollo takes the form of Hector's friend Phaenops and urges Hector to fight Menelaus. Zeus takes up the aegis and sends lightning and thunder to terrify the Greeks (17.593–96). But when Ajax prays to

Zeus to lift the fog that surrounds them, Zeus takes pity on his tears and scatters the cloud and mist.

When Achilles learns that Patroclus has been killed, his mother, Thetis, hears him crying and comes with her sisters from the bottom of the sea. She leads them in lamentation: while he lives Achilles will be miserable, and she knows that he will never return home from Troy alive. Even though Zeus has done what he asked for, there is no pleasure for him now that Patroclus is dead and Hector has taken his armor. He will soon die himself, because his own end is destined to follow Hector's. Achilles is prepared to die because he was not there to help Patroclus and the other Greeks, and he blames himself for the resentment that caused him to withdraw from the battle. "I shall receive my fate whenever Zeus and the other gods decide to bring it about," he says. "For not even Heracles escaped death, and he was dearest to lord Zeus son of Cronus. No, fate crushed him and the cruel anger of Hera" (18.115–19).

Unlike Heracles, however, Achilles has Hera on his side, and she sends Iris to get Achilles at last to join the fighting. Since he cannot enter the battle without armor, Iris advises him simply to show himself to the Trojans. Athena wraps the aegis about his shoulders and crowns his head with a golden cloud, from which a bright flame shines out (18.203–6). He stands in front of his tent in this brilliant light and shouts three times; Athena also cries out. The Trojans retreat in disorder, and Achilles helps the Greeks drag the body of Patroclus out of the battle. At this point Hera brings the day to an early end by sending the sun god Helios, against his will, to bring his chariot to the streams of Ocean. Hector, although the Trojan leader Poulydamas advises him to return to the city, remains outside the walls, along with the other Trojans, thinking that they will be victorious. Homer's remark on this is, "Fools, for Athena had taken away their wits!" (18.311).

While Achilles leads the lament for Patroclus, Zeus remarks to Hera that she has at last brought about the return of Achilles to the battle. Some gods intervene only to save their own children, but Zeus observes that, in Hera's case, "all the long-haired Achaeans must be your own children" (18.358–59). Hera replies that if mortals can sometimes get their way, even though they do not know so much as the gods, she has a right to get her way as well, since she is wife and sister of the ruler of the gods. She has not forgotten the judgment of Paris against her: "Why should I not be angry with the Trojans and devise trouble for them?" (18.367).

Meanwhile Thetis goes to Hephaestus and asks him to make new armor for Achilles. Hephaestus is indebted to her because Thetis and the goddess Eurynome kept him safely in a hollow cave when Hera, in her anger, wanted to hide him away because he was lame. Hephaestus says that he will do as she wishes; he cannot save Achilles from death, but he can give him beautiful armor that will cause men to wonder. The shield that he makes for Achilles shows the gods in action among men. Athena and Ares lead an army, "both wrought in gold and wearing golden garments, both beautiful and large with their weapons, standing out

Hephaestus, left, gives Thetis new armor for Achilles; on the shield is a
Gorgon's head (the artist did not have space to depict the scenes described
by Homer). (Red-figure amphora, 500–450 B.C., by the Dutuit Painter.
© 2002 Museum of Fine Arts, Boston, Francis Bartlett Collection, 13.188.)

clearly, like gods" (18.517–19). The goddesses Strife, Confusion, and cruel Death are present on the battlefield.

Even though Zeus has now done what Thetis asked him to do and stopped helping the Trojans, the other gods are still involved in the fighting. Thetis brings Achilles his immortal armor and keeps the body of Patroclus from decaying, while Achilles arms himself and gets ready to enter the battle, telling the Greeks that he has ended his anger. Agamemnon delivers an apology, which places the blame on the gods rather than on himself for causing so many deaths and injuries: "I am not to blame; rather, it was Zeus and Fate and the Erinyes who walk in mist, who in the assembly put savage Atē into my heart, on that day when I took his prize away from the son of Peleus. But what could I have done? A goddess brought all this to pass, Atē, the oldest daughter of Zeus, who brings delusion [atē] to all, a destructive goddess" (19.86–92). Atē once tricked even Zeus.[20] This destructive goddess comes to one man after another, walking silently over their heads so they do not realize that what they are doing is wrong.

Achilles also blames Zeus for what happened: "Father Zeus, you give delusions that cause damage [atas] to men, otherwise the son of Atreus would not have caused anger to remain in my heart, and stubbornly taken my girl away from me against my will. But perhaps Zeus wished that so many Achaeans would die" (19.270–74). When Zeus sees that Achilles cannot be comforted, he takes pity on him and calls Athena: "You have completely abandoned this man of yours! Has Achilles a place in your heart no longer?" (19.342–43). Athena has already been eager to go help him; she comes down like a hawk and gives him the gods' food, nectar and ambrosia, to strengthen him. As Achilles goes into battle, he asks his immortal horses, Xanthus and Balius, to bring him and his charioteer back safely. Hera allows the horse Xanthus to speak to Achilles. This speech has great dramatic effect, because the horses, as immortals, have greater knowledge than any man: "We are not to blame, but it is the great god and powerful Fate. It was not because we were slow or remiss that the Trojans took the armor from the shoulders of Patroclus. No, it was the most mighty god, the son of Leto, who killed him in the front lines and gave the glory to Hector. We two could run along with the speed of the West Wind, which they say is the fastest of all. But it is your fate as well to be beaten down by a god and a mortal" (19.409–17). Achilles realizes from what the horse says that Patroclus would not have died as he did if Zeus had not sent Apollo to Troy; then the Erinyes take away the horse's voice (19.418).

Up to this point all has gone according to the plan of Zeus, but he nonetheless tells the goddess Themis to call all the gods, even those who do not live on Olympus, to an assembly. Poseidon asks why he has summoned them, since it is now clear that the war will soon end. Zeus says, "I still care about the mortals, even though they are about to die" (20.21). He tells the other gods to go down to help either side as they choose. He is afraid that if the gods do not interfere, Achilles will be able to take Troy now, before it is fated to fall. So Zeus stays on Mount

Olympus, and Hera, Athena, and Poseidon go to help the Greeks along with Hermes and Hephaestus, while Ares, Artemis, Apollo, their mother Leto, Aphrodite, and the river Scamander go to help the Trojans.

Before the gods joined the battle, the Greeks had been winning. Once the gods arrive, the conflict intensifies, not only between the two armies, but also among the gods themselves. Apollo, disguised as Lycaon, advises Aeneas to fight Achilles, assuring him that his mother, Aphrodite, is a more powerful goddess than Thetis, the mother of Achilles. Nonetheless, when Aeneas sets out to find Achilles, Hera becomes concerned. She asks Poseidon and Athena to consider helping Achilles so that he will not be afraid when Apollo comes to oppose him in the fighting. Poseidon advises her to wait. Wrapped in thick mist, "the gods on either side sat considering their plans; both sides hesitated to take the lead in sorrowful war, and Zeus seated on high gave the orders" (20.153–55).

When Aeneas confronts Achilles, however, Poseidon intervenes to save not Achilles but Aeneas, even though he is a Trojan. The god takes pity on him because Apollo did not come to help him: "Why does this man, who is not to blame, suffer for the sorrows of others? He has always given pleasing gifts to the gods, who hold wide heaven" (20.297–99). Zeus might be angry if Aeneas were to die, because then the line of his beloved son Dardanus would perish when Troy is destroyed. The poet surely knew of the legend that Aeneas survived to rule elsewhere in the area near Troy, and he now has Poseidon say: "Zeus has come to hate the race of Priam, and now mighty Aeneas will rule over the Trojans, and his children's children who will be born in the future" (20.306–8).[21] So Poseidon goes to the battlefield, clouds Achilles' eyes with mist, and takes away his spear. He tells Aeneas to withdraw; then he lifts the mist from Achilles' eyes. Achilles realizes that Aeneas is "dear to the immortal gods" and lets him go (20.347).

As the battle resumes, Achilles kills Hector's younger brother, so Hector confronts him even though Apollo has warned him not to, and throws his spear at him. Athena blows the spear away simply by breathing softly, with as little effort as when she brushed aside the arrow Pandarus shot at Menelaus in Book 4. Then Apollo snatches Hector away, "easily, as a god can," when Achilles rushes after him (20.444). Achilles understands that Apollo has intervened. His words echo what Diomedes said when he threw his spear at Hector's head, and Hector was able to survive because he was wearing a helmet that Apollo had given him: "Now you have escaped death, you dog! Indeed evil has come near you; but now again Phoebus Apollo has saved you, he to whom you pray when you come near to the thud of spears. But I will finish you off when I meet you again, if some god comes to me also to help me. Now I shall pursue other Trojans, anyone I can catch" (20.449–54). Like Diomedes before him, Achilles recognizes that Hector would never have been as successful on the battlefield without the assistance of the gods.

The river god Xanthus, another son of Zeus, becomes involved in the battle;

the poet uses the name the gods give him, though mortals call him the river Scamander (20.74). Hera sends down a heavy fog to keep the Trojans who have fled to the river from escaping. As Achilles slaughters them, the river god takes the form of a man and speaks to him from his depths: "Achilles, you are the strongest, and of all men you do the most evil. For the gods themselves always help you" (21.214–15). The river complains that his waters can no longer flow to the sea because Achilles has filled them with Trojan corpses. When Achilles goes on with the killing, Xanthus calls on Apollo to help him: "You are not carrying out the plans of the son of Cronus; he told you many times to stand beside the Trojans and defend them, until evening comes on when the sun sets late, and casts shadows over the rich fields" (21.229–32).

When Apollo does not respond, the river himself surges against Achilles, pursues him onto his banks, and follows him over the plain. At this point even Achilles prays to Zeus to pity him and save him from the river. Poseidon and Athena immediately come to help him, taking human form and grasping his hands. Poseidon tells him who they are, and that they come with the approval of Zeus. He assures Achilles that the river will not kill him, but that he will drive the Trojans back into their city, and return to his ships after killing Hector. "We are giving you this glory," the sea god says (21.297).

Athena gives Achilles strength, but the river Xanthus asks his brother the river Simoeis to help him drown Achilles. Hera calls on her son Hephaestus to fight against the rivers by kindling a great fire. When the fire burns the plain and threatens to destroy the river, Xanthus promises that he will withdraw from the fighting and let Achilles continue his slaughter. With his waters now boiling, the river prays to Hera, and swears that he will do nothing more to defend the Trojans. Hera tells Hephaestus to stop: "It is not fitting to mistreat an immortal god for the sake of mortals" (21.379–80).

As soon as Hephaestus stops his attack on Xanthus, the other gods become involved in the conflict. Zeus is delighted to see the gods fighting one another; he can take pleasure in their battles because there can be no tragedy or lasting sorrow when they cannot suffer death or serious injury. Ares attacks Athena with his spear, but she hurls a stone at him and knocks him down: his body spreads out over some sixteen acres of land. When Aphrodite comes to lead him back to Olympus, Hera urges Athena to pursue her. Athena strikes Aphrodite on her breasts and knocks her down. Poseidon challenges Apollo, but Apollo refuses to fight with him: "Earthshaker, you would say I was not sound of mind if I were to fight with you for the sake of mortals, poor creatures, who like leaves now flourish brilliantly, when they eat the fruit of the fields, and then wither away lifeless! Let us withdraw from battle, and let the mortals fight with one another!" (21.462–67). When Apollo's sister Artemis, goddess of the hunt, scolds him for his cowardice, Hera seizes her by the wrists and, with a smile, boxes her ears with her bow and scatters her arrows. Artemis runs away, but Hermes refuses to fight with her mother, Leto, and Leto withdraws after gathering up her daughter's arrows. Artemis goes to Zeus and complains of how Hera has treated her: "It is because of her that strife and contention have arisen among the immortals" (21.513).

Apollo now returns to Troy to protect the Trojans, who are still fleeing from Achilles. Had he not intervened at that point Achilles might have taken Troy. The god stops Achilles by encouraging the Trojan warrior Agenor to stand and confront him, later taking Agenor away before Achilles can harm him and assuming Agenor's form himself. Thus disguised, Apollo lets Achilles chase him across the plain and along the banks of the river Scamander while the Trojans retreat behind the walls to safety.

Only Hector remains outside the city, for "cruel fate chained Hector to remain there in front of Ilion and the Scaean gates" (22.5–6). Apollo now tells Achilles who he is and assures him that "you cannot kill me; I am not a subject of Fate" (22.13). Achilles is angry with Apollo for depriving him of glory, and frustrated because he cannot take vengeance against this powerful god. As Achilles runs back toward Troy, Hector's father and mother urge him to come inside the walls; but Hector refuses. He is ashamed to admit that he should have taken the advice Poulydamas had given him, to retreat before Achilles returned to the fighting. He is also afraid of what people would say about him. He knows Achilles will not accept any settlement he might offer him, so he waits. But when Achilles closes in on him, he loses his courage and runs away with Achilles in pursuit.

Zeus pities Hector, because he has always honored the gods, and he asks the other gods whether they should save him or let him die. This time it is not Hera but Athena who warns him: "This is a mortal man, long ago fated to die; do you now wish to save him from cruel death? Do it, but none of the rest of us gods will approve it!" (22.179–81). Zeus assures her that he did not mean what he said, and gives her leave to do as she wishes. Apollo, for the last time, has come to help Hector and given him the strength and speed to elude Achilles (22.202–4). But when they come around for the fourth time to the springs of the river Scamander, Zeus takes out his scales. Hector's day of death sinks down, and Apollo leaves him. Athena intervenes, first going to Achilles and telling him to rest while she persuades Hector to stop running. Then she assumes the form of Hector's brother Deiphobus. She offers to confront Achilles alongside him, and leads him forward with her deception. Achilles throws his spear and misses; Hector throws his spear but hits only his foe's shield. Hector turns to Deiphobus for another spear but finds that he has disappeared, and the great defender of Troy realizes what the gods have done to him. "Alas, now indeed the gods are calling me toward death," he says. "For I thought that the hero Deiphobus was here with me, but he is within the wall, and Athena has deceived me. Now evil death is near and not far away, and there is no escape. For indeed in the past this was what Zeus and his son Apollo always wanted, they who in time past gladly protected me, but now fate

Achilles, with Athena standing behind him at left, defeats Hector, while Apollo, holding an arrow at right, begins to move away. (Red-figure hydria, 490 B.C., by the Eucharides Painter. Vatican Museum, H 502.)

has come to me. But I will not die without effort or without glory; rather I will do a great deed that men to come will remember" (22.297–305).

Hector charges Achilles with his sword, but he is wearing the Greek's old armor that he stripped from the dead Patroclus. Achilles looks for the place where he knows the armor is weakest and drives in his spear at that point. Hector, dying, asks Achilles to return his body to Priam, but Achilles refuses. With his last words, Hector speaks of the impending death of Achilles, and warns him that his cruelty may anger the gods: "Watch out, I may be a cause of anger to the gods on that day when Paris and Phoebus Apollo kill you, great as you are, at the Scaean gates" (22.358–60). But Achilles is not moved. "Die!" he says. "I shall await my death, whenever Zeus and the immortal gods wish it to happen" (22.365–66). He strips his own armor from Hector, and drags the Trojan's body in the dust behind his chariot: "Then Zeus allowed his enemies to defile his body in his own homeland" (22.403–4).

Although the Trojans' best fighter is dead and it seems certain that Troy will be destroyed, the gods continue to keep close watch on what is happening in the Greek camp. As Thetis leads the lamentation for Patroclus his ghost appears, asking Achilles to bury him. Achilles tries in vain to embrace his friend and discovers that only a semblance of a man exists after his death, without substance. Achilles wants to give Hector's body to dogs and let them eat it, but Aphrodite keeps them away all night, anointing the dead man's skin with immortal oil. Apollo meanwhile surrounds the body with a cool mist so that the skin will not decay. When the pyre built for Patroclus will not burn, Achilles calls on Boreas the North Wind and Zephyrus the West Wind to fan the flames. Iris hears his prayers and goes to the house of Zephyrus, where the winds are feasting, and asks them to go to Troy.

After the burned remains of Patroclus have been collected, Achilles holds funeral games for the Greeks. He does not take part, and neither do his immortal horses, who are still grieving for Patroclus. Even though matters of life and death are not involved, Apollo and Athena continue to intervene, helping the men they favor in the games and harming the men they hate: Apollo knocks a whip from the hands of Diomedes, but Athena sees what has happened and gives it back to him, and then gives strength to his horses and drives his opponent's horses off the course. She intervenes again in the footrace, answering a silent prayer for Odysseus by giving him speed, and causing Ajax to slip in cattle dung. Ajax realizes what has happened: "Alas, the goddess has hurt my feet; she has always stood beside Odysseus like a mother and helped him" (23.782–83). Teucer, a half-brother of Ajax, fails to win the archery contest because he forgets to promise a sacrifice to the archer god, Apollo (23.863–64). But Meriones makes a vow to the god, and hits the target.

Finally, the gods intervene one more time to protect Hector's body and allow his father, Priam, to bring it back to Troy. Achilles has been dragging the body around the tomb of Patroclus, then leaving it lying face down in the dust. Apollo takes pity on Hector and covers him with the aegis, so that his body will be unharmed (24.18–21). Some of the gods now suggest to Hermes that he steal the body, but Hera, Poseidon, and Athena object, because "they still hated the Trojans, as at first they had hated holy Troy and Priam and his people because of Alexander's atē; he had insulted the goddesses when they came to his cattle yard, and praised the one who had given him sorrowful lust" (24.27–30). But on the twelfth day after Hector was slain Apollo speaks out on the dead soldier's behalf, reminding the other gods of his piety. Achilles, he says, "has killed pity, and he has no sense of respect, which can harm men greatly or help them. A man will lose someone very dear to him, a brother born from the same mother, or a son, but he puts aside his weeping and sorrow, for the Fates have given humankind an

Achilles sits on a couch with his armor on the table before him; Hector's body lies under the table while Priam enters from the right, followed by Hermes. (Black-figure hydria, 600–550 B.C. Archäologisches Institut, Universität Zürich, no. 4001. Photo: Silvia Hertig.)

enduring heart" (24.44–49). Hera is not persuaded; Hector's mother was mortal, but Achilles is the son of a goddess, and all the gods came to the wedding of Thetis and Peleus. Zeus agrees that the two men should not receive equal honor, but he pities Hector because he always honored Zeus.

So Zeus thinks of a resolution that will satisfy the honor of all involved. He does not send Hermes to steal the body, because Thetis would see it and realize that the other gods were acting without her consent. Instead he sends Iris into the depths of the sea to fetch Thetis. She comes and is received by Hera and the other gods with kindness. Zeus sends her to Achilles to tell him that Zeus is angry with him because he has not returned Hector's body to his father. Achilles agrees to do what Zeus has ordered (24.140).

Then the gods help Priam to accomplish his difficult journey to the Greek camp. Zeus sends Iris to tell the Trojan king not to be afraid, and to explain that Hermes will come to guide him to Achilles. When Priam's wife, Hecuba, and his family try to stop him from going, Zeus sends the omen of a black eagle (24.315–16). The god watches the old man as he sets out on his journey, sending Hermes to guide him, as he had promised. Hermes puts on his sandals and takes the wand he uses to wake men or put them to sleep (24.340–42). Taking the form of a young Greek warrior, Hermes speaks kindly to the old man and gives an account of himself that is designed to reassure him. It is only after he has easily pulled back the heavy bolt that secures the door of Achilles' hut that Hermes tells Priam who he is: "I shall go back now, so that I do not come into Achilles' sight, for it might anger the gods for an immortal god to greet mortals face to face" (24.462–64).[22] He tells Priam to clasp Achilles' knees in supplication and speak to him of his father, mother, and child, to move his heart.

Achilles thinks of his father when he sees Priam and tries to comfort him. He tells him about the two jars on the threshold of Zeus's house; one is full of good things, the other of evil. Zeus can give a man a combination of evil and good, or just evil (24.527–30). Zeus gave a mixture to Peleus, father of Achilles, and also to Priam, who once ruled a great kingdom. Achilles knows that a god has brought him, because otherwise he could never have entered his hut. He advises Priam to eat, and tells him the story of Niobe, who ate even after Apollo and Artemis had killed all her children (24.602–17). Both men and gods now sleep, except for Hermes, who wakes Priam early and guides him away from the camp as far as the river Xanthus. Then he goes back to Olympus, as Dawn with her yellow robe spreads over the earth. The Trojans mourn Hector for nine days, and on the tenth day they bury him.

So, with the funeral of Hector, the *Iliad* ends. Since Hector was killed the gods have stayed away from Troy, because their presence was no longer needed. Achilles at last has ended his terrible anger. The Trojans have lost their best defender. The will of Zeus has been accomplished.

Zeus determines the general course of the action, but even he never has absolute control. He can postpone the destruction of Troy because he owes Thetis a favor, but ultimately he must let the Greeks win because that is what he has always promised Hera and Athena. He and the other gods also must reluctantly yield to Fate, who does not allow mortals to live beyond the time allotted to them. Hera will not let him prolong the life of his son Sarpedon, and Athena will not let him keep Achilles from killing Hector. When Achilles finally returns to the fighting, Zeus does not permit him to capture Troy, for other events must take place first, including Achilles' own death.

Zeus pays attention to what the other gods say, and he tries whenever possible to avoid conflicts with them, but he is not afraid to threaten them with violence if they oppose his will. In the case of mortals, he is not always so scrupulous. He sees to it that his will is accomplished in the long run, but he does not always concern himself with the daily course of human affairs. His attention can be diverted from the battlefield at Troy, as when Hera deliberately sets out to seduce him. The other gods respond to some prayers, and refuse to listen to others. They respect piety, ignore the mortals who neglect them, and punish the mortals who fail to honor them. But mortals cannot count on the gods' help or their antagonism, because, as Achilles says, they are free from cares (24.526). They also take time off for rest and feasting. Often they are not around, or their attention is diverted when they are most needed. They care for some individuals, but not for humankind in the aggregate; they are not everywhere at every time, but present only at specific times and places.

The gods of the *Iliad* speak to some mortals directly, as Thetis does to Achilles, and Athena to Diomedes, but much more often their communications are made through indirect means. Zeus never speaks to mortals himself, instead sending messages to them through Iris and Hermes. The other gods prefer to come in the form of a trusted friend or ally to offer needed advice to mortals. On occasion they will send a message through a dream. They will offer general support or send general warnings through omens, like a thunderclap, or the sudden appearance of birds or other animals. But they rarely share all the knowledge they have with human beings. Some gods may not even know what Zeus has intended; of all of them, only he seems to have certain knowledge of the future.

Thetis tells Achilles that he will die if he remains at Troy, but she does not warn him that his withdrawal from the fighting will lead to the death of Patroclus. Athena lifts the mist from Diomedes' eyes in Book 5, but not at other times. Hector occasionally seems aware that he is being helped by one of the gods, but often he assumes that he, rather than a god, is responsible for his success; in Book 22 Hector does not realize until it is too late that Athena has tricked him into taking a stand against Achilles. Other mortals understand even less of what is going on around them. It is a condition of mortality to lack complete understanding of what is happening in the present, let alone what will happen in the future.

The gods are aware of all the disabilities of mortal existence, but they do not try to make any permanent change in the conditions of human life. They allow mortals to suffer and to die, and assume that most mortals can endure the losses and deaths that are inherent in their condition. As Apollo says, "a man will lose someone very dear to him, a brother born from the same mother, or a son, but he puts aside his weeping and sorrow, for the Fates have given humankind an enduring heart." The gods may pity a mortal, or even weep for someone close to one of them, as Thetis does for Achilles, but the poet never lets them be sad for very long. They may get angry, and even strike out at one another, as they do in Book 21, but without doing any lasting damage. Hera quarrels with Zeus, and Iris taunts Hera. But soon they return to their feasting, and they sleep soundly every night in the comfort of their homes.

As the poet imagines it, the life of the gods is a highly idealized form of human life; it is what human life would be if mortals were deathless, ageless, and strong, if they had continual access to plentiful supplies of nourishing food, and could move swiftly from one place to another and change shape and appearance at will. In Book 13 Poseidon can come in four steps from Samothrace to his palace near Aegae at the bottom of the sea. He then rides in his chariot straight to a cave between the islands of Tenedos and Imbros near Troy. Of course no mortal can move across space so quickly and efficiently. In Book 24 Priam must make careful preparations for his journey to the Greek camp: his sons must get the mule cart ready and load it with gifts for Achilles. Then they must yoke the mules to the cart, along with Priam's own horses. Then Priam needs to reassure his wife and offer prayers to Zeus. The distance between Troy and the camp is not far, but it is fraught with danger, and the fearful old man reaches his goal only because Hermes is there to help him. The cruel realities of mortal life stand out more strongly against the background of the blessed existence of the gods.

Like all mortals, Priam cannot count on help from the gods or easily recognize such signs and help as the gods choose to send him. Mortals can hope for the gods' favor and do what they can to secure it, by offering sacrifices and prayers, and they can try to find reassurance in omens and portents, which they may or may not interpret correctly. But on the whole the gods are not concerned with the affairs or feelings of most human beings. That is why they do not seem to object if a mortal complains about how the gods have treated them. When the Trojans' ally Asius accuses Zeus of being "a lover of untruths," the god pays no attention because he is intent on giving glory to Hector (12.164, 12.173–74). The gods concentrate on those few mortals who are important to them, but they are prepared to abandon even their favorites when it is time for them to die. Communication with the gods is brief and lacking in comfort, even for the gods' children and other favored mortals. The Greeks learned from the *Iliad* that the gods did not exist to make them happy, and that at best human life involved suffering: not even the mortal children of the gods are free from sorrow. They also saw how more often than not mortals were unable to see, and did not understand, what the gods were doing. Only in retrospect might they realize that what happened was all part of the plan of Zeus.

CHAPTER 4

The Gods in the *Odyssey*

The gods were willing to let the Greeks conquer Troy, because the Trojans did not return Helen when Paris took her from Menelaus. But they soon had reason to punish the Greeks as well. During the sack of Troy, Ajax son of Oileus (a different Ajax from the one who fought in the *Iliad*) raped a Trojan princess, Priam's daughter Cassandra, in Athena's temple, and the Greeks did not punish him for this offense to the goddess. So Athena asked Poseidon to send a storm to destroy and scatter their fleet as they returned home, and she struck Ajax son of Oileus with lightning. Menelaus was driven far away from Greece, to Egypt, and Agamemnon landed in the territory of a cousin who had reason to be hostile to him. Odysseus too was driven off course. The *Odyssey* is the story of his wanderings, and his long-delayed return to reclaim his kingdom on the island of Ithaca, off the west coast of Greece.

As the epic begins, Odysseus has been away from home for twenty years; he spent the first ten of those years in the siege of Troy, and after that it took him another ten years to return to Ithaca. In his absence his neighbors have violated the basic laws of hospitality. On the presumption that he is dead or will never return, they have sought to marry his wife, Penelope, against her will, and they have remained in his house, eating his livestock, while they wait for her to decide which of the suitors she will take as her new husband.

In the *Iliad* many gods are involved in the affairs of mortals and they intervene with deftness and urgency, because time is short and death is constantly near at hand. The events of the *Iliad* are crowded into some fourteen days and take place in one locality.[1] In the *Odyssey*, however, the gods have time to speak with the mortals they have come to assist, and the inclination to explain their actions. The events described in the first half of the *Odyssey* take place all over the Mediterranean, during a period of more than ten years.

The differences in pacing in the two epics might make it appear that they were composed by two different poets. But it is also true that each narrative requires different responses from the gods. In the *Odyssey*, as in the *Iliad*, the gods intervene to ensure that human history follows a certain course. They are concerned with justice, and with making sure that crimes are punished. For the purpose of this discussion I will not try to question the ancient assumption that both epics were written by the same poet, and I will assume that both epics were composed about the same time and that we cannot know which was composed first. I discuss the *Odyssey* after the *Iliad* only because the story it tells happened after the fall of Troy.

In the *Odyssey*, as in the *Iliad*, the gods do not approve of adultery or the misappropriation of another man's property. But in the *Odyssey* only four of the Olympian gods play an active role: Zeus, Athena, Hermes, and Poseidon. Hermes makes a few brief appearances as a guide and messenger, and Zeus and Poseidon intervene only indirectly, at a distance. Athena, however, intervenes frequently, often in disguise, sometimes directly as herself, and other times indirectly, by putting a thought in someone's mind or by causing weapons to fall short of their target. In the *Iliad* she is concerned primarily with harming the Trojans in any way that she can; in that epic we see the violent and destructive side of her character. In the *Odyssey* she is a much more beneficent presence: she is an adviser, counselor, and guide, a worker of miracles. She shows the warlike side of her character only in connection with the suitors; otherwise she is concerned with bringing peace and reconciliation to Odysseus and his family, and comforting them when they are in distress. In the *Iliad* she is the goddess of war. In the *Odyssey* she is the goddess of the palace and champion of the values of a civilized life.

⊁| ZEUS AND ATHENA AGAINST POSEIDON (BOOKS 1–12) |⊱

Throughout the *Odyssey*, Homer repeatedly reminds us of the presence and the power of the gods. He begins by asking the Muse to tell him the story "of the man of many turns, who wandered very much, and sacked the holy city of Troy; he saw the cities of many men and understood their minds, and on the sea suffered many sorrows in his heart while saving his own life and bringing his comrades home" (*Odyssey* 1.1–5). Odysseus did not save his comrades, in fact, because they perished through their own folly; they ate the cattle of the god of the sun, and "he took away from them the day of their return" (1.9). The poet asks the Muse to begin the tale from any point she wishes, and the narrative takes up with Odysseus in the middle of his wanderings, as he is being prevented from going home by the goddess Calypso, a daughter of Atlas.

Calypso has kept Odysseus in her cave because she wanted him to be her husband. When the time comes that the other gods have ordained for him to return, they all take pity on him, all except Poseidon, who is angry with Odysseus for blinding the Cyclops Polyphemus, who is the sea god's son. But at the moment Poseidon has gone to visit the Ethiopians for a festival and is enjoying the sacrifices, while the other gods are together on Mount Olympus. Zeus begins to speak to them; he has been thinking about Aegisthus. While Agamemnon was away at Troy, back home Aegisthus had been busy making love to Agamemnon's wife, Clytemnestra. The gods had warned Aegisthus not to kill Agamemnon and marry his wife while he was in Troy; they even sent Hermes to tell him that Agamemnon's son Orestes would avenge his father's death, but Aegisthus would not listen. He murdered Agamemnon when he came home from Troy, but now in turn Aegisthus has been killed by Orestes. Zeus says to the assembled Olympians: "How mortals blame the gods, and say that evils come from us! But they themselves because of their own folly have sorrow beyond what was fated for them" (1.32–34).

Athena responds: "May anyone who does such things suffer the same fate! But my heart grieves for clever Odysseus, ill-fated, who far from his friends suffers sorrows on a sea-girt island" (1.47–50). Odysseus longs for home and wants to die if he cannot return there: "And you have no concern for him in your heart, Olympian. And did not Odysseus do you honor in sacrificing beside the Argive ships in wide Troy? Why are you so angry with Odysseus, Zeus?" (1.59–62). This last question has a special sting, because the word the goddess uses for "be angry with" (odusao) echoes the sound of Odysseus's name.[2] Zeus replies that he is well aware of the piety of Odysseus, but that Poseidon has a right to be angry with the man because of what he did to the Cyclops. As in the *Iliad*, the gods take advantage of another's absence to embark on a new course of action. Zeus says, "Poseidon will give up his anger. He cannot fight alone against the will of all the immortal gods" (1.77–79).

Athena suggests that Zeus should get Calypso to release Odysseus. Then she herself goes to Ithaca, the home of Odysseus, to encourage his son Telemachus to call an assembly. She wants Telemachus to speak out against the suitors, who are slaughtering his father's sheep and cattle. Then Athena will send Telemachus to Pylos and Sparta to learn about his father and win glory for himself. To accomplish her purpose, she intervenes directly, putting on her sandals and taking the powerful spear that she uses in battle. When she comes to the threshold of Odysseus's home in Ithaca, she takes the form of Mentes, leader of the Taphians; the name Mentes suggests a person who has come to offer advice and support.[3] In this disguise, simply by her persuasive speech, she sets in motion the events of the next several books.

While the suitors eat and drink, and the bard is singing, Athena (as Mentes) speaks with Telemachus, claiming to be a friend of his father and telling him that if Odysseus were there he would kill them. Mentes encourages Telemachus to call an assembly and ask the suitors to leave, and then advises him to go to Nestor in

Pylos and to Menelaus in Sparta to learn what he can from them about Odysseus. Taking the form of a bird, the goddess leaves by flying up through a vent in the roof. Telemachus has new strength and courage; he thinks of his father more than before, and he realizes that it was a god who had spoken with him (1.319–23).

Even when Athena is away from the scene of the action, she takes an interest in the welfare of the wife and son of Odysseus. Following her advice, Telemachus asks his mother, Penelope, to return to her room, where she weeps for Odysseus until "Athena threw sweet sleep on her eyelids" (1.364). The goddess manages to be present whenever she is needed, as when she invests Telemachus with divine beauty before he goes at dawn to address the assembly (2.12).

After Telemachus has told the suitors to leave his house, Zeus sends two eagles over the assembly to indicate his approval (2.146–54). A trusted friend of Odysseus named Mentor tells the men of Ithaca that it is evident that there is no reward for kings who are just and kind to their people, since his people have now forgotten Odysseus and are allowing the suitors to plunder his house (2.230–34). When the assembly breaks up without taking any action, Telemachus goes to the seashore and prays to Athena. The goddess now takes the form of Mentor, whose name, like that of Mentes, suggests his power as an adviser. As Mentor, Athena advises Telemachus to pay no attention to the suitors and begins to make the arrangements necessary for his journey to Nestor and Menelaus (2.270–95). Telemachus assures his old nurse Eurycleia that "this plan is not without sanction from a god" (2.372). Next Athena disguises herself as Telemachus and recruits a crew for the ship. She then makes the suitors so sleepy that they return to their homes, and, once again as Mentor, summons Telemachus to embark (2.401–6). She leads him onto the ship and sits beside him, sending a favorable southwest wind as the men pour libations to the gods, and especially to Athena (2.420–21, 432–33).

When the ship arrives in Pylos, Athena, disguised as Mentor, leads Telemachus ashore and encourages him to go directly to Nestor. Telemachus is afraid that he will not know what to say, but Athena assures him that a god will advise him: "For I do not believe that you have been born and raised without the help of the gods" (3.27–28). She even joins Nestor and his men in praying to Poseidon, and gives Telemachus the courage to speak to Nestor (3.75–77). Nestor replies that he hopes Athena will favor Telemachus as much as she cared for Odysseus: "For I have never seen gods so favorable as Pallas Athena when she stood by that man openly. If she wanted to favor you thus and care for you in her heart, then each suitor could forget about his marriage" (3.221–24).

Athena's affection for Odysseus and his family is extraordinary, especially since she is not his mother or his lover. When Telemachus says that the goddess could never show him such favor, Athena as Mentor objects that "a god can easily save a man, even from a distance," adding however that "not even the gods can ward off death the leveler from a man they love, when the cruel fate of sorrowful death takes him" (3.231, 236–38). Athena suggests that they offer prayers to Poseidon, who will try to block the return of Odysseus, and says she will stay near the ship while Telemachus goes to Nestor's house to sleep. As soon as she has spoken, she leaves in the form of a vulture. All are amazed at the sight, and Nestor states that even though Telemachus is young he has the gods as escorts; he recognizes that this was Athena, and he prays to her and offers a sacrifice of a heifer. Athena hears his prayer, and on the next morning she comes to accept the sacrifice when it is offered (3.375–85, 435–36). After the ritual meal, Telemachus sets out on his journey across country to see Menelaus.

Athena does not join Telemachus for the trip to Sparta, because she is not needed there. He is accompanied instead by Nestor's son Pisistratus, and when they arrive they are welcomed by Menelaus and Helen, herself (like Athena) a daughter of Zeus, now reunited with her husband after the long Trojan War. The story Menelaus tells of his return from Troy reminds Homer's audience of the power of the gods. As he relates it, the sea goddess Eidothea took pity on Menelaus when his ships were becalmed near Egypt, and she advised him to consult her father, the god Proteus, the old divinity of the sea. The old god warned him that he should have sacrificed to Zeus, and now he needed to make amends for it. Proteus told Menelaus that Aegisthus had killed his brother Agamemnon, and that Odysseus was being held against his will by the goddess Calypso. But Proteus also said that in the end Menelaus would be rewarded by the gods, not because of his own virtues, but because he was married to a daughter of Zeus, and the gods are partial to their children and their families: "You are not fated to die or to pursue your destiny in Argos that nourishes horses, but the gods will send you to the Elysian Fields and the ends of the earth, where blond Rhadamanthys dwells; there existence for mortals is at its easiest; there is no snow, or heavy storm or rain, but always Oceanus sends the breezes of the light-breathing west wind to keep men cool, because you are Helen's husband and in the gods' eyes the son-in-law of Zeus" (4.561–69).

Meanwhile, back in Ithaca, the suitors are conspiring to ambush Telemachus on his way home and kill him. The herald Medon hears them plotting and tells Penelope, who prays to Athena. The goddess sends a phantom that resembles Penelope's sister Iphimede to speak to Penelope in a dream: "The gods who live at their ease do not allow you to weep or lament, since your child will return home, because he has done no wrong to the gods" (4.805–7). When Penelope asks about Odysseus, the phantom assures her that "such an escort goes along with him as other men have prayed might stand by them, Pallas Athena, and she can save him, because she pities you in your sorrow" (4.826–28). But the phantom does not tell her whether Odysseus is alive or dead, because if Penelope knew too much she might reveal Athena's plan to the suitors.

As we have seen in the *Iliad*, it is not at all usual for a god to take such close interest in the day-to-day existence of mortals. In the *Iliad* Thetis was the only goddess who offered comfort to a mortal, and that was because he was her son. Athena is a much more powerful goddess than Thetis, but even so she cannot change the conditions of mortal life: she can ward off harm, but ultimately she cannot keep her mortal friends from dying. Although she can somewhat alleviate their sorrows, she cannot stop their suffering altogether, because death and suffering are inevitable in human life.

As another day begins, Dawn rises from her bed beside Tithonus, the mortal man she abducted to be her consort. The myth has a direct relevance to the story of Odysseus, who is still being held against his will by Calypso. The gods again hold council. Athena is thinking of Odysseus, and she reminds them of his sorrows; "she was concerned that he was still in the house of the goddess" Calypso (5.6). She repeats what Mentor said to the assembly in Ithaca, that there is no reward for kings who are just and kind to their people, since his people have now forgotten Odysseus and are allowing the suitors to plunder his house. Zeus assures her that she has the power to bring Telemachus home safely, and he tells his son Hermes to order Calypso to let Odysseus build a raft and begin his voyage home.

So Hermes puts on his immortal sandals, which carry him across the sea from Olympus to Calypso's island. The goddess is in her cave, singing as she weaves, and Hermes stops to admire the beautiful setting. Calypso remarks that Hermes does not often come there, although she receives him kindly. But when he tells her why Zeus has sent him she is angry, complaining that the gods do not allow goddesses to take mortal men as husbands. Dawn chose Orion, but Artemis killed him; Zeus struck Demeter's lover Iasion with a thunderbolt. She herself had saved Odysseus from a shipwreck and wanted to make him immortal and ageless. "But since there is no way for another god to avoid or escape the will of Zeus who holds the aegis, let him go across the barren sea, if Zeus commands and orders it" (5.137–40). She cannot send him herself, because she has no ships, but promises to advise and help him. Hermes cautions her not to change her mind, and to avoid the anger of Zeus.

When Calypso goes to Odysseus to tell him that she will let him go, he insists that she swear an oath not to "plan any other evil sorrow for me" (5.179). Calypso swears by the Styx: "For I too have a mind that is just, nor is the heart in my breast made of iron, but it can feel pity" (5.190–91). Calypso takes Odysseus back to the cave and gives him the kind of food mortal men eat (not the nectar she had offered Hermes). Then she reminds him of what he will suffer before he can return home, although he could have stayed with her and become immortal. She asks why he longs to see his wife, who could not compete with her, an immortal goddess, in appearance.

The reply Odysseus makes to her brings out one of the most important differences between gods and mortals. Humans have ties to each other, and to their homeland and property, and the intensity of these ties is all the stronger precisely

Calypso offers a chest to Odysseus, who is sitting on a couch. (Red-figure
Lucanian hydria, ca. 390–380 B.C. Museo Nazionale, Naples, 81839 [H 2899].)

because they cannot last. "Great goddess," he says, "do not be angry with me! I
myself know very well that wise Penelope is inferior to you in appearance and
stature, for she is mortal, and you are immortal and ageless. Yet even so I wish
and desire every day to go home and to see the day of my return. If a god wrecks
me on the wine-dark sea, I will bear it, because I have an enduring heart in my
breast. I have already suffered and toiled greatly on the sea and in war; let these
new troubles be added to those" (5.215–24). The goddess and the mortal then go
to bed together, but on the next morning Calypso gives him gifts and Odysseus
starts work on his raft.

On the fifth day, Calypso bathes Odysseus, provisions him with food and supplies, and sends him on his way as she dispatches a favoring wind behind him.
Odysseus sails for seventeen days, but just as he begins to see the land of the
Phaeacians, Poseidon catches sight of him while returning to Olympus from the
land of the Ethiopians. The god takes advantage of the opportunity to send a
storm, since he knows that once Odysseus reaches the Phaeacians, "his fate is to
reach the limit of his misery and escape from it" (5.288–89). The raft is destroyed, and Odysseus almost drowns. But he is saved by the intervention of a sea
goddess, Ino, also known as Leucothea. Ino advises him to take off his clothes
and abandon the raft, and gives him a shawl to support him as he swims to shore.
Odysseus hesitates because he is not sure whether he can trust the goddess; then
Poseidon sends a great wave that breaks the raft into pieces. Poseidon departs for

his palace at Aegae, leaving Odysseus swimming; but soon Athena arrives and stops the winds.

Odysseus swims for two more days straight; on the third day at last he comes near to shore, where he would have been overwhelmed by a large wave if Athena had not given him the forethought to approach through the mouth of a river. Odysseus prays to the river god, and the god calms the waves. As soon as he has recovered his breath, he puts Ino's shawl into the river so that it can be carried out to sea. No gods assist him once he is on shore, as he uses his keen intelligence to find a safe resting place in a thicket of wild and domestic olive trees.

While Odysseus sleeps, Athena goes to the city of the Phaeacians. The king there had a beautiful daughter, named Nausicaa, who was soon to be of marriageable age. Athena takes the form of a companion of the young princess and tells her that she should ask her father for a wagon and go to the sea to wash her clothes. Leaving the excitement on earth, the goddess then returns to the peace and beautiful surroundings of Olympus. As Nausicaa and her companions leave for the seashore, "Athena thought of another plan, that Odysseus might wake up and see the beautiful girl, who might lead him to the city of the Phaeacians" (6.112–14). The goddess gives her courage so that she does not flee when Odysseus emerges from the olive thicket, holding a branch in front of him to cover his nakedness (6.139–40). After the girls have given him clothes, Athena makes him appear taller and more handsome, which Nausicaa understands to be the work of a god (6.240–41).

Athena comes to meet Odysseus at the outskirts of the city, where he is waiting in a grove of poplars that is sacred to her. Odysseus prays to Athena: "Listen to me now, since before you did not listen to me when I was being shipwrecked, when the famous Earthshaker was wrecking me; grant that the Phaeacians may receive me as a friend and take pity on me!" (6.325–27). Athena hears him, but she does not appear to him face to face in deference to Poseidon, her father's brother, who will remain angry with Odysseus until he reaches his homeland. Instead she comes to him disguised as a young girl who leads him into the town, and shrouds him in mist so that none of the inhabitants see him as he enters. She also explains who the rulers are, and how to approach Nausicaa's mother; then she leaves him and goes across the sea to Marathon and Athens, where she enters the house of the Athenian king Erechtheus.

In the morning, Athena again makes plans for Odysseus to return home. Disguising herself as a herald, she calls the Phaeacians to an assembly, at which she makes Odysseus appear taller and more handsome so they will treat him with respect (8.15–23). Alcinous, the king, orders a ship to be made ready to take him home, and a banquet is prepared. Athletic competitions are held, during which Athena takes the form of a man who calls out that the throw Odysseus makes has surpassed all the others. As the banquet begins, Odysseus asks the bard Demodocus to sing the story of the wooden horse that the Greeks used in the final assault on Troy, "which Epeius made with the help of Athena, and Odysseus brought to the acropolis as an ambush, after filling it with men" (8.493–95). Odysseus weeps, as he had earlier when the bard sang about Troy. His sorrow suggests to the Phaeacians that he is someone who played an important role in the Trojan War, as in fact he did, having contrived the clever scheme of hiding Greek soldiers inside the huge horse that the Trojans took inside the city, which brought about the final downfall of Troy. Alcinous notices him, and asks him to tell them his name and where he comes from.

So Odysseus begins to tell the long narrative of his journeys so far. He is the principal speaker in the next three books, and he tells the story from his own perspective, which is both more personal and narrower than that of Homer, since Odysseus does not claim to know what men do and think, and cannot describe the actions and thoughts of the gods.

He starts his tale by mentioning how Calypso tried to make him her husband and keep him from returning home; but "there is nothing sweeter than one's homeland and parents," he says, "even when one is living in a wealthy house in another land far from one's parents" (9.33–36). Zeus, as he sees it, is responsible for the hardships he and his party of men encountered soon after they left Troy for home. They first landed at a place inhabited by people called Cicones, whose city they sacked. But more Cicones arrived early the next day and attacked the Greeks when they were unprepared: "Then an evil doom from Zeus came to us who were ill-fated, so that we suffered many sorrows" (9.52–53). Odysseus and most of his companions managed to escape, but six men from each of his twelve ships were lost. Then Zeus sent a violent north wind, compelling them to wait on shore for two days. When they set off again, another north wind drove them south to the land of the lotus-eaters. There three of his men couldn't resist eating the lotus flowers that grew there, and it made them forget about their homeland and not care about going back, although the others forced them to come with them.

They next came to the land of the Cyclopes, who have no laws or agriculture but live off the land and the rain Zeus sends them. At first the men thought they had found a safe harbor there, and that "a god led them through the dark night" (9.142–43). The nymphs sent them some mountain goats, which they killed and ate. But instead of leaving directly, Odysseus took his own ship and sailed off to the inhabited part of the island to see if the people would offer them some hospitality. There they found a cave with sheep and goats outside it; no one was inside, so they took some cheese from the cave and prepared to drive some of the lambs and kids back to their ships.

Before they could abscond, however, the owner of the cave returned, and he was no ordinary mortal but a monstrous one-eyed Cyclops whose name was Polyphemus. Odysseus explained that they were driven off course and came to him as suppliants, which meant they were protected by Zeus, to which the Cyclops answered, "We Cyclopes do not care about Zeus or the other blessed gods, since we are much stronger" (9.275–76). The Cyclops then proceeded to eat two of his men. Trapped in the cave, Odysseus was in even greater danger than he had been at Troy, because Athena was not ready to help him. The Cyclops was much too strong for him to try to kill, and only the Cyclops could move aside the huge rock he used as a door to the cave. The next day, the Cyclops ate two more men, but after that Odysseus began to think of a scheme. While the Cyclops was away from the cave with his flocks, Odysseus and his men took the giant's tremendous olivewood walking stick and sharpened it to a fine point at one end. When the Cyclops returned—and ate two more men—Odysseus offered him some wine. This pleased the Cyclops, who then asked for his name. Odysseus had the sense to refrain from giving his real name, saying instead that he was called Noman. As the gift of hospitality that Odysseus had been hoping for, the Cyclops promised to eat him last.

Presently the Cyclops, who was drunk from the wine by this time, lay down to rest, and once he was truly asleep Odysseus and his men got out the olivewood stake and drove it into the giant's huge eye, blinding him. The monster bellowed ferociously in his pain, and cried out, "Noman is killing me by deception, not by violence" (9.408). Odysseus then turned his attention to devising a way to get out of the cave. Each of the men bound three rams together with long twigs; in this way, each man could ride underneath the middle one, holding on to its coat of wool above. When Polyphemus turned his flock out to graze in the morning, he was clever enough to feel the backs of the animals to make sure the men weren't taking advantage of his blindness to escape by riding on them, but it never occurred to him to check underneath the beasts. Thus Odysseus, hanging from the biggest ram, and his remaining men made it to safety, even without the intervention of the gods, driving the sheep back to their ship as they went.

But as they left the harbor Odysseus made the mistake of taunting the Cyclops, yelling that "Zeus and the other gods have punished you" (9.479). The Cyclops threw a huge rock at them, almost driving the ship back to the shore. The desire to boast had terrible consequences, for, against the advice of his men, Odysseus insisted on telling the Cyclops his real name, so he would know who had blinded him. Polyphemus prayed to his father, Poseidon, to prevent Odysseus from ever returning home, or, if it was his fate to return, that he might reach his home late and unfortunate, having lost all his comrades, on a ship belonging to others, and finding troubles in his house. And Poseidon saw to it that the second part, at least, of the prayer was fulfilled.

On board his ship, Odysseus made a sacrifice to Zeus of the big ram he took from the Cyclops, but Zeus ignored his offering; "rather, he was considering how all the ships might be destroyed and also my trusty companions" (9.554–55). As the god of hospitality, Zeus protects both host and guest, and Odysseus had taken food from the Cyclops without his permission. As Odysseus said to Alcinous when he first came to his palace, "There is nothing more shameless than the belly, which forces a man to remember it even when he is miserable and has great sorrow in his heart" (7.216–18).[4] His eagerness to get food from the Cyclops caused the death of some of his companions and nearly led to his own as well; later, when they reached the Island of the Sun, those of his fellows who still remained let their greed get the better of them once more, this time fatally.

After escaping the land of the Cyclopes, Odysseus and his men came to the island of Aeolus, the god of the winds. Even minor gods like this one enjoyed a life infinitely easier and happier than that of the most fortunate of men. Aeolus lived on his island in safety and contentment with his wife and sons and daughters: "They are always feasting with their dear father and kind mother; there is unlimited roast meat for them, and the hall is fragrant with smoke and resounds to the sound of the pipe, every day" (10.8–11). Aeolus was kind enough to help Odysseus on his way by tying all the winds in a bag, which he gave to the sailor, and providing a western breeze to send him home.

But human folly wrecked the genial god's well-intentioned plan. As the ships neared Ithaca, Odysseus fell asleep and his men—thinking the bag contained treasure he had not wished to share with them—opened it to have a look. The winds rushed out, and a terrible storm ensued. In despair, Odysseus thought of killing himself, but he endured the storm and when they landed again on the island of Aeolus he asked the god to help him once again. This time, however, the god refused, sending him on his way saying, "It is not right for me to accompany or escort a man who is hateful to the blessed gods; go away, since you have come here hated by the immortals" (10.73–75). In this state, without the assistance of any god, the wanderers came to the land of the Laestrygonians. These turned out to be giants and cannibals, and they speared Odysseus's men like fish and carried them off to eat. Odysseus escaped in his ship with only a few men; all the rest were lost.

Finally he came to the island of Circe, "a dreadful goddess who speaks to humans," a daughter of the sun god (10.136–39). On the first day there, Odysseus killed a stag to feed his men, and on the next he divided his companions into two groups. One group went to Circe's house; she received them kindly and fed them, but the food contained drugs she had mixed in that turned them into pigs and made them forget their homeland. When Odysseus heard this, he took his sword and went straight to Circe's house, but before he could come to any harm Hermes came to help him, disguised as a young man. The god gave Odysseus a magic herb to ward off Circe's drugs. "The gods call it moly," according to Odysseus, "but it is hard for mortal men to dig up. Gods, however, can do anything" (10.305–6). Hermes said to threaten Circe with his sword, and then make her swear an oath not to harm him.

When he met with Circe in her home, she of course fed him her drug, expecting it to turn him into a swine. When it didn't work, thanks to the magic herb of Hermes, she was impressed with Odysseus, guessed who he was, and invited him

Odysseus, among men with animal heads, approaches Circe, who stands naked, holding a cup. (Black-figure kylix, 560–550 B.C., by the Painter of Boston Circe Acheloös Cup. © 2002 Museum of Fine Arts, Boston, Henry Lillie Pierce Fund, 99.519.)

to come to bed with her. Afterward, her servants bathed him and fed him, and he made Circe return his comrades to human form. Circe washed and fed them all too, inviting them to remain and recover their spirits after the exhaustion and misery of their journey. So they remained with her, eating and drinking, and the men enjoyed themselves with her for a year before they began to long for home again and asked Odysseus to return them there. Circe agreed to let him go, but she said that he must first visit the house of Hades to consult the spirit of the seer Tiresias about his journey. She gave him precise directions for the trip to Hades, which he could never have accomplished without her help.

Circe sent a favorable wind that carried them past the land of the Cimmerians to the edge of the stream of Oceanus, right up to the borders of Hades. There they offered sacrifices according to Circe's instructions, and the blood from these attracted many of the spirits of the dead. The first ghost to approach Odysseus was his former comrade Elpenor, and Odysseus wept to see his old friend because he had not known that he had fallen from the roof of Circe's house and broken his neck. Odysseus then saw the ghost of his mother, who had been alive when he left Ithaca, but before he could speak to her he had to consult with the spirit of Tire-

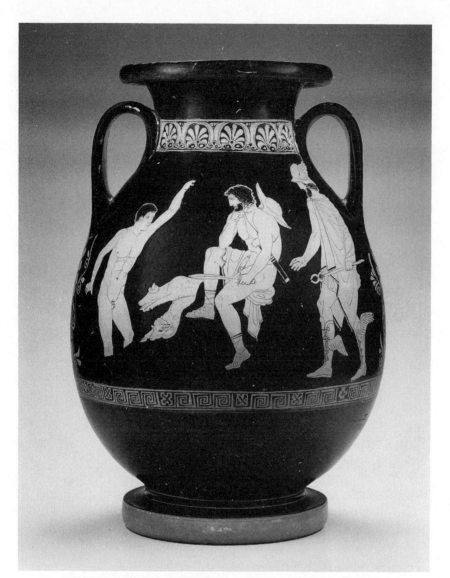

Odysseus holding a sword at the entrance to the world of the dead,
with Hermes behind him. (Red-figure pelike, 440 B.C., by the Lykaon Painter.
© 2002 Museum of Fine Arts, Boston, William Amory Gardner Fund, 34.79.)

sias for advice about how he and his men could get home. The ghost of Tiresias
informed him that Poseidon would make it hard for him to return home, and that
none of them would ever get there if they made the mistake of eating any of the
cattle that lived on Thrinacia, the Island of the Sun, for they belonged to the sun
god. In any case, Tiresias said, it would be a long time before he could return, and
if he did get home he would find the suitors in his house, wooing his wife, and
even though he was destined to kill them he would still have to set off on another

Odysseus, tied to the mast of his ship, listens to the Sirens' song; one Siren
is plunging to her death. (Red-figure stamnos, 500–450 B.C., by
the Siren Painter. British Museum, London, E440, 1843.11–3.31.)

journey to find a land where the people do not know about the sea. Tiresias said
that someone would ask him if the oar he is carrying is a winnowing fan, and
when that happens he must plant the oar in the ground and offer a sacrifice to
Poseidon, and only then would he be able to return home and offer sacrifices to all
the gods.

Odysseus listens to two of the Sirens sing while he is bound to the mast.
(Red-figure krater, ca. 330 B.C. Staatliche Museen, Berlin,
Antikensammlung, no. V.I.4532. Photo: Jutta Tietz-Glagow.)

After receiving these portents from Tiresias, he talked with the spirit of his mother, learning about his family. He spoke also with dead heroes from the long campaign at Troy, among them Agamemnon and Achilles; he saw spirits who had lived in the generation before the Trojan War, including some who were being punished eternally for their crimes against the gods. Odysseus would have stayed to talk to more heroes, but he became afraid that Persephone would send a Gorgon's head at him.[5] So at last he returned to his ship and sailed on, back to Circe's island.

There, Circe took Odysseus aside to question him about his visit to the house of Hades and to advise him about the rest of his journey: "Do you listen, as I tell you, and the god himself will remind you!" (12.37–38). The first peril he would face, she told him, would be the Sirens, whose gorgeous voices and wonderful song enchant men and lead them to their deaths. As she explained it, however, there might be a way for him to hear the Sirens' song and not be killed by them: he must stop up his comrades' ears with wax so they can't hear, and have them tie him to the ship's mast so that he cannot escape. Once past the Sirens, he would have to decide whether to pass through the rocks called the Wanderers or to go by the monster Scylla and the whirlpool Charybdis. Odysseus asked if he might fight against Scylla, but Circe advised him to avoid her: "You are thinking of the works of war, and fighting—will you not yield to the immortal gods? She is not mortal, but an immortal evil, dreadful and harsh and savage and not to be fought against" (12.116–19). Instead, Circe said, he should sail past Scylla and pray to her mother Cratais. Then he would come to Thrinacia, the island where the sun god Hyperion keeps his cattle. (In other stories Helios is called the sun god; in the *Odyssey* the sun god is identified as Hyperion, one of the Titans and the father of Helios.) She repeated the warning Tiresias had already given him, to leave the sun's cattle alone, for if any of the cattle should be harmed his companions would never return home, even if Odysseus himself should contrive to escape.

Thanks to Circe's advice, Odysseus was able to resist the temptation of the Sirens' song as they tried to lure him to their rocks with flattery and offers of knowledge about Troy and the rest of the world. But when he and his men came to Scylla and Charybdis, Odysseus forgot the instructions the goddess had given him and donned his armor (12.226–27). No god was there to remind him of Circe's warning not to try to fight against an immortal god. Scylla snatched up six of his companions, who held out their hands and called to him, and then he watched the monster eat them. "This was the most pitiable sight my eyes have seen of all that I suffered in my journey on the paths of the sea" (12.258–59).

Those who survived this torment came at last to the island where the sun god kept his cattle. Odysseus tried to prevent the men from landing there, but they refused to listen. Adverse winds kept them there for a month, and they ran out of food. Odysseus went to pray to the gods, and then he fell asleep, just as he had done when his ship drew near to Ithaca in Book 10; again his men took advantage of his absence to disobey his orders. They rounded up some of the sun god's cattle and they sacrificed them with prayers and libations. When Odysseus woke up and smelled the delicious aroma of the meat, he exclaimed: "Father Zeus and you other gods who live forever, again you have lulled me into destruction with a cruel sleep" (12.371–72). Odysseus learned later from Calypso, who heard it from Hermes, that Hyperion the sun went to Zeus and threatened to descend and shine among the dead if Zeus and the other gods did not punish the men of Odysseus, so Zeus promised to strike his ship with a thunderbolt (12.374–90). Meanwhile there were terrible omens: the animals' hides creeping on the ground, the meat lowing on the spits, a sound of cattle in the background.

After feasting for six days, Odysseus and his men set sail again, but Zeus sent a storm, and the mast fell on the helmsman; the god then hurled his lightning bolt, and all the men were thrown overboard. Odysseus himself survived only by tying the mast and the keel together and using them as a raft. He was blown by the wind back past Scylla, and he would have been sucked down into Charybdis had he not held on to a branch of a fig tree until his raft came back up again from the whirlpool. He escaped death only because Zeus did not allow Scylla to see him (12.445–46). From there, he drifted for ten days, until he arrived on Calypso's island.

With that, Odysseus finished telling the Phaeacians the tale of his adventures since leaving Troy. As we already know from the account of his journey from Calypso's island, with Poseidon, Hyperion, and Zeus against him, Odysseus needed the active intervention and support of other gods, particularly Athena, to get to the land of the Phaeacians. Even with all his great intelligence and ingenuity, he could not save his men and barely managed to keep himself alive. He made the mistake of invading the home of the Cyclops, and then insisted on telling him his name, so that Polyphemus could call on his father Poseidon to punish him. Even when Odysseus had Circe's guidance, he forgot her advice, challenging Scylla by putting on his armor, resulting in the loss of six of his men. Once he finally reaches Ithaca, his ability to reclaim his home and property requires the close supervision of Athena herself throughout the rest of the story.

→{ ATHENA TAKES CONTROL (BOOKS 13–24) }←

The events related in the second half of the Odyssey take place over the course of only six days.[6] During that brief time Athena takes control of the action, supported by her father, Zeus. Poseidon appears only once, briefly. After Odysseus reaches Ithaca, Athena's attention to his family is constant, until he has killed the suitors and a peace treaty has been arranged with their families. With her sympathy for Odysseus and her concentration on his problems, she appears to be kinder and gentler than the Athena of the Iliad—but she is just as determined to see that justice is done. She does not support everything Odysseus does; at the end of the Odyssey she even threatens him with destruction if he does not obey her orders.

The Phaeacians, in their sympathy for Odysseus and his harrowing wanderings, load a ship with gifts for him and use it to take him back to Ithaca. They come into the island's harbor through an entrance reserved for the gods, and they carry him ashore while he sleeps, leaving his gifts concealed behind an olive tree. Poseidon is still angry with Odysseus, however, and is determined to take revenge on the Phaeacians for bringing him home. He complains to Zeus that they have dishonored him by doing so, and asks to be allowed to destroy their ship and surround their city with a mountain so they will no longer be able to give passage to strangers. The honor of the god is thus satisfied, even though the people who die in the process are not guilty of any direct wrongdoing. Odysseus has no way of knowing about the damage his presence has caused to his kind hosts.

As soon as Odysseus wakes up, Athena comes to him disguised as a young shepherd. Since Odysseus does not yet realize where he is, he greets her with great deference: "I pray to you as a god, and approach your knees as a suppliant" (13.230–31). Athena describes the land he has come to but holds back its name until the end of her speech. Odysseus is delighted when he finds out he is home, but he does not tell her who he is. Instead he says he has come from Crete as an exile because of a murder he committed, bringing with him his booty from Troy, and that he has been brought here and abandoned by Phoenician sailors.

At this, Athena takes the form of a woman, and she smiles and strokes his hand. She explains that she takes a particular interest in him because of his intelligence and cunning, qualities that she shares: "Let us not go on talking in this way; we both are experienced in deceit, since you are by far the best of all mortal men at planning and talking, and I among all the gods am renowned for my intelligence and deceits. But you did not recognize Pallas Athena, the daughter of Zeus, who always stands by you everywhere and watches over you, and who made you a friend of all the Phaeacians" (13.296–302). She now reveals her plan: he must hide the treasures that she made the Phaeacians give him and conceal his identity, even though he will need to suffer in silence because of his disguise.

Odysseus replies that the goddess is hard for even a knowledgeable mortal to recognize. He knows that she was kind to him when he was at Troy, but he says that he never saw her afterward, during all the years of his journey home, until she met him outside the city of the Phaeacians. So he asks her again if what she has told him is the truth. The goddess answers: "You always have the same thoughts in your heart, and so I cannot abandon you when you are unfortunate, because you are always clever and devious, and have your wits about you" (13.330–32). She explains that she knew that one day he would return home, but she could not intervene on his behalf because she could not fight against her uncle Poseidon, who was angry with him for blinding the Cyclops.

Then Athena and Odysseus sit down by the olive tree and plan his revenge on those who have wronged him in his home while he was away. "If you were to stand beside me as eagerly as you did at Troy," he tells her, "I could fight against three hundred men with you, great goddess, when you are determined to help me" (13.389–91). Athena says: "Indeed I shall be with you, I shall not forget you, whenever we work on these matters" (13.393–94). Her plan calls for Odysseus to disguise himself as a beggar and first go to the swineherd Eumaeus, who has remained loyal to him. Meanwhile she will go bring Telemachus back from Sparta;

Athena speaks to Odysseus. (Red-figure pelike, ca. 450 B.C. Staatliche
Museen, Berlin, Antikensammlung, no. F 2354. Photo: Jutta Tietz-Glagow.)

the suitors' plot to ambush him will not succeed. The goddess touches Odysseus
with her wand and makes him look like an old man, giving him worn and dirty
clothes to wear, and then she goes off to Sparta to find Telemachus.

When Odysseus visits Eumaeus he learns that he can count on the swineherd's
loyalty. Their conversation also reminds the audience of the importance of piety
in this epic. Eumaeus treats his guest kindly, "because all strangers and beggars

belong to Zeus" (14.57–58). Such piety contrasts sharply with the treatment Odysseus received from the Cyclops, whose attitude was that he did not "care about Zeus or the other blessed gods."

During the same night, Athena has gone to Sparta, where she has found Telemachus awake, thinking about his father. She does not assume a disguise this time, speaking to him directly and telling him to ask Menelaus to send him home at once. She warns him that the suitors are waiting to ambush him between Samos and Ithaca, but that they will not succeed.[7] He must avoid the islands, and must sail at night; the god who guards and protects him will send a favorable wind. She also tells him to go first to Eumaeus before he returns home, because she wants him to discover that Odysseus has returned. When Telemachus expresses the wish that he may find his father at home, and be able to tell him about his journey, an eagle flies by on the right holding a goose in its talons (15.160–62). Menelaus says that this is an omen that Odysseus will return and exact vengeance (15.177). The omen of the eagle is the first of many signs sent by the gods to predict the doom awaiting the suitors.

When Telemachus returns to Pylos and offers a sacrifice before boarding his ship, a young man, Theoclymenus, approaches him. Theoclymenus is a descendant of the seer Amphiaraus, who was shown particular favor by Zeus and Apollo, and Apollo made the young man's father, Polyphides, "by far the best prophet since Amphiaraus" (15.252–53). Theoclymenus has been exiled from his home for killing a kinsman, so he comes to Telemachus as a suppliant and asks him to take him to Ithaca. Once he arrives there, Theoclymenus will make dramatic use of his prophetic gifts. Telemachus offers him hospitality with the same alacrity he showed to Mentes in Book 1, and so they set sail, with Athena sending them a favorable wind (15.292).

In the morning, after Telemachus arrives safely in Ithaca, Theoclymenus prophesies the return of Odysseus. Telemachus suggests that his new friend should stay with the suitor Eurymachus, although he expresses the hope that Eurymachus will not live to marry his mother (15.521–24). As Telemachus is speaking, a bird flies by from the right, a hawk, the swift messenger of Apollo. It holds a dove in its talons and is tearing off its feathers, scattering them down on the ground between the ship and Telemachus himself (15.525–28). Theoclymenus declares: "This bird has come from the right with the blessing of the god; I knew when I saw it that it was a bird of omen. No other family has more right to be king in Ithaca than yours; no, your family will always be rulers" (15.531–34). Telemachus now asks his comrade Peiraeus to offer hospitality to Theoclymenus and goes to see Eumaeus.

It is Athena who makes it possible for Telemachus to discover that his father has returned. As soon as Telemachus has sent Eumaeus to tell Penelope that her son is back safely, Athena takes the opportunity to disguise herself as a woman and make herself visible to Odysseus—Telemachus cannot see her. The goddess tells Odysseus to reveal himself to his son, and changes his appearance so that he looks taller and younger, and well dressed. Telemachus thinks the stranger must be a god and approaches him as a suppliant: "You now appear to be someone other than you were before, you have different clothes and your skin is not the same. You must be one of the gods who hold broad heaven: be kind to me, and we will give you sacrifices and gifts wrought in gold; spare us" (16.181–85). Odysseus replies that he is not a god but his father, and, when Telemachus is still reluctant to believe him, he explains that Athena was responsible for the transformation: "She can make me appear however she wishes, at one time like a beggar, and at another like a young man with fine clothes on his body; it is easy for the gods, who hold wide heaven, to make a mortal honorable or repulsive" (16.208–12).

Their reunion is joyful, and Odysseus recounts how the Phaeacians brought him to Ithaca by ship. Father and son discuss how to deal with the suitors. Telemachus warns him that they will need help in fighting against all the suitors in his house: there are one hundred and eight of them, plus eight servants, their bard, and their herald. But Odysseus reminds him that they will have the two most powerful gods on their side. "Will Zeus and Athena be enough for us," he wonders, "or should we consider another helper?" (16.260–61). Their scheme is for Odysseus to pretend to be a beggar and endure whatever abuse the suitors greet him with; meanwhile Telemachus must hide all the suitors' weapons and tell no one about the presence of his father. Once this is settled, Eumaeus returns home to find Odysseus, who once again looks like a beggar. Athena, just in time, has touched him with her wand; she now seems to appear whenever she is needed to help Odysseus make his revenge on the suitors.

With their design in place, Odysseus returns to his house and enters disguised as a beggar; Athena tells him to go to each man to beg "so that he may know which of the suitors was just and which unjust, and not even so was she about to allow any of them to escape destruction" (17.363–64). The suitors each give him something to eat, all except Antinous, who refuses to give him anything, and when Odysseus replies that he too is eating another man's food Antinous throws his footstool at him. The reason he must beg for food, Odysseus observes, is on account of his "cruel belly, a wretched thing, which gives many troubles to mankind; but if poor men also have gods and furies on their side, then the fate of death could come to Antinous before his marriage" (17.473–76). The other suitors warn Antinous that the beggar might be a god in disguise: "The gods in the likeness of strangers from other lands appear in every form and go through the cities observing insolence and good behavior among men" (17.485–87).[8]

Odysseus tries to warn another suitor, Amphinomus, that the owner of the house may be near, and says he hopes that a god will take Amphinomus back home before there is bloodshed. Amphinomus goes off brooding and shaking his head, because he has a premonition of trouble to come. "But even so," says the poet, "he would not escape death. Athena had bound him to be subdued forcibly by the hands and sword of Telemachus" (18.155–56). Continuing with her plan, Athena puts it into Penelope's mind to show herself to the suitors, but first she causes Penelope to fall asleep. All along Penelope has refused to wash or dress up because she was mourning for her husband, but while she sleeps the goddess makes her more beautiful, using Aphrodite's own oil on her face and making her taller and her skin whiter. When they see her, the suitors are overwhelmed with desire for her.

Athena sees to it that Odysseus knows which of the people in his house have been loyal to him and which are basically hostile, however agreeably they might speak. Odysseus learns that he cannot trust his slave Melantho even though Penelope had treated her with special kindness. Melantho has become the concubine of Eurymachus, and she now speaks insultingly to the beggar. To steel his resolve for revenge, Athena also "does not let the proud suitors refrain from hurtful insults, so that the pain would sink still further into Odysseus's heart" (18.346–48). Even Amphinomus, the most fair-minded and moderate of the suitors, must perish, for he knows that what the others are doing is wrong and should have taken no part in it (18.155–56).

Odysseus is left in the main room of the house, "plotting with Athena the slaughter of the suitors" (19.2). He and Telemachus move all the men's armor and weapons into a storeroom; "Pallas Athena went before them, and holding a golden lamp, created a beautiful light" (19.33–34). Telemachus is amazed by the sight of the armor shining as if with blazing fire: "One of the gods must be present, who hold the wide heaven," he says (19.40). Odysseus confirms that "this is the way of the gods, who hold Olympus" (19.43).

Penelope now invites the beggar to speak with her. After making sure that he is seated comfortably, she tells him the story of how she fooled the suitors. She told them she would marry one of them when she finished weaving a shroud for Odysseus's father, Laertes, but every night she unraveled the work she had done on it that day, until she was betrayed by one of her serving women. When the beggar tells her he has seen Odysseus in Crete, Penelope weeps, but still he does not reveal his true identity. He tells her he has heard that Odysseus is near, in the land of the Thesprotians, but Penelope does not believe him. She describes for him a dream she has had about a great eagle that swept down and killed all her geese, which were then stretched out dead together in her hall. In her dream she wept and mourned for the geese, but the eagle told her that they were the suitors, and he was her husband (19.536–50). Odysseus says that the dream will come true, but Penelope insists that it is one of the false dreams that come through the gate of ivory, not a dream from the gate of horn that will be fulfilled.[9] She is resigned, she says, that the time has come for her to pick a husband. She declares that there will be a contest: her new husband will be whoever can draw the bow of Odysseus and shoot an arrow through the shaft holes of twelve ax heads set in a line.[10] The beggar assures her that Odysseus will arrive before any other man can even string the bow, let alone accomplish the difficult task of shooting. Penelope, accompanied by her women, goes to her room and "Athena casts sweet sleep on her eyelids" (19.603–4).

Odysseus lies down to sleep on the porch, but he becomes angry when he hears the slave women who have been sleeping with the suitors laughing and talking. As he lies awake thinking how he can kill the suitors, Athena descends from heaven and stands above his head, taking the form of a woman. He tells her that he is thinking about how he might win against so many suitors, and then, if he does kill them, about how he can escape the vengeance of their relatives. Athena reminds him that he cannot fail as long as she is protecting him: "Strange man, another man would trust a less capable comrade, who is a mortal and does not know what I know. But I am a god, who continually watches over you in all your troubles. I will say this openly: if fifty companies of mortal men surrounded us, striving like Ares to kill us, even so you could drive off their cattle and strong sheep" (20.45–51). Then she sends him to sleep.

Meanwhile Penelope prays to Artemis to come, so that she can die before she has to marry someone other than Odysseus. She tells the story of the daughters of Pandareus, who were raised by the goddesses but were carried off to the Furies by storm winds before they could be married. She says she dreamed that someone like Odysseus was sleeping next to her, and in her dream she was happy. Odysseus hears her weeping and thinks that she has recognized him and is standing beside his head. He prays to Zeus for a good omen. Zeus hears him and thunders. There is also another omen from inside the house. A woman who is grinding grain on the millstones realizes that thunder without rain is a sign from the gods, so she prays to Zeus that this meal for which she is grinding the grain may be the suitors' last. Odysseus rejoices when he hears her prayer, for he is now certain that he can take vengeance on the wrongdoers (20.98–121).

The next day, when the suitors are plotting to kill Telemachus, an eagle flies toward them from the left, holding a dove in its talons. Amphinomus interprets this as a bad omen and suggests that they spend their time feasting instead. Animals are brought and sacrificed, but once again, as in Book 18, "Athena did not let the proud suitors refrain from hurtful insults, so that the pain would sink still further into Odysseus's heart" (20.284–86). She makes the suitors laugh uncontrollably and act as if they are out of their minds. As they laugh, their meat becomes spotted with blood, their eyes fill with tears, and they think thoughts of grief. The prophet Theoclymenus exclaims: "The walls and rafters are dripping with blood, and the porch and hall are full of ghosts rushing down to the darkness of Erebus; the sun has disappeared from the sky, and a dark mist surrounds you" (20.354–57). All the suitors laugh at him, and Eurymachus offers to send him home. But he leaves without an escort, because he sees "evil coming on you, which no one of the suitors can escape or avoid" (20.367–69). The contrast between the suitors' hysterical merriment and the seer's dire prediction heightens the tension. The suitors continue to enjoy their meal, but the poet observes that "there would be no meal less happy than the one that the goddess and the powerful man would set before them; for the suitors without provocation had committed disgraceful acts" (20.392–94).

Athena puts the thought in Penelope's mind that she should now set the bow of Odysseus and the axes before the suitors for the contest that marks "the beginning of their slaughter" (21.4). Each suitor tries to string the bow, and each one in turn fails. When Odysseus asks if he can try it, the suitors are furious, but he strings the bow easily, as a musician would tune a lyre. The suitors are frightened. "Zeus thundered loudly and sent Odysseus a sign, and then much-suffering godlike Odysseus rejoiced, because the son of Cronus the crooked-minded had sent him the portent" (21.413–15). He takes an arrow and shoots through all twelve of the axes. He tells Telemachus it is time for the banquet, and Telemachus puts on his sword and picks up his spear.

Odysseus throws off his rags, praying to Apollo that he might hit his next target. He shoots the leading suitor, Antinous, as he is lifting his cup, completely unaware of what is happening. The suitors rush around looking for their armor, thinking that the beggar has made a mistake, but Odysseus reminds them of the way they have treated his property and his serving women, and how they sought to marry his wife while he was still alive, and tells them that he will kill them. Eurymachus tries to put the blame on Antinous, but Odysseus shoots him as well. Amphinomus now attacks, but Telemachus kills him with his spear, as Athena planned it in Book 18. Odysseus keeps killing the suitors until he runs out of arrows, and then he, Telemachus, and the two loyal servants prepare to fight against all those who still remain alive.

It is only at this point, when Odysseus and the others appear to be in need of reinforcement, that Athena intervenes, taking the form of Mentor. Odysseus sees Mentor and rejoices, "because he knows it is Athena, saver of peoples" (22.210). One of the suitors, Agelaus, threatens Mentor with death if he helps Odysseus. Athena is angry and mocks Odysseus, accusing him of having lost the strength he had when he was at Troy. "So she spoke, and yet she did not fully grant them a mighty victory, but she was still making trial of the power and strength of Odysseus and of his glorious son" (22.236–38). She takes the form of a swallow and flies up to the rafters to watch the battle, keeping close watch over the fighting.

The remaining suitors attack, thinking that Mentor has disappeared, but Athena makes their weapons miss their mark. Then Odysseus and his companions attack, and again Athena blocks the spears thrown by the suitors. In this way she is easily able to fulfill the promise she made to Odysseus in Book 20, that together with her he could defeat fifty companies of men (20.49–51). When Telemachus kills the suitor Leocritus, "above them, from the roof, Athena holds up the man-destroying aegis, and the suitors' minds become distraught" (22.297–

98). Odysseus, Telemachus, and Eumaeus proceed to kill the ones who are still standing; only the herald Medon and the bard Phemius are spared.

Even though the suitors are all dead, Athena still feels the need to assist Odysseus. She has to be sure that he is reunited with Penelope, and she also has to protect him from the vengeance of the suitors' relatives by arranging for some sort of lasting peace between them. Penelope at first is reluctant to believe Eurycleia when she tells her that Odysseus has returned. Penelope looks at Odysseus, but she sits down at a distance from him. He thinks that she does not recognize him because of his clothes, so he gets himself washed and puts on new clothes. Athena makes him look taller and more handsome; the poet uses the same lines to describe the transformation that he used in Book 6 when Odysseus washed in the river and put on the clothes Nausicaa gave him. When he comes from his bath he looks like one of the immortal gods (23.163).

But Penelope still does not believe he is Odysseus, so she devises one more test for him by telling Eurycleia to move his bed out of his bedroom. Odysseus is disturbed when he hears this, explaining that he himself made the bed from the trunk of an olive tree and that no one could have moved it unless they sawed it through, and going on to describe exactly how he built it. Only he could have given this answer, so Penelope is finally convinced he is her husband; she embraces him at last and tells him why she was so cautious. Someone might have tried to seduce her, and she might have betrayed her husband, as Helen had done. Both Penelope and Odysseus begin to weep. Her joy and relief at seeing her husband is compared to the welcome sight of land to sailors whose ship Poseidon has wrecked, a simile that suggests her understanding of all that Odysseus has suffered. Husband and wife would have wept all night had Athena not held golden-throned Dawn back by the stream of Oceanus, keeping her from yoking her horses to bring light to men (23.243–46).

Some scholars, both ancient and modern, have been tempted to try to end the narrative here, since Odysseus has finally returned home and been welcomed by his wife.[11] But even though Odysseus and Penelope have been reunited, the poem must continue because there is still the problem of the vengeance that will be demanded by the suitors' relatives. Homer needs to explain how they and Odysseus agree to a truce, and he must show that Zeus is satisfied that justice has been done and that the gods have approved of the peace settlement.

Because Athena has kept Dawn from setting out in her chariot, Odysseus has time to tell Penelope about his journey. He begins with the Cicones, as he did when he told the story to the Phaeacians, but this time he gives only a short summary of what happened. He mentions how the Cyclops revenged himself on Odysseus by eating his men, but says nothing about Poseidon's anger. He tells Penelope that Zeus destroyed his ship with a thunderbolt, but not how Poseidon sent a storm that smashed his raft on his way to the Phaeacians. After describing briefly how the Phaeacians honored him and brought him home, he falls asleep.

"Now Athena thinks of another plan; when she supposes that Odysseus has enjoyed his wife's bed and sleep as he had desired, then she urges golden-throned Dawn, who rises early, to bring the light to mortals" (23.344–48). Odysseus tells Penelope that he must now go to his orchard farm to see his father, and that she must stay secluded in her room for safety.

Meanwhile Hermes takes the souls of the suitors past the streams of Oceanus and the White Rock near the gates of the sun and the land of dreams, to the meadow of asphodel. This meadow is the dwelling place of the shades of the heroes of Troy, whom Odysseus had visited seven years earlier, before his ship was destroyed and he went to Calypso's island. Achilles and Agamemnon are talking about the funeral of Achilles and how much better it was to die in Troy than to have Zeus devise that one would be killed on one's return, as Agamemnon was by Aegisthus and Clytemnestra. Agamemnon reflects on the good fortune Odysseus enjoyed in having a wife like Penelope, so different from Clytemnestra, who will give a bad name to all women, even when they are virtuous.

After Odysseus is reunited with his father, Laertes, Athena is present to make Laertes seem taller and more handsome, and he wishes that he were young again. As the relatives of the suitors gather, Medon the herald warns them that he saw an immortal god standing next to Odysseus in the likeness of Mentor. An old man named Halitherses reminds them that Mentor had urged them to stop the suitors from destroying the property of Odysseus and wooing Penelope. Some are persuaded, but Eupeithes, the father of Antinous, leads the others in an attack on Odysseus. Athena asks Zeus whether he plans an extended war between the two sides, or will he make friendship between them? Zeus reminds her that the vengeance against the suitors was her plan; he will let her do as she wishes, but his advice is to let them make a truce. Odysseus is to rule over them, and the gods will make them forget about the slaughter of their sons and brothers (24.478–86).

Athena rushes down from Olympus, again taking on the likeness of Mentor and joining Odysseus. Mentor advises Laertes to pray to Athena and Zeus, and gives him the strength he needs to kill Eupeithes. Odysseus and Telemachus attack the others and would have killed them all, "but Athena, daughter of Zeus who holds the aegis, shouted, and held back the whole army: 'Stop the harsh war, citizens of Ithaca, so that you can reach a settlement without bloodshed as quickly as possible'" (24.529–32). All drop their weapons in fright at the sound of her voice. When Odysseus begins to rush after them as they retreat, Zeus throws a thunderbolt that falls at the feet of the goddess, and she calls to Odysseus: "Son of Laertes, Odysseus of many wiles, stop this quarrel in war that destroys both sides alike, lest wide-seeing Zeus the son of Cronus become angry with you!" (24.542–44). Odysseus gladly obeys, and Athena in the form of Mentor arranges the truce. There will be no continued revenge, and Odysseus will rule Ithaca in peace. There the story ends.

Gods have helped Odysseus throughout his journey: Aeolus tied up the winds;

Hermes gave him the herb that enabled him to confront Circe; Circe gave him directions to Hades, so he could learn about the future from Tiresias. Circe also told him how to avoid the Sirens and warned him not to touch the cattle belonging to the sun. Calypso rescued him, and eventually helped him to begin his voyage home. The sea goddess Ino gave him the shawl that helped him swim to safety after Poseidon wrecked his raft. But it is only after Athena begins to intervene actively on his behalf that he is able to return home. Athena saw to it that the Phaeacians would welcome him. She also made it possible for him to regain his kingdom, even though his house was occupied by his enemies. She told him to hide his treasures when he arrived in Ithaca and thought of the plan that allowed him, with the help of Telemachus and two loyal servants, to kill all the suitors in spite of the overwhelming odds against him. She helped his father kill the father of Antinous, the chief suitor. In the end Athena commanded both sides to reach a truce and stopped Odysseus from pursuing his vengeance further.

That Odysseus needed the help of the gods does not detract from his own achievements. He shows incredible fortitude and determination throughout, as well as considerable ingenuity, even without the intervention of the gods. He thinks of a way to get out of the cave and escape the Cyclops alive. He knows how to build his own raft so he can leave Calypso's island. He understands how to use words to the greatest possible effect, without any prompting from Athena. It is because of these qualities that Athena is so fond of him and comes down from Olympus again and again to help him, his son, his wife, and his father.

But perhaps the most remarkable of these qualities is one that Athena does not mention when she compliments him in Book 13 for his use of wiles and trickery. What distinguishes Odysseus from other heroes, and particularly from Achilles, is his understanding of the positive values of mortality. He refuses Calypso's offer to make him immortal and ageless, because he would rather return home. Calypso warns him of the great troubles he will face when he leaves her. His reply is tactful: he does not emphasize how much he wishes to return to the wife he "longs for every day," as Calypso puts it, but rather states that he wishes to go home (5.210). Similarly, in the presence of Alcinous, the king of the Phaeacians who wanted to make him his son-in-law, he stresses how much he wants to see Ithaca, and describes the island to them in some detail, saying "there is nothing sweeter than one's homeland and parents, even when one is living in a wealthy house in another land far from one's parents." His behavior when he does return makes it clear that he is as eager to see Telemachus and Penelope as he is to see his parents. He is willing to face death and old age, and prepared to work to maintain his land and acquire possessions, rather than live eternally cut off from his home and family. Also, it is the excitement of living that appeals to him, as opposed to the continual sameness of existence on Calypso's island. It gives him pleasure to tell the Phaeacians about his adventures, and he is eager to tell Penelope what has happened during the twenty years of his absence.

In contrast to the change and uncertainty that is characteristic of human life, there is the eternal comfort of the life of the gods. Even minor gods like Calypso, Aeolus, and Circe live on beautiful islands with all their wants supplied. For the Olympian gods the days are always radiant, and there is never a shortage of food or drink or comfort, and their home is not disturbed by winds or rain or snow (6.42–44). The gods meet and talk in Zeus's house on Olympus, and the *Odyssey* begins and ends with conversations between Athena and Zeus. Their relationship in the *Odyssey* is close and not marked by discord as it is in the *Iliad*. Athena cares about Odysseus, and Zeus respects her concern, but their affections are tempered by the security of their existence. They never weep or rejoice as Odysseus does when he sees his mother in Hades, or when he is reunited with Telemachus, Penelope, and Laertes. Even the gods' anger has limitations. Poseidon stops persecuting Odysseus when he reaches the Phaeacians. Athena is eager to punish the suitors, but she is reluctant to exact further vengeance on their families.

In general, modern readers can look on the actions of the gods in the *Odyssey* with a more ready sympathy than they can find for the gods in the *Iliad*. This response is understandable. Not only do Athena and Zeus appear primarily as benevolent figures, but also the gods' justice seems to be administered more fairly, because in the world of the *Odyssey* right and wrong are more clearly marked. With only occasional exceptions (such as Odysseus's invasion of the cave of the Cyclops and the eating of the sun god's cattle), the heroes behave nobly and the villains dishonorably. The signals the gods send are clear and readily understood by anyone who is prepared to see them.[12] Although the poet allows us the great satisfaction of seeing Odysseus return home with the support of the gods, he leaves us with no illusions that mortal life is easy. Even though he has Athena's support and counsel, Odysseus must fight to return home and fight to regain his kingdom. He cannot remain and live happily ever after because he must go to a place so remote from the sea that no one knows what an oar is, and there build a temple to Poseidon, the god who has persecuted him. And he must die, now that he has given up the immortality that Calypso had offered him.

CHAPTER 5

The Gods in Drama I

APOLLO AND ORESTES

The traditional myths about the gods also provide the background for most ancient dramas. In ancient Athens dramatic performances were literally religious events, meant to honor the god Dionysus at his festival, as well as all the other gods with whom he was associated. Honoring the gods meant recognizing and acknowledging that Zeus, and the gods whom he favors, have all the power to do what they want and the knowledge of what will happen in the future, while nothing that any human being accomplishes endures. Mortals must learn to recognize their limitations, even though in reality they rarely do so. Virtually every surviving ancient Athenian drama brings out this strong distinction between human understanding and the power of the gods.

Nowhere do gods play a more important role than in the action of drama, but they are not as visible to audiences as they are in the epic poems because of the conventions of the stage. We do not know how and why these conventions were agreed upon, but all the dramas that have come down to us conform to them. All action takes place on earth, usually in front of a palace or temple. The audience can learn about anything that happens outside the stage only from the report of an eyewitness. It cannot see inside the building in front of it. Unlike an epic poet, the dramatist cannot let the audience eavesdrop on conversations on Olympus and then direct its attention quickly back to earth.

What the audience hears is speeches, with some formal exchanges in dialogue, in interludes or episodes divided from one another by choral songs. The chorus consists of a group of gods or mortals who have some connection with the main characters. Although the chorus usually plays the role of interested onlooker, it is also a character in the drama (and not the voice of the poet), despite its collective identity. In that role it comments on what is happening onstage and reflects on the actions of the gods in the past. The main characters in the play are almost always members of the same family, and the poets take their plots from the many myths that describe family conflicts. When gods appear as characters, they come for a purpose, to make an immediate change in the course of human action. Most often they appear at the end of the plays to inform the mortals of the consequences of what the mortals have done, and to describe what will happen to them in the future.

Because the poets tend to concentrate on human action, some critics have been tempted to imagine that the presence of the gods is merely symbolic, and that humans are able to direct the course of their lives without their immediate intervention. The technical term *deus ex machina* (the god from the machine) contributes to the notion that gods are somehow artificial and external to the drama.[1] But in fact the gods' presence and actions are central to Greek drama, even when they are not visible to the audience. The outcomes of the dramas show that the characters ignore the gods only to their great peril.

Poets almost always chose to set the dramatic action during the heroic age, the period in Greek mythology when gods regularly involved themselves in mortal life. The gods do not appear directly in the one surviving drama that deals with an almost contemporary event, the *Persians* of Aeschylus, which describes the aftermath of a war that had taken place some eight years earlier. But even there the presence of the gods and the power of Zeus's justice are clearly acknowledged by the characters in the play.

The discussions of drama in this chapter and the next continue to concentrate on the roles played by the gods, showing how in all the dramas known to us the gods intervene in human life in the same ways and for the same reasons that they did in Homer. I shall discuss dramas by each of the three great dramatic poets whose works have come down to us: Aeschylus (525–456 B.C.), Sophocles (ca. 496–406 B.C.), and Euripides (ca. 480–406 B.C.). These works show that Sophocles and Euripides had no intention of encouraging their audiences to question the gods' existence, nor did they mean to suggest that their audiences adopt new forms of worship, even though they devoted even more time and space to the description of human suffering than Aeschylus did. Rather, the purpose of their dramas, and all drama, is to remind the audience that the gods ultimately control human action and are determined to see that justice is done in the end, even when they appear to mortals to be indifferent to human suffering or when they seem to intervene on behalf of those who do not appear—at least to us—to deserve their support.

This chapter considers the role of the gods in the dramas that describe how Orestes avenged the death of his father, Agamemnon: the *Oresteia* trilogy (*Agamemnon*, *Choephoroe*, and *Eumenides*) by Aeschylus, *Electra* by Sophocles, and *Electra* and *Orestes* by Euripides. This basic story was familiar to every Greek from the *Odyssey*, where the fate of Agamemnon's family is repeatedly compared and contrasted with that of Odysseus. In his first speech in the *Odyssey*, Zeus explains that he sent Hermes to warn Aegisthus not to kill Agamemnon, because Orestes would return from exile to kill him in turn. But Aegisthus did not listen, and he died as the gods had predicted. As Zeus says, when mortals ignore the advice of the gods they bring troubles on themselves.

More details of the story of the revenge of Orestes are revealed during the course of the narrative. Menelaus learns from the god Proteus that Aegisthus had treacherously killed Agamemnon and his comrades at a feast, when they were unable to defend themselves (*Odyssey* 4.535–37). The shade of Agamemnon tells Odysseus of the horror of seeing his comrades slaughtered around him, and the whole floor running with blood, and describes his wife Clytemnestra's role as a willing accessory to the crime (11.421–34). Nestor explains to Telemachus that Aegisthus seduced Clytemnestra, arranged for the death of the bard whom Agamemnon had left to keep watch over her, and then ruled Mycenae for seven years, until Orestes came from Athens to kill him (3.306–10).

Homer does not give the rest of the family's history, since he relates only the aspects of the myth that have a bearing on the lives of Odysseus and his family. But in fact the troubles in Agamemnon's family had begun much earlier, when his grandfather Pelops murdered his charioteer Myrtilus. The sons of Pelops, Atreus and Thyestes, became bitter enemies. After the death of Pelops, Atreus claimed the kingdom because a golden lamb had been born among his flocks; Thyestes stole the lamb and seduced Aerope, the wife of Atreus. After the sun and the stars turned backward in their courses because of these actions by Thyestes, Atreus became king and his brother went into exile. Atreus later welcomed him back with a feast, but the meat he served him was the flesh of the exile's own children. The only child of Thyestes to survive was Aegisthus, who was determined to avenge the wrongs Atreus had done to his father. Agamemnon, as the son of Atreus, paid the price. Clytemnestra, his wife, also had reason to be angry with Agamemnon, for he had killed her first husband and child, and then he had sacrificed their daughter Iphigenia to appease Artemis, whom he had offended.

Dramatists were drawn to the myth of the house of Pelops because of the many questions it raised about the workings of divine justice. Why did the gods allow so many murders to be committed? Was there a curse on the family? How would the gods bring the cycle of revenge to an end? Of the ancient Greek dramas that have come down to us, thirty-three in all, eight deal with the story of Agamemnon and his family, and the myth is alluded to in others. The Athenian dramatist Aeschylus wrote at least four dramas about Agamemnon and his family, the *Iphigenia*, which is lost, and the trilogy known as the *Oresteia*, about the murder of Agamemnon and the revenge of Orestes.

In the version of the myth told by Aeschylus, the moral issues become more complicated than they were in Homer, because the god Apollo orders Orestes to kill not only Aegisthus but also his own mother, Clytemnestra. Apollo is present throughout the *Oresteia* trilogy, at first indirectly through his oracles, and finally as a character in the last of the three plays. Apollo, through his oracle at Delphi, has told Orestes that he must kill his mother as well as Aegisthus if he is to avenge his father's death. When he does murder his mother, he commits another crime, the shedding of kindred blood, which incurs the wrath of his mother's Erinyes, or avenger goddesses. The Erinyes persecute Orestes until Apollo, with the help of his sister Athena, sees to it that he is absolved of guilt for his mother's death. Unlike Homer, who tells the story in retrospect, after Orestes has avenged the murders and the justice of Zeus has been enforced, the dramas of Aeschylus take place in present time, before the audience's eyes. The poet compels us to see the action from the point of view of the people who witness and commit the murders, without knowing for sure what will happen in the future. We see their uncertainty and fear, and listen to them as they express doubts and concerns about the involvement of the gods.

In the first play of the trilogy, *Agamemnon*, the mortal characters can only hope to understand what the gods want them to do from signs that are interpreted by other human beings. At the beginning of the play, a watchman asks the gods for deliverance from his toils (*Agamemnon* 1). He has been watching for a year for the beacon lights that will signal that Troy has been taken, and at last the signal has come. The chorus is made up of the old men who were left behind when Agamemnon, the king of Argos, took all the younger ones with him to fight at Troy. The old men know that the gods support those who have been wronged, and that Zeus, the god of host and guest, sides with Agamemnon and his brother Menelaus against Paris (Alexander) because of his perfidy. But they also have reason to believe that the gods are hostile to Agamemnon, because two eagles attacked and killed a pregnant hare at the start of the expedition to Troy, while the Greek ships were assembled at Aulis; the prophet of the Greek army, Calchas, took the omen to mean that the two sons of Atreus would take Troy, but that at the same time Artemis, the goddess who protects wild animals, was angry with them. The omens were favorable but not faultless. Calchas called on Apollo in his role as healer to intercede with his sister Artemis, because he saw that the signs were prophetic of another sacrifice, this time of a child.

The old men find it hard to understand or describe the will of Zeus: "Whoever Zeus may be, if this name is pleasing to him, by this name I address him. I can compare with him, measuring all things against him, none but Zeus, if from my mind the vain burden may be cast in all sincerity" (160–66).[2] Even understanding brings pain to humankind: Zeus makes it "a valid law that by suffering they shall learn" (177–78). When the expedition could not sail to Troy because the winds were unfavorable, the prophet said there was only one remedy, one so awful that it caused the two brothers to weep and beat the ground with their staffs. If Agamemnon wished to save the expedition, he would need to sacrifice his own daughter. In doing so, he made a disastrous choice: "For mortals are made reck-

Iphigenia being led to the scene of her sacrifice by Agamemnon. (White-figure lekythos, ca. 470 B.C., by Douris. Museo Regionale, Palermo, Italy, NI 1886.)

less by the evil counsels of merciless infatuation. And so he steeled himself to become the sacrificer of his daughter Iphigenia, to aid a war fought to avenge a woman's loss, and to pay beforehand for his ships" (222–26).

The old men know that the sacrifice took place and that justice will prevail, but they are still uncertain about the outcome of the war. Clytemnestra responds to

Agamemnon approaches Iphigenia with a knife as she stands before an altar;
behind her is the deer Artemis has sent to take her place as the sacrificial victim.
(Red-figure volute krater, fifth century B.C. British Museum, London, no. F 159.)

their doubts with assurance. She knows that Troy has fallen, and she knows exactly how the beacons were relayed from Troy to Argos across the mountaintops. She describes the scene in Troy vividly, as if she had seen it herself. Although she is a woman, the chorus says that she speaks "wisely, like a prudent man" (351). The old men prepare to sing in praise of the gods, something that so far Clytemnestra has failed to do. They give the credit for the victory to Zeus, who has punished the Trojans for Paris's violation of the laws of hospitality. Zeus "has accomplished it as he ordained," they sing. "Men have said that the gods did not deign to attend to mortals by whom the grace of things inviolable was trampled; but such men are impious" (369–72). Paris is responsible for the fall of Troy: "His prayers none among the gods will hear, and him that has dealings with such men Justice brings down" (396–98). There is reason to fear for the fate of the victors as well: "The killers of many do not go unwatched by the gods; and the black Erinyes in time consign to darkness him who is fortunate without justice. . . . The burden of excessive praise is heavy; for by the eyes of Zeus the thunderbolt is hurled" (461–70).

After the chorus has learned from a messenger about the miseries the Greeks endured during the long siege, and about the terrible storm that struck their ships after they left Troy, the old men sing of how great prosperity leads to woe, and injustice breeds destruction: "A spirit irresistible, unconquerable, is brought forth, the recklessness that is *atē*, black for the house, like to its parents" (768–72). As they speak about justice, Agamemnon enters and offers thanks to the gods for punishing Troy (821–23). Clytemnestra asks her servants to spread precious tapestries on the ground for Agamemnon to walk on, so that Justice may lead him home. She concludes with an ominous prayer, not in thanks for the victory, but for what may happen in the future: "And for the rest, may forethought not overcome by sleep accomplish all justly with the gods' aid as it is fated!" (912–13).

At first Agamemnon is reluctant to ruin the tapestries by treading on them; he does not wish to act like a barbarian. "It is the gods you should honor with such things," he says, "and to walk, being a mortal, on embroidered splendors is impossible for me without fear. I tell you to honor me with honors human, not divine" (922–25). He asks her to welcome with kindness the stranger he has brought with him, Priam's daughter Cassandra, the war captive given to him by the Greek army; in the *Iliad* he says explicitly that he preferred the war captive Chryseis to his wife Clytemnestra (*Iliad* 1.113–15). But Clytemnestra persuades him, despite his scruples, to walk on the tapestries into the house. As Agamemnon enters the palace, she again prays for help in the future: "Zeus, Zeus with power to accomplish; accomplish my prayer; and may what you are about to accomplish be your care" (*Agamemnon* 973–74). Addressing Zeus as "accomplisher" (*teleios*) suggests sacrifice and killing: *telein* means bring to completion; *telos* can be an end or death as well as an achievement.

Even though Agamemnon has returned, the old men hear a dirge of the Erinyes. Good fortune can quickly lead to ruin, abundance can lead to famine, unless Zeus brings a harvest. Cassandra asks Apollo to tell her where she is; she calls him by his cult title as a god of prophecy, *aguiates* (god of the roadside), and interprets his name as meaning "my destroyer" (*apollōn emos*), "for you have for a second time easily destroyed [*apōlesas*] me" (1081–82). She insists that this is "a house that hates the gods, one that knows many sad tales of kindred murder" (1090–91). First came the children that Agamemnon's father, Atreus, killed, and then cooked and served to their father, his brother Thyestes. Then there is the murder that is about to happen, of a husband who will be sacrificed by his wife, in a bath, trapped in a net; then Cassandra speaks of her own death, of Paris and Troy, and of the many sacrifices offered to the gods by her father.

Cassandra speaks in a more controlled manner about the Erinyes, the Furies "bred with the family," and of the crimes they avenge, mentioning specifically the killing of the children by Atreus because of the seduction of his wife by his brother (1190). When the chorus is amazed that she knows this history of the family, she explains that Apollo has taught her. Once, in the past, the god had approached her, and she agreed to give herself to him. The god, in return for the favor she was about to grant him, gave her the gift of prophecy. But when she then refused to have intercourse with him, in retaliation Apollo made it so no one would believe her prophecies, even though they were always true. Cassandra now sees the ghosts of the children that Atreus slaughtered and their father ate, and then the one child that was spared, Aegisthus, who has been waiting for Agamemnon's return. Clytemnestra has made a long speech of welcome, but in reality she is a monster, waiting to kill him.

Because the god has given her the gift of prophecy, Cassandra can also see that Clytemnestra will kill her along with Agamemnon, and she cries out, "Ah, ah! It is like fire, and it comes over me. Oh, Lycian Apollo, woe is me!" (1256–57). She throws down the staff and the hair bands that are the insignia of her prophetic office. But she also predicts that "a son who slays his mother, an atoner for his father," will avenge her (1281). She has seen Troy fall, and now she is about to die. The gates of the palace are like the gates of Hades. She talks about the smell of blood and slaughter in the house: "Alas for the affairs of men! When they are fortunate, one may liken them to a shadow; and if they are unfortunate, a wet sponge with one dash blots out the picture. And I pity this far more than that" (1327–30).

It is at this point that Agamemnon cries from inside the house that he is being struck a mortal blow. Before the old men can decide what to do, Clytemnestra appears with the dead bodies of Agamemnon and Cassandra. She describes how she killed her husband when he was defenseless, while he was taking the bath that wives traditionally prepared for their men when they returned from battle. She threw a cloth over him and struck him three times. She speaks of the murder as if it were a sacrifice to Hades, god of the underworld, "a votive offering for the Zeus below the earth, the savior of corpses" (1386–87). She has taken pleasure in

Aegisthus, holding a sword at left, is about to kill Agamemnon, who is emerging from his bath draped in a fine cloth. Behind Aegisthus is Clytemnestra, rushing to his side with an ax in her hand (out of view at far left). (Red-figure calyx krater, ca. 460 B.C., by the Dokimasia Painter. © 2002 Museum of Fine Arts, Boston, William Francis Warden Fund, 63.1246.)

the blood that splattered over her as the crops rejoice when Zeus sends rain. It would be just to pour a libation over the corpse in blood, rather than in wine: "Such a mixing bowl of evils, sprung from the curse [kakōn araiōn] did he fill up in the house and return himself to drain" (1397–98). The curse she refers to is the consequence of the series of crimes committed by Atreus and Thyestes that Cassandra has already mentioned.

Clytemnestra believes that she has acted in accordance with justice: "I swear by the justice accomplished for my child, and by Atē and the Erinyes, to whom I sacrificed this man, for me no expectation walks the hall of fear," so long as Aegisthus lives (1432–34). But the old men suppose that Agamemnon has died because of the curse on Agamemnon's family, which has been sent by Zeus: "Mighty for this house is the spirit you tell of, heavy his wrath! Alas, alas, evil is your tale, never satiate of baneful fortune. Woe, woe, through the act of Zeus, cause of all, doer of all; for what is accomplished for mortals without Zeus? Which of these things is not god-ordained?" (1481–85). The chorus knows that the curse cannot end here: "But it abides, while Zeus abides upon his throne, that he who does shall suffer; for it is the law. Who shall cast out the brood of curses from the house? The race is fastened to destruction" (1563–66).

Justice has been defined in different ways by the characters. Clytemnestra blames Agamemnon for the sacrifice of Iphigenia, "he holding it of no special account, as though it were the death of a beast, where sheep in their fleecy flocks abound, sacrificed his own child, a travail most dear to me, to charm the wind of Thrace" (1415–18). Artemis demanded the sacrifice (201–4), but why has Zeus allowed Iphigenia to be sacrificed and Agamemnon to be murdered? The play leaves these questions unanswered, but the audience has heard Cassandra's prophecy that Orestes would return to avenge his father's death. Other than that, there has been no indication that the gods will ensure that justice will be done, and no indication of how the curse on the house of Atreus will come to an end.

The question about the return of Orestes from exile is answered at the beginning of the next play in the trilogy, the *Choephoroe* (The Libation Bearers). The first lines of the play are lost, but where the text begins, Orestes and his friend Pylades are already standing before Agamemnon's tomb. Orestes offers his father a lock of hair "in token of my mourning" (*Choephoroe* 7). He prays to Zeus that he may avenge his father's death and that the god may be his willing ally. They stand back as his sister Electra enters, along with the chorus of Trojan slaves who serve Clytemnestra. They have come to the tomb because Clytemnestra saw a dream during the night that made her cry out and set her hair on end. The prophets in the palace have said that "those below the earth make angry complaint and harbor wrath against the killers" (40–41). Electra calls on the gods of the earth, Hermes and Earth herself, to pray that Orestes may return: "For us convey upward good fortune, by the grace of the gods and earth and justice triumphant!" (147–48).

The speed with which Electra's prayers are answered makes it clear that the gods are listening. Electra notices a lock of hair on the tomb and immediately recognizes that it belongs to Orestes. Sister and brother are reunited, and they each pray to Zeus to protect them and to rescue the fortunes of their house. Orestes explains that he is following the orders of Apollo in avenging his father: "Never shall I be betrayed by the mighty oracle of Loxias [one of Apollo's epithets], which commands me to pass through this danger" (269–70). If he refused to avenge his father, not only would he never recover his possessions; he would be afflicted with disease, pursued by his father's Erinyes, unable to participate in ritual, without friends or honor.

Looking for guidance and strength, Electra and Orestes, with the help of the chorus, seek to establish contact with Agamemnon's ghost. In the course of the ritual, they remind themselves of what he and they have suffered, gathering courage for the revenge that Orestes must now take. Orestes invokes Hades, the Zeus of the underworld, by saying, "You who send up from below late-avenging ruin to the reckless violence of men; nonetheless debts to parents must be discharged" (382–85).[3] The chorus warns him that bloodshed must be avenged. Orestes asks Zeus to tell him where to turn, and he calls on the powerful curses of the dead to look after him and his sister. Together the two of them call on the gods of the lower world, and on Persephone, and they beg Agamemnon himself not to let their family perish.

Clytemnestra had dreamed she gave birth to a snake that sucked blood from her breast along with milk. Orestes sees that he is the snake and that the dream predicts that he will kill her. Apollo has told him to use the kind of treachery Clytemnestra and Aegisthus used against Agamemnon, so he decides that he and Pylades will pretend to be strangers from Phocis, where Orestes had been in exile. When they arrive, Clytemnestra receives the strangers hospitably. Orestes explains that they have come with news of the death of Orestes, and that they have brought his ashes home. Clytemnestra speaks sadly of the curse upon the house. She leads these men, whom she supposes to be strangers, inside without displaying any other sign of sorrow about the death of her son. Her cruel indifference is immediately contrasted with the real grief expressed by an old nurse of his, who comes out in tears because she has heard the news of his death.

The chorus tells the nurse to go to bring Aegisthus the news so that he will return to the house, hinting that all will soon be well, and they call on Zeus to help Orestes. When Aegisthus returns, uncertain if he should believe that Orestes is dead, they urge him to enter the house. Soon we hear the death cry of Aegisthus, and a slave runs out to say that he has been killed. When Clytemnestra enters and learns what has happened, she realizes that Orestes has returned, and she cries for an ax with which to defend herself.[4] But before anyone can bring her a weapon, Orestes enters and tells her that she can join Aegisthus in death.

Orestes hesitates, however, when Clytemnestra says he owes her the respect that a son owes his mother. She bares her breast, as Hecuba did to Hector in Book 22 of the Iliad in a vain attempt to keep him from fighting against Achilles (Iliad 22.79–80). The audience of the Choephoroe knows that Clytemnestra's appeal is false, because we have seen that it was his nurse, not his mother, who looked after him when he was young and wept when she thought he was dead. But her plea gives Orestes pause, and he asks his friend Pylades if he should kill her. Pylades is the son of the king of Phocis, the region near the Delphic oracle. So far he has been silent, but now he states that Orestes must kill his mother because Apollo

Orestes, center, kills Aegisthus, as Clytemnestra threatens her son with an ax from behind and Electra reaches out to him at right. This scene appears on the other side of the vessel seen in the preceding figure. (Red-figure calyx krater, ca. 460 B.C., by the Dokimasia Painter. © 2002 Museum of Fine Arts, Boston, William Francis Warden Fund, 63.1246.)

has ordered him to do so, speaking with great dramatic effect: "Where henceforth shall be the oracles of Loxias declared at Pytho and the covenant you pledged on oath? Count all men your enemies rather than the gods!" (*Choephoroe* 900–902). Clytemnestra tries to dissuade her son, but he reminds her of her crimes, and then leads her into the house.

The chorus sings a song of triumph that acknowledges the power of the gods:

"There came Justice in time to the sons of Priam; there came a heavy retribution; and there has come to the house of Agamemnon twice a lion, twice a god of war! Altogether he has driven to the end of the course, he the exile prompted by Pytho, well sped on his way by the counsels of the gods!" (935–41). Hermes helped them with their cunning plot, and Athena guided Orestes' hand, and Apollo saw that justice was done. In the words of the chorus: "It is right to proclaim the power that has the mastery of heaven" (960). But the chorus is now apprehensive about the future: "None among mortals shall pass his whole life free from suffering, unpunished to the end. Alas, alas! One sorrow comes today, another shall come tomorrow" (1018–20). Orestes admits that he does not know where it will end; he thinks he is losing control of his wits, even though he still believes that he acted with justice. He sees "ghastly women, like Gorgons, with dark raiment and thick-clustered snakes for tresses" (1048–50). The women of the chorus cannot see the beings that he is talking about and suggest that they are "fancies" (doxai, 1051). But Orestes realizes that these are his mother's Erinyes, her "wrathful hounds," from whom he must try to flee (1054). Only Apollo's touch can free him from his troubles.

As Orestes leaves, the chorus speaks of this third storm that has come upon the house: the first was when Atreus slaughtered the children of Thyestes; the second when Clytemnestra murdered Agamemnon in his bath; and now "there has come a deliverer, or shall I say a doom? What shall be the decision, what the end of the might of destruction, laid at last to rest?" (1073–76). The final word of the play is "destruction" (atē). The curse on the house of Atreus has not ended, and we do not yet know how Apollo can save Orestes from the powerful goddesses who are pursuing him. How can a conflict between an Olympian god and the gods of an earlier generation be resolved without violence?

These questions are answered in the third play of the trilogy, the Eumenides, or "The Kindly Ones," a title given to the Erinyes because their true name is too dreadful to utter.[5] Finally the audience is allowed to see the gods who in the first two plays were present only at a distance. Apollo's priestess at Delphi, the Pythia, opens the play by describing the ancient shrine in which she serves the god. The first god to prophesy there was Earth, and then came Themis; Themis turned it over to Phoebe, another Titan god, and she gave it to her grandson Phoebus Apollo. Zeus established Loxias (Apollo) as the fourth prophet god, but the priestess also honors other gods at the sanctuary: the nymphs of the Corycian cave, Athena, Dionysus, the river Pleistos, and Poseidon.

Near the beginning of the Eumenides, the Pythia opens the doors to the temple, but then she turns back again in horror, grasping the walls to steady herself. She has seen Orestes, with his bloody hands, and the Erinyes, "not women, but Gorgons I call them, no not even to the shape of Gorgons can I compare them" (Eumenides 48–49). Her description confirms that what Orestes said about them at the end of the Choephoroe was not an illusion caused by his disordered mind. The

Erinyes are asleep, snoring, with their eyes dripping a foul liquid. The Pythia refuses to enter; only the god Loxias can cleanse the temple of this new pollution.

So the temple doors open to reveal the god Apollo himself. He speaks to Orestes, assuring him that "I will not abandon you; but I will guard you to the end, whether by your side, or far removed, and I will not grow gentle to your enemies" (64–66).[6] He explains that he has caused the Erinyes to go to sleep so that Orestes can escape. They will continue to pursue him, the god says, until he comes to Athens and takes hold of Athena's statue as a suppliant. In Athens there will be judges, and Apollo will find a way of rescuing him, since it was he who ordered him to kill his mother. The god also asks his brother Hermes to protect Orestes and guide him. Although Apollo has promised to give Orestes the same personal attention that Athena gave to Odysseus in the Odyssey, Orestes is not yet entirely confident that he has the god's support: "Lord Apollo, you know how to be righteous, but since you have that skill, learn also not to be neglectful! But your strength renders sure your power for good" (85–87).

As soon as Apollo and Orestes leave, however, the ghost of Clytemnestra comes to rouse the Erinyes from their slumber and urge them to pursue her killer. The chorus of Erinyes slowly awakens, after which they blame Apollo and the younger generation of gods: "Ah, son of Zeus! You are a thief! Young as you are, you have ridden us down, aged divinities, respecting the suppliant, a godless [atheos] man, hateful to parents" (149–52). "Such are the actions of the younger gods," they say, "whose might goes altogether beyond justice" (162–63). But Apollo returns to drive the Erinyes away by threatening to wound them with his arrows. They belong where there are murders, blight, and mutilation, he tells them, and such creatures should inhabit a lion's den rather than pollute those present at his oracle. When the Erinyes insist that they are right to pursue a murderer, Apollo asks why they did not pursue Clytemnestra when she murdered her husband, dishonoring Hera, the goddess of marriage, Zeus, the god of hospitality, and Aphrodite, the goddess of love. The Erinyes reply that in murdering her husband Clytemnestra did not shed kindred blood.

Although the action of most dramas occurs in one place, in this case the scene shifts from Delphi to Athens; the audience learns of the new location from what the characters say. Orestes addresses the statue of Athena in her "house," that is, her temple on the Athenian Acropolis.[7] The Furies are close behind him and threatening to suck his blood, but Orestes tells them that Apollo has purified him with pig's blood, and that time has purified him as well. He calls on Athena to appear. Meanwhile the Erinyes surround him, singing a binding song and calling on their mother, the goddess Night, to punish him: "Over our victim we sing this song, maddening the brain, carrying away the sense, destroying the mind, a hymn that comes from the Erinyes, fettering the mind, sung without the lyre, withering to mortals" (328–33). Zeus has tried to ignore them and deprive them

Erinyes stand on either side of Orestes, who sits as a suppliant before the statue of Athena. (Red-figure Apulian bell krater, 415–390 B.C. Staatliche Museen, Berlin, Antikensammlung, no. 4565.)

of honor, but the ancient law about revenge remains, and the gods beneath the earth still honor the Erinyes.

Athena herself enters, having come from Troy, where the Athenians have established a new cult for her. She explains that she was able to arrive with such speed because the winds carried her across the sea, holding herself aloft by her aegis. She is not afraid of the Erinyes, despite their appearance. She asks who they are and listens to their complaint dispassionately, and then she does not drive them away. Rather, she asks them to accept her as judge, to which they agree. Then she turns to Orestes, addressing him formally as "stranger" (xenos), and asks him who he is even though she knows already, just as she knew who the

Erinyes were. By asking she allows them to speak for themselves, and by this tactic she contrives to make herself appear impartial.

Athena displays no favoritism to either side: "The matter is harder than any mortal thinks to judge of; it is not right even for me to decide a trial for murder that brings down fierce wrath" (470–72). Orestes has come to her temple as a suppliant, and the Erinyes can cause grievous harm to Athens should they fail to get their revenge. Instead of judging the matter by herself, she decides to hold a trial. She goes off to select the best of the citizens of her city, Athens. The Erinyes sing of how the gods punish murderers: "And those he calls on shall not hear him as he struggles in vain amid the whirling waters; the god's laughter mocks the reckless man . . . he has run aground on the reef of Justice the vessel of his former happiness; he is lost forever, unwept for and unseen" (558–65).

Now the scene changes again, from Athena's temple on the Acropolis to the nearby Hill of Ares (Areopagus). The judges have been chosen, and Athena orders the herald to tell them to take their places. She asks for silence, and for the people to learn the ordinances of her court for all time to come. Apollo states his case: Orestes is his suppliant, so the god himself is responsible for the death of the man's mother. Athena asks the Erinyes as prosecutors to describe what happened, and they question Orestes about his mother's death. Orestes in turn asks them why they did not pursue Clytemnestra for the murder of Agamemnon, and they reply that she was not kin to Agamemnon. If a father is to be considered more important than a mother, why was Zeus permitted to bind his father Cronus? Apollo points out that Cronus, because he is a god, could be released at any time, but that "once a man is dead, and the earth has sucked up his blood, there is no way to raise him up" (647–48). Apollo also argues that the male parent should have priority. As proof, he offers the example of Athena herself, who was not nurtured in a womb or born from a mother. Apollo uses this argument because he hopes it will be persuasive not only to the men who are judging the case but also to the goddess herself.[8] He further adds what amounts to a bribe: he assures Athena that he sent Orestes to her rather than to another god so that Orestes and his descendants, the Argives, would forever be the allies of Athens. (When the trilogy was performed, Argos was allied with Athens.)

After the arguments on both sides have been presented, Athena casts her vote in favor of Orestes so that he will win in case of a tie in the judges' votes. Announcing her decision before the votes of the human judges are counted makes her appear more impartial, because she is not casting the final deciding vote.[9] And in fact when the votes are counted, the judges are deadlocked, because each parent of Orestes has a valid claim on justice. Half of the human judges were not persuaded by the arguments advanced by the Erinyes about the shedding of kindred blood; the others were not persuaded by Apollo's argument about the primacy of the male parent. Nonetheless, because of Athena's single vote, Orestes is acquitted. He offers thanks to the goddess for preserving his house and allowing

Athena and Apollo stand on either side of Orestes, protecting him from one of the
Erinyes at far right. (Red-figure column krater, 475–425 B.C., by the
Duomo Painter. Réunion des Musées Nationaux/Art Resource, New York, K 343.)

him to return home, and he promises that his people will always be the allies of
her city.

Next, however, Athena must deal with the wrath of the Erinyes. The audience
knows that she can play the role of peacemaker, because at the end of the *Odyssey*
she stopped Odysseus and Telemachus before they could kill all the relatives of
the suitors, and in the guise of Mentor she arranged the peace settlement. But in
Athens, after the trial of Orestes, Athena cannot simply tell the Erinyes what to
do, because they are gods. Instead, she must try to persuade them not to harm her
citizens. She makes this case by telling the Erinyes that they did not lose, because

the votes of the judges were divided equally, and she further promises them a home in Athens where they will receive honors from her people. Finally, when they continue to threaten harm and complain of being dishonored, she remarks that she has keys to the house where Zeus keeps the lightning. In the end they agree to accept the home and the honors she offers, and they promise to protect Athens. They sing, "For the city I make my prayer, prophesying with kind intent, that in plenty the blessings that make life prosperous may be made to burgeon from the earth by the sun's radiant beam" (921–26). The Erinyes vow they will prohibit untimely deaths, ask the ruling gods to let all maidens find husbands, and prevent civil wars and murders. At the end of the play the citizens escort them by torchlight to their new homes. Athena has successfully persuaded them that by accepting these new honors they have won a victory equal to that of Orestes.

In the course of the three dramas Aeschylus has shown that without the intervention of the gods human ignorance and selfishness would have prevailed. Orestes would not have been acquitted, and the curse on the house of Atreus would have gone on claiming new victims until all members of the family had been eliminated. The gods bring other benefits as well: Apollo confronts the Erinyes to protect Orestes, and Athena takes pity on him as well. She manages to bring the conflict with the Erinyes to an end by offering them new honors, which is the strategy that Zeus, her father, used to establish his hegemony among the gods. Without her intervention the conflict among the gods would have continued, with terrible consequences for the city of Athens.

Aeschylus ensures that his audience understands the importance of the role played by the gods in the story by making them the principal characters in the last play of the trilogy. But even if the *Choephoroe* had been the only play from the trilogy to survive we would have a clear sense of the gods' presence behind the scene. There is, first of all, the frightening dream about the blood-sucking snake that causes Clytemnestra to send Electra and the slave women to Agamemnon's tomb with libations. Then there is the moment when Pylades, who has remained silent during all the preceding action, suddenly speaks out to tell Orestes to count all men his enemies rather than the gods. After Orestes has killed Aegisthus and Clytemnestra, he reveals that Apollo has instructed him to go to Delphi to be purified. And, finally, he begins to see his mother's Erinyes.

Perhaps a generation after the *Oresteia* of Aeschylus was first performed in 458 B.C., the great tragic poet Sophocles wrote a drama about the story of the killing of Clytemnestra. Since Sophocles was the most consistently successful poet in the tragic competitions of his time, his characterization of the gods may reflect what other Athenians were prepared to believe. In his *Electra* no god appears as a character, and nothing is said about what happened to Orestes after he committed the murders.[10] Instead, during the course of the drama he concentrates on the effects that the process of revenge has had on the lives of Electra and Orestes. But even though the gods do not intervene directly in the action, the poet nonetheless shows that, as always, they will see that justice is done, even if slowly and painfully for the mortals involved.

In Electra, as in the Oresteia, Apollo is the primary mover, albeit behind the scenes. Orestes says that Apollo has told him through his oracle at Delphi that "without the help of armed men and of an army, I should accomplish by cunning the slaughter done by a righteous hand" (Sophocles, Electra 36–37).[11] He expresses no concern about murdering his mother, and he prays to the gods of the land and to his ancestral home to receive him in good fortune, "for I come in justice to cleanse you, sped on my way by the gods" (69–70).

Electra, his sister, prays to the gods of the underworld and to the Erinyes to see that her father's death is avenged. She is joined by a chorus of Argive women who try to comfort her; they tell her, "Zeus is still great in heaven, he who surveys all things and rules them," urging her to "make over to him your grievous anger" (175–77). Hades, too, has not forgotten about Agamemnon, they point out, but nothing they say can console her. Electra's sister Chrysothemis reveals that she has been sent by Clytemnestra to offer libations at Agamemnon's tomb. Clytemnestra had a dream in which Agamemnon came and took his staff away from Aegisthus and planted it beside the hearth, and from it grew a bough that overshadowed the land of Mycenae. The chorus understands the dream to mean that Justice is on the way: "She shall come, with many feet and many hands, she who lurks in dire ambush, the brazen-clawed Erinys" (489–91). The misery of troubles has not left the house since Agamemnon's grandfather Pelops threw his charioteer Myrtilus into the sea; this murder was followed by a series of other revenge killings that culminated in the bloody death of Agamemnon.[12]

Clytemnestra reminds Electra that Agamemnon sacrificed her sister to the gods, so that he could bring back the wife of his brother Menelaus. But Electra insists that Artemis demanded the sacrifice because she was angry that Agamemnon had boasted of killing a stag in her sacred grove, and that he "sacrificed her, against his will, and after much resistance, not for the sake of Menelaus" (575–76). Clytemnestra has come out of the house to bring sacrificial offerings to the statue of Apollo. Usually prayers are spoken out loud, so that all can hear, but Clytemnestra prays to the god privately about the ambiguous dreams she had in the night, asking him to fulfill them if they are favorable, and if they are not, to turn them back on her enemies, especially if someone has come to rob her of the great wealth that she now enjoys. Unlike Clytemnestra in the Agamemnon, she is less concerned about Iphigenia than she is about herself and her own happiness: "Hear this, Lycian Apollo, with kindness, and grant to all of us that which we are praying for! The rest I think that you, who are a god, know well, even if I say nothing, for the children of Zeus can surely see all things" (655–59).

At first her prayer to the god seems to have been fulfilled. The old slave who has come with Orestes enters and announces that Orestes is dead, and tells in detail an exciting story about how he was killed competing in a chariot race at the

Pythian games. The chorus laments for the destruction of the family, but Clytemnestra, though briefly sad to learn of the death of her son, is grateful that she no longer needs to live under threat, either from Orestes or from Electra. Electra is despondent, thinking she has lost her only hope of revenge.

When Chrysothemis rushes in to tell her that she has seen flowers and offerings on Agamemnon's tomb, and that this means Orestes has returned, Electra insists that someone else must have put them there. She asks Chrysothemis to join her in killing Aegisthus and, when Chrysothemis refuses, insists that she will do it alone. The chorus sings about the duty of children to help their parents, and praises Electra for her loyalty to the dead: "I have found you enjoying no happy fate, and yet winning the highest prize in the observance of the greatest laws, by your piety toward Zeus" (1095–97).

Orestes and Pylades come in carrying a funeral urn. They tell Electra it contains the ashes of Orestes and listen while she laments that she was not with him when he died, and could not prepare his body for the funeral pyre. But just when everything appears to be hopeless, Orestes, who has seen that Electra is still loyal to him, takes the urn away from her and explains that he is in fact alive. There is no time for celebration, however; as Orestes and Pylades enter the house, Electra prays to Apollo: "But now, Lycian Apollo, with such offerings as I have, I ask, I fall before you, I implore, be an active helper in this plan and show mortals with what wages the gods reward impiety" (1379–83).

Immediately it becomes clear that the god has listened to Electra's prayer and not to Clytemnestra's. From offstage Clytemnestra is heard calling for Aegisthus and asking Orestes to take pity on her; but Electra tells her brother to strike his mother twice as hard, if he has the strength (1415).[13] She wishes he were killing Aegisthus at the same time. The chorus sings that the curse on the house of Atreus is being fulfilled: "The curses [arai] are at work! Those who are beneath the ground are living, for the blood of the killers flows in turn, drained by those who perished long ago!" (1418–21). Orestes reports that "in the house all is well, if Apollo prophesied well" (1424–25). Then Electra sees Aegisthus approaching in the distance, and Orestes and Pylades go inside to wait for him.

When Aegisthus discovers that Clytemnestra is dead and Orestes has returned, Orestes orders him to go inside so he can die in the place where he killed Agamemnon. Aegisthus asks: "Is it needful that this house should witness the present and the future woes of the house of Pelops?" (1497–98). Orestes replies, "It shall witness yours, at least; I am a good prophet in this matter" (1499). As far as the women of the chorus are concerned, the death of Agamemnon has been avenged: "Seed of Atreus, after many sufferings you have at last emerged into freedom, made complete by this day's enterprise" (1508–10). There is no need for further deaths or retaliations.[14] There is, furthermore, no reference to Clytemnestra's Erinyes or the trial of Orestes in Athens. The messages Apollo has sent to

Electra and Orestes through oracles and dreams referred only to the return of Orestes to reclaim his kingdom, and now his revenge has been accomplished.

Euripides, the third major tragic poet of ancient Athens, also wrote two plays about the return of Orestes to Argos: *Electra*, written about 420 B.C., and *Orestes*, which was completed in 408.[15] Gods appear onstage in Euripides with greater frequency than in the plays of either Aeschylus or Sophocles, but it is also true that in his dramas characters are inclined to question the gods' motives and even their existence. The resulting contrast between the doubts of mortals and the decisive action of the gods is both theatrically effective and deeply unsettling. Although the gods in Euripides behave like the gods in Homer, the audience becomes more aware of their limitations because of what the characters in the plays are prepared to say about their actions and the nature of divinity in general. In both of these dramas the poet returns to the version of the story Aeschylus told, in which Orestes must suffer because he killed his mother, be purified by Apollo, and be tried in Athens. But like Sophocles (and unlike Aeschylus) he does not bring the Erinyes on stage or give an extended account of what happens to Orestes after he flees from Argos. In both plays Orestes and Electra learn about what is to come from gods who appear at the end of the plays, after Aegisthus and Clytemnestra are dead.

The action of Euripides' *Electra* takes place outside a peasant's hut in the countryside of Argos. Agamemnon is already dead, and Aegisthus and Clytemnestra have gotten Electra out of their house by marrying her off to a poor farmer. But this man, despite his poverty, respects her, so that she is still a virgin. Orestes has come from "the god's initiations" (*ek theou mysteriōn*) to Argive soil in secret, "to exact payment for the murder of my father with murders" (Euripides, *Electra* 87–89). By speaking of the process of obtaining an oracle as an initiation, and by not saying what Apollo told him, Orestes gives the impression that his contact with the god has been more indirect than it was in the *Choephoroe*.[16]

When Electra comes out of the farmer's hut, Orestes thinks she is a slave woman because she is carrying a water jar. In a soliloquy she explains who she is; she wonders where Orestes is, and sings about the murder of her father. The Argive women who form the chorus ask her to come with them to the festival of Hera in Argos, wearing borrowed clothes, so that she can honor the goddess: "Do you think that with your tears, without honoring the gods, you can defeat your enemies? You will acquire your day of happiness not by lamentation, but by reverence toward the gods in prayer" (193–97). Electra replies that "none of the gods pays attention to my voice in my misery, or to my father's blood shed long ago" (198–200).

Electra sees Orestes and Pylades approaching, but she thinks they must be criminals, so Orestes has great difficulty persuading her that he is in fact a friend. Electra's husband invites them into his house, where Orestes says that he still hopes Orestes might come: "For the oracles of Loxias are secure, though I have no regard for mortals' prophecies" (399–400). In order to offer the strangers enough food, they need to send for another farmer, Agamemnon's former slave, who had rescued Orestes from Clytemnestra and Aegisthus when he was a child. When the old man arrives, he is excited because he has seen a lock of hair on Agamemnon's tomb that resembles that of Orestes; he asks Electra to compare it with her own. This time Electra is not persuaded by the same tokens that the Electra of Aeschylus's *Choephoroe* was prepared to accept as genuine. Even when the old man recognizes Orestes, she still refuses to believe. "Lady Electra, my daughter, pray to the gods!" he says to her, and she replies, "For what in the world?" "To have the prize you long for, which the god reveals," he answers. Again she quibbles with him: "See, I am calling on the gods. But what are you saying, old man?" (563–66). Finally the old man is able to persuade her that her brother has come by pointing to a scar beside the young man's eyebrow. The chorus is overjoyed, understanding, unlike Electra, that the presence of Orestes is a sign that at last the gods are seeing to it that Agamemnon's death will be avenged: "A god, a god now brings victory for us, dear friend; raise your hands, lift your voice, send prayers to the gods, that with good fortune, good fortune, your brother may enter the city" (589–95).

Orestes, the old slave, and Electra now plan the murders of Aegisthus and Clytemnestra. They pray to Zeus and Hera, the goddess of Mycenae and Argos, and to Hades and Earth, and to Agamemnon's ghost. The chorus sings of the golden lamb that was born in Mycenae, and of the story of how after Thyestes stole the lamb and also Atreus's wife, the sun and the stars reversed their courses, and Egypt was deprived of its rains. The chorus is reluctant to believe that such things would happen for the sake of justice for a mortal, although such frightening tales can be used to encourage mortals to worship the gods.

But just at the moment that the chorus has expressed these doubts about divine justice, its members hear a death cry far off. A messenger reports that Orestes has killed Aegisthus and proceeds to give a detailed account of his death. Aegisthus was sacrificing an ox to the nymphs and invited the two strangers to join in the feast. He allowed Orestes to carve up the meat, but when he examined the sacred parts of the animal he saw that the liver had no lobe and the gall bladder was damaged, and he became fearful. Orestes asked for a cleaver, and he killed Aegisthus while he was examining the entrails. When he told the servants who he was, they rejoiced.

The chorus dances, and Electra calls on the light, the brightness of the sun, and Earth and Night. Orestes returns, bringing the body of Aegisthus to show his sister that her enemy is dead.[17] Electra greets Orestes as a victor, but her brother replies: "First you must think of the gods as the ones who brought this good fortune, and then praise the man who assisted the gods and the success" (890–92). But Orestes hesitates to kill his mother and questions the advice that he received at Delphi: "Phoebus, your oracle uttered much unwisdom." Electra replies: "If Apollo is wrong, who is wise?" (971–72). Orestes wonders if an avenging deity pretended to be the god, but Electra accuses him of cowardice, and urges him to kill Clytemnestra as she killed Agamemnon.

When Clytemnestra arrives in her chariot, she expresses some remorse. She forgives Electra for her partiality toward her father, "for I do not take so much pleasure in what I have done" (1105–6). When she goes into the house the chorus sings, "There is requital for evil; the winds of the house have changed direction" (1147–48). But when Electra and Orestes come out of the house, spattered with blood, they are both unhappy, and Electra blames herself. Orestes questions the god: "Alas, Phoebus, dark is the justice of which you sang, but manifest the sorrows you have accomplished, and bloody the lot you have given to me, far from the land of Greece" (1190–93). They describe how Clytemnestra called out to them, and how Orestes covered his eyes as he killed her.

As Orestes and Electra cover up their mother's body, the chorus sees that spirits or gods have appeared on the roof of the house and asks who they are. One of them, Castor, explains that they are the Dioscuri, the twin brothers of Clytemnestra and Helen, who have become gods.[18] They had been attending to other human problems, saving ships in a storm, but now they have come to Argos: "We observed the slaughter of our sister, your mother. She has been punished justly, but you did not act justly. Phoebus, Phoebus—but he is my lord, and I am silent. He is wise, but his oracle did not advise you wisely" in encouraging Orestes to kill his mother (1242–46).

Although no god will interfere with what another god, especially a more powerful god, has done, the Dioscuri make it clear that they do not approve of Apollo's actions. Castor tells Electra and Orestes what will happen to them in the future: Electra will marry Pylades, and Orestes, pursued by the avenging goddesses, must go to Athens, where he will be tried in the court of the Areopagus. Apollo will defend him, and he will be acquitted. Once Orestes has fulfilled his destined fate, he will be happy and released from sorrow. Menelaus and Helen will bury Clytemnestra; Menelaus brought Helen back with him from Egypt, for in this telling of the story she never went to Troy. "Zeus sent her image to Troy," Castor says, "so that there would be strife and bloodshed among mortals" (1282–83).[19]

Orestes and Electra now ask the twin gods if they may speak to them; Castor replies that they are not polluted by the murder, "because I hold Phoebus responsible for this bloody deed" (1296–97). Orestes asks them why they did not come to help their sister and her children: "Since you both are gods and brothers of the dead woman, why did you not keep the gods of death from the house?" (1298–1300).[20] Castor answers: "Fate and Necessity led to what happened, and the unwise utterance of the tongue of Phoebus" (1301–2). Electra asks: "Which Apollo, which oracles allowed me to become my mother's murderer?" (1303–4). Castor tells her that she is a victim of the family curse: "Your deeds are shared, and your fates are shared, but a single atē from your ancestors has crushed you both" (1305–7).

The gods' answers offer little comfort to Orestes and Electra. They must now be separated from each other, and both must leave Argos. Orestes will be pursued by the Erinyes, and he asks Electra to sing a song of lamentation for him as if he were dead. The god Castor expresses his sorrow: "Alas, alas, what you have said is dreadful to hear even for the gods; for the heavenly gods and I too have pity for mortals and their many sorrows" (1327–30). But there is little time for further conversation. Castor tells Orestes to flee, because he sees the Erinyes coming with their "harvest of dreadful pains" (1346). As the mortals prepare to set off on their long and difficult journeys, the Dioscuri will effortlessly take themselves off to the distant Sicilian sea: "We two are going through the expanse of the sky; we come to the rescue not of the polluted, but of mortals who care about what is holy and just in their lives—these we release from their difficulties and rescue. So let no one wish to do wrong nor sail with those who have broken their oaths; as a god, I address you mortals" (1349–56).

The chorus responds: "Farewell; a mortal will live a good life if he is able to fare well and not suffer from disaster" (1357–59). But that general reflection could apply only to the most retiring and insignificant of human beings. It has no relevance to Electra or Orestes, or anyone in their family.

In this play Orestes has none of the assurances that he had in the *Choephoroe* of Aeschylus or the *Electra* of Sophocles. Apollo's oracle ordered Orestes to kill Clytemnestra, but the god sent no signs or dreams to guide him along the way. Until the end of the play, Electra and Orestes are on their own, aided only by the chorus, the farmer, and the loyal slave. The only hint given of what is to come is the damaged liver and entrails of the sacrifice offered by Aegisthus, and Orestes begins to doubt whether Apollo himself was responsible for the oracle (979). Without the god's direct support, Orestes and Electra would have regarded the murder of their mother as a brutal crime and not as an act of justice. In spite of Electra's doubts ("Which Apollo, which oracles?"), Castor reveals that in fact it was Apollo who ordered Orestes to do what he did.

By blaming Apollo for the murder of Clytemnestra, Castor makes it clear that (contrary to what Zeus says at the beginning of the *Odyssey*) it is not just mortals who bring trouble on themselves. The gods also make life hard for them, because they can be indifferent to mortal suffering and tend to treat too lightly the ties of affection that bind mortals together. Castor is critical of Apollo for what has happened to his niece Electra and nephew Orestes, but nonetheless he too has acquired a similar divine aloofness from the concerns of mortal life. When he was a mortal, he had been engaged to marry Electra, but now that he is a god he shows her no special favor. He feels pity for her and for Orestes, but then he returns to the sky without promising any further aid to his mortal relatives in Argos. His action is wholly in keeping with the attitudes of gods throughout the myths. Gods may express sympathy for humans, but they do not attempt to alleviate their suffering, because suffering and misery are inherent in the condition of being mortal.

In 408 B.C., Euripides produced another play, *Orestes*, about the moral issues raised by Apollo's demand that a son murder his mother. The action of this drama takes place on the sixth day following Clytemnestra's death. Orestes is lying on the ground, sick; he is having fits of madness that have been sent by the Erinyes. The city of Argos has decreed that no one shall offer Orestes and Electra hospitality, and a vote is about to be taken on whether or not to execute them by stoning. Electra asks: "But how can one accuse Apollo of wrongdoing? He ordered Orestes to kill his mother, who had given him birth, a deed which did not bring him honor in the eyes of all, but he did not disobey the god's orders" (*Orestes* 28–31). Electra blames Helen and then Apollo for her suffering: "Phoebus sacrificed us, offering our blood as a miserable sacrifice for the mother who murdered my father" (191–93). Orestes thinks that he sees his mother and the Erinyes attacking him and calls on the god: "Phoebus, the hideous ones will kill me!" (260). He asks for the bow that Apollo gave him to defend himself against the Erinyes, and he seems surprised that the goddesses do not flee from its arrows: "Blame the oracles of Phoebus [for the crime]!" (276). The chorus of Argive women observes that "great happiness does not endure among mortals, but it is like the sail of a swift boat that a god shakes and swamps in the deadly roaring waves of the sea" (340–44).

The young man's uncle Menelaus blames Apollo for the murder, saying, "The god is rather ignorant about right and justice" (417). Orestes replies: "We are slaves to the gods, whatever the gods are" (418). But Menelaus asks why the god has not come to help him. Orestes says, "He is on his way: that is what gods are like" (420). The god, however, sends no sign that he supports Orestes: "Cannot the god be depended on to release me from the pollution? Where is there any escape, if the one who ordered the murder will not rescue me from death?" (597–99). When Menelaus will not help him, his friend Pylades advises him to appeal directly to the people of Argos, but the Argives vote to condemn Orestes and Electra to death, although they are also allowed the option of killing themselves rather than be subjected to stoning. Electra blames the curse of the family of Pelops: "Last of all it has come upon me and my father in the many sufferings and struggles of the house" (1010–12). Pylades proposes that they kill Helen, who is hiding in the palace, and take her daughter Hermione hostage so that they will have a chance of escaping with their lives. Orestes and Electra call on Agamemnon's shade to help them, and Pylades prays to their common ancestor Zeus and to the holiness of Justice.[21]

While Orestes and Pylades seize Helen and Hermione and begin to set fire to the palace, the chorus again blames the family curse for the present catastrophe:

"The god has the outcome for mortals; the outcome will be as he wishes. But the avenging deity also is a great power; these halls have fallen, fallen in blood, because of the fall of Myrtilus from the chariot" (1545–49). Orestes threatens to kill Hermione and set fire to the house unless Menelaus goes to the Argives and asks them to spare him. It is only now, at this moment of ultimate crisis, that Apollo appears above the house, accompanied by Helen, whom he has liberated from her captors.[22]

The god's intervention brings about a peaceful resolution to this desperate situation in a way that none of the mortal participants in the action could have predicted. He begins by telling Menelaus not to be angry with Orestes, and orders Orestes not to kill Hermione. He explains that Zeus has told him to save Helen. As the daughter of Zeus, Helen will be made immortal, and she will join her brothers Castor and Polydeuces as a saving god for sailors.[23] The gods sent Helen so that the Greeks and the Trojans would fight and kill one another, and "rid the Earth of the insult of its unstinted supply of human beings" (1641).[24] Orestes is to go into exile for a year. Then he will stand trial in Athens, accused by the three Erinyes, but the gods will acquit him of his mother's murder (1652). After that, he is to marry Hermione, "the one at whose neck you are holding your sword" (1653). Electra is to marry Pylades. Orestes will then return to rule over Argos, and Menelaus will return to Sparta, free of Helen and the trouble she has brought him. Apollo even promises to "set things right" with the Argives who had wanted to kill Orestes and Electra (1664).

Orestes immediately agrees to follow the god's orders: "Prophetic Loxias, you did not prove to be a false prophet of your own oracles, but a true one. I had begun to fear that I was hearing some god of vengeance rather than your voice. But all is well in the end. I shall obey your commands" (1666–70). Menelaus addresses Helen as a divinity, promises his daughter Hermione to Orestes, and ends his quarrel with him. Apollo sends Menelaus and Orestes on their separate ways, ordering them to honor Peace, the "fairest of divinities" (1682–83). And he takes Helen with him to Olympus.

By waiting until the last moment to make his appearance, Apollo illustrates in the most vivid manner possible the difference between divine and mortal understanding. Before he came forth accompanied by Helen, all the human characters believed that Orestes and Pylades had killed her; none of the mortals realized that Helen had in fact been saved by Apollo himself. Throughout the course of the drama Orestes was never sure that the god would support him. When the Argives condemned him to death, he took matters into his own hands and did not wait for the god to come or give him orders. He was prepared to kill Helen and Hermione and burn down his ancestral home. By intervening just in the nick of time the god prevents him from committing new murders and causing further destruction.

Apollo also promises that the outcome of the trial in Athens will be more secure and honorific than it was in Aeschylus, in the *Eumenides*. In that drama the vote of the (human) Athenian jurors was evenly divided, and it was only because Athena cast the deciding vote that Orestes was acquitted. In the *Orestes* the god says that he will be tried by the gods, and acquitted by a majority vote. "The gods as justices for your case will split their vote most righteously; for there you are fated to win," he says (1650–52). His support for Orestes is sure and unequivocal. If the god had intervened sooner in the action, or sent clear signs that he would make things go right in the end, his intervention might have seemed less significant. But coming when it does, at the last possible moment, it draws attention to the importance of the god, even though the delay has increased the mortals' suffering and sense of isolation.[25] If once again the gods appear to have behaved unjustly, it is because they are like Homeric gods, who have their own interests, favorites, and even relatives. They are not concerned with achieving an abstract good, like God in the creation story in Genesis. In *Electra*, Castor takes Orestes and Electra's side because he is their mother's brother.[26]

In both *Electra* and *Orestes* Apollo's interventions have great practical importance. He makes arrangements for Helen's relatives that befit members of this privileged family. In the *Odyssey* also, Menelaus is assured that he will not die but will go to the Elysian plain, where "existence for mortals is at its easiest"; he is granted this favor not because of any particular virtue or past service but because he is the son-in-law of Zeus (*Odyssey* 4.561–69). In the *Orestes*, Menelaus is allowed to keep Helen's dowry and to marry again, while his daughter Hermione is married to Orestes. The god quickly disposes of Achilles' son Neoptolemus, the man Hermione had been engaged to marry; he will be killed at Apollo's shrine in Delphi (*Orestes* 1655–57).

Thus the *Orestes* ends on a much more positive note than the *Electra*. In the earlier play, Electra and Orestes, separated for so long, will never see each other again, and both will be exiled from their fatherland because of the murder. But in the *Orestes* the human beings are left to their new, more closely connected fates. The troubles of the houses of Atreus and Tyndareus are brought to an end. Orestes is vindicated. Helen never went to Troy and now will be made a goddess. Although there has been much talk onstage about death and destruction, in the course of the drama no one has been injured or murdered. Despite all appearances to the contrary, and all the doubts expressed about the gods throughout the drama, Apollo's intervention is a triumphant demonstration both of Zeus's justice and of his support for the mortal who has obeyed his command. It is and has always been in accordance with Zeus's plan that human beings will suffer and die. In the hands of Euripides, the story of Apollo's orders to Orestes demonstrates powerfully the terrible cost to mortals of accomplishing the gods' plan.

Perhaps it is because Apollo appears so late in the *Orestes* that he appears not to care about the mortals involved in the action. In the *Eumenides* of Aeschylus, Apollo comes to tell Orestes what to do, and sends him to his sister Athena for protection. Athena also intervenes on behalf of Orestes, by casting her vote in his favor at his trial. But in Euripides' drama Apollo makes no attempt to advise Orestes before he appears in front of the Argive assembly, or before he makes his desperate attempt to escape from the palace. Of the two portrayals of the god, unquestionably it is that of Euripides that seems more characteristic of human life in the post-Homeric age. Apollo speaks through his oracle in the *Electra* plays of Sophocles and Euripides, but he never appears in these dramas. The gods have stopped intervening personally in the lives of mortals, and instead they speak to them only briefly and from a distance.

CHAPTER 6

The Gods in Drama II

APOLLO, ATHENA, AND OTHERS

In the *Iliad*, Athena and Apollo are the most powerful of all the children of Zeus, and they are the gods who together bring about the resolution of the action in the *Oresteia* of Aeschylus. Athena is the principal divinity of Athens, but Apollo has an even more prominent role in drama than she because he is the god who can tell mortals about what will happen in the future. He has special access to his father, Zeus, as the Pythia says in the *Eumenides*: "Loxias is the spokesman [*prophētēs*] of his father Zeus" (19). Apollo knows what will happen, but it is up to mortals to interpret the signs that he sends them, and it is their responsibility to consult his oracle and not try to influence it. He describes his role in some detail to Hermes, his half-brother, in the Homeric Hymn to Hermes:

> I have sworn a mighty oath that no one aside from me among the gods who live forever shall know the wise counsel of Zeus. And you, brother of the golden wand, do not ask me to tell the decrees that Zeus of the broad brows devises. One man I will harm, and help another, as I drive like sheep the many tribes of unenviable humans. A man shall derive advantage from my voice, if he comes accompanied by the voice and flight of favorable birds. He will derive advantage from my voice; I shall not deceive him. But the man who trusts in birds who chatter in vain and wants to make an inquiry of my oracle against my will, and to know more than the gods who live forever, that man, I say, shall make his journey in vain, though I would receive his offerings. (Homeric Hymns 4.535–49)

Mortals can try to act in accordance with the will of the gods by consulting oracles. They can also use the various arts of divination to help them determine whether or not their present plans have any chance of success. The contrast between divine knowledge and mortal ignorance is vividly portrayed in *Prometheus Bound*, a drama by Aeschylus written around 460 B.C. All the characters in the play are gods, with one exception, Io, a beautiful young woman who has been pursued by Zeus. In the play Prometheus explains to the daughters of the god Oceanus, who form the chorus, that it was he who taught men to interpret dreams, to discern the hidden meaning in utterances they might overhear, to understand the flights of birds, to examine the entrails of sacrificed animals, and to read the signs in flames (*Prometheus Bound* 484–99). But even though mortals have all these gifts at their disposal, in many dramas they seem to do everything they can to ignore or disregard them, especially when they do not want to hear what the prophecies or omens are telling them.

In *Prometheus Bound*, when Io tells Prometheus the story of her encounter with Zeus, it is clear that she has not understood the messages the gods have sent her. Dreams come to the maiden Io saying that Zeus is in love with her. She consults her father, who sends messengers to the oracles at Delphi and Dodona. At first the oracles send back riddling answers, but at last they tell him to drive his daughter from his house (661–68). Then her body and mind are transformed; she has horns on her head, and pursued by a gadfly she rushes with maddened leaps away from her home.

The chorus members, who are goddesses, understand what has happened. They say that they would not choose to be a partner of Zeus: "I fear a maidenhood without a husband's love, when I look on Io's maidenhood crushed by cruel wandering and suffering from Hera" (898–900). Io, however, because she was not a goddess, had no power to refuse the god's advances, and she did not seem to realize that if she had sexual relations with Zeus she would incur the wrath of his wife Hera. Only after much suffering and long wandering does she learn from Prometheus, who can see far into the future, that Zeus's love for her will ultimately bring her a great reward. She will bear a son who will found a colony in Egypt; one of her descendants will be Heracles, who will release Prometheus from his chains (813–15).

By resisting the god's commands, Io only increases her suffering. Yet she and many other mortals are unwilling to do what the gods tell them to do. Resistance to the will of Zeus and the other gods, at its best, is a heroic assertion of free will against a cruel fate. But it can also take the form of an obstinate folly, or a simple refusal to understand that the gods have the mortal's welfare in mind. Whatever the reasons for a mortal's resistance, the gods inevitably triumph. They see that their orders are obeyed, either through the actions of the mortals themselves or (as in *Eumenides* and *Orestes*) through direct interventions. In this chapter I want to show how the gods treat mortals who are reluctant to accept their commands or accede to their wishes, and to describe the many ways the gods can intervene to influence the outcome of events.

Even when Apollo helps a mortal being, the assistance or information he gives may not make the person's life happy or easy, as the case of Orestes shows. Apollo ordered Orestes to kill his mother, and by obeying him Orestes incurred the wrath of the avenging goddesses the Erinyes, as well as the anger of many mortals also. There is clear hostility against him in the *Eumenides* of Aeschylus, where half the jury of mortals votes against Orestes; in the *Orestes* of Euripides his uncle Menelaus and grandfather Tyndareus refuse to help him, and the Argive people vote to condemn him to death.

In *Oedipus Tyrannus*, by Sophocles, Apollo's prophecies warn of even greater suffering. When Oedipus, who had thought he was the son of Polybus, the king of Corinth, learned that he might have been adopted, he went to the oracle at Delphi to ask who his true parents were. The god did not answer his question, instead telling Oedipus that he would kill his father and marry his mother. Oedipus tried to keep the prophecy from coming true by not returning to Corinth, but this decision led him to fulfill the prophecy anyway, first by killing an old man who later proved to be his real father, and then by marrying the widow of Laius, the king of Thebes, who had been killed on his way to Delphi; this woman turned out to be his mother.

Apollo plays a critical role in *Oedipus Tyrannus*, even though he does not appear in person. From the quick and angry reactions Oedipus has to the other characters, it is clear that he is the type of person who would have responded violently when insulted, as he did when he met the old man on the road to Delphi. The play begins, like the *Iliad*, with a description of a plague. Since Oedipus became king of Thebes when he married the old king's widow, the priest of Zeus and the people of Thebes come to him as suppliants, because the people and the crops are dying. Oedipus assures the priest that he has already sent Creon, his wife's brother, to Delphi to ask the god's advice. Creon returns with the god's message: "The lord Phoebus orders us plainly to drive out from the land a pollution, one that has been nourished in this country, and not to nourish it so that it cannot be cured" (*Oedipus Tyrannus* 96–98).[1] According to Creon, the god also said that the killers of King Laius must be driven out, and that they are living in Thebes.

The chorus of old Theban men is frightened and prays to Apollo: "What thing will you accomplish, perhaps new, perhaps coming again with the revolving seasons? Tell me, child of golden Hope, immortal oracle!" (155–58). When the prophet Tiresias says outright that Oedipus himself is the killer, Oedipus refuses to believe him. At first Tiresias speaks only in riddles, like the god himself. Finally he predicts exactly what will happen: Oedipus will be revealed as the killer of his father, husband of his mother, brother and sister to his children; he will be blinded and driven out of Thebes. "Go inside and think this over," he says, "and if you find me to be mistaken, you may say at once that I have no wisdom in prophecy" (460–62).

Again the chorus sings about Apollo's "oracular rock of Delphi," and how the god will pursue the killer: "For armed with fire and lightning there leaps upon him the son of Zeus and after him come dread spirits of death that never miss their mark" (464, 469–72). The words of Tiresias have frightened them, but they remain loyal to Oedipus. He says, "Zeus and Apollo are wise and know the affairs of mortals, but when it comes to men, one cannot tell for sure that a prophet carries more weight than I" (497–501).

Oedipus's wife, Jocasta, claims that she can prove there is no truth in prophecies: although the oracle had said that her first husband, Laius, would be killed by their son, Laius was killed by robbers at the place where three roads meet. Their son had been exposed to die on the mountainside three days after he was born: "Thus did the voices of prophecy outline the future; pay them no regard, for when the god needs a thing and looks for it, he will easily reveal it by himself" (723–25).

Oedipus does not find any reassurance in Jocasta's words, because he now suspects that the old man he killed long ago at the place where three roads meet was in fact King Laius. He wonders if the prophecy of Tiresias was accurate after all: "Would one not be right who judged that this came upon me by the action of a cruel deity? Never, oh sacred majesty of the gods, may I see that day, but may I vanish from among men before I see the stain of such a disaster come upon me!" (828–33). His only hope is that the old slave who witnessed the death of Laius will repeat his statement that the killing was done by robbers rather than a lone individual. The chorus is also troubled by Jocasta's skepticism about the oracle. It sings of the laws of Olympus, of justice, and of punishment for wrongdoing: if unjust actions are to win respect, why should they honor the gods with dances, or go to Delphi or any of the shrines of the gods? "But, oh ruler, if you are rightly thus called, Zeus, lord of all, may this not escape you and your ever deathless power! For already the oracles of Laius are fading and are being expunged, and nowhere is Apollo manifest in honor, but the power of the gods is perishing" (903–10).

Jocasta explains to the chorus that she is bringing offerings to the temples of the gods, because she is concerned about Oedipus. First she approaches the statue of Apollo in front of the house: "I come as a suppliant to you, Lycian Apollo, since you are our neighbor, with these accompaniments of prayer, that you may provide us with some solution that will purify" (919–21). But just at that moment a messenger arrives from Corinth to say that Polybus has just died and Oedipus has inherited the kingdom of Corinth. Oedipus supposes that the news has proved that Jocasta was right about the unreliability of oracles: "Ah, ah! Lady, why should one look to the prophetic hearth of Pytho, or to the birds that shriek above us, according to whose message I was to kill my father?" (964–67).

But his supposition about the oracle is quickly disproved. When Oedipus expresses concern that he could still marry his mother, presuming her to be Merope, the queen of Corinth, the messenger assures him that she is only his adoptive mother. The messenger himself had brought him to Corinth as a baby and given him to the king and queen. He had taken him from a Theban shepherd, who proves to be the same old slave who witnessed the death of Laius. Jocasta realizes what has happened and urges Oedipus not to inquire further, but he refuses. She leaves the stage with a warning: "Ill-fated one, may you never find out who you are!" (1068).

The old men of the chorus prophesy that it will soon be discovered that Oedipus is the offspring of the god Pan, or Apollo, or Hermes or Dionysus (1084–1109). But then the old shepherd arrives, reluctantly reveals that the baby he gave to the man from Corinth was the king's son; the king and his wife exposed it because they were afraid of the prophecies that the child would grow up to kill its parents. Inexorably the terrible prophecy has been fulfilled, and everything the prophet Tiresias said has proved to be true. The chorus sings: "Ah, generations of men, how close to nothingness I estimate your life to be! What man, what man wins more of happiness than enough to seem happy, and after seeming to decline?" (1186–92).

More terrible revelations quickly follow. A messenger reports that Jocasta has killed herself, and that Oedipus has blinded himself with the golden pins from her dress. Oedipus comes out of the house, blind, uncertain where he is and to whom he is speaking. When the chorus asks which god has attacked him, he replies: "It was Apollo, Apollo, my friends, who accomplished these cruel, cruel sufferings of mine! And no other hand struck my eyes but my own miserable hand! For why did I have to see, when there was nothing I could see with pleasure?" (1329–35). Thus far, blinding himself is the first action he has undertaken that was not ordained by the god.

Oedipus reflects that he is the mortal most hated by the gods; how much better it would have been if he had not been saved by the shepherd! Creon now urges him to go inside the house, so as not to expose his pollution to the sun god, and refuses to let him leave until he has learned from Apollo what they should do. The chorus speaks the concluding lines: "So one should wait to see the final day and should call none among mortals fortunate, till he has crossed the boundary of life without suffering grief" (1528–30). There is no need for them to say anything further about the accuracy of Apollo's oracle, or the importance of prophecy.

If Apollo knows the will of Zeus, and through his oracle makes it known to mortals, why is it that mortals do not seem to be able to understand the god's message? In the case of Oedipus, the problem was that the message was so awful: Who would wish to kill his father and marry his mother? Why should Oedipus, who had committed no crime, be punished in this way? The answer is that he was the victim of a family curse, like Orestes, and that if justice is to be accomplished in the long run, the innocent must suffer.[2] This form of justice offers little comfort to Oedipus, or to the chorus, or indeed to any mortal, unless it be the cold comfort that comes from understanding. He is now blind, penniless, about to be sent into exile; but he does understand that he cannot control everything (1523). The god, who is so much more powerful than he, has made it impossible for him to avoid committing the crimes he was so determined not to commit.

The example of Oedipus, however, does not stop his brother-in-law Creon from supposing that he can ignore the ancient customs of burial ordained by the gods. In another play by Sophocles, *Antigone*, Creon, the brother of Jocasta, has just become king of Thebes. He is faced with a decision whether or not to bury the body of a son of Oedipus, Polynices, who had died while attacking his homeland, Thebes, in an attempt to reclaim the kingship from his brother Eteocles. The assault on Thebes failed, and Polynices and Eteocles have killed each other. Creon decrees that whoever attempts to mourn or conceal the body of Polynices in a grave shall be subject to death by stoning. The old men of the city, who form the chorus, regard the defeat of Polynices as evidence of the gods' justice: "For Zeus detests the boasts of a proud tongue" and Ares has shattered the army of Polynices; the chorus calls on Bacchus, "who shakes the land of Thebes," to rule their city (*Antigone* 127, 153–54). "The gods," says Creon, "have threatened the city's fortunes with a heavy shaking, but now they have set them right once more" (162–63). He wishes to show by his decision to leave his nephew Polynices unburied that he regards him as an enemy of the city, even though he is his close relative.

But soon Creon learns that "someone has just gone off after burying the body, sprinkling its flesh with thirsty dust and performing the necessary rites" (245–47). The old men of the chorus are aware that, for all their many accomplishments, humans sometimes do wrong in the eyes of the gods: "Skillful beyond hope is the contrivance of his art, and he advances sometimes to evil, and at other times to good. When he applies the laws of the earth and the justice the gods have sworn to uphold he is high in the city; outcast is he with whom the ignoble consorts because of his recklessness. May he who does such things never sit by my hearth or share my thoughts!" (365–75). At this point the guards bring in a captive: Antigone, daughter of Oedipus. The guards explain that they had removed the dust from the body, but in the heat of the day there was a sudden whirlwind, "a godsent affliction" (421). After it subsided, Antigone saw that they had stripped the body, and she returned with more dust and water for a threefold libation. When Creon asks her why she has refused to obey his law, she explains: "For it was not Zeus who made this proclamation, nor was it Justice who lives with the gods below that established such laws among men, nor did I think your proclamations strong enough to have power to overrule, mortal as they were, the unwritten and unfailing ordinances of the gods. For these have life, not simply today and yesterday, but forever, and no one knows how long ago they were revealed" (450–57). Antigone believes that she is acting in accordance with the gods' will, but the old men of the chorus regard what she has done as senseless defiance. Creon is particularly angry because she is a member of his household.

The chorus now reflects on the troubles of the family: "For those whose house is shaken by the gods, no part of ruin is wanting, as it marches against the whole of the family. . . . From ancient times I see the troubles of the dead of the Labdacid house falling hard upon one another, nor does one generation release another, but some one of the gods shatters them, and they have no means of deliverance" (584–97). In their view, what has happened to Antigone is a consequence of the family curse. The old men do not mention any individual names, but everyone in the audience knew the story of Oedipus, and that the god told his father Laius not to beget a child. Now, with the deaths of Eteocles and Polynices, the sons of Oedipus, and the condemnation of his daughters Antigone and Ismene by Creon, the last root of the house of Oedipus has been cut down "by the bloody chopper of the infernal gods, folly in speech and the Erinys of the mind" (602–3). The Erinyes do not need to make an appearance in this drama, because as Sophocles sees it they are already present in the human mind. Unlike the gods, who enjoy their eternal existence in the brightness of Olympus, no mortal can have great prosperity without suffering disaster.

The final stanza of their song provides a devastating description of human ignorance: hope brings profit, but it also deceives, so that mortals cannot see disaster approaching. The chorus sings: "And a human knows nothing when it comes upon him, until he sets his foot in blazing fire. For in wisdom someone has revealed the famous saying, that evil seems good to him whose mind the god is driving toward disaster; but the small man fares throughout his time without disaster" (618–25). Only the man who entertains no hopes and no ambitions can avoid the sufferings that are experienced by the families of rulers and heroes.

When Creon's son Haemon tries to persuade his father not to kill Antigone, Creon refuses to listen to his son's sensible advice, and accuses him of being driven by passion, because Antigone had been engaged to marry Haemon. But he will not ask the citizens to stone Antigone to death. Instead he will place her in a cave, with sufficient food so that she will live long enough to allow him to escape the pollution of having killed a relative. The chorus sings about the god Eros, from whom no man can escape and who drives men insane; they blame the god for having caused the quarrel between Creon and his son. Haemon, as they see it, has been overcome by desire for Antigone.

When Antigone is led in, the chorus offers an explanation instead of solace. She is the victim of a family curse: "Advancing to the extreme of daring, you stumbled against the lofty altar of Justice, my child! And you are paying for some crime of your fathers" (853–56). Antigone claims that she will be welcomed by her family when she comes to Hades. She regards her obligations to her family as a law (nomos): "Such was the law for whose sake I did you special honor, but to

Creon I seemed to do wrong and to show shocking recklessness" (908, 913–15). Yet preferring the law of the gods to a law made by a man has led to her death. "What justice of the gods have I transgressed?" she asks. "Why must I still look to the gods, unhappy one? Whom can I call on to protect me? For by acting piously I have been convicted of impiety. Well, if this is approved among the gods, I should forgive them for what I have suffered, since I have done wrong. But if the others are the wrongdoers, may they not suffer worse evils than those they are unjustly inflicting upon me!" (921–28). Although she will not live long enough to find out, or to see what the audience will soon see, the gods approve of what she has done, and they intend to punish Creon.

In all this time there has been no sign from the gods, unless one supposes that they sent the whirlwind that covered Polynices with dust after the guards had cleaned it off (421). But now the blind prophet Tiresias describes the terrible omens he has witnessed: birds fighting, sacrificial meat that would not burn. Creon himself is responsible, because carrion birds and dogs have dropped pieces of Polynices' body on the altars. The gods will not accept the Thebans' prayers, and the birds will not give signs because they have eaten the polluted fat. When Creon refuses to believe these prophecies, Tiresias predicts what will happen: Creon will lose his own child in return for having entombed Antigone unjustly. The Erinyes and the gods are waiting to destroy him; soon there will be wailing and lamentation in his own house.

The chorus reminds Creon that Tiresias has never proved to be wrong and urges him to relent. Creon rushes off to rescue Antigone, but he arrives at the cave just too late to save her: a messenger reports that she has hanged herself. Creon's son Haemon is so furious that he tries to kill his father, and then kills himself. Creon had once been happy; now he has lost both his sons, Haemon and Megareus, who had sacrificed himself during the recent battle on behalf of Thebes. Eurydice, his wife, hears the messenger's description of her son's death and leaves without responding. When Creon returns with Haemon's body another messenger reports that Eurydice also has killed herself. The chorus says: "Alas, you have seen justice only late" (1270). Creon prays for death, but the chorus replies: "Utter no prayers now! There is no escape from fated calamity for mortals" (1337–38).

Had Creon been less eager to establish his authority, he could have prevented all the deaths by observing the laws of the gods and allowing Polynices to be buried, or by asking Tiresias what to do before he made his decision not to burn the body, or by consulting the oracle at Delphi. If Antigone had been less impetuous, she might have tried to persuade Creon to see that she was right to follow the gods' laws by covering the body, or urged him to consult Tiresias, and she might not have decided to hang herself as soon as she was put in her tomb. But even if Creon and Antigone had behaved more sensibly and deliberately than they did, the gods would have found a means of ensuring that the earlier deaths in the family were avenged; as the chorus has said, "For those whose house is shaken by the gods, no part of ruin is wanting, as it marches against the whole of the family." So the gods did not save Antigone from death, even though she did what was right when she buried her brother, because her death served as a means of punishing Creon, by causing in turn the deaths of his son and his wife. Apollo could have encouraged his prophet Tiresias to arrive earlier, before Antigone had a chance to make her second attempt to bury the body, or before she was taken off to her tomb. But by not intervening directly to prevent the mortals from making further mistakes, as Apollo does so memorably in Orestes, the gods see to it that the earlier crimes of the family of Oedipus are avenged, and so they determine the terrible outcome of the drama.

But direct intervention is usually required when the gods want to bring about a more positive outcome, as they do in Orestes. In another of the plays of Euripides, Ion, Apollo arranges for his son Ion to become king of Athens. The boy's mother, Creusa, had abandoned the baby after the god deserted her. Unbeknownst to her, however, Apollo would not let his son die. Instead he sent Hermes to bring the baby to the temple of Delphi, where the child was raised by the priestess of Apollo and later became a temple attendant. The play begins just as Apollo is about to restore the child to his mother. Creusa, the daughter of Erechtheus, king of Athens, has married Xuthus, who was an ally of the Athenians in their war against the Euboeans; now, as her husband, he rules Athens. Since Xuthus and Creusa have had no children, they have come to consult Apollo's oracle. Hermes tells us in the prologue of the play that Apollo has arranged to make Xuthus believe that he is the father of the god's son, but that Creusa will recognize the young man privately as the baby she abandoned long ago. He is called Ion, and he will become the ancestor of the Ionians, the Greek settlers in Asia Minor.

But Apollo's plans are almost wrecked by the mortals involved in the story. Creusa still believes that she has been abandoned by the god and considers him to be unjust: "You did not save your child whom you ought to have saved and, although you are a prophet, did not answer its mother when she asked if she should honor him with a tomb if he were dead, or should he be alive, if she would ever see him" (Ion 386–89). Xuthus tells Creusa that he has learned from the oracle of Trophonius that neither he nor she will return to Athens without a child (408–9).[3] But Creusa is still resentful, and when she joins Xuthus in offering prayers to the god, she complains: "Loxias, if he is now willing to make up for his wrongdoing in the past, I would not consider in all respects a friend, but I will accept what he wishes, for he is a god" (425–28).

Creusa has been speaking to the young man who serves as the attendant of Apollo's temple, telling him the story of a "friend" of hers who had intercourse with Apollo and bore his child, and then exposed the child. The young man is horrified and begins to question the god whom he has served so happily all his life: "I must admonish Phoebus; what has happened to him? Does he take maidens by force and abandon them? Does he beget children in secret and abandon them to die? Do not do that, but rather, since you have the power, pursue virtue, for if the gods punish mortals who prove to be evil, how is it just that you who yourselves wrote the laws for mortals can be accused of lawlessness? If—though it will not happen, but for the sake of argument—you gods paid the penalty to mortals for violating marriages, you and Poseidon and Zeus the ruler of heaven would empty your temples by paying the fines for your wrongdoing" (436–47).

Xuthus meanwhile has learned from Apollo's oracle that the first person he meets when he comes out of the temple will be his son, and this person proves to be Ion. Creusa is jealous and resentful, because this son, who would not be related to her by blood, could claim the kingdom that Xuthus has acquired by marrying her. Creusa blames the god for her misfortune:

> To this light I shall speak in reproach against you, son of Leto. You came to me, with your hair shining with gold, when I was gathering saffron petals in the folds of my gown, to reflect the golden light in their flowering. You grasped the pale wrists of my arms and you led me to a bed in the cave, while I cried out "Mother!" a lover god in your shamelessness, granting a favor to Cypris [Aphrodite].4 And I in my misfortune bore you a son, and out of fear for my mother I threw him on your couch, where you had lain with me in my misfortune, in my sadness on our sad bed. Alas, and now he is gone, stolen, a feast for the birds, my child and yours, you wretch, and you play the lyre and sing your paeans. (885–906)

Creusa's old tutor, who has come with her from Athens, suggests that she burn down the god's shrine, but when she demurs, his next suggestion is that she kill the child her husband has just claimed for himself.

Before she can do so, however, the god about whom Creusa is complaining intervenes to save his child. The old man puts poison in Ion's wine cup, but as Ion holds the cup up to pour his libation one of the servants utters a word of ill omen (blasphēmia, 1189). Ion, who had been raised in a temple with Apollo's prophets, interprets it as an omen (literally, "a bird," oiōnos, 1191) and orders a new bowl of wine to be prepared. Meanwhile a bird drinks the wine Ion had poured in libation to the god, and dies in agony.

Having seen this, Ion and the citizens of Delphi go in pursuit of Creusa, who takes refuge at the god's altar. Once again the god intervenes, this time to prevent Ion from unwittingly killing his mother. As Ion complains of the law that protects suppliants, the priestess arrives with the basket in which she found Ion and the tokens that were in it; these Creusa is able to identify, and mother and son are joyfully reunited. "This was the god's work," says Ion; "now may we be happy in what remains of our fortune, just as the past was unfortunate" (1456–57).

Again though, just as it looks as if the god's plan has succeeded, human doubt threatens his arrangements. Ion is not yet sure that he is really the son of Apollo, as Creusa swears he is. As Ion goes into the temple to ask the oracle, Athena appears above the temple: she has come "in urgent haste" from Apollo, "who did not think it right to be seen by you, lest blame for the past come out in the open, so he sends me to deliver his message to you" (1556–59). Athena tells Ion that he is indeed the god's son, and that he will be the ancestor of the Ionians, and that Xuthus and Creusa will now have children of their own. She confirms what Hermes said in the prologue, that Apollo did not abandon his son Ion but preserved him from death so he could in time be restored to his mother: "Apollo nobly brought all this to pass" (1595). Creusa says: "I praise Apollo even though I did not praise him in the past, because he has given me the child he had abandoned; I am glad to see the temple doors and the god's oracle, which were hateful to me in the past" (1609–12). Athena is pleased that Creusa has changed her mind about Apollo. "The gods' actions take time," Athena says, "but in the end they are not without power" (1615). At the end of this drama, as in the Eumenides and the Odyssey, she uses her diplomatic skills to bring about a peaceful resolution.

The chorus closes the drama with a reflection on the importance of adjusting human expectations to the gods' timetable: "If your house is going through a time of troubles, take heart and honor the gods, for in the end good people get what they deserve, and the bad, because of who they are, could never fare well" (1620–22). The chorus's attempt to understand, however well intentioned, is less than a complete appraisal of what has happened in the course of the drama. It is true that mortals need to be patient, because gods take their time, as Athena herself has said. But the play also makes it clear that being "good" in itself would never be enough to guarantee that a mortal could get what he or she deserves. Apollo rescued Ion after he was born and again when Creusa's old tutor tried to poison him, and prevented him from killing his mother—not just because Ion was good, but because he was the god's own son, and Creusa is his son's mother.

What the chorus of the Ion fails to observe is that the gods' code of ethics differs in important particulars from that of mortals. The gods, as we have often seen, have a more leisurely timetable than mortals, and they stir themselves to timely action only when it is absolutely necessary, as at the end of the Orestes or at several critical points in the Ion. They can be indifferent to human suffering for long periods of time; and they allow mortals to experience isolation and despair even when they are looking out for their welfare. Apollo lets Creusa believe that their child is dead and for years says nothing to her about the bright future he has in store for him. Because gods can take a longer view than short-lived mortals, they are content to wait to administer their justice and to postpone revenge even for several generations. They are partial also to their own kin and those connected with them by blood or marriage. And, as we have seen, they are prepared to rescue these privileged mortals even when other mortals might judge them to be unworthy.[5]

When Athena appears in the action of dramas, it is without warning, as at the end of *Ion*. Unlike Apollo, she has no oracle she can employ to send messages to mortals but must rely on direct intervention, or on dreams, and that is not a strategy that can be used at the last moment. Only Apollo has the capacity to send instant messages to mortals, either through his oracle or through prophets like Calchas and Tiresias, or through the flights of birds. Athena, by contrast, enters the action directly, as helper or mediator, as she does at the end of the *Ion*.

She also materializes suddenly at the end of another of the dramas of Euripides, *Iphigenia Among the Taurians* (ca. 413 B.C.). Iphigenia explains in the prologue that she has been rescued by the goddess Artemis who, just as her father Agamemnon was about to sacrifice her, had substituted a deer in her place. The goddess then brought Iphigenia to the Crimea, the land of the Taurians, a barbarian people, to serve as the priestess of her temple and to preside over human sacrifices. Meanwhile her brother Orestes and his friend Pylades have been sent by Apollo to bring the statue of Artemis to Athens. But the Taurians attempt to stop the ship in which Iphigenia, Orestes, and Pylades are trying to escape, and adverse winds drive the ship close to the rocks. Athena intervenes just in the nick of time and saves them.

Athena tells the king of the Taurians to allow Orestes to carry off the image of the goddess, because "it was fated in the oracles of Loxias" (*Iphigenia Among the Taurians* 1438).[6] She has asked Poseidon to make the waters calm so that the Greeks can escape. Because she is a goddess, she can make Orestes hear her even though he is on the ship and cannot see her. The king of the Taurians, Thoas, willingly complies with the orders of the goddess. "Lady Athena," he says, "the man who hears the commands of a god and disobeys them is out of his mind" (1475–76). Athena thanks him: "Necessity has power both over you and over the gods" (1486). Athena uses her authority to bring about a peaceful resolution of the conflict and confusion in which the mortals have been involved, and the humans readily comply, as they do at the end of the *Odyssey* and the end of the *Ion*.

But in other dramas Athena plays her other Homeric role, that of partisan and advocate. In the drama *Rhesus*, by an unknown author, Athena takes the Greek side, as she did in Book 10 of the *Iliad* when she guided Odysseus and Diomedes on their excursion to the Trojan camp and helped Diomedes kill the Thracian prince Rhesus and steal his horses. In the *Rhesus*, Athena diverts the attention of Paris by pretending to be his patron goddess Aphrodite, while Odysseus and Diomedes go inside the tent where Rhesus sleeps.[7] She tells Paris just what a mortal would want to hear from a god: "Take heart, I, Cypris, am protecting you; I am well disposed toward you; I care about your war, and I have not forgotten the honor you bestowed on me, and I praise you because you have been good to me" (*Rhesus* 646–48). Deceitfully, Athena promises that she will take good care of him and see that the Trojans prosper: "And you also will be aware of my readiness to help you" (667). As soon as Paris leaves, the goddess tells the Greeks to make their escape.

The Ajax, a drama by Sophocles, also has Athena assuming her Homeric role as advocate of the Greek cause and special protector of Odysseus. This drama begins just after the Greeks have awarded Achilles' armor to Odysseus rather than to Ajax. Athena tells Odysseus that Ajax had intended to kill the other Greek leaders because he was angry over not being awarded the armor. But the goddess has intervened to save Odysseus and the others, not by attacking Ajax directly with her own hand, but by driving him mad, so that he imagines that the cattle he was slaughtering were the sons of Atreus, Agamemnon and Menelaus, and the other leaders. Athena summons Ajax to come out so that Odysseus can see him and tell the other Greeks what he has witnessed; she fixes it that Ajax cannot see Odysseus watching him. Odysseus observes: "Indeed anything can happen if a god contrives it" (Ajax 86).[8] When Ajax boasts to the goddess that he has killed Agamemnon and Menelaus, the goddess cunningly leads him on and asks him what he plans to do with Odysseus, and Ajax describes how he will torture him before he kills him. Athena sends Ajax back inside his hut and then asks: "Do you see, Odysseus, how great is the power of the gods?" (118).

Because Odysseus is a mortal, however, he pities Ajax, even though he is his enemy, "thinking not of his fate, but of my own; because I see that all of us who live are nothing but ghosts, or a fleeting shadow" (124–26). Athena responds, "Look then at such things, and never yourself utter an arrogant word against the gods, nor assume conceit because you outweigh another in strength or in profusion of great wealth. Know that a single day brings down or raises up again all mortal things, and the gods love those who think sensibly and detest offenders" (127–33).

Why did the goddess choose such a particularly cruel means of punishing Ajax and derive such pleasure from taunting him? She was angry because Ajax had boasted when he left home that he was confident that he could win glory even without the help of the gods. He made the same boast a second time when Athena urged him to attack the enemy: "'Queen, stand by the other Argives; where I am the enemy never will break through.' By such words as these he brought on himself the unappeasable anger of the goddess, through his more than mortal pride" (774–77).

In Euripides' drama Trojan Women (415 B.C.) anger again causes Athena to turn against the Greeks after the sack of Troy, despite her unwavering support for them during the whole of the Trojan War. Poseidon also had been on the side of the Greeks, but in the prologue to the Trojan Women he speaks with regret about the destruction the Greeks have wrought in Troy. The shrines of the gods have been desecrated: "When desolation takes hold of a city, the worship of the gods is neglected and receives no honor" (Trojan Women 26–27). He blames Athena for the devastation of the city: "If Pallas the child of Zeus had not destroyed you, you would still be standing on your foundations" (46–47).

But suddenly Athena appears and tells Poseidon that she wants "to delight the Trojans who were hateful to me in the past, and impose a bitter return upon the Greeks" (65–66). When Poseidon asks her why she has changed her mind, she explains that she and her temples have been treated insolently. Ajax the son of Oileus raped Cassandra in her temple but was not punished or even admonished for his impiety by the Greeks. She tells Poseidon that Zeus at her request will send rain, hail, and storm winds against them, and that he has given her the thunderbolt so she can burn the Greek ships. Although Poseidon had been Athena's rival for the honor of being the patron god of Athens, she asks him to stir up the Aegean Sea "and fill the hollow bay of Euboea with corpses, so that in the future the Greeks will know that they should show proper respect to my power and should respect the other gods" (84–86). Poseidon agrees to help her, for the gods cannot tolerate impiety. He states: "Foolish is the mortal who sacks cities, temples, tombs, and the sacred places of the dead. If he lays them waste, he himself perishes afterward" (95–97).

Meanwhile, the women of Troy are in despair because they know nothing about the punishment that lies in store for the Greeks. They were not on stage to hear the conversation between Athena and Poseidon in the prologue. No god appears at the end of the drama to tell them what will happen in the future. When Cassandra prophesies that she and Agamemnon will be murdered, the Trojan women do not believe her. Her mother, Hecuba, wonders why the gods allowed Helen to survive the fall of Troy but have done nothing to prevent the death of her husband, Priam, and all her children. She has begun to wonder who controls the course of justice. Is it Zeus, or fate, or human intention?[9] "Sustainer of the earth and you who have a base on earth, whoever you are, most difficult to know, Zeus, or necessity of nature or the mind of men, I address you in prayer," she says. "For as you go along your silent path, you direct all mortal affairs according to justice" (884–88). As Hecuba prepares to leave her city, she is overcome by despair: "Oh Troy, once so proud among barbarian cities, you will soon lose your famous name. They are setting you on fire, and they lead us along the earth as slaves! Oh gods! But why do I call on the gods? When I called on them before, they did not hear me" (1277–81).

The Trojan women of the chorus suppose instead that Zeus has betrayed his temple and altars in Troy: "Gone are the sacrifices and the pious songs of the choruses and the all-night festivals to the gods, the golden images and the holy moon-cakes of the Phrygians, twelve in number. I wonder, I wonder, if you think about these things, Zeus, as you sit upon your heavenly throne, and the city is destroyed, attacked by the blazing force of fire" (1071–80). They do not appear to realize that offering sacrifices and performing rituals was not enough. The gods allowed Troy to be destroyed because the Trojans allowed Paris to keep Helen.

Ajax the son of Oileus, sword in hand, pulls Cassandra away from the statue of Athena, where she has taken refuge. (Red-figure hydria, ca. 480 B.C., by the Cleophrades Painter. Museo Nazionale, Naples, no. 81669/H 2422.)

The gods are now about to see to it that the Greeks themselves will suffer for the sacrilege of Ajax son of Oileus against Athena. In spite of the Trojan women's doubts, there is justice in the world, even though it will bring them little comfort. Neither they nor Hecuba have the satisfaction of knowing that gods are in fact watching, and that Athena has already intervened to punish the Greeks for their impiety.

⇥ GODS DEFENDING THEIR HONOR ⇤

Gods intervene in human affairs to see that justice is done and to protect their relatives, but they also intervene to defend their honor. Euripides emphasizes the importance of honoring the gods in two dramas, the *Hippolytus* and the *Bacchae*. Euripides composed *Hippolytus* toward the beginning of his career, in 428 B.C., and *Bacchae* at the very end, 407–406 B.C., but there is no significant difference in the way he portrays the nature of divinity in the two plays. In both plays a god becomes angry because a mortal refuses to pay him or her due proper tribute; in both the god sees to it that the mortal dies a painful death, and that members of his family are responsible for killing the offender. In the *Hippolytus* Aphrodite states: "I respect those who honor my power, but I throw down those who regard me with arrogance. For this is true even among the race of gods: they enjoy receiving honor from men" (*Hippolytus* 5–8). She is angry at Hippolytus, the son of the hero Theseus and the Amazon Hippolyte, because Hippolytus says that Aphrodite is "the lowest of divinities"; he has no interest in sex and will not consider marriage. Instead, he "honors Phoebus's sister Artemis, the daughter of Zeus, and regards her as the greatest of divinities" (13–16). Aphrodite does not object to his spending his days hunting with Artemis, "but for the wrongs he has done me, I shall take my revenge on Hippolytus on this very day. I have already done most of the work; I have no need of great effort" (21–23).

Like Athena in the *Ajax*, Aphrodite has chosen to let mortals do most of the work for her. She has made Phaedra, wife of Theseus and stepmother of Hippolytus, fall in love with him. Aphrodite will not allow her to perish in silence: she will see to it that Theseus learns about it, and that he will then kill his son with one of the three curses that his father Poseidon gave to him. Aphrodite does not hesitate to let the innocent Phaedra die in the course of getting her revenge on Hippolytus: "Phaedra will keep her honor, but die nonetheless. For I do not attach greater value to the harm done to her than to my rendering justice to my enemies in a way that is satisfactory to me" (47–50). As Hippolytus enters, Aphrodite reminds the audience of the cruel limitations of human knowledge: "[Hippolytus] does not know that the gates of Hades are open, and the light he looks upon will be his last" (56–57).

Hippolytus and his hunters sing a short hymn of praise to Artemis, and Hippolytus brings a wreath for her statue. He has made the wreath from grasses and flowers that grow in a meadow sacred to Artemis, which only virtuous mortals have access to: "Now, dear mistress, receive this garland for your golden hair from a pious hand. For it is my privilege alone among mortals to be with you and converse with you, hearing your voice, but not seeing your face. May I reach the end of life's race as I have begun it!" (82–87). An old slave asks if he may offer him advice. Mortals dislike proud people and like affable people, the slave says, and he suggests that gods are the same. "Yes," says Hippolytus, "if mortals use the same laws as gods" (98). The old man suggests that he address the holy goddess Cypris, who stands near his gates, but Hippolytus says, "I greet her from a distance since I am pure" (102). Different men, he argues, like different gods, and he does not like a god who displays her powers at night. The old man replies, "My son, one must give honors to the gods" (107). But Hippolytus says to the old man, "To your Cypris I say farewell" (113). The old man asks Aphrodite to forgive him: "If someone because he is young has a grudge against you and talks nonsense, pretend not to hear him. Gods ought to be wiser than mortals" (118–20). But, as we know, the goddess will not forgive Hippolytus.

Phaedra tries not to give in to her passion, but her old nurse, without her permission, tells Hippolytus about it. To protect her reputation Phaedra writes a letter to her husband, Theseus, saying (falsely) that Hippolytus has raped her. When Theseus reads the letter, he asks his father Poseidon not to let Hippolytus survive the present day, and in addition, he sends him into exile. The hunters see Hippolytus off as he leaves his home.[10] They know that he is virtuous and want to believe that the gods will protect him, but they are overwhelmed by the sudden change in his fortune: "Greatly does the gods' concern, when it comes to my mind, offer relief from sorrow, but I fail to hold my understanding hidden in hope, when I look upon the fortunes and affairs of mortals; for one thing comes after another, and the life of man changes place, always straying on" (1104–10). The women of the chorus add, "Would that in response to my prayers fate from the gods would provide the fortune of wealth and a heart untried by sorrow! May my thoughts be steadfast and not counterfeit, and changing my ways for tomorrow's time, may I be ever happy in my life" (1111–19). As far as Hippolytus is concerned their reflections are useless. A messenger reports that he is near death; his horses, frightened by a bull that has risen out of the sea, have upset his chariot so that he has been dragged along in the reins over the rocks. While Theseus exults in his revenge, the chorus sings a hymn to Aphrodite: "You lead the unyielding hearts of the gods and of men, Cypris" (1268–69). She and Eros rule over earth and sea, young and old: "Whatever the earth nourishes and the blazing sun looks down upon, over all this, Cypris, you alone have power" (1277–80).

Suddenly Artemis appears above the stage building. She tells Theseus the terrible truth, that his wife lied to him and that he killed his son impiously. As she observes, all her revelations can accomplish is to bring him pain, because she cannot save Hippolytus. Theseus has done awful things, although it is still possible for him to be forgiven even for what he has done. Artemis explains: "Cypris wanted things to happen as they did, gratifying her passion. The custom among the gods works in this way: no one is willing to oppose the determination of another's wish, but we always stand aside" (1327–30). It was only because Artemis was afraid of Zeus that she allowed the mortal dearest to her to die: "For the gods are not happy when pious men die; it is the evil ones that we destroy along with their children and households" (1339–41).[11]

When Hippolytus is carried onstage, the goddess tells him that Cypris devised his death: "She found fault with you for doing her no honor, and she hated you because you were chaste" (1402). Although she cannot save him, Artemis can get her revenge by killing the mortal who is dearest to Aphrodite with her inescapable arrows. She does not mention his name, but she must mean Adonis, who will be mortally wounded when he is out hunting; it is not a concern to Artemis that her victim is not in any way responsible for the death of Hippolytus.

Artemis ensures that Hippolytus will be honored after his death: maidens before their marriage will offer him a lock of their hair and remember him in their songs. She tells Theseus and Hippolytus to forgive each other, and then takes her leave: "Farewell, for it is not right for me to look upon the dead or to let dying breaths pollute my eyes; and I see that you are near this evil" (1437–39). There are few lines in Greek tragedy that express more poignantly the difference between the affections of gods and those of men: "Farewell to you also, fortunate maiden. Easily you leave our long relationship" (1440–41). What seems long to mortals is only a moment in the existence of someone who is immortal and ageless.

The angry deity in Euripides' drama *Bacchae* (the name means women celebrating the rites of Bacchus, or Dionysus) is Dionysus, son of Zeus. In this play, Dionysus has returned to Thebes in the form of a mortal. It is here, before the palace, that his mother Semele was struck by lightning, because (as he says) of Hera's immortal outrage toward her (*Bacchae* 8–9).[12] Dionysus commends his grandfather Cadmus, his mother's father, because he has turned the place where Semele was killed into a sacred precinct. Dionysus has been in Asia, establishing his rituals in all the eastern lands. Now he has come back to Thebes, posing as a stranger, because his mother's sisters, "who are the last people who ought to have done so, have said that Dionysus is not the son of Zeus, but that Semele was made pregnant by some mortal man and put the blame on Zeus, a story contrived by Cadmus, on account of which Zeus struck her with lightning, because she lied about her pregnancy" (26–31). Because his mother's sisters do not believe that he is the son of Zeus, he has driven them mad and forced them to dress as his devotees. He has driven all the other women of Thebes mad as well, and they have gone to the mountains: "For this city must understand, even if it does not want to, that it has not been initiated into my Bacchic rites, and I must make the case for my mother's defense and appear to mortals as a god whom she bore to Zeus" (39–42). Pentheus, a first cousin of Dionysus, is now king of Thebes. He is the son of Agave, Semele's sister. But Pentheus, despite his close relation to Dionysus, "fights against the gods as far as my cult is concerned and will not offer libations to me, and does not mention me in his prayers; for this reason I will show him and all the Thebans that I am a god by birth" (45–48).

The god in his disguise as a stranger is accompanied by a band of women who have come with him from Lydia in Asia Minor. These Asian women are the Bacchae, the devotees of the god. They call on Thebes to join in the rituals of Dionysus by wearing fawn skins and carrying the thyrsus, a stalk of fennel crowned with ivy, and they sing of the blessings the god bestows on his worshipers: "Blessed is the fortunate man who knows the rituals of the gods and leads a pious life and places his soul in the sacred band, celebrating the rites of Bacchus in the mountains, and who, observing the rites of the great goddess Cybele, brandishing the thyrsus, crowned with ivy, is an attendant of Dionysus" (72–82).[13] They describe the dances and the music of the pipes, and how Dionysus the thunder god leads his followers to the mountain, with torches and joyful cries, in rituals that make one feel young again: "Then joyfully like a colt beside its mother as she grazes, the bacchant lifts her swift feet in her leapings" (163–65).

Tiresias, the seer of Thebes, advises Pentheus to worship Dionysus, trying to persuade him that this god is as important for humankind as Demeter. According to legend, when Semele was destroyed by lightning, Zeus took his infant son Dionysus from her womb and secured it in his own thigh with golden pins until it was time for the child to be born, and Tiresias urges Pentheus not to make fun of this myth by appealing to reason. That story, he says, is based on confusion between the portion of heaven that Zeus gave Hera as a hostage (homēros) and the word for thigh (mēros).[14] "You take pleasure when the crowd stands before the gates and the city glorifies the name of Pentheus; the god also, I think, enjoys being honored" (319–21). Cadmus, grandfather of both Dionysus and Pentheus, suggests that the king should worship Dionysus even if he is not a god, because the story will bring honor to the family. He also reminds him of the fate of his cousin Actaeon, the son of Cadmus's daughter Autonoe, who was torn to pieces by his own dogs because he boasted that he was a better hunter than Artemis (337–40). "Come with us and give honor to the god," Cadmus says (342). Pentheus, however, refuses to join the ritual, whereupon Tiresias tells him he is insane: "May Pentheus not bring sorrow (penthos) into your house, Cadmus; this is not a prophecy but a statement of the facts. Pentheus is a fool and talks foolishly" (367–69).

In fact the god has given and continues to give Pentheus every opportunity to change his mind and pay him due honor. But Pentheus, like Hippolytus, has his own notions of what a divinity should be, and he is concerned that Dionysus is leading the women of the city astray. This drama, like Hippolytus, illustrates that mortals cannot choose what they want their gods to be like. Instead the chorus recommends an unquestioning piety toward the gods: "Of unbridled mouths

The infant Dionysus is born from Zeus's thigh while Hermes looks on.
(Red-figure lekythos, ca. 460 B.C., by the Alkimachos Painter.
© 2002 Museum of Fine Arts, Boston, Catharine Page Perkins Fund, 95.39.)

and unlawful folly the end is misfortune; but the life of calm and thought remains unshaken and holds the house together. Furthermore, the heavenly beings, though they live in the sky, see the doings of mortals. Being wise is not wisdom, and thinking more than mortal thoughts is a short life. In addition whoever pursues great ambitions does not preserve what he has. Such in my opinion is the behavior of madmen and people who make foolish judgments" (386–401).

Pentheus questions the stranger who has come to Thebes with the Asian women, asking him about Dionysus without ever realizing that the stranger is the god himself (500–502). When Pentheus tries to imprison the god, the palace is shaken and the fire on Semele's tomb blazes up. Pentheus in his delusion ties up a bull, thinking he has caught the stranger, while the stranger stands by watching. He tells the chorus: "Calmly I stepped outside of the house and came to you, without giving a thought to Pentheus" (636–37). The ease with which he does things is a sure sign of his divinity.

A messenger now offers an eyewitness account of what has been happening on Mount Cithaeron, where the women of Thebes have gone, abandoning their homes. The women, led by Agave, mother of Pentheus, wearing their fawn skins and carrying their thyrsoi, fed themselves on milk, and the ivy in their hair dripped honey. The messenger tells Pentheus about the women's supernatural strength: "So, if you had been there and seen it, you would have approached with prayers the god whom you now attack" (712–13). When the men tried to capture them, the women drove them off without difficulty; then they attacked the herds and tore cattle to pieces. They sacked two villages and carried off the children; whatever they carried stayed on their backs without being tied down. Fire flashed from their hair, and the weapons the villagers threw at them missed them: "Women wounded men and made them flee, not without the help of a god" (763–64). Because he has seen these miracles, the messenger concludes: "This god, master, whoever he is, receive him in this city, for they say that he is great also in this, as I understand, that he gives the vine to mortals that releases them from care. When there is no more wine there is no Aphrodite nor any other pleasure for mortals" (769–74). But Pentheus still is not persuaded; he gives orders to send his army after the women.

Unlike Aphrodite, who has already decided in Hippolytus that the man who has offended her must die, Dionysus makes a last attempt to bring about a peaceful resolution. He advises Pentheus to sacrifice to him, and not to resist his authority, "since you are mortal and he is a god" (794–95). It is only when the mortal refuses to listen that the god offers to take him to the mountain, where he can see the women of Thebes for himself. The stranger says that Pentheus must dress like a woman—as a Maenad, or maddened devotee of the god. The stranger promises to lead him through back streets so the Thebans will not laugh at him. The god already knows that Pentheus will take his advice: "The man is being brought into the snare; he will go to the Bacchants, where he will be punished by

Dionysus, center, holding a wine cup, dances with his Maenads.
(Red-figure kylix, fifth century B.C., by the Triptolemos Painter.
Réunion des Musées Nationaux/Art Resource, New York, G 250.)

death; Dionysus, you have the power, for you are not far off. Let us punish him"
(848, 847, 849–50). The god predicts exactly what will happen: "I shall go and
put on Pentheus the dress he will wear when he goes to Hades, after his mother
has killed him; he will come to realize that Dionysus is the son of Zeus, a god who
is most terrible in his authority, but most gentle to mankind" (857–61).

Some choruses in Greek drama, particularly those composed of old men,
stand somewhat outside the action onstage and offer advice to both sides in any
controversy. In this play, however, the chorus of Asian Bacchants is devoted to its
god, and remains hostile to anyone who opposes him. The Bacchants sing of the
pleasures of revenge: "What is being wise? Or what among men is a nobler reward from the gods than to hold one's hand in power over the heads of one's enemies? What is noble is always dear to us" (877–81). They then describe the nature of divine justice, using the same kind of language that Antigone used in her
appeal to the unwritten laws that humans ought to observe (*Antigone* 450–57,
908). The chorus of Bacchants sings: "The power of the gods moves slowly, but

nonetheless it is sure; it corrects those mortals who honor willful ignorance and refuse to honor the doings of the gods by their insane thinking. But the gods conceal in intricate ways the slow foot of time and hunt down the irreverent man. One must recognize that one is not stronger than the laws and observe them. It is a small expense to believe that these have power: the divine, whatever it is, and the law that has existed always in the long course of time and in nature" (Bacchae 882–96). Although they speak of "the divine, whatever it is," as the chorus of old men in the Agamemnon spoke of "Zeus, whoever he may be," the chorus of the Bacchae is certain that justice will be done.

The stranger now leads Pentheus out of the house in his woman's dress, telling him what he wants to hear, in much the same way that in the Ajax Athena encouraged Ajax in his madness, and in the Rhesus she encouraged Paris to believe that Aphrodite was protecting him. The chorus sings: "Go, swift dogs of Madness, go to the mountain, where the daughters of Cadmus have their sacred band! Drive them in frenzy against the man in the dress like a woman's, the maddened spy upon the Maenads!" (977–81). The chorus sees, without pity, that his mother will kill him, and it sings this refrain celebrating the god's revenge on Pentheus: "Let Justice go triumphant, let her go forth with a sword straight through the lungs, slaughtering the godless, lawless, unjust earth-born son of Echion!" (991–96).

A messenger comes from the mountain, mourning the fall of the house of Cadmus; he cannot understand why what he says gives the chorus of Asian women so much pleasure. He tells them how Pentheus has died: the stranger pulled down the top of a pine tree and seated Pentheus at its top, where the Maenads could see him; the god's voice gave them directions, and the women uprooted it so that Pentheus fell to the ground. He took off his headdress so his mother would recognize him, and he then understood what had happened and realized that he was in real danger: "Take pity on me, mother, and do not kill your child because of my mistakes" (1120–21). But his mother, Agave, thought he was a wild animal. Foaming at the mouth, with her eyes rolling, out of her mind, she was in a Bacchic trance and did not listen to him. Agave and her sisters tore Pentheus limb from limb, scattering his body over the mountain. Agave returns to Thebes in triumph with his head on her thyrsus, not realizing that what she has killed is not a mountain lion but her own son.

When Agave's father, Cadmus, returns from searching for the remains of the king's body on the mountain, she cannot understand why he does not take pleasure in her accomplishments. He replies simply: "Alas for our sufferings, yours first of all, and then mine. The god has destroyed us with justice, but in excess, the lord Bromius [Dionysus], one of our own kindred" (1248–50). When Agave comes back to her senses, Cadmus explains: "Pentheus was like you and your sisters; he did not honor the god, and therefore the god attached the same blame to all of you, you and him, so that my house is destroyed" (1302–5).

A Maenad holds a thyrsus in her left hand and a leopard in her right hand, as depicted on the inside of a kylix. On the side of the vessel (facing page), Dionysus sits with wine cup in hand while the women of Thebes dance around him holding pieces of the body of Pentheus. The other side shows the women with pieces of his body. (Red-figure kylix, ca. 480 B.C., by Douris. Kimbell Art Museum, Fort Worth, Texas, no. AP 2000.02.)

Dionysus now addresses the characters from above the stage building, speaking not as the stranger but as a god. About fifty lines of his speech are lost, but where the text resumes he tells the mortals what will happen to them in the future. Cadmus and his wife, Harmonia, the daughter of Ares and Aphrodite, will be changed into snakes. Later, after resuming his human form, Cadmus will destroy many cities in the East with a large army. The army will be punished for sacking a shrine of Apollo, but Ares will rescue his daughter Harmonia and Cadmus and settle them in the Elysian Fields; like Menelaus, Cadmus is fortunate in being the son-in-law of a god. "Thus I have prophesied, I, Dionysus, born of no mortal father, but of Zeus. If you had known how to be sensible, when you were unwilling, you would have been happy, having the son of Zeus as your ally" (1340–43). Cadmus tries in vain to get the god to take pity on them: "'Dionysus, we beseech

you, we have wronged you.' 'Too late you have understood; but you did not know me when you should have.' 'We realize our mistake, but you have set upon us too harshly.' 'But you insulted me although I am a god.' 'Gods ought not to be like mortals in their anger.' 'Long ago my father Zeus agreed to these plans'" (1344–49). Cadmus is forced to leave Thebes, the city he founded. He will never see Agave again. As they embrace for the last time, Agave wonders what she will do without him, and he answers: "I do not know, child; your father is little help to you" (1367). Their affection for each other is in stark contrast with the god's implacable indifference. Such lack of concern for human suffering is not uncharacteristic of divinity, as we have seen: Aphrodite allows Phaedra to suffer and die, even though she is innocent, and the gods do not rescue Antigone even though she had done what was right.

The play ends with lines that are also appended to the conclusion of several other plays: "Many are the forms of divinity; the gods bring many things to pass unexpectedly. And what we thought would happen did not come to pass, but the god found a means to bring about what we did not imagine. That is how this action went" (1388–92). The same lines also appear, with a slight variation, at the end of the *Medea*, another drama in which a mother kills her offspring. In two other plays the same lines are spoken after a happy ending. They remind the audience that at a basic level the outcome of a drama, whether for better or for worse, depends on the actions of the gods. Mortals cannot anticipate what the gods will do: "the gods bring many things to pass unexpectedly"; "what we thought would happen did not come to pass"; "the god found a means to bring about what we did not imagine." Pentheus, Agave, and her sisters were certain that Dionysus could not be a god; Cadmus was not sure if he was a god but thought it prudent to participate in his cult. Dionysus proved that he was a god by using his special powers: he is the patron of the theater, where men pretend to be gods and mortals other than themselves. So in this drama he made Agave believe that she was a hunter and he made Pentheus dress like a woman, reversing their roles, so that a woman could kill a man. Many proofs are given in the course of the drama that Dionysus is a god, but perhaps the most powerful of all is the unexpected, deadly effect of all these strange transformations.

Of course such tag lines as those that conclude the *Bacchae*, about the many forms of divinity, describe only the general nature of divine action in Greek drama. They say nothing about the anger that motivates some of these sudden changes or the pain and suffering they cause to mortals. Cadmus complains that the punishment Dionysus metes out to his family members far exceeds their crimes; Hippolytus also pays with his life for neglecting to give due honor to a goddess, even though that goddess is not harmed or injured in any way by his neglect. The tag lines say nothing about the suffering of innocent victims like Phaedra, or Oedipus, who tried to avoid the terrible fate of killing his father and marrying his mother. Human beings, even in the ancient world, could be more forgiving than the gods, even in the case of far more serious crimes than a slight to honor, and mortals are more hesitant than the gods to take revenge upon those who have not directly harmed them.

Dramas bring out even more vividly than the Homeric epics the ruthlessness of the gods in pursuit of their own honor. The most poignant example of such divine persecution is the intervention of Hera in Euripides' *Heracles*. Hera is determined to do harm to Heracles, because of Zeus's partiality for his mother, Alcmena. She sends Iris to order Lyssa, the goddess of violent insanity, to drive him to kill his wife and children, even though he has rescued them from death just a short time before. Athena intervenes and stops him by throwing a stone at his chest and sending him to sleep, before he can kill Amphitryon, his mother's husband, the man he regards as his father (*Heracles* 1004–6). When Heracles comes back to his senses he wants to kill himself, but his friend the Athenian hero Theseus persuades him not to and offers him asylum in Athens.

Like Hecuba and other characters in deep despair, Heracles believes that there is no justice in the world.[15] He is Zeus's son, and the greatest of all the heroes, but his father has not protected him. He says to Theseus and Amphitryon: "Zeus, whoever Zeus is, begot me to be hated by Hera (do not be angry at me, old man, since I think of you as my father rather than Zeus). . . . Who would offer prayers to a goddess like her? She was angry at Zeus because he slept with a mortal woman, so she has destroyed the benefactors of Greece, even though we are not in any way to blame" (1263–65, 1308–10). Heracles even goes so far as to believe that the traditional myths about the gods are untrue: "I do not believe that the gods seek out illicit unions and bind each other in chains; I do not suppose and I will not believe that one god is master of another. For a god, if he is truly a god, needs nothing. These are the miserable tales of poets" (1341–44). At this stage in his life Heracles cannot know what the audience knows, that Zeus does care for his son, and that he will ultimately make him immortal, even though he must still undergo even more terrible sufferings. The play demonstrates that the gods do exist, and that the poets have described them accurately. But, like the *Bacchae*, the drama also illustrates that the gods do not care for mortals with anything like the kind of sympathy or kindness that mortals can show for one another.[16]

Dramas offer repeated reminders of human ignorance, but they also deliver explicit messages about the difference between divine and mortal ethics. Gods have all the power, and they do not hesitate to use it. They demand honor and see that they receive it. Since they like to live at their ease, they allow human beings to do their work for them whenever possible. Because of their superior intelligence and foresight, they are able to devise cunning plots that pit members of families against one another, and cause parents to kill their children. They are in control, and mortals are like the nightingale that the hawk holds in its claws in Hesiod's *Works and Days*. The hawk has the power to kill the nightingale, if he chooses, or to let it go. All the nightingale can do is sing. Even though she cannot persuade the hawk, she can at least hope that some other mortal creature may be listening. When Cadmus says to Dionysus, "We realize our mistake, but you have set upon us too harshly," he fails to change the god's mind. The god is obdurate, but meanwhile the mortal spectators have heard what Cadmus has to say. They can agree that his punishment is too harsh, and even if they are powerless to help they can derive some comfort from knowing that life was hard even for the great heroes.

CHAPTER 7

The Gods in Hellenistic Poetry

In the fourth century B.C., most of the exciting and influential accounts of the ancient myths were written not in Greece but in the Greek city of Alexandria in Egypt. After 321 B.C., Egypt was ruled by a dynasty of Macedonian Greeks who sponsored literature and scholarship, while mainland Greece was still suffering from the effects of a series of wars. The Alexandrians began to make a collection of all the important literature that had been composed in the past, and because the settlers of the city had all come from many different parts of the Greek world they were eager to preserve the traditions of their original homes and to tell others about them. They produced a literature that is respectful of older traditions but at the same time more modern. They saw the gods in a larger perspective, as if from a greater distance, and in comparison with what they had learned about the gods of the other peoples with whom they had come into contact.

In the myths told by poets of this later period, the Hellenistic age, the mortals seem less conscious of the presence of the gods, but the gods are still in charge. Like Dionysus in the *Bacchae* of Euripides, many of the gods in these later narratives appear to be more interested in their own honor than in the accomplishment of the justice of Zeus. Zeus is present, but much more in the background than he is in Homer, as if the poets imagined him to be less inclined than he was in the *Iliad* to intervene or to check the anger of the gods who are intent on their own revenge. At the same time, the interventions of the gods often take less naturalistic forms than in the *Iliad*, where gods often appear in disguise and make their wishes known through natural phenomena, such as thunder and lightning or the flights of birds. Hellenistic poets seem deliberately to call attention to the more fantastic elements of the supernatural: the keel of a boat speaks out loud, a horse rushes from the sea, gods dissolve into dust before our eyes. These incidents, by their sheer lack of realism, call attention to the relative powerlessness of the mortals who witness them.

The mortals themselves also seem to be less like the heroes and heroines of old than like ourselves. The Hellenistic poets learned from the dramatists, and in particular from Euripides, that human beings, for all their aspirations, are ignorant, vulnerable, and morally flawed. Jason, the principal hero of the epic poem *Argonautica*, does not have the stature or powers of an Achilles or the ingenuity and craftiness of an Odysseus. Jason can be brave, but at other times he is apprehensive and fearful, and he could never have managed to achieve his goals without the assistance both of the gods and of a human being who possesses supernatural powers.

⊁| THE GODS IN THE ARGONAUTICA |⊱

Only one mythological epic written in Alexandria during this time has survived intact, the *Argonautica*, or *Voyage of the Argo*, by the third-century poet Apollonius of Rhodes.[1] Ancient sources tell us very little about Apollonius, although we know he was librarian of the Alexandrian library and a tutor of the heir to the Egyptian throne. He appears to have been a friend or associate of another influential poet, Callimachus, who had written a poem (now lost) about the rivers of the known world.[2] The story the *Argonautica* tells, of the first sea voyage by Greeks into the Black Sea, was of particular interest to Alexandrian audiences, who liked to hear about geography. Along the way Apollonius recounts the history of Greek settlements and religious cults throughout the region. In spite of his interest in places and customs, however, the *Argonautica* is not just a travelogue or an adventure story; it has a serious ethical element, and the gods are active in the world that it describes.

The poem begins with an invocation, not to a Muse, but to Apollo. The Argonauts rely on prophecy to set their course, and the voyage itself was inspired by a prophecy. Pelias, the king of Thessaly, in northeastern Greece, had been told by Apollo's oracle to beware of a man with one sandal. As Pelias was offering a sacrifice to the gods, including his own father, Poseidon, he paid no attention to Hera.[3] Then Jason appeared, the son of the king's half-brother Aeson. Jason had lost one of his sandals while crossing the river Anaurus, so Pelias devised an ordeal for him, in the expectation that he would never return: he sent him on a long and dangerous voyage to bring back the Golden Fleece.[4] This was the skin of a golden ram with magical powers, sent by Zeus to rescue Pelias's cousin Phrixus and his sister Helle from their cruel stepmother Ino. Phrixus and Helle flew east from their home in Iolcus (modern Volos) on the ram's back. Helle fell off into the sea, in what was afterward called the Hellespont. Phrixus came to the city Aea, in the region of Colchis on the east coast of the Black Sea, where he sacrificed the ram to Zeus and hung its fleece in a sacred grove.

The task of retrieving the Golden Fleece was daunting because no one besides Phrixus had yet traveled that far. Also, the king of Aea, Aeëtes, a son of Helios, the

Phrixus and Helle ride over the sea on the golden ram. (Red-figure calyx krater, fourth century B.C. Museo Nazionale, Naples, 82411 [H 3412].)

sun god, was a violent man and known to be hostile to strangers. But the gods come to Jason's rescue. With the advice of Athena, the craftsman Argos builds a ship, which is called the *Argo*. Heroes from all over Greece, many of whom are the sons of gods, come to help Jason on his quest. The powerful goddess Hera also is on Jason's side. On his way to Iolcus, when Jason lost his sandal, he was helping an old woman cross the river; this woman was Hera in disguise. Hera herself tells the story in Book 3 of the *Argonautica*, to explain to Aphrodite why she is eager to help him (*Argonautica* 3.66–73).

From the start, Apollo's oracles determine the course of the action. Before the voyage begins, Jason offers a sacrifice to Apollo, the god of embarkation: "Hear me, lord of Pagasae and the city Aesonis, which is named for my father, you who told me when I inquired at Pytho that you would show me the end and means of the journey, for you yourself were responsible for my ordeal" (1.411–14). Jason considers Apollo accountable because the god's oracle had warned Pelias about a man with one sandal. Apollo's son the prophet Idmon interprets the bright flames surrounding the sacrifice as a favorable omen. He predicts that they will return home, after many ordeals, but he already knows that he himself will die in Asia.

All the gods look down on the Argonauts from heaven as they set out on their voyage; the nymphs watch from the peaks of Mount Pelion, and so does the centaur Chiron, holding the infant Achilles in his arms. First the Argonauts arrive on the island of Lemnos. The women there had neglected to give due honor to Cypris, or Aphrodite. The goddess in anger then caused their husbands to sleep with slave women instead, and the women of Lemnos murdered all the men. When Jason arrives, he is wearing a beautiful cloak that Athena made for him. He is welcomed by the new ruler of Lemnos, the old king's daughter Hypsipyle, who asks him to remain and become king in her father's stead, and the women invite the Argonauts into their homes. Because Lemnos was the site of the most important shrine to Hephaestus, the story goes, "Cypris aroused sweet desire in them, as a favor to Hephaestus, so that again in future time Lemnos would not be deprived of males" (1.850–52). The Argonauts would have remained indefinitely, but among them is the great hero Heracles, who sternly reminds them of their mission, and Jason takes leave of Hypsipyle and returns to the ship and sets sail.

The Argonauts come next to the land of a people called the Doliones, whose king, Cyzicus, receives them hospitably. But after the Argonauts depart, during the dark night they are driven back again to the same harbor. They do not realize where they are and when the natives, not knowing who they are, attack them, the Argonauts kill the king who had treated them so kindly. Poseidon has protected the Doliones from their monstrous neighbors known as the children of the Earth, but not from the Argonauts: "For the gods have ordained that mortals cannot avoid their fates; a great net is spread all around them; thus when King Cyzicus thought that he had escaped any threat from the heroes, destiny caught him in

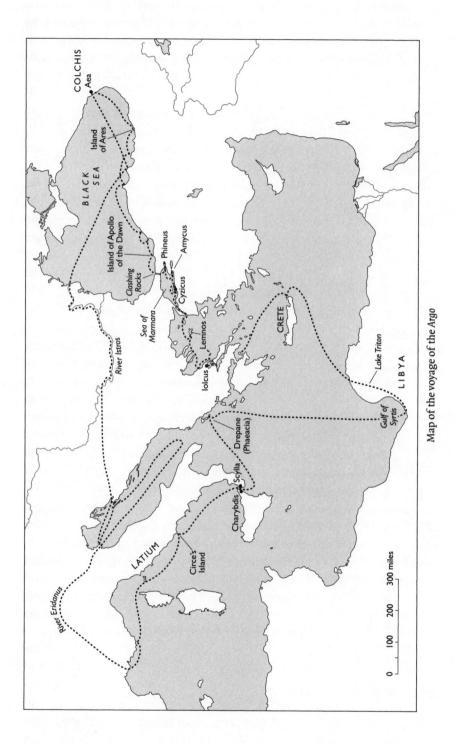

COLCHIS
Aea

Island of Ares

BLACK SEA

Island of Apollo of the Dawn

Clashing Rocks

Phineus

Amycus

Cyzicus

Sea of Marmara

Lemnos

Iolcus

River Istros

CRETE

Lake Triton

LIBYA

Drepane (Phaeacia)

Gulf of Syrtis

Scylla

Charybdis

LATIUM

Circe's Island

River Eridanus

0   100   200   300 miles

Map of the voyage of the Argo

her net on the same night, fighting against them" (1.1035–39). But soon a divinity sends a sign: a kingfisher flies over Jason's head, and the seer Mopsus interprets the omen to mean that if they build a shrine to Rhea (here identified with Cybele, the mother of the gods), the adverse winds will abate. Cybele sends an indication of her favor by creating a spring in land that previously had no flowing water.[5]

Soon after the Argonauts set off again, however, another disaster occurs. The oar used by Heracles breaks, and he goes into the forest to uproot a tree to make himself a new one. While he is gone, the Argonauts sacrifice to Apollo, and a companion of Heracles, the boy Hylas, goes to get water from a spring. There Aphrodite causes a water nymph to fall in love with him and pull him into the spring. When Heracles learns that Hylas has not returned, he rushes off to search for him, and it is only after the Argonauts have set out early in the morning to take advantage of a favorable wind that they realize they have left Heracles behind. When the Argonauts blame one another and begin to fight among themselves, the sea god Glaucus suddenly emerges from the depths to tell them that Zeus did not want Heracles to travel with them (1.1315–25).

Another son of Zeus, Polydeuces, now rescues his fellow Argonauts when they encounter on the south coast of the Sea of Marmara the brutal Amycus, king of the Bebryces, who forces men to box with him. After Polydeuces kills Amycus, the Argonauts reflect that Heracles might have defeated him even more effectively; but, as the poet observes, "everything has happened according to the plans of Zeus" (2.154). On the north coast of the Sea of Marmara they come to the seer Phineus. Phineus has been taught the art of prophecy by Apollo, but he did not show due reverence for Zeus when he gave his prophecies, so Zeus took away his sight, and did not even let him enjoy the food his neighbors brought him; whenever he tried to eat something, everything on his table was snatched away, or fouled, by hideous winged monsters called Harpies. Phineus, although blind, knows who the Argonauts are and realizes that they will rescue him. He thanks Apollo, and begs the young heroes to free him from his plight: "In the name of Zeus, god of suppliants, who treats wrongdoers most sternly; I beseech you for Phoebus Apollo's sake and for Hera herself, who more than any other god cares for you on your journey" (2.215–17). The Argonauts are sympathetic, so two of them, Zetes and Calais, the sons of the North Wind, drive the Harpies away, and they would have killed them too, against the will of the gods, but Iris intervenes and swears that the creatures will never return to bother Phineus (2.284–94).

The fate of Phineus provides a clear illustration of how important it is to pay close attention to the wishes of the gods. Phineus was blinded because he told other mortals more than the gods wanted them to know. Now he realizes that he cannot tell the Argonauts everything they need to know, even though he would like to help them (2.311–12).[6] His warnings about dangers to come fill the young men with fear, and they ask if they will then be able to return home. He tells them:

"The divinity will lead you on another voyage back from Aea, and after Aea you will have escorts enough. But look for cunning help from Cypris; in her lies the glorious conclusion of your struggle. Do not ask me to reveal more than that" (2.421–25).

Since he can no longer recover his sight, Phineus now asks that a god send death to him directly, "since in death I will be at the peak of happiness" (2.447). But the gods do not grant his wish. In the world of the *Argonautica*, any comfort an individual may receive comes from other mortals. One such mortal is a neighbor of Phineus, Paraebius, who has constantly come to help him in return for a kindness Phineus had done him.[7] Before they leave, the Argonauts offer a sacrifice and pray to Apollo, the god of prophecy, and they build an altar to the twelve Olympian gods before they undertake their journey into the Black Sea.

Thanks to the advice of Phineus, they know how to survive the next peril they faced, the Clashing Rocks that open and close, crushing any who try to pass between them. But when they reach the rocks they are also helped by Athena, "who has kindly intentions toward the oarsmen," although they do not see her because she comes as quickly as the thought of home passes before the eyes of a traveler (2.536–48).[8] The goddess pushes the ship through the rocks just as they are about to close on it. The men row along the coast through the day and night, and at dawn they land on an island. It is then that they see Apollo, who is traveling from Lycia on the south coast of Asia Minor to the land of the Hyperboreans in the north. He is both beautiful and terrifying to behold: "The whole island shook beneath his feet, and waves rolled over the dry land. The men were stunned when they looked on him, and no one could bear to look into the god's beautiful eyes. They stood still and looked down at the ground. The god went through the air far away toward the sea" (2.679–84). The men name the island after Apollo of the Dawn and build an altar to him on the shore.

After they pass the cave of Hades and the mouth of the river Acheron, the prophet Idmon, who has foreseen his own death, is killed by a boar. Then the helmsman Tiphys dies, but Hera encourages another of the men, Ancaeus, to take his place so the ship can sail on without further delay (2.865–66). As they pass the river Thermodon, Zeus sends a breeze that keeps them away from the land of the Amazons. Instead they come to Aretias, the "island of Ares," where Phineus earlier told them they should land, and here they discover why: the sons of Phrixus are washed ashore there after their ship has been wrecked "with the advice of the gods" (2.1110). They are Jason's cousins and can guide them on the rest of their journey to Colchis. Jason says: "In truth Zeus oversees everything, and we men never escape his notice completely, whether we are godfearing or unjust" (2.1179–80). As they approach Colchis they see Zeus's eagle flying toward the Caucasus Mountains, where Prometheus has been chained to the rock (*Theogony* 521–31). The Argonauts hear the cries of the god as the eagle tears out his liver (*Argonautica* 2.1246–59).

Now, though, just as the Argonauts have arrived at their goal, the poet keeps his audience in suspense for a while by concentrating on the actions of the gods. He begins Book 3 with a new invocation, this time to the muse Erato, rather than to Apollo. Apollonius chooses to call on this particular muse because her name is connected with *eros*, sexual passion, which plays a role in the story that unfolds next. "For you also have a part in Cypris's doings," he says, "and you charm unmarried maidens because you care for them; that is why the name of love is attached to you" (3.3–5).[9] While the heroes are hidden in the dense reeds of a marsh, Hera goes to Athena. Both goddesses want to help Jason, and they agree to call on Cypris, the goddess of love. Cypris is in her bedroom, combing her hair, and she is amazed to see Hera and Athena on the porch coming to call on her. Hera explains that she hates Pelias, because he has not honored her with sacrifices, and wants to protect Jason, who carried her across the swollen river Anaurus when she was disguised as an old woman to test men's behavior (3.56–75). Cypris agrees to help, so she goes to Zeus's orchard to find her son Eros. He is busy playing knucklebones with Ganymede, and winning. Cypris scolds him, and then promises to give him a golden ball made by Hephaestus if he goes to shoot his arrows at Medea, a daughter of Aeëtes, so that she will fall in love with Jason.[10] Eros leaves Olympus and flies through the sky to Colchis.

The Argonauts, waiting in their ship, do not know that the gods are planning to intervene. Hera conceals them in mist so they will not be seen entering the city, Aea, just as Athena wrapped Odysseus in mist when he entered the city of Alcinous. Hera dispels the mist as the heroes enter the palace, and there the Argonauts see the daughter of the king, Medea, and King Aeëtes himself. Ordinarily, Medea would have been at the temple of the goddess Hecate, whom she served as priestess (3.250–52). But Hera has kept Medea at home so that she will be in the palace when Jason arrives. Apollonius expects his audience to remember the scene in the *Odyssey* where Athena sees to it that Nausicaa is there to welcome Odysseus (*Odyssey* 6.20–40). Hera has seen to it that Medea will not just help but also fall in love with Jason: "Eros came through the gray mist, excitedly, like the gadfly that comes upon young heifers as they graze, which the cowherds call *myops* [or 'shut-eye']" (*Argonautica* 3.275–77). As the simile makes clear, Eros will bring Medea pain and misery. Unseen, he kneels at Jason's feet and shoots an arrow at her. She is struck dumb, and the god laughs as he flies out of the palace. "The arrow burned inside beneath her heart, like a flame" (3.286–87). Medea can think only of Jason; she blushes frequently; her mind has lost control of her body (3.298).[11]

Aeëtes says he will give Jason the Golden Fleece only if he passes a test of strength and courage. He must yoke two fire-breathing bulls with bronze hooves, plow the plain of Ares, and sow the teeth of a serpent into the furrows. From the teeth will grow a crop of armed men, whom Jason must kill single-handedly. Only then will he be permitted to take the Fleece. Jason hesitates, but he accepts the challenge. After he leaves to return to his ship for the night, Medea keeps thinking of him: "Many thoughts, everything that the Passions [Erōtes] urge one to think about, stirred her heart" (3.451–52). She does not want to betray her father, but she prays to Hecate to let Jason escape. Meanwhile, Jason's friends urge him to appeal to Medea for help, because she is skilled in using drugs, "with Hecate's encouragement" (3.478). Argos, son of Phrixus, offers to return to the palace to speak to his mother, Chalciope, another daughter of Aeētes. "Perhaps a god may favor my attempt," he says (3.539). At that very moment the gods send an unambiguous sign: a dove, chased by a hawk, falls into Jason's lap, while the hawk impales itself on the ship's sternpost. Mopsus says that the sign means they must depend on Cypris, because the dove is her bird.

Homer's characters tell us what they plan to do in speeches, but Apollonius lets us see directly into the human mind. King Aeētes regrets that he ever welcomed Phrixus to his land when the golden ram brought him there, but Zeus sent Hermes to order him to do so. Now he is afraid of an oracle his father Helios had revealed to him, that a member of his family will betray him. Medea, in the meantime, dreams that she harnesses the bulls and completes the labor for Jason. She cannot sleep: "The pain inside continually tormented her, burning through her flesh and around her delicate nerves and deep beneath the base of her neck, where the anguish hurts most deeply, when the untiring Erōtes thrust their pains into the mind" (3.761–65). She does not know whether to let Jason die or to help him or to kill herself. She takes out the casket where she stores her drugs, with the thought of poisoning herself; but then she changes her mind at Hera's urging and is no longer uncertain about what she should do (3.817–19). As soon as dawn comes she orders her maidservants to harness mules to a wagon. She takes from her casket "the drug they say is called Promethean," which makes a mortal man invulnerable, though only for a day (3.845). The drug is made from the root that grows from the ichor flowing from the torn liver of Prometheus. When Medea cut the root from the ground, Prometheus groaned in pain (3.865–66).

When Medea sets out for the temple of Hecate, to meet there secretly with Jason, the poet compares her to Artemis driving her chariot through the hills, surrounded by her nymphs. In the *Odyssey*, Homer similarly compared Nausicaa to Artemis with her nymphs playing around her and her mother, Leto, rejoicing (*Odyssey* 6.102–9). But in the *Argonautica* the Artemis simile has a darker, more sinister tone: "Around her the whimpering beasts fawn and tremble as she goes by" (*Argonautica* 3.883–84).[12] As Jason comes to the temple, he is an alluring figure: "None of the men of the past, neither the sons of Zeus nor the offspring of other gods, looked so handsome as the wife of Zeus made Jason look that day or spoke more persuasively" (3.919–23). The seer Mopsus hears a crow mocking him for not being willing to leave Jason and Medea alone. The seer understands the bird's warning as a good omen.[13]

When Jason goes off alone to meet Medea, the poet compares him to Sirius, the Dog Star, "who rises beautiful and bright to look upon, but sends unending pain to the flocks" (3.958–59). He asks Medea for her help, telling her how Ariadne helped Theseus, but without mentioning that Theseus later abandoned her. Medea promises to help him by giving him the drug, with careful instructions so that he can survive the ordeal. Jason tells her that he would like to take her with him and marry her. The poet adds that Medea would not for long refuse to live in Greece, "for that is what Hera was planning for her" (3.1134).

That night Jason sacrifices to Hecate. He hears the goddess come out to receive the sacrifice, surrounded by torches and howling dogs; he does not look at them. The next morning, when Jason enters the field of Ares, he does not need the help of the gods, because Medea has already done everything for him that he will require. He resembles Ares or Apollo as he enters the field, naked, to yoke the bulls. With great courage he follows Medea's instructions precisely. When he sows the serpent's teeth and the armed men immediately rise up from the furrows, he throws a huge stone among them. The armed men run around the stone like swift dogs, shouting. They attack each other, and fall onto their mother, the Earth. Jason annihilates the survivors, just as a farmer cuts down his crop at harvest time. With Medea's help, he has accomplished his impossible task.

But neither Jason nor Medea will derive much pleasure from his achievement. Book 4 begins with a grim invocation: "Yourself, tell, goddess, of the suffering and sorrows of the Colchian maiden, Muse, daughter of Zeus! For my mind whirls within me and I am unable to speak, as I struggle to say whether it was the cruel pain of delusive desire or shameful panic that caused her to leave the people of Colchis" (4.1–5). Since Aeētes is furious at Medea for helping Jason, Hera now intervenes: "Hera threw the most terrible fear into Medea's heart; she took fright, as in the shelter of a deep wood a delicate fawn is driven to flight by the barking of dogs" (4.11–13). In her terror Medea would have killed herself by taking drugs, frustrating Hera's plans, but the goddess urges her to flee. Medea is able to escape because she can cause the doorbolts of the palace to open by means of her incantations.

As Medea hurries to the ship, the goddess Moon, who is just rising, is delighted to see her suffering: "Now I am not alone when I burn with desire for fair Endymion," her mortal lover, who cannot respond with passion equal to her own (4.58).[14] The Moon is angry because Medea had often made her hide with her incantations. "You yourself must endure a similar fate," the Moon says, "and a god with evil intention has sent Jason to trouble you. Go off and suffer miserable sorrow, despite all your cleverness!" (4.62–65). The Moon's observation that Medea's suffering has been caused by a hostile god reminds us that Hera did not have Medea's welfare in mind when she asked Cypris to send her son Eros to Colchis. To Hera, Medea is a means to an end—the punishment of Pelias.

Medea advises the Argonauts to sail to the grove where a serpent guards the

Golden Fleece. At dawn they come to the altar where Hermes ordered Phrixus to sacrifice the ram, for near there its Golden Fleece is kept, hanging in a tree. The dreadful serpent rolls toward Jason and Medea menacingly. Medea, however, fixes it with her gaze and bewitches it with an incantation, calling on the god Sleep and on Hecate. As the serpent falls asleep, Medea sprinkles drugs on its eyes as she sings, keeping the beast under her spell until Jason is able to pull the Fleece down from the tree where it hangs. They hurry to the *Argo* with their prize, and they and the ship set sail for Greece. Aeëtes, meanwhile, has discovered their treachery, and in a rage he sends his ships to pursue them. Hera sends a favorable wind behind the Argonauts, "so that Medea of Aea may reach the Pelasgian land [Greece] to bring harm to the house of Pelias" (4.242–43).

The Argonauts decide not to return by the route they came by, along the south coast of the Black Sea. Instead they head for the mouth of the river Istros (the modern Danube), which was then believed somewhere north of Greece to divide into two streams, one of which flowed toward the north, and the other into the Adriatic. Hera sends a favorable omen of approval, a track of light through the sky in the direction they are to take (4.294–97).[15] The Argonauts travel across the Black Sea to the northern mouth of the Istros, but they are pursued by the Colchians, who enter the Istros by its southern mouth and meet them on the northern side of the island formed by these two streams at the mouth of the river.

Although the Colchians, led by Medea's half-brother Apsyrtus, could easily defeat the heroes, they agree that the Argonauts are entitled to keep the Fleece, but they insist that Medea should be kept in the temple of Artemis until one of the kings who make judgments can decide her fate. Medea, however, appeals to Jason, threatening him with her Erinyes if he betrays her. He suggests that instead they ambush Apsyrtus and kill him. They send Apsyrtus gifts, including a robe made by the Graces, which Hypsipyle had given to Jason. They invite him to come to the temple to meet them secretly, saying that they will be prepared to return the Golden Fleece. Medea sprinkles the air and breezes with attractive drugs so powerful that they could bring wild animals down from the mountain.

At this point the poet interrupts the narrative with a dramatic invocation to the god Eros: "Cruel Eros, great sorrow, great plague to mankind; you are the source of deadly quarrels, groans and tears, and you stir up many sorrows in addition to these. Rise up and come down on the heads of my enemies, as you did when you threw deadly ruin into Medea's mind!" (4.445–49). Apsyrtus comes to the temple, but just when he has reached an agreement with Medea, Jason comes out of hiding and kills him. His blood stains Medea's dress; the Erinyes see what they have done. Jason cuts off the dead man's extremities so that his soul cannot follow him, and he tries to expiate the crime by licking up the blood and spitting it out three times. Then the Argonauts attack the ship that Apsyrtus had led and kill all its crew. They escape by rowing along the Istros until it emerges at the mouth

Medea charms the serpent that guards the Golden Fleece, while
Jason watches. (Red-figure squat lekythos, ca. 320–310 B.C.
Ruhr-Universität, Bochum University, S 1080. Photo: I. Berndt.)

of the Eridanus (the modern Po) and then sail down the western coast of the Balkan Peninsula. Hera keeps the remaining Colchians from searching for them by sending thunderbolts from the sky.

Now the poet asks the Muses to explain why the Argonauts did not return home directly but instead went on to the seas west of Italy (4.552–56). The poet observes: "No doubt Zeus himself was furious at what they had done, when the great body of Apsyrtus fell" (4.557–58). Zeus decides that Jason and Medea must be purified by Circe, Medea's aunt, whose home is on the west coast of Italy. The Argonauts continued, sailing down toward what is now Albania, and "then Hera understood Zeus's plans for them and his great anger. She considered how they might complete their journey, and sent adverse winds" to drive them back again to the mouth of the Eridanus (4.576–80). As the ship rushes along, a plank in the ship's keel speaks to the Argonauts with a human voice and tells them of the anger of Zeus and the need to be purified by Circe. The plank was made from a prophetic oak tree at the oracle of Zeus at Dodona, and it had been placed in the ship by Athena (1.526–27).

The Argonauts spend days in the marsh at the mouth of the Eridanus, near the rotting corpse of Phaethon, who had once asked his father, Helios, to borrow his chariot and had fallen to his death there (4.596–606). From the Eridanus they enter the stream of the Rhodanus (now the Rhone). They are about to head north on a tributary, in a direction that would have led to their destruction in the stormy lakes in the land of the Celts, when Hera leaps down from the sky and screams at them from the Hercynian Rock.[16] They are terrified, "and there was a dreadful roaring in the great sky" (4.642). They are able to pass safely by the tribes of Celts and Ligurians because Hera shrouds them in mist (4.645–48).

The Argonauts come to the island of Circe, Medea's aunt, the sister of King Aeëtes. The goddess welcomes Jason and Medea, until she learns that they have committed murder. She purifies them according to the laws of Zeus, offering sacrifices so that the anger of the Erinyes may be averted and Zeus may treat them kindly. Then she asks them to leave her house. Hera knows that Circe is sending them away, because she has sent Iris to watch for them. Now she sends Iris to summon the goddess Thetis and tell Hephaestus to dampen his fires on Aetna until the *Argo* has sailed past them, and to have Aeolus send Zephyrus, the West Wind, to bring the ship to Phaeacia.

When Thetis arrives Hera reminds her of how she has respected her in the past, and asks her to see that the ship gets safely past Scylla and Charybdis (the modern straits of Messina). She tells Thetis that her son Achilles is destined to marry Medea when he comes to the Elysian Fields after his death in Troy. She also reminds Thetis that her former husband Peleus, father of Achilles, is on the *Argo*. Hera insists that Thetis was wrong to be angry with Peleus and to desert him because, when he saw her putting their son in the fire, he did not understand that she meant to make him immortal. So Thetis goes to the *Argo* and speaks to

Peleus, making herself visible only to him. She tells him that they should leave the coast of Latium in the morning and of Hera's plans to keep the ship safe. Then, with the lack of sympathy that gods often show toward mortals, "she vanished, dove into the depths of the sea, and Peleus was stricken by cruel grief" (4.865–66).[17]

Zephyrus, meanwhile, takes the ship quickly past the Sirens while the Argonaut Orpheus, the son of the muse Calliope, plays a song that keeps them from luring the men onto their rocks; only two men succumb, and one of them, Boutes, is rescued by Cypris, who takes him to her shrine in Lilybaeum (modern Marsala), on the west coast of Sicily. On Mount Aetna, Hephaestus stops his labor, and Thetis and her Nereid sisters surround the *Argo*, passing the ship from hand to hand, holding it above the waves until it is safely past Scylla and Charybdis (4.930–32). Thetis keeps the ship straight on its course as Hephaestus watches them. "Standing high in the shining sky, the wife of Zeus threw her arms around Athena, because she was so frightened when she looked at them" (4.958–60).

By showing how concerned Hera is as the Argonauts pass Scylla and Charybdis, Apollonius reminds his audience that she has helped the Argonauts at almost every crucial point along the way, providing omens and guidance. Odysseus, at the same point in his journey, was trying to follow Circe's advice but was otherwise unassisted by any god. Zeus was angry with Odysseus because he had violated his laws of hospitality, and he had refused to accept the sacrifice of the Cyclops's ram. In the *Argonautica*, Hera did not intervene to stop Jason and Medea from murdering Apsyrtus, even though it was a terrible crime, because she wanted to bring Medea to Greece in order to punish Pelias.

Thetis and the Nereids, once they have helped the Argonauts past the dangerous straits, disappear into the depths of the sea, and the Argonauts sail safely past the meadow of Thrinacia, where the cattle that belong to the sun god are grazing. The Argonauts head across the Ionian Sea to Drepane (now Corcyra or Corfu), the land of the Phaeacians. The island of Drepane was named after the sickle (*drepanon*) used by Cronus to lop off his father Heaven's genitals, long ago in the age of the Titans. About that incident, Apollonius says: "Forgive me, Muses, against my will I tell a story told by the men of old" (4.984–85). By calling attention to this painful story, just before the Argonauts arrive, the poet indicates that their visit to the Phaeacians will be less happy than the encounter Odysseus had with these people in the *Odyssey*. According to Apollonius, the Phaeacians were born from the blood of Heaven, a genealogy that neither Homer nor Hesiod mentions.

King Alcinous welcomes the Argonauts, but soon afterward a force of Colchians arrives, demanding Medea's return. Medea comes to the Phaeacians' queen, Arete, as a suppliant. While her husband the king sleeps, Arete sends her herald to tell Jason that Alcinous has said they must hand over Medea, unless she has already been married to Jason. In response to this information, the Argonauts immediately hold a wedding ceremony for the couple. Jason and Medea had hoped to wait until they reached his home in Greece. The poet comments: "Indeed we, the races of unfortunate mortals, never tread upon joy with a sure foot, but some bitter woe always walks alongside our delights; even so they, though they were taking their pleasure in sweet love, were gripped by fear about the decision that Alcinous would make" (4.1165–69). But Hera sends out advance word of the marriage; the heroes sing, and the nymphs form a circle and sing "in honor of you, Hera, for it was you who put it into Arete's mind to speak to Alcinous a telling word" (4.1198–1200).

After a week in Drepane, the Argonauts sail south, but just as they are about to approach the Peloponnesus, a deadly blast from Boreas the North Wind drives them off course for nine days, and brings them to the Gulf of Syrtis (modern Sirte), on the north coast of Libya. In despair, the Argonauts prepare to die in what appears to be a wasteland, but three heroines, shepherd goddesses and the daughters of Libya, appear to Jason. They know everything that has happened to him (4.1319–21), just as the Sirens told Odysseus they knew everything that had happened at Troy (*Odyssey* 12.189–91). But unlike the Sirens, the heroines have kind intentions, and they tell Jason that they will be saved. But he cannot understand what they tell him, namely to repay their mother for her long labors, when the goddess Amphitrite releases the chariot of her husband Poseidon. Their meaning becomes clear only when "the most amazing of portents" appears (*Argonautica* 4.1364). A giant horse with a golden mane rushes from the sea to the land and gallops off. Peleus understands the omen: the chariot of Poseidon, Amphitrite's husband, has been loosed, and the Argonauts must pick up and carry their "mother," the ship that held them in its belly for so long, in the direction taken by the horse. The story is incredible, but the poet remains faithful to the traditional tale, as he did when he told the story about why Drepane was named for a sickle. Yet while professing his obedience to the Muses, he reminds us, just as Hesiod did near the beginning of the *Theogony*, that they can tell lies as well as the truth (4.1381–92). As goddesses, they have both the knowledge and the power.

The heroes go off to search for drinking water, and along the way they come upon a sacred plain near Lake Triton. There the snake Ladon used to guard a tree with golden apples, and the daughters of Hesperus, the god of the evening, used to sing as they went about their daily tasks. Until the day before the Argonauts came, it had been a place of legendary beauty: Zeus brought Hera to this place after they were married, "where the holy land with her gifts of wealth magnifies the happiness of the gods," as Euripides says (*Hippolytus* 750–51). But Heracles had come there the previous day and broke into the paradise. He killed the snake, and the Argonauts find flies dying in its wounds from the blood that was poisoned by Heracles' arrows. The Hesperids turn to dust before the Argonauts' eyes, and then change into trees and then again into their original forms. They blame Heracles for coming and destroying their peace with such brutality. His violence proves beneficial, however, at least for the Argonauts. When he was there he had kicked a rock and found a spring. Thus, "even though he was far away Heracles has saved his comrades when they were dying of thirst" (*Argonautica* 4.1458–59). Nothing could illustrate more clearly the dual nature of heroic achievement, in both its destructiveness and its power to rescue by means of destruction.

The Argonauts set sail, but they cannot find a way out of Lake Triton until they leave as an offering to the local gods a tripod that Apollo had earlier given to Jason. One of the gods of the sea, Triton, appears in the form of Eurypylus, a son of Poseidon, shows the Argonauts how to sail out of the lake, and gives them directions for their journey home. Once under way, the Argonauts offer Triton another sacrifice, and this time he appears to them in his true form, which is half god and half sea monster, and leads them out to sea.[18]

When the next danger appears, it is Medea who saves them from it with her magic. The island of Crete is guarded by Talos, the last of the bronze generation of men. He is invulnerable, covered with bronze, except for one vein in his ankle. Medea, using incantations, spells, and the power of her eyes, causes Talos to hit his ankle on a rock, and he falls to the ground, strengthless. The poet asks, "Father Zeus, my mind is adrift with astonishment: does death come to us only from diseases and wounds, or can someone strike us from far away, as that man, though he was made of bronze, was brought down by the force of Medea with her magic?" (4.1673–77).

Since Crete is no longer guarded by Talos, the Argonauts are free to sail to the northeast corner of the island. In the blackness of night, unable to navigate, Jason calls on Apollo; the god comes down from the sky and stands on a rock, holding his golden bow in his right hand, with the bow shedding a brilliant light in all directions. On the nearby island of Anaphe, the heroes build a sanctuary to Apollo the Gleamer (4.1701–18). This is the last time a god needs to intervene to help them on the journey; after that they sail back to Iolcus in Thessaly without incident. The end of the voyage is the end of the epic, and the poet concludes by saying to the Argonauts: "Happily you stepped upon the shores of Pagasae" (4.1781).

The poet says nothing about what happens after that, but the audience knows that Medea will use her magical skill, first to make Jason's father, Aeson, young again, and then to bring about the death of Pelias. To accomplish this, she tells the daughters of Pelias that she can make the old young again, and, to show them how, she cuts an old sheep into pieces and cooks it with her drugs, whereupon it emerges rejuvenated as a young lamb. She encourages the daughters to use the same means to make their father young, but when they try it they are unable to revive him, and by that time Medea is gone and Pelias is dead. Hera has her revenge on Pelias, and she does not even need to intervene directly to get it.[19]

After Pelias dies, however, Jason and Medea do not end up living happily ever after. Because she is responsible for the death of Pelias, they must go into exile and settle in Corinth, where they have no source of money. In Euripides' drama *Medea* (431 B.C.), Jason seeks to leave Medea to marry the the daughter of the king of Corinth; Medea then sends the princess a poisoned robe, which kills both her and her father, and then Medea kills her own two sons. She goes off to Athens in the sun's chariot to live with King Aegeus, leaving Jason behind in Corinth. Helios the sun god rescues Medea because she is his granddaughter.

As Helios rescues Medea, Hera also protects her favorites in the *Argonautica* in numerous ways. She did not intervene to prevent the murder of Apsyrtus, and she abandoned Jason and Medea once she saw that Pelias had been punished. Zeus, too, makes sure that in the end both Jason and Medea suffer for their crimes, but not in ways that would bring much satisfaction to the families of their victims. Aside from Zeus, who is displeased by the murder of Apsyrtus, the gods in the *Argonautica* do not intervene to see that justice is done. Athena plays only a minor role. Apollo intercedes primarily in his role as a prophet. Hera and Aphrodite, the goddesses who do the most to help the Argonauts, are mainly concerned with up-holding their own honor and supporting their friends, much as they do in the *Iliad*. And some gods, notably Eros and the Moon, even take pleasure in seeing human beings suffer.[20]

The *Argonautica*, like the *Odyssey*, describes a voyage. As in the *Odyssey*, much of the action occurs in places that no humans have ever seen, or which in reality bear little resemblance to the poet's accounts of them. But whereas in Homer even the islands inhabited by gods look like places in the world of men, the landscape of the *Argonautica* includes men sown from dragon's teeth, and a terrible serpent who guards the Golden Fleece. There are portents and omens like the *Argo*'s talk-ing keel, or the giant horse that emerges from the sea. Thetis and the Nereids pass the *Argo* from hand to hand to get it past Scylla and Charybdis. The heroes (al-though the poet claims not to believe it) are said to carry their ship from Syrtis to Lake Triton. Even so, in the midst of the fantastic world of the epic, the heroes Apollonius writes about seem more like ordinary men than their counterparts in Homer. Jason is less sure of himself than Odysseus, and he is openly afraid of many of the challenges before him. He frequently relies on the other Argonauts to help him, and he could not have recovered the Golden Fleece without Medea's help. The other heroes are quick to find fault with him and with each other.

In other respects as well, these heroes inhabit a world that this poet's audience could easily recognize. Apollonius mentions traditions, cults, and place-names that were established as a result of the voyage. His similes often describe the lives of poor people like the farmer or plowman exhausted from their labors (1.1172–73), and ordinary things that anyone might have seen, like light dancing on the surface of water (3.756–58). He describes disappointment, anguish, and pain with almost clinical accuracy. He clearly visualizes exactly what it might feel like to carry an object as ungainly and terrifying as the Golden Fleece, when Jason lets it hang down from his shoulder, or gathers it up in a ball: "He was afraid that some man or a god might come and take it from him" (4.181–82).

There is also a greater element of realism in this poem's descriptions of the gods, compared with older works. We see Aphrodite at home, combing her golden hair, and look in on her son Eros as he takes advantage of Ganymede in a game of knucklebones. Circe is troubled by dreams, in which she has seen her house dripping with blood. As the Argonauts pass by Scylla and Charybdis, Hera is so concerned that she throws her arms around Athena. But even though the gods in the *Argonautica* are sometimes less interested in justice than mortals would like them to be, they remain terrifying and powerful nonetheless. Like Homeric gods, they take an interest only in certain human beings and do not concern themselves with the pain or damage they may cause to the lives of others. At the same time, the gods Apollonius describes are more remote from mortals than the gods in Homer's epics. In the *Iliad* and the *Odyssey* the gods appear among mortals with much greater frequency, even talking directly to the people they favor. The Argonauts cannot look at Apollo, and do not dare to speak to him directly when he appears to them. They do not see Athena or Hera when they help them, and only Peleus can see Thetis when she comes to visit him.

The heroes in the *Argonautica* do not seem to expect the kind of direct intervention from the gods that Odysseus appears to take for granted. Occasionally a minor god will appear, as Triton does in Book 4, first in disguise and then in his true form, to give advice or encouragement. But for the most part the heroes are unaware of the actions of the more important gods. Jason does not seem to know that the old woman he carried across the river was really Hera. He learns from the seer Phineus that Hera "more than any other god cares for you on your journey" (2.216–17). But Jason never discovers that she arranged the interventions of Eros and Thetis on his behalf. He does not know that she wrapped him and his companions in mist when they arrived in Aea, that she kept Medea at home when he arrived and put ideas into her mind, that she sent favorable and adverse winds, and signs, and even saw to it that Arete spoke to Alcinous about Medea. But whether or not he is aware of it, without Hera's aid he would never have survived the voyage, or even have had the assistance of Medea's powerful spells and drugs. In the heroic world that Apollonius describes, the gods remain powerful, even though mortals are only occasionally conscious of their presence.

⇥ GODS IN CALLIMACHUS ⇤

To some extent—it is impossible to know how much—Apollonius may have been influenced by his contemporary Callimachus. Callimachus also takes particular interest in the origins of cults and customs; in fact these are the subjects of his most famous poem, the *Aetia* (Causes), which now survives only in fragments.

Erysichthon holds his ax aloft, while Demeter implores him not
to cut down her tree. (Red-figure pelike, ca. 450 B.C. Archäologisches
Kunstmuseum der Universität Bonn, no. 2661. Photo: Wolfgang Klein.)

In the *Aetia* Callimachus tells the story of the origin of Apollo's name Hieios: Jason prayed to Apollo with the ritual cry, Iēie, when he was lost in the darkness north of Crete (*Aetia* 1.18.5–7).[21] Jason reminds the god that it was because of his oracle that he and his mates embarked on the *Argo* and set up the altar to Apollo, the god of embarkation, at Pagasae (1.18.9–12).[22] Callimachus also provides memorable accounts of the ways in which gods punish human beings. No one who knows the story of Hera's resentment against Pelias will be surprised at how Demeter in another poem by Callimachus, the *Hymn to Demeter*, treats a young Thessalian prince who has offended her. This was Erysichthon, who cut down a tree in a grove sacred to the goddess. "Demeter felt it, because a tree sacred to her was in pain; she was angry and said, 'Who is chopping down my beautiful trees?'" (*Hymn to Demeter* 6.40–41).

In this hymn, the goddess gives Erysichthon a chance to make amends. Instead of confronting the young man directly, she takes the form of one of her priestesses and begs him to respect the goddess and his parents: "Child, you are cutting trees that are dedicated to the gods; hold back, child that your parents prayed for, stop, and send your servants away, lest Lady Demeter be angry with you, because you are destroying her sacred grove" (6.46–49). But Erysichthon threatens her, saying he needs the trees to build a banquet hall for his friends. "Demeter was unspeakably angry and became a goddess again. Her footsteps touched the ground but her head touched Olympus. The mortals were half-dead with fear when they saw the Lady" (6.57–59). The goddess inflicts a punishment on him appropriate for a crime against the goddess of the harvest: insatiable hunger. Finally his father calls on his father, Poseidon, asking him to cure Erysichthon or let him die, but the god does not hear him (6.96–110).

Any mortal who breaks the rules is punished, even if his crime is not intentional. In his *Hymn to Athena*, Callimachus calls on the goddess to come, and summons the maidens of Argos who have been chosen to pour the water for Athena's bath. But he warns the men of Argos to stay away: "The man who sees Pallas [Athena] naked will look upon Argos for the last time" (*Hymn to Athena* 5.53–54). He now tells a traditional story. Athena was once a close friend of a nymph in Thebes, Chariclo: "But even so for her many tears remained, although she was the beloved companion of Athena" (5.68–69). One day when the goddess and the nymph are bathing, Chariclo's son Tiresias comes to drink from the same spring; he has been hunting, and is thirsty: "Miserable creature, he did not wish to see but saw what was forbidden" (5.78). Athena is angry, and strikes him blind. Chariclo, in anguish, complains to Athena: "The penalty you have inflicted is great in return for something small; you lost a few deer and roe, but you have taken my son's eyes" (5.91–92).

Athena takes pity on her friend but insists that she is not responsible: "It was not I that made your son blind. It gives Athena no pleasure to take away children's eyes. But these are the laws of Cronus; whoever sees an immortal, when the god does not wish it, pays a large price" (5.98–102). Athena cannot change the fate of Tiresias; she points out that Actaeon will be punished even more cruelly when he sees Artemis bathing (he was torn to pieces by his own dogs).[23] But because of her friendship for his mother, the goddess will give Tiresias the gift of prophecy, a great staff that will take his feet where they need to go, a long life, "and only he, when he dies, will go among the dead with his senses intact, honored by the great Leader of the Dead" (5.129–30). Athena then nods her head to indicate that she has made her decision, and what she decides will happen. She alone of Zeus's daughters has this decisive power.

Athena treats Tiresias with greater consideration than Demeter treats Erysichthon, because Tiresias did not intend to commit an impious act. But he is not given a chance to explain or apologize, or make any atonement. All that mortals can do to avoid misfortune is to honor the gods with prayer, ritual, and sacrifice. Callimachus ends his *Hymn to Athena* by encouraging the girls of Argos to welcome the goddess, and calling on her to protect the city. His *Hymn to Demeter* also ends with a warning: "Demeter, may the man you hate not be a friend of mine or live in the same house; evil neighbors are my enemies!" (*Hymn to Demeter* 6.116–17). Then he calls on the maidens and women to welcome the goddess, so that she will bring them fruitful seasons and protect them for another year.

Still, it is clear that in the myths, as in life, piety alone does not protect mortals from divine anger. Zeus raises this same troubling question in the *Iliad*, when he sees Hector facing Achilles in single combat: "Alas, I see before me a man dear to me being pursued around the wall. My heart grieves for Hector, who has burned many thigh bones of cattle on the peaks of Mount Ida with its many valleys, and again at other times in the citadel of Troy" (*Iliad* 22.168–72). He asks the other gods if he should save Hector, but Athena replies: "This is a mortal man, long ago fated to die; do you now wish to save him from cruel death? Do it, but none of the rest of us gods will approve of it!" Traditional religion and the myths connected with it offer no means of resolving the question of why the good must suffer. It is simply assumed that human beings will suffer, and that only a few will receive compensation or be given relief during their lifetimes. Those who suffer will probably no longer be alive when justice is finally done, and the wrongs that they suffered are at long last righted.

CHAPTER 8

The Gods in the *Aeneid*

The enduring question of piety and its postponed rewards is central to Virgil's *Aeneid*. Virgil (70–19 B.C.), although he wrote in Latin, drew on Greek poetry for his subject matter. He had an intimate and detailed knowledge of Greek literature, and he chose to live in Naples, where Greek was still spoken. By the time he wrote, it had long been believed that after the fall of Troy, Aeneas went to Italy and founded a settlement there. He was regarded as the ancestor of the first kings of Rome, and had a hero cult in Latium, the region of west central Italy that includes Rome. Virgil intended the *Aeneid* to be a great national epic, an *Iliad* for speakers of Latin.[1] For his description of the journey of Aeneas into a new and unknown world, he recalls scenes not only in the *Odyssey* but also in the *Argonautica*.

Like Homer in the *Odyssey*, Virgil begins his narrative some years after the fall of Troy. Aeneas is exhausted from his travels, and doubts whether he will ever reach the distant shores where the gods have directed him to found a new settlement. He discovers that he has landed in Carthage, on the north coast of Africa. Carthage has recently been founded by refugees from Phoenicia; their leader is the beautiful Queen Dido, who falls in love with Aeneas and wants to keep him in Carthage. Although mortal, she proves to be almost as alluring to Aeneas as Calypso was to Odysseus. But the gods see to it that Aeneas leaves Dido, and sails away to Italy to fulfill his destiny. Their encounter has terrible consequences, not only for Dido, who kills herself, but also for Aeneas himself, and for Rome. Carthage was for centuries Rome's most powerful rival and deadly enemy.

We can recognize in the *Aeneid* the gods of the *Odyssey* and the *Iliad*, but we can also see especially in Virgil's characterization of Juno (as the Romans called Hera) the strong passions that Apollonius attributed to her in the *Argonautica*. In the *Aeneid*, however, the role Juno plays is antagonistic and vengeful, not supportive, as it was in the *Argonautica*. The goddess is still angry with the Trojans, as she was in the Iliad, because of the way Paris insulted her honor. But in the Aeneid Jupiter (Zeus) plays a much more prominent role than he did in the Argonautica, where he never appears directly and never interferes with Hera's plans for Jason. Jupiter sees to it that Aeneas survives to become the ancestor of the first rulers of Rome, and that Rome itself will in time come to rule the known world. But he does not intervene to make life easy for Aeneas, and Aeneas does not survive long enough to see more than the very beginnings of the settlement he has struggled so hard to establish. Like Jason in the Argonautica, he is not always aware of what the gods have in store for him. But Virgil, who is a far greater poet than Apollonius, makes it possible for us to see what it is like to try to carry out a great mission in the face of divine hostility, with only occasional encouragement from favorable deities. Aeneas derives little pleasure from his existence. He chooses to survive not for himself but to ensure that his son Ascanius and his descendants will obtain the future that is promised for them.

The story that Aeneas was fated to survive the Trojan War derives from Homer. In the Iliad Poseidon sees that Aeneas is ready to fight Achilles, and says: "Why does this man, who is not to blame, suffer for the sorrows of others? He has always given pleasing gifts to the gods, who hold wide heaven." Poseidon then predicts that Aeneas and his children's children will rule over the Trojans. Aphrodite speaks virtually the same words to Anchises, in the Homeric Hymn to Aphrodite, after they have slept together and she has become pregnant with the son who will be called Aeneas. In the Aeneid, Apollo delivers a version of Poseidon's lines to Aeneas as a prophecy, but with a significant change: "The house of Aeneas will rule over the whole of the world" (Aeneid 3.97–98).

Virgil makes it clear in his opening lines that divine persecution will be a central theme of his epic: "I sing of arms and the man, who first from the shores of Troy came as an exile by fate, to Italy and the coast of Lavinia. He was driven hard on land and on sea by the power of the gods, on account of the unforgetting anger of Juno, and he suffered much in war also, until he could found a city and bring his gods to Latium" (1.1–6). The poet asks the Muse to tell him the reasons for Juno's anger: "Or what was the slight to her godhead, for what sorrow did the queen of the gods force a man known for his piety to undergo such misfortunes and to undertake such labors? Is there such anger in the minds of the heavenly ones?" (1.8–11). Juno persecutes Aeneas because she is particularly fond of the city of Carthage, and she knows that his descendants in Italy are fated to destroy it. But there are other causes as well: "The reasons for her anger and the cruel pain had still not left her heart; there rankled in the depths of her mind the judgment of Paris and his rejection of her beauty, and the race she hated, and the honors bestowed on Ganymede after he was carried off" (1.25–28). Juno is not angry with Aeneas for any personal reason, as she had been with Pelias because he failed to offer sacrifices to her. Aeneas as an individual has done nothing to offend her. Juno hates him because he is a Trojan. She is still angry with Paris for choosing

Venus (Aphrodite), and jealous of Ganymede because Jupiter chose him as his lover and made him immortal.

Venus, as the mother of Aeneas, comes to his rescue in the *Aeneid*, as she does in the *Iliad*, and other gods also are ready to assist him. When Juno bribes Aeolus, the god who controls the wind, to send a storm down on the fleet of Aeneas as the ships are heading toward Italy, Neptune (Poseidon) intervenes and drives the winds away from his territory. Aeneas is discouraged, because he believes that all but one of his ships are lost, and despairs of ever reaching Italy, where he is destined to found a new Troy. So Venus appeals to Jupiter, reminding him of what he had promised to Aeneas. She asks him when the suffering of this man will end: "His ships have been lost, which is unspeakable; because of one goddess's anger we are betrayed and kept far from the shores of Italy. Is this the reward for piety? Is this how you are restoring us to power?" (1.251–53). Jupiter assures her that there has been no change in Aeneas's destiny, that he will reach Italy, defeat his opponents, and found a city. His son Ascanius will move the kingdom to Alba Longa; Romulus will found the city of Rome, and he will grant the Romans a kingdom without end. "Indeed fierce Juno, who now terrorizes the sea, earth, and sky," Jupiter says, "will change her mind for the better, and along with me will cherish the Romans, rulers of the world, and the people dressed in togas" (1.279–82). He sends Mercury (Hermes) to Carthage to ensure that Queen Dido and her citizens will receive the Trojans hospitably.

But Venus, for all her concern for her son, seems as indifferent to mortal sensibilities and feelings as she is in the *Iliad* and in the Homeric Hymn to Aphrodite. When Aeneas goes ashore and does not know where he is, Venus comes in disguise as a huntress to help him find his way. Aeneas does not quite recognize her; he thinks she is a goddess, possibly Diana (Artemis) or a nymph, and he promises to honor her. Venus assures him that she is not a goddess. Virgil's readers would recognize the allusion to the Homeric Hymn to Aphrodite, where the goddess tells Anchises, father of Aeneas, that she is not a divinity, as he supposes, but a mortal princess. In the Homeric Hymn to Aphrodite she needed to deceive Anchises, because, as he says later, he would have been afraid to sleep with a goddess. But there is no such compelling reason for Venus to conceal her true identity from her own son when she meets him in the woods in Carthage. She tells him about Carthage and its queen, Dido. When she leaves, Venus assumes her normal form, and Aeneas realizes that he has been talking to his mother. He asks for an explanation: "Why do you repeatedly deceive your son with false illusions? You too are cruel! Why am I not permitted to take your hand and hear you speak to me in your true voice?" (1.407–9). Venus does not answer, but she takes steps to ensure that he will be safe. She sends her son Cupid (Eros) to make Dido fall in love with him, as Aphrodite sent Eros to shoot Medea with one of his arrows in Book 3 of the *Argonautica*. Venus is not concerned about the effect this passion will have on Dido. She is only interested in seeing that her son reaches Italy.

Aeneas tells the story of the fall of Troy to Dido and the guests assembled at her palace. He describes how Laocoön, the priest of Neptune, advised the Trojans not to bring into their city the wooden horse left behind by the Greeks, when they appeared to have abandoned their siege. Aeneas reflects: "If divine fate, if the gods' minds had not been adverse, he would have compelled us to break into the Greeks' hiding places with our swords, and Troy would now be standing, and Priam's high tower would still exist" (2.54–56). But Minerva (Athena) sent serpents that killed Laocoön and his two young sons, and the Trojans thought he had been punished for striking the wooden horse with his spear (2.228–31).[2]

Aeneas says that he would have died in Troy had it not been for the action of the gods. He was determined to die fighting, until his mother appeared to him: "She put herself before me so that I could see her more clearly than ever before. In the darkness my kindly mother was surrounded by light. She revealed herself as a goddess, as the dwellers in heaven see her, and in her full stature" (2.589–92). Venus told him that he must flee, and she took away the cloud that dulls mortal vision.[3] Now he could see the gods destroying Troy: Neptune, savage Juno, Minerva, and Jupiter himself were all involved. "She spoke and hid herself in the scattered shadows of night," he recalls; "I saw the cruel faces and the great and powerful gods, hostile to Troy" (2.621–23).

When Aeneas went to find his family, his father, Anchises, refused to leave. Aeneas then decided to return to the fighting, but the gods would not let him remain. Suddenly his son Ascanius appeared with his hair on fire. Anchises saw this as a sign, and prayed to Jupiter to confirm the omen. The god responded directly, by a clap of thunder and a falling star, with a trail of light.[4] So Aeneas was able to leave Troy, carrying his father and holding his son by the hand, with his wife, Creusa, following behind them.

But Venus had not warned Aeneas that he would be unable to take his wife with him on his journey. When he reached the sanctuary of Ceres (Demeter), Aeneas discovered that she had been separated from them. He returned to Troy to look for her; then he saw her shade and was terrified. Creusa told him that the gods would not let her come; a long exile and voyage awaited him before he reached Hesperia, as Italy was called, and the Tiber River, where he was fated to have a happy settlement, a kingdom, and a royal wife. Creusa instructed him not to mourn for her. She would not be taken captive by the Greeks, but the mother of the gods would keep her near Troy (2.776–89).

Aeneas sets sail from Troy, "onto the sea as an exile with my followers, my son, and the great gods of my household" (3.12).[5] He now needs to find his way to a land that neither he nor his followers have ever seen. For guidance he must rely entirely on prophecy, because at this point no god, not even his mother, intervenes in person to help him. The Trojan refugees are told by Apollo's oracle on the island of Delos to return to their ancient mother. Anchises supposes that the god means they should go to Crete, the birthplace of Jupiter, the ancestor of the

Aeneas carries his father, Anchises, on his back, while his son Ascanius, at left, walks with him beside his shield. (Hydria, 480 B.C., by the Cleophrades Painter. Museo Nazionale, Naples, no. 2422.)

Trojan race. But when they get to Crete, the Penates, the household gods that Aeneas brought from Troy, tell him that Apollo meant that they should go not to Crete but to Italy, since it was from there that Dardanus, ancestor of Aeneas, had come.

Aeneas and his followers sail on to the Strophades Islands, off the west coast of the Peloponnesus, but just as they are about to eat their meal they are attacked by Harpies, who steal and foul the food as they did to Phineus in the *Argonautica*. Aeneas and his men drive them off, but the Harpy Celaeno delivers a dire prophecy: Apollo has told her that they will be stricken by famine before they can enter Italy, and they will gnaw at the edges of their tables (3.250–57). In Epirus they find Priam's son Helenus, a prophet. Helenus is able to give Aeneas more information about his future, but not all that he needs to know. He tells him the sign that will indicate that they have reached their goal, and assures them that they need not be afraid of eating their tables: "The fates will find a way and Apollo will come when you call on him" (3.395). Following these instructions from Helenus, they pass safely through Scylla and Charybdis, and travel south, past the Cyclopes on Mount Etna, past Syracuse to Drepanum on the northwest corner of Sicily. But here Anchises dies. Aeneas laments and wonders why the gods did not warn him of his father's death: "There, oh best of fathers, you deserted me in my exhaustion; in vain I had saved you from great dangers. Helenus the prophet did not warn me about this sorrow, although he told me about many terrible things, and neither did dread Celaeno" (3.710–13). After they leave Drepanum, they are struck by the storm described in Book I and driven southwest to Carthage.

After this long journey, without any direct contact with his mother or any other gods, we can understand why Aeneas is discouraged, and why when he arrives in Carthage he is impatient with Venus when she comes to meet him playfully disguised as a young huntress. He does not know that Venus has sent Cupid to make Dido fall in love with him. And he does not realize that Juno is eager to keep him in Carthage, so that he does not go on to found Rome. In order to detain him, Juno proposes to Venus the arrangement of a marriage between him and Dido. Venus agrees, because she does not trust the Carthaginians, even though remaining in Carthage will delay his arrival in Italy. Juno arranges it so that Dido and Aeneas, while out hunting, are caught in a thunderstorm, and find themselves in the same cave.

For Dido "that first day was the cause of her death and the cause of her troubles" (4.169–70). Although she does not realize it, both her life and that of Aeneas have been controlled by the gods. Juno is no more concerned with Dido's welfare than Hera was with Medea's. Iarbas, the king of the Moors, is furious; he had let Dido have land on which to build her city, hoping that she would marry him. He complains to his father Jupiter about her relationship with Aeneas. Jupiter sends Mercury to deliver a message to Aeneas, reminding the messenger god: "He is not the man that his mother, the most beautiful of goddesses,

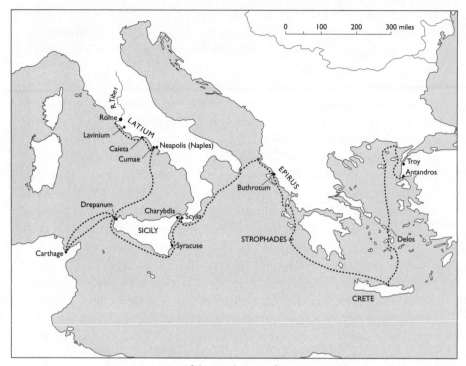

Map of the wanderings of Aeneas

promised to us and twice saved from the Greeks in battle; rather, he was to be the man to rule Italy pregnant with empire and intent on war. He was to continue the race descended from the high blood of Teucer, and to place the whole world under its laws" (4.227–31).

As Mercury descends, he passes Atlas, who stands holding up the world, beaten by wind and rain. He finds Aeneas building a citadel and new houses, wearing a purple cloak woven by Dido. The god appears in person, not in disguise, to deliver his message: "Alas, you have forgotten your kingdom and all that was to be yours" (4.267). He reminds him of his son, and of Italy and the land of Rome. Aeneas is terrified. "He burns to take flight and leave these sweet lands" (4.281). He does not know what to say to Dido, but he begins secret preparations for his departure.

When Dido learns what is happening and confronts him, Aeneas explains that he must think of his father and his son, and the promised kingdom. He saves the most telling reason for last: he has no choice but to follow Jupiter's orders. Mercury came to him: "In clear light I saw the god with my eyes coming into the city and with my ears drank in his voice. Stop inflaming both me and yourself with your complaints! It is not of my own free will that I seek Italy" (4.358–61). But

Dido is in love with him, and she is not persuaded by what he says. When it becomes clear that he will not listen to her entreaties, Dido decides to kill herself.

Aeneas leaves without trying to see her again; Mercury has come to him in a dream, warning him of danger, and suggesting that Dido is preparing to attack him. Aeneas tells his men: "A god has been sent from the sky above to hasten our departure and urges us once again to cut the ropes. We are following you, blessed deity, whoever you are, and again we rejoice in obeying your orders. Stand by us and give us your kind help, and bring us favorable stars in the sky" (4.574–79).

When Dido sees Aeneas leave, she calls on the sun, Juno, and Hecate. Like the Cyclops in the *Odyssey*, she curses the man who has ruined her life, praying that if he reaches Italy he will suffer in war, die before he can enjoy his kingdom, and lie unburied on the sand. Dido's curse is the origin of Rome's later wars with Carthage, and of the almost successful invasion of Italy by the Carthaginians under Hannibal. She calls on her people to be the enemies of Aeneas's descendants; an avenger will rise from her bones to attack the Romans in their own land. "I pray that our shores be opposed to their shores," she says, "our seas against their waves, their armies against our armies; may they and their descendants be at war with us" (4.628–29).

Dido builds a funeral pyre, pretending that she is conducting a magical rite to rid herself of her passion for Aeneas, and then she falls on her sword. Her death is slow and painful, until at last Juno sends Iris from Olympus to take a lock of her hair to Dis (Hades), the king of the dead. "So Iris, moist with dew, flies down through the sky on her saffron wings, trailing many colors behind her against the sun" (4.700–702). In contrast with the gorgeous flight of the goddess, Dido's death is silent, unnoticed. Her life simply disappears into the winds.

Aeneas returns with his ships to Drepanum in Sicily and holds funeral games for his father. Even this interlude in their voyage, however, cannot pass without disaster. While the men are praying at the tomb of Anchises, Juno sends Iris, "seen by no one as she hastens through the rainbow with its many colors" (5.609–10). She disguises herself as an old woman, and urges the women of Troy to set fire to the ships. But even after the women have come to their senses, and "Juno is shaken out of their hearts," the fire still rages (5.679). It stops only when Aeneas prays to Jupiter to save them or destroy them. Jupiter immediately sends a storm with pouring rain, thunder, and lightning. Only four ships are lost.

Now the gods once again begin to help Aeneas on his way. Anchises appears to Aeneas in a dream and tells him to take the bravest men with him to Italy; he also says that before Aeneas can go to his future home in Latium, he must descend to the underworld and meet with him in the Elysian Fields, where he now dwells (5.722–39). Venus goes to Jupiter to ask him to give Aeneas a safe passage to the harbor of Avernus in Italy, the entrance to the underworld. Jupiter does as she asks, although one man is lost on the way. Neptune goes across the waves in his chariot, followed by all the gods of the sea. During the crossing to Italy, the god of sleep causes Palinurus, the Trojan helmsman, to fall into the sea, so that Aeneas must bring the ship into the harbor himself. He does not know that the disappearance of Palinurus had been ordained by Jupiter and caused by the direct intervention of the god Sleep.

After the Trojans land on the west coast of Italy, near the modern city of Naples, Aeneas goes to the cave of the Sibyl of Cumae, the priestess of Apollo and Diana. She is to guide him to the lower world so he can see his father. He prays to Apollo to help the people of Troy, as he has done in the past, and promises to build him an oracular shrine. The god then compels the Sibyl, against her will, to prophesy: she foresees a war that will be fought over a woman, like the Trojan War, with a second Achilles as his opponent; "nor will Juno ever be absent as an infliction on the Trojans" (6.90–91). But help will come, surprisingly, from a Greek city. She tells Aeneas that before he can descend to the lower world he must pluck a golden bough from a hidden tree in a grove sacred to Proserpina (Persephone): if the branch comes off easily, he will be able to make the journey. She tells him also that a friend of his has died, and he must find and bury the body. The dead man proves to be the Trojan Misenus, who once roused the Trojans with his war chant (6.164–65). The god Triton killed him, because Misenus foolishly claimed that he could play on a conch shell better than the god, although the poet adds, "if the story is worthy of belief" (6.173). This disclaimer calls attention once again to the violence of divine resentment.[6]

Aeneas and his men cut down trees to build a funeral pyre for Misenus. Just when Aeneas is beginning to wonder how he can find the golden bough, two doves appear and settle at his feet. He recognizes his mother's birds, and realizes that she has sent them to guide him: "And you, goddess mother, do not fail me in this uncertain situation," he says (6.196–97). The doves lead him directly to the tree. The branch is reluctant, but Aeneas breaks it off and brings it to the Sibyl. When they have performed the funeral rites for Misenus, the Sibyl takes Aeneas into the cave that leads to the lower world.

The scene is distantly reminiscent of the visit of Odysseus to the world of the dead in Book 10 of the *Odyssey*. But the tone of the journey in the *Aeneid* is even more somber. Among the shades waiting to cross the river Styx, Aeneas meets the helmsman Palinurus. But he cannot turn back to bury his comrade, and the Sibyl warns him: "Do not hope that the fates determined by the gods can be changed by prayer" (6.376). Aeneas and the Sibyl ride with Charon in his dark boat across the Styx. Aeneas sees the monster Cerberus, and the souls of those who have died before their time. In a grove with the shades of mortals who have killed themselves, he sees Dido in the dim light and tries to speak with her, but she turns her back and returns to her former husband, Sychaeus. The heroes of Troy are also there, and he barely recognizes the mutilated form of Priam's son Deiphobus, who had married Helen after the death of Paris. The Sibyl will not let Aeneas linger in conversation, however. They move on past a place guarded by the Fury Tisiphone. Offenders against gods are confined there, condemned to eternal punishment. One of these is Phlegyas, whose daughter Coronis had been unfaithful to Apollo, so the god killed her with his arrows, and Phlegyas then tried to set Apollo's temple on fire. "Miserable Phlegyas admonishes everyone and proclaims in a loud voice through the shadows: 'Be warned, learn that you must be just and not scorn the gods!'" (6.618–20).

After he has witnessed the torture of the impious, Aeneas comes to the Elysian Fields. When he sees his father he tries, and fails, three times to embrace him, like Odysseus when he met the shade of his mother (*Odyssey* 11.204–6). But here the souls of the blessed are not merely insubstantial wraiths. They have a second chance at life, after they have been punished for their wrongdoings and have been purified. Anchises shows Aeneas the shades of those who will become the founding fathers of Rome and her great leaders. Among these are Julius Caesar and Quintus Fabius Maximus, who by delay will end Hannibal's series of triumphs, and Marcellus, who will win the first Roman victory over Hannibal. The sights "set his mind on fire with passion for the glory to come" (*Aeneid* 6.889). Anchises also advises him about the battles and trials immediately ahead of him.

After Aeneas has spoken with his father, he and the Sibyl leave the underworld. No prophet had explained how Aeneas and the Sibyl would manage their departure, but the Sibyl had warned him that supernatural help would be required: "The descent to Avernus is easy; the doors of dark Dis are open night and day; but to retrace your steps, and to come out again in the upper air, that is the challenge, that is the labor" (6.126–29). Aeneas and the Sibyl leave the lower world through the gate of ivory, the Gate of False Dreams. The mode of their departure lends an air of mystery to the experiences in the lower world that have preceded it.[7] But what they have just seen is not a false dream, since Virgil's audience knows that much of what Anchises describes to Aeneas is historically true. The transition back to reality is abrupt. Aeneas returns directly to his ships, and prepares to depart for Latium.

Aeneas could never have reached Italy without the aid of the gods. He also needs their help to establish his new settlement in Latium. Neptune keeps them away from Circe's island (which the poet locates near the coast of Italy), and they enter the Tiber at dawn. The poet now calls on the muse Erato to help him describe the battles and the kings that Aeneas and his men will encounter (7.44–45). The region of Latium was inhabited by Latins and Rutulians, who would dispute the Trojans' right to settle there, although the gods have already foretold the outcome of the war that must be fought. Among the Latins portents predicted the arrival of a stranger who would marry Lavinia, the daughter of Latinus, the king of Latium, even though she had been betrothed to Turnus, the prince of the Rutulians. The forest god Faunus, father of Latinus, confirmed through his oracle that the prophecies were true. The Harpy Celaeno's prophecy is fulfilled when the

Trojans realize that they have arrived at their destination: Ascanius sees them eating their meals off wheat cakes, and he exclaims that they are eating their tables. Aeneas offers thanks to the gods. Jupiter thunders three times, and with his own hand shows them a cloud burning with golden light. King Latinus understands that Aeneas is the man of whom his father Faunus has spoken, and he gives the Trojans presents.

Juno will not allow a peaceful settlement, however, because she has not ceased to hate the Trojans. As in the *Iliad*, anger is the cause of death and sorrow, but here it is a god's anger, and thus more powerful and irrational than the wrath even of the greatest of mortal warriors, Achilles. Juno sees from the sky that the Trojans have started to build houses, and she says, "I am being defeated by Aeneas, but if my divine powers are not strong enough, I can hardly hesitate to call on whatever there is: if I cannot stir up the gods above, I shall move Acheron" (7.310–12). She goes to earth to find the Fury Allecto to shatter the peace and stir up war. Allecto goes first to throw a serpent into the heart of Amata, Lavinia's mother. Then, disguised as a priestess, she appears to Turnus in a dream, and when he refuses to believe that Latinus has promised Lavinia to Aeneas, Allecto assumes her true form and throws a burning torch into the prince's heart. Then she sends the hounds of Ascanius after a tame stag, which Ascanius wounds. When the farmer sees that his daughter's pet stag has been wounded, he calls on his neighbors to attack the Trojans. Allecto goes to Juno and asks permission to do even more damage. But Juno is satisfied that the causes of war are now established, and she sends the Fury back to the lower world. Juno herself comes down from the sky to throw open the iron Gates of War.

The river god Tiber comes to encourage Aeneas, who is disheartened by the prospect of war. "Here your home is assured, and your household gods," Tiber says. "Do not depart! Do not be afraid of the threats of war! The violence and rage of the gods have yielded" (8.39–41). To confirm that his message is not illusory, the river god tells Aeneas that he will see a portent, a white sow with a litter of thirty piglets. The sign presages the founding of Alba Longa (the "long white" city) by his son Ascanius thirty years hence. He tells him to make a treaty with Evander, a Greek from Arcadia, and to make appropriate offerings to Juno: "Overcome her anger and threats with prayers of supplication" (8.60–61).

After Aeneas has offered thanks to the Tiber, he sees the remarkable omen the god has described to him in his dream, and sacrifices the sow to Juno. The Tiber then reverses his current to help Aeneas make his journey upstream to Evander on the future site of Rome. While Evander is showing them the land on which the city of Rome will later be built, Venus asks her husband Vulcan (Hephaestus) to make armor for Aeneas. When he hesitates, she takes him to her bed. Before the night is over Vulcan has commanded the Cyclopes to prepare the armor.

Evander sends his son, Pallas, with four hundred men to join Aeneas. Venus sends a sign, thunder in a clear sky, which Aeneas understands as a favorable omen, though he laments the suffering that the war will cause and fears that Pallas, Evander's only son, will not return to his father. Evander prays to Jupiter to protect his son, but after offering his prayer he collapses. On this somber note, Aeneas and his army ride out of Evander's settlement.

When Venus sees that Aeneas has gone off by himself, she brings him his new armor, revealing herself to him and speaking to him directly, without disguise or pretense. She seeks his embrace and places the armor beneath a tree, but Aeneas says nothing to his mother. He cannot take his eyes off the armor. The shield tells the fate of Italy and the triumphs of Rome, from its beginnings with Romulus down to Virgil's own time, with the battle of Actium in 31 B.C., and Augustus Caesar's triumph over Antony and Cleopatra. The Roman gods defeat those of the Egyptians, "every type of monstrous god and barking Anubis" (8.698). Apollo draws his bow, and the nations of the East flee before him, and as Augustus rides into Rome, Apollo receives the offerings of the subject peoples: "Such events were upon Vulcan's shield, his mother's gift to him. Aeneas marveled at the scenes without understanding them, and rejoiced as he lifted onto his shoulder the glory and the fate of his descendants" (8.729–31).

While Venus is bringing Aeneas his armor, Juno sends Iris down to have Turnus make a surprise attack on the Trojan camp. Turnus sees that the sky is divided, with the stars wandering in the heavens, and prays to the gods. He and his men prepare to set fire to the Trojan ships, but again a goddess intervenes to help the Trojans. Cybele asks Jupiter to preserve the Trojan fleet intact for all time, because the ships are made of timber she gave to Aeneas when he left Troy.[8] Jupiter is reluctant to interfere with the Fates: "Should ships made with mortal hands enjoy immortal rights? Should Aeneas gaze in certainty on uncertain dangers? What god possesses such power?" (9.95–97). Even though he cannot allow Aeneas to enjoy safety and security, Jupiter keeps Cybele's trees from harm by promising that they will turn into sea goddesses when they are no longer needed by the Trojans. As Turnus and his men approach with their torches, the sky darkens and Cybele's voice warns the Trojans not to defend their ships; the ships plunge into the water like dolphins, and they are changed into nymphs. Turnus sees the transformation as a sign that gods are on his side, since the Trojans cannot escape.

Turnus and his Rutulians kill the Trojans Nisus and his young friend Euryalus when they make a heroic attempt to take a message to Aeneas, but after that the gods see to it that the tide of battle turns against the Latins and their allies. The gods remain active in this phase of the fighting. Ascanius, who has never before been in a battle, prays to Jupiter. Jupiter thunders in support, and when Ascanius shoots Remulus through the temples, Apollo looks down from the clouds and exclaims: "My blessings on your new manhood, my son; this is the way to glory! You are the descendant of gods and will have gods as your descendants" (9.641–42).

As Iulus, the name by which Ascanius was later known, he is the ancestor, and Apollo the patron god, of the Julian family, and of Julius and Augustus Caesar, who were to be honored as gods in Virgil's time.

Apollo now disguises himself as Butes, Anchises' old armor-bearer, and advises Ascanius to leave the field. The god dissolves into thin air, as the Trojans realize that he is Apollo when they hear the sound of his arrows and quiver as he flies away. The Latins rally, encouraged by Mars (Ares), the god of war. When the Trojan Pandarus casts his spear at Turnus, Juno deflects it, and Turnus defends himself bravely. But Juno does not dare to keep renewing his strength, because Jupiter sends Iris down to command her to let Turnus retreat. He rushes into the Tiber, who returns him to his comrades.

Virgil never lets us forget that this war was caused by a goddess and could be stopped by an agreement among the gods. Book 10 opens with Jupiter calling a council of the gods. He asks, "Great dwellers in heaven, why have you reversed your decision, and why are you fighting so, with hatred in your hearts? I had forbidden Italy to clash in battle with the Trojans. Why has conflict arisen against my orders?" (10.6–9). He suggests that the time will come for war, and hatred and plunder will be needed, when Hannibal invades Italy. Venus complains that the Italians have surrounded the Trojan camp in the absence of Aeneas. She describes the trouble that Juno has caused: the Trojans' ships burned in Sicily (Book 5), the storm caused by Aeolus (Book 1), the message brought from Juno to Turnus by Iris (Book 9), and Juno's enlistment of Allecto (Book 7). She asks Jupiter to protect Ascanius, to let Aeneas spend the rest of his life in safety at one of her shrines, and to take pity on the Trojans and let them return to Troy. Then Juno speaks, "driven by violent anger" (10.63). She asks why it is wrong for Turnus to defend his native land against invaders. Since Jupiter can work miracles, such as transforming ships into sea nymphs, why should he not help the Italians? She reminds him that she (unlike Venus) was not responsible for the adultery of Paris or for the Trojan War. When the gods fail to reach an agreement, Jupiter declares that at present he will take no action: "Jupiter is king for all men alike; the Fates will find a way" (10.112–13).

Jupiter's withdrawal leaves the way open for the other gods to intervene. Aeneas has been joined by Etruscan forces, and as he sails along the Italian coast, together with their thirty ships, the sea nymphs who had once been the Trojans' ships tell him that Ascanius and the Trojans have been besieged by the Latins. Aeneas offers his thanks to Cybele. As he returns, a flame shines down from his head and great fires emerge from the golden boss of his shield (10.270–73). He is like Sirius, the Dog Star, bringing thirst and disease to sick mortals.[9] The battle now claims the life of Pallas, Evander's young son, who is killed brutally by Turnus. Aeneas in his anger hacks down everything near him with his sword, and in his fury he cuts a swath through the enemy ranks.

At this point in the fighting Jupiter remarks to Juno that the Trojans have been sustained by Venus. Juno asks him to let her rescue Turnus, which Jupiter allows, but he warns her that he will not alter the outcome of the war. Juno creates a shade that resembles Aeneas.[10] Turnus follows it onto a ship, and Juno sends the ship out to sea. Latin envoys come to Aeneas asking for a truce, and both sides mourn their dead, but the truce expires before the Latins reach a decision about the war. Queen Amata and her daughter Lavinia, "the cause of this great disaster," and the mothers of the soldiers pray to Minerva for the death of Aeneas (11.480).

A beautiful and brave warrior maiden named Camilla comes to join Turnus in the fighting. The goddess Diana knows that Camilla will die in battle, so she gives her bow and arrow to the nymph Opis for use later in avenging Camilla's death. Camilla's onslaught against the Trojans is stopped only when Jupiter intervenes and gets the Etruscans to rally. The Etruscan Arruns prays to Apollo to let him kill Camilla with his fatal spear that never misses its mark, and to let him return home safely. But the god grants only the first part of his prayer. When Camilla falls, Opis is watching. She says (even though Camilla can no longer hear her): "Your queen has not left you without honor in your last hour, your death will not be un-known among the peoples of the world, and you will not be known as someone who has died unavenged" (11.845–47). Opis shoots Arruns with one of Diana's arrows, and then flies back to Olympus. Turnus returns from the woods, "in a frenzy (and that is also what the fierce divinity of Jupiter demands)" (11.901). But it is too late in the day for the two armies to begin fighting.

The next day, Turnus and Aeneas agree to engage in single combat. Juno knows that Turnus is fated to lose and goes to Juturna, sister of Turnus, whom Jupiter has made a goddess in return for her virginity. To Juturna, Juno says she can no longer protect Turnus, but she urges the weeping Juturna to try to help him. As the leaders of the two armies pray to the gods and state the terms of their agreement, Juturna takes the form of the Rutulian leader Camers, rousing the men of Turnus. She shows them a portent, "which more than any other sign con-fused the Italians' minds and deceived them with what they saw" (12.245–46). An eagle, the bird of Jupiter, flying along the shore, scattering the other birds be-fore him, seizes a swan. But as he carries the swan away the other birds surround him, until he is forced to drop his prey. "This is the sign that I have often sought in my prayers," says the Rutulian seer Tolumnius (12.259). Now the Latins attack the Trojans and their allies, breaking the agreement about single combat. When Aeneas stands up to protest, he is hit by an arrow.

Old Iapyx, a physician, comes to help the wounded Aeneas. Apollo had loved Iapyx and promised to teach him the arts of song, prophecy, and archery, but Iapyx instead chose the art of medicine. Even Iapyx cannot heal the wound Aeneas has received, however; "no Fortune shows the way, nor does his patron Apollo come to his aid" (12.405–6). Aeneas is cured only because his mother Venus intervenes. She picks some dittany on Mount Ida in Crete, and brings it to Latium. She is surrounded by a dark cloud so that no one sees her, and Iapyx does not know that the herb has been added to the water he was using to bathe the wound. As soon as Aeneas recovers, Iapyx exclaims: "This cure was not brought about by human efforts or with a doctor's skill, nor did my right hand save you, Aeneas; a higher power is behind it, and sends you on to greater accomplishment" (12.427–29). Aeneas tells the joyful Ascanius: "My son, learn courage and hard work from me, but fortune from others; now my right hand will protect you in war and lead you to great rewards. And you must remain mindful, when increasing time has ripened you, to turn your mind to the examples of your countrymen; and let your father Aeneas and your uncle Hector inspire you" (12.435–40). Certainly Aeneas is justified in thinking that his accomplishments have been won by his own endurance and determination. But even if he is not prepared to acknowledge it, fortune has been on his side as well, because he is the son of a goddess who has repeatedly come to assist him.

When Aeneas returns to the fighting, Juturna takes the form of her brother's charioteer and goes to assist Turnus. Aeneas calls on Jupiter, and he is also aided by Mars. But why (the poet asks) does Jupiter want the war to continue? "Which god shall reveal to me in song these cruel events, the many killings and deaths of leaders, which now Turnus, and now the Trojan hero, were inflicting over the whole plain? Jupiter, was it pleasing to you that peoples rushed at each other with such violence who were to live in eternal peace in the future?" (12.500–504). Amata, Lavinia's mother, kills herself after Venus, "his most beautiful mother," has put it into Aeneas's mind that he should attack the walls of the city Latinus rules (12.554–56). When Turnus tells his charioteer, who is actually Juturna, to drive him toward the walls, she tries to keep him away from Aeneas. Turnus sees through his sister's disguise, and he says with great courage since he has no illusions about his chances of success, that he prefers to die rather than be disgraced: "Now at last the fates are too strong; do not hold me back any longer. Let us go where the god and cruel Fortune call us" (12.676–77).[11]

The gods keep a close watch on this final phase of the battle. As Turnus advances to meet Aeneas in single combat, Jupiter takes out his scales to weigh their fates before they begin to fight, as he did in the *Iliad* when Hector and Achilles were about to clash. When his sword shatters against the shield of Aeneas, Turnus starts to flee, and Aeneas pursues him five times around the battlefield. Aeneas hurls his spear, which becomes embedded in the trunk of an olive sacred to the god Faunus, King Latinus's father, and Turnus prays to the god to keep hold of the spear. The god hears his prayer, and while Aeneas struggles to free the spear Juturna comes forward to bring Turnus a sword. Venus, angry that the nymph has been allowed to intervene, comes and pulls the spear out of the roots of the tree (12.786–87).

At this point Jupiter asks Juno when she plans to leave off intervening, for Juturna never could have returned the sword without her help. "You have reached the limit. You have been able to drive the Trojans across land and sea, and to ignite

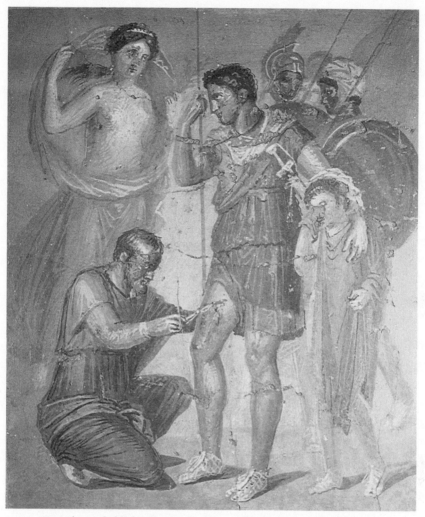

Venus hovers behind Iapyx with the dittany while he treats Aeneas's wound, and Ascanius stands weeping beside his father. (Wall painting from Pompeii, first century A.D. Museo Nazionale, Naples, no. 9009.)

this awful war, to wreck a home and to mingle wedding songs with lamentations. I forbid you to attempt anything more" (12.803–6). Juno admits that she has given up, and that it was she who told Juturna to intervene. She agrees to the marriage between Aeneas and Lavinia, but she asks Jupiter to let the Latins keep their name and not become Trojans: "Let it be Latium, let there be Alban kings through the centuries, let the Roman race be strong with the courage of Italy. Troy has fallen; allow it to fall along with its name" (12.826–28). Jupiter honors her request, and he also promises that the Latins will surpass other nations in honoring her. Juno redirects her thoughts and leaves the sky. Again, the ease with which the gods can resolve a long-standing quarrel is contrasted with the grim struggles of mortals.[12]

Jupiter then summons the Dirae, the three winged daughters of Night who guard his throne. One of them goes to earth in the form of a bird of ill omen and flies again and again in the face of Turnus. Turnus is terrified; his sister recognizes the Dira and realizes that Turnus is about to die. She wishes that Jupiter had not given her immortality; now her suffering and mourning will never end. She covers her head with a blue veil and hides herself in her river. Aeneas taunts Turnus: "Pray to chase the steep stars or to hide yourself in the hollow earth" (12.892–93). But no god is present to help him escape.

When Turnus sees that he has no place to run, and no sister to help him, he is paralyzed with fear. Aeneas hurls a great stone at him, which brings him down. Turnus appeals to Aeneas to return him to his father, since he knows how much he cared about Anchises, or at least to give his body back to his people: "You have defeated me, and the people of Italy have seen me in defeat stretch out my hands to you. Lavinia is your wife. Do not stretch your anger beyond this" (12.936–38). Aeneas hesitates. But then he sees on his opponent's shoulder the baldric Turnus took from Pallas when he killed him. In his anger, Aeneas buries his sword in the foe's breast, saying that Pallas is taking his revenge.

The last lines of the *Aeneid* echo the lines that describe Hector's death in the *Iliad*. "His limbs were loosened by the chill of death," in Virgil's description, "and with a groan his life fled, in anger, beneath the shadows" (12.951–52). In the *Iliad* Hector's death presages the death of Achilles. For Aeneas also there will be no happy ending, and only a short time to enjoy the victory he has won. By ending the epic with the description of the death of Turnus, Virgil emphasizes the grim limitations of human existence. The goddess Juno, who is responsible for the suffering and bloodshed, can depart in joy, looking forward to future honors. Aeneas instead has the memory of Pallas, his ally now dead at the hands of Turnus, and his enduring sorrow and anger.

In the world of the *Aeneid*, the gods retain the powers they have in Homer, and they intervene in much the same ways and with almost the same frequency. Venus guides her son to Carthage and sees that Dido falls in love with him. She ensures that the seas are made smooth for him when he goes to Italy. She sends her doves to guide him to the golden bough, so he can gain entry to the lower world. She brings him the immortal armor he needs in war and in his single combat with Turnus. She sees that his wound is healed and pulls his spear out of the oak tree where the god Faunus has been holding it. But even though he is her son, he has less real contact with her than Odysseus does with Athena in the *Odyssey*. Achilles can go to the seashore and expect his mother Thetis to come to him, but Aeneas never seems to be sure when Venus will appear. He is not fully aware of all the action his mother has undertaken on his behalf.

Like Zeus in the *Iliad*, Jupiter sees that justice is done in the end. He has ordained that Aeneas will settle in Italy, that he will win the war against the Latins, and that his descendants, the Romans, will rule the world. But he does nothing to make life easy for Aeneas. When Mercury tells Aeneas in Book 4 that he must leave Dido and Carthage, he does not take into consideration at all whatever feelings Aeneas might have about it. When Cybele is concerned about the Trojans and their ships, Jupiter tells her that he will not interfere with the Fates, asking, "What god possesses such power?" Even when a Trojan victory is certain, Jupiter will not allow a peaceful settlement, leaving the poet to wonder whether it simply pleased the god to witness such violence.

Virgil does not answer his own question directly, but he leaves his audience with the impression that Jupiter is even less concerned than Homer's Zeus with the fate of individual human beings. Jupiter in the *Aeneid* does not shed tears of blood for any dying mortal, as the god did for his son Sarpedon in the *Iliad*. He does not regard Juno's violent hostility toward the Trojans as a matter of great urgency. When Venus appeals to him on her son's behalf in Book 1, he merely reassures her that his plans remain the same, and that "fierce Juno, who now terrorizes the sea, earth, and sky, will change her mind for the better." Jupiter does not intervene when Juno tries to keep Aeneas in Carthage, when she gets the Trojan women to set fire to the Trojan ships in Book 5, when she sends Allecto to stir up the Latins in Book 7, or when she tries to keep Turnus out of Aeneas's way in battle. Perhaps it is because Jupiter takes such a long view of human achievement that he seems less sympathetic to individual mortals than Zeus in the *Iliad*, who is not concerned with what happens beyond the end of the Trojan War.

The gods in Homer also seem less remote, and more sympathetic to mortals, because we see more of them and can watch them eating, drinking, putting on armor, and riding in chariots. Virgil describes how Venus uses her sexual appeal to get Vulcan to make armor for Aeneas, but there is nothing in the *Aeneid* that has the humor and lightness of the scene in the *Iliad* where Hera seduces Zeus, or in the *Argonautica* where Hera and Athena visit Aphrodite and find her in her bedroom combing her hair. The greater element of fantasy in the *Aeneid* adds to the sense of distance. The keel of the *Argo* utters a brief prophecy in the *Argonautica*, but there is nothing in Apollonius to match the sudden transformation of the Trojan ships into sea nymphs when the mother of the gods gives her command. That miracle, along with many actions that mortals are unaware of, reminds the audience that while anything is possible for the gods, by comparison mortals can accomplish very little, even when they act with divine assistance. Watching from her golden cloud, Juno does not feel the chill atmosphere around her, and she is unaffected, like the other gods, by the weight of gravity that keeps mortals down (12.792).

Because the world of the *Aeneid* is controlled by gods who have such limited interest in and understanding of the mortal condition, we are far more absorbed in the experience of the human characters who must exist in such a universe, and who are only partially aware of the forces that rule their lives. Aeneas realizes at least some of the time that his mother has been helping him, but he does not see Neptune calming the winds, or Cupid sitting in Dido's lap. Dido remains unaware of what Juno and Venus have done to her; Turnus sees Allecto only in a dream. At the end of the *Aeneid*, he does not know which god has caused the bird to fly at his head. It is because they are driven to do what they do by forces beyond their control that we can sympathize with them, even though both Dido and Turnus become enemies of Aeneas. The same fact of human powerlessness enables us to be sympathetic toward Aeneas even when he leaves Dido, and ultimately when he drives his sword into the breast of Turnus.

By emphasizing not only the weakness but the misery and loneliness of the human condition, Virgil makes it clear that traditional religion offers little comfort to humankind, and very little in the way of hope. At best, human beings may be remembered for what they have done, like the helmsman Palinurus, who will have the region where he died named after him (6.373–83). Piety is not always rewarded, and prayers are not always heard, or are heard only in part. Even the son of a goddess cannot expect that his mother will come to him if he wishes to speak with her. The outward forms of traditional religion in this later period have not changed, but the poets have begun to make us more keenly aware of its deficiencies.[13]

CHAPTER 9

Changes

One of the great strengths of traditional Greek religion is that it allowed its adherents to complain to the gods if they thought they were being treated unfairly, and to call attention to the great disparity between the happy existence of the gods and the inevitable suffering and loss borne by humankind. Another strength is that it was not exclusive: worshipers of the old gods could also worship foreign gods, and even associate them with the gods they already knew. New gods were welcomed, so long as the old gods were not neglected in any way. Such openness to change encourages inquiry and discussion, and the creation of poetry that explores the limitations of the human condition. But openness also encourages thinkers to come up with new answers to the old questions. Why do the gods behave in ways that seem to us immoral? Why should we worship gods who do not seem sufficiently concerned about the welfare of humankind?

The first questioners of the traditional religion were Greeks who lived outside mainland Greece, on the fringes of the Greek world, in Asia Minor (now the west coast of Turkey) and the southern coastal regions of Italy and Sicily. It is possible that these people had come into contact with foreigners from different religious traditions. After the mid–sixth century B.C., many Greeks in Asia Minor lived under Persian domination. The Persians were worshipers of a single god, Ahuramazda (the Wise Lord). Xenophanes of Colophon in Asia Minor, writing in the late sixth century B.C., attacked the epic poets for saying that the gods behaved in ways that among humans would be considered immoral. "Homer and Hesiod ascribed to the gods all the actions that among humans cause reproach and blame, lies, adulteries, and deceptions of one another," he wrote. Instead of telling stories about the gods, he proposed that men should spend their time praising the achievements of other men. He advised that "one should not tell about the battles of Titans and giants and centaurs—these are fictions invented by the men of old—or violent quarrels, for there is nothing useful in these narratives. It is good always to have consideration for the gods." The phrase "for there is nothing useful in these narratives" is particularly telling: stories should set good examples of behavior for humankind. By demanding "consideration" for the gods he seems to have meant that only good should be said about them. In his view, the traditional myths had no practical utility.[1]

Instead, Xenophanes argued for the existence of a single all-powerful divinity—monotheism over polytheism. He wrote that "there is one god, who is greatest among gods and men, who is not like mortals in appearance or in intelligence." This god "sees as a whole, thinks as a whole, hears as a whole." Gods, in the opinion of Xenophanes, would not look like mortals: humans only suppose "that gods are born and have clothes and voices and shapes like themselves." Horses would suppose that gods looked like horses, Ethiopians that their gods had black skin and flat noses, and Thracians that their gods were green-eyed and red-haired.[2]

Around the time that Xenophanes raised his questions about traditional notions of the gods, Theagenes of Rhegium (the modern Italian city Reggio di Calabria) proposed that the gods represented forces in nature. Apollo, the sun god Helios, and Hephaestus were fire, while the sea god Poseidon and the river god Scamander were water, and so on. In that way the conflicts between the gods in myth could be understood as the opposition of physical forces. Dry is in conflict with wet, hot with cold, and light with heavy. Making such statements was not regarded as impious, because it involved no physical demonstration of disrespect, such as defiling or destroying temples or the sacred images within them, cutting down trees in sacred groves, or harming a priest or priestess.[3]

Around 500 B.C. Heraclitus of Ephesus, another thinker from Asia Minor, expressed his concerns about the way the poets described the gods in a strikingly different fashion. Heraclitus agreed that god was a unity and did not resemble a human being, but he described the unity of that god as a tension between polar opposites: "The one which alone is wise wishes and does not wish to be called by the name of Zeus." What Heraclitus seems to be saying is that despite appearances, the divine consists not of many different entities but of one controlling intelligence, not unlike Xenophanes' notion of a divinity who "sees as a whole, thinks as a whole, hears as a whole." Heraclitus blamed the epic poets for misleading their audiences about the nature of reality: "The wise is one thing, to understand judgment, how all things are steered through all." Although most people learn about the creation of the world from the poet Hesiod, he did not understand that "god is day night, winter summer, war peace, plenty famine." "They think [Hesiod] knows more than anyone, but he does not know day and night; for it is one." In defining divinity as an intelligence controlling all things, Heraclitus argued that what happened in the world was not determined by conflicts of will and interests among the gods, as in Hesiod and Homer. He was searching for something that was less subject to whim and caprice, and which could be seen operating in the forces of nature.[4]

Since only fragments of what Heraclitus wrote have come down to us, we have no way of knowing all the reasons why he rejected the traditional notions of the gods. But it is at least clear that he sought to stop people from turning to Homer and Hesiod as authorities, and to listen to writers like himself, who spoke on his own authority and did not seek to learn what the gods might want in the usual ways, through dreams or oracles. He wanted to make the ways of the god immediately intelligible to humans, and he wished to discover what the god was through the process of his own reasoning and sense perception. His single divinity, and that of Xenophanes as well, was more accessible to humanity than the gods of the traditional religion, and it ran the world in ways that were more acceptable to human beings and could be more readily understood by them. The fifth-century thinker Protagoras of Abdera said, "Man is the measure of all things: of the things that are, that they are, of the things that are not, that they are not." That statement seems completely reasonable to us today, but in antiquity many religious Greeks must have been shocked by it, because Protagoras fails to acknowledge that human knowledge and judgment had its limitations. Most of his contemporaries would have been distinctly uneasy about the idea that humans, and not the gods, should be the judge of the nature of reality.[5]

Virtually all subsequent critics of the traditional religion concentrate on the problems that the early thinkers identified: the incredible elements in mythology, like the centaurs, and the immoral and capricious behavior of the gods. Plato (429–347 B.C.), in his *Republic*, used some of the arguments first employed by Xenophanes. The gods set bad examples for mortals: "A young person should not hear that he was doing nothing remarkable if he were to commit the greatest crimes, not even if he were to punish his father without restraint for doing wrong, because that is what the foremost and greatest of the gods might do" (*Republic* 378b). Nor should a young person hear that "gods have wars, plan campaigns, and have battles with gods—that isn't true" (378c). In the ideal city that he describes in the dialogue, Plato advocated censorship of the myths and elimination of poetry altogether: "We must not admit into our city battles between the gods such as the ones Homer has written about, whether or not they are written as allegories" (378d). Poets were to be replaced by philosophers who spoke on their own authority, without the traditional acknowledgment to the Muses. Plato was determined to banish the poets from his ideal state, because most people still knew the traditional narratives and were reluctant to abandon them.

Plato also had no use for allegories, because they provided a reason to keep on teaching and learning the traditional narratives. In the fifth century writers like Theagenes of Rhegium used allegories to suggest that the gods represented elemental forces working in the world. In the last quarter of the fourth century, Euhemerus of Messene in Sicily devised an allegorical theory of myth that turned the gods into human beings. Zeus, his father Cronus, and his grandfather Uranus had originally been kings, whose grateful subjects worshiped them as gods. Around the same time, a popular writer who was later known as Palaephatus (Ancient Prophet) suggested in his treatise *On the Unbelievable* that irrational stories about the gods came into being because "certain events occurred that the poets transformed into the incredible and miraculous in order to astound people" (Palaephatus, *On the Unbelievable*, preface). For example, the winged Sirens who attempt to seduce Odysseus were not women with the wings and feet of birds; they were courtesans who were adept at singing and music. They carried off all their clients' wealth, which is why they were said to be like birds.

In effect, such interpretations transform the extraordinary events of myth into the familiar and ordinary. How could anyone believe that Paris, a mortal, was asked to decide which of the goddesses Athena, Hera, and Aphrodite was the most beautiful? Palaephatus proposed instead that what Paris actually did was to write poems praising the three goddesses (10). Palaephatus objected strongly to the irrational elements in myths, such as the notion of monsters like the one-eyed Cyclops and combinations of men and animals such as centaurs. They could never have existed, because the shapes and forms we see now must also have existed in the past.

Theories like these encouraged later writers to use allegory as a means of removing all elements of the irrational, including the gods, from the *Odyssey*. Another writer called Heraclitus, whose exact dates are unknown, proposed that the goddess Calypso could not have offered to make Odysseus immortal; rather, what she wanted was for him to have a luxurious and brilliant style of life (Heraclitus, *On the Unbelievable* 32). The Cyclops, Heraclitus suggested, did not have just one single eye: he was a man whose only means of perception was his ability to see (11). Circe was not a goddess but a courtesan who managed to entice and conquer everyone, including Odysseus (16). Another writer, who is now known as Pseudo-Heraclitus (first century B.C.), argued in his treatise *Inquiries into Homer* that such allegories were intended to allow people to enjoy reading the *Iliad* and the *Odyssey* by keeping the narratives "clean and purified of every pollution" (*Inquiries into Homer* 2.1).[6]

Absurd as some of these suggestions may seem, they do at least show us that some educated people were uncomfortable with how the poets had portrayed the gods, and that an easy solution to the problem was to turn the gods, or at least the minor gods, into human beings. But in the process of making myths credible, the allegories deprive the myths of their religious content, and of the irrational elements that appeal to the human imagination. If gods are just like humans, or even were humans, why worship them?

One logical solution was to disregard the myths entirely, and to treat them as the inventions of foolish mortals. In the school of philosophy known as Stoicism, which had a wide influence from the time of its founding in the early third century B.C. into the early centuries A.D., the myths were unworthy of belief because of their immorality. Divinity did not have a human form but was made of intangible qualities, such as mind and soul. When the Stoic philosopher Cleanthes (331–232 B.C.) wrote his *Hymn to Zeus*, he praised the god for his goodness, his reasoning, and the order he brings to the universe, without reference to any of the traditional myths.[7] Cicero (106–43 B.C.), in his treatise *On the Nature of the Gods*, makes the poet Lucilius say that the traditional pantheon of gods is deceptive and fictional, because in it they act just like mortals: "We believe in the gods' desires, illnesses, and angers, and indeed that they engage in wars and battles, both when two armies are opposing each other, as in Homer, and when they fight their own wars with the Titans and the Giants" (*On the Nature of the Gods* 2.70). Not even old women believe in Centaurs and Chimaeras or monsters in the lower world like the three-headed Cerberus (2.5). As Pliny the Elder (A.D. 23–79) wrote, echoing Xenophanes, "It goes beyond shamelessness to suppose that the gods committed adultery among themselves, and then fought with and hated each other, and that there were actual deities of theft and crimes." Instead he suggests that "for a mortal to help mortals—this is a god," and (following the line of argument suggested by Euhemerus) that the mortals who do the most for other mortals, such as Emperor Vespasian, should be honored as gods (*Natural History* 2.5.17–19).[8]

An even more radical solution to the deficiencies of the traditional religion had already been proposed by the philosopher Epicurus (361–270 B.C.). The gods existed, but they had nothing to do with the world in which humans live. Everything that happened in the world could be explained in terms of physical causation, the movements and configurations of atoms and nothingness. Epicurus made it possible to observe the traditional pieties and speak about the gods with respect, but at the same time he enabled people to suppose that their lives were controlled by forces in nature rather than by the whims of divinities. In the first half of the first century B.C., the Roman poet Lucretius showed how it was possible to do both at once in his epic poem *On the Nature of Things* about the theories of Epicurus. It begins with an invocation to Venus, "mother of Aeneas's race, joy of gods and men" (Lucretius 1.1). Lucretius describes how Venus gives life upon the earth and brings peace both to men and to the war god Mars (1.45–49). But then he continues: "It must be that all the nature of the gods flourishes in perfect peace in immortal time, removed in itself from our [mortal] affairs and distantly separated; for free from all sorrow, remote from danger, divinity is rich in its own wealth, and needs nothing from us. It is not won over by our devoted services to it nor troubled by our anger" (2.646–51).

If the gods are so remote from human life that they have no influence over it, and cannot be appealed to by mortals because they need nothing from us, is there any reason to fear them, or to continue worshiping them? Inevitably, allegorical theories lead to the same questions. Why worship gods who resemble human beings in conduct and are distinguished from us only because they are immortal, ageless, and powerful? The Roman poet Ovid (43 B.C.–A.D. 17) offers a frivolous answer: we worship the gods because they are what we would be if we had the chance. In his *Ars Amatoria* (The Art of Love) Ovid suggests that mortal lovers should model themselves on Jupiter: "Jupiter made a practice of swearing false oaths by the Styx; you profit by his example! It is useful that gods exist, and as it is useful, let us think that they do exist, and let wine and incense be given to the ancient altars" (*Ars Amatoria* 1.635–38). In Ovid's most influential work, the *Metamorphoses* (or *Transformations*), the gods have lost their traditional dignity. Human beings, on the other hand, have a higher place in the universe than other creatures, and they were created deliberately, as in the Hebrew Bible. Whoever the god was (Ovid does not say) that was responsible for creation, he decided that "an animal more holy than his earlier creations and capable of high thinking was still missing, a being that could rule over the others, and man was born," perhaps from divine seed, and molded from earth and water by Prometheus (Ovid, *Metamorphoses* 1.76–78).

In the *Metamorphoses* Ovid frequently compares gods to mortals. Rome is the model for Olympus. The minor gods live on the outskirts, but the aristocratic gods have houses near Jupiter's royal palace: "This is the place, which if I could speak boldly, I would not hesitate to call the Palatine Hill of the great sky" (1.175–76). In practice, the gods hold mortals to a higher standard of behavior than they impose on themselves. Jupiter appears on earth in disguise to test humanity, and when Lycaon offers him meat from a human sacrifice, Jupiter sends a flood to destroy humankind. He allows only the most virtuous mortals, Deucalion and his wife Pyrrha, to renew the human race, but unlike God in Genesis, he does not offer them a covenant. Nothing exists to stop him or the other gods from preying on humans or from exploiting them.

Ovid's other gods are much reduced in stature. In the Homeric Hymn to Apollo, the archer god dispatched the female serpent with a single arrow; but Ovid's Apollo shoots almost every arrow in his quiver before the monster expires (1.441–44). The poet relates in a few lines how the god then founded the Pythian games. He spends much more time telling the story of Apollo's unsuccessful love affair with Daphne, the mortal daughter of the river Peneus. Cupid shoots a golden arrow into Apollo but only a leaden arrow into Daphne, so that instead of being attracted to Apollo she prefers to remain a virgin. But Apollo does not take Daphne's own wishes into consideration: he sees her and pursues her. She flees, but when he catches her, she prays to her father the river god: "Because my beauty has made me too pleasing, destroy it by changing it" (1.547). Her father changes her into a tree, which the god embraces. From then on, the daphne, or bay, is his sacred tree.

Daphne the maiden exists no longer, but she receives the traditional consolation given to mortals whose lives have been destroyed by the gods: a memorial.

Pursued by Apollo, Daphne turns into a tree. (Roman mosaic from Antioch, late third century A.D. Princeton University Art Museum, Gift of the Committee for the Excavation of Antioch, no. 65–219. Photo: Bruce M. White.)

Hippolytus, in Euripides' drama, seemed grateful when Artemis told him that from then on young girls in Troezen would cut off locks of their hair so that his story would not be forgotten.[9] As Ovid tells the story of Daphne, however, when the river gods of Greece gather, "they do not know whether to offer their congratulations or consolations" to Daphne's father Peneus (1.578). One river, Inachus, is not even present. He is in his cave, weeping for his daughter Io: "He mourns for her as one who is lost; he does not know if she is alive or among the dead" (1.585–86). Jupiter has seen his beautiful daughter and abducted her. Juno was suspicious, so Jupiter turned Io into a white heifer ("she was also a beautiful cow"; 1.612). Juno then asked her husband to give her the heifer, and set the hundred-eyed monster Argos to keep watch over her.[10]

As a cow, Io's life is hardly happy. She cannot speak or otherwise express herself; her new voice frightens her, and she is terrified when she sees her own reflection in the water. No one recognizes her, although her father strokes her. Finally she is able to tell him who she is by using her hoof to trace her name in the dust. Her father is disconsolate: "Now the herd will provide your husband, and your child will belong to the herd" (1.660). The women Odysseus meets in the world of the dead are proud of their liaisons with the gods, but as the result of Jupiter's intervention Io has been deprived even of her humanity.

But Jupiter rescues Io by sending Mercury to put her guardian, Argos, to sleep, and then Mercury kills Argos and puts his eyes in the tail of Juno's bird, the peacock. At last the goddess is mollified, and Io is permitted to resume her human form. "She is afraid and hesitates to speak, lest she moo like a heifer," as Ovid tells the story; "timidly she again attempts the words she had not used" (1.745–46). Now she is a goddess worshiped in Egypt, along with her son Epaphus, "who is believed to be born of Jupiter's seed" (1.748–49). In Ovid's time, Io had long since been identified with the Egyptian goddess Isis, and Io's son Epaphus with Osiris, son of Isis. But Ovid seems to cast doubt on even this happy ending by suggesting that Epaphus is only "believed" to be Jupiter's son.

The question of divine paternity causes even more sorrow in the next story, the tale of how the mortal Phaethon wanted to be sure that the sun god, who is Apollo in Ovid's telling, would recognize him as his son. (Apollo was occasionally identified as the sun god in literature as early as the fifth century B.C.)[11] The boy climbs up to his father's brilliant palace, but he cannot come too near the throne because he is blinded by the light. The sun, to show that he acknowledges Phaethon as his son, allows him to make a wish, so the boy asks to drive his father's chariot. The sun tries to dissuade him, but once Phaethon has made his request his father cannot refuse to honor it. Phaethon cannot control the sun's immortal horses; the careening chariot scorches the earth, and Phaethon falls to his death in flames. He lands in the West, on the shores of the river Eridanus, far from his home in the East. His sisters come there to mourn for him, and in their grief they are turned into poplar trees. The sun in his fury threatens to shroud the earth in darkness: "In his grief Phoebus rages at his horses with goads and a whip (for he was furious) and put the blame on them for his son's death and held them responsible" (2.399–400). Even when a god tries to be kind to a mortal, his powers bring misery and destruction, and his wrath is inflicted on innocent people and on animals.

As Jupiter surveys the earth after this disaster, he sees one of Diana's maidens sleeping in a glade and decides to seduce her.[12] He approaches her disguised as Diana, but he betrays himself when he embraces her. "If only you had seen this, Juno; you would have been kinder to her! Indeed she fights, but what girl, what man, could overpower Jupiter?" (2.435–37). She manages to hide her secret from Diana for nine months, but once the goddess sees her naked, she sends her away from her sacred band. Juno waits until the girl's son is born and then flies at her, throwing her to the ground and transforming her into a bear. Although the girl is deprived of the power of speech, she is aware of who she is and what she was, because "her mind remains as it was" (2.485). For sixteen years she haunts the forests where she had hunted when she was a maiden. Then her son comes upon

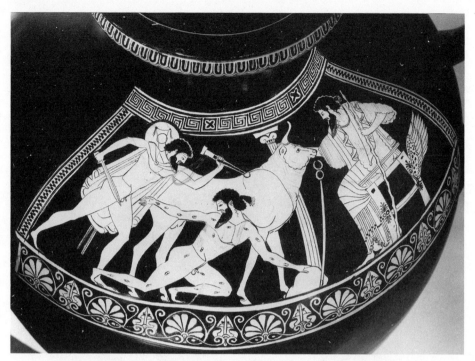

Hermes prepares to kill Argos with a sword, while Zeus strokes the cow Io
with his right hand. (Red-figure hydria, 500–450 B.C., by the
Eucharides Painter. Martin v. Wagner-Museum der Universität Würzburg,
Leihgabe Sammlung Fujita, Tokyo, no. ZA 48. Photo: K. Oehrlein.)

her while he is out hunting. But just as he is about to kill her, Jupiter takes both
son and mother away and turns them into stars, the Great Bear and the Little Bear.
Juno is still furious, and she asks the sea gods never to let those stars descend into
the sea. She departs in her chariot, which is drawn by peacocks. Their tails are
decorated with the eyes of Argos, who had kept guard over Io. Ovid does not want
us to forget about this other victim of Jupiter's lust and Juno's anger.

There are many other, similar examples of inhuman behavior on the part of
Ovid's gods. Diana is as cruel as her brother Apollo. Actaeon, looking for a cool-
ing spring in unfamiliar woods, comes upon her while she is bathing with her
nymphs, for "that is where the Fates were taking him" (3.176). The nymphs surround Diana to shield her from Actaeon's gaze. The goddess does not have her
bow with her, but she throws water in his face, saying, "Now tell that you saw me
without my clothes! If you can do it, you have my permission" (3.192–93). As she
speaks he is turning into a stag. When he looks into the water and sees what he
looks like, "he was about to say 'poor me,' but no voice came. He moaned; that
was his voice, and his tears flowed down a face that was not his own; but still his
mind remained as it had been" (3.201–3).

Diana's maiden Callisto watches as her hands and feet turn into bear paws. (Red-figure Apuleian pitcher, 360 B.C. The J. Paul Getty Museum, Malibu, California, no. 72.AE.128.)

In Ovid, however, the metamorphosis is only the first stage of Actaeon's punishment. While he is deciding what to do next, his own hounds see him. We know what will happen, but before it does, Ovid tells us all their names, along with the details about their lives that Actaeon would have known. Actaeon "is hunted in the places where he has often hunted. Ah! the master is pursued by his slaves! He would like to shout, 'I am Actaeon! Recognize your master.' His mind brought forth no words, and the air echoed with barking" (3.228–31). His dogs attack, all of them; he cries out and waves his head, as if stretching out his arms to them. His friends rush up, calling his name as if he were not already there. "It is said that not until his life had been put to an end with many wounds was the anger of Diana, the archer goddess, satisfied" (3.251–52).

Perhaps this particularly cruel punishment might have had greater justification if, instead of coming upon the goddess by chance, Actaeon had insulted the goddess by boasting that he was a better hunter than she was (as he did in Euripides' *Bacchae*). When Tiresias accidentally sees Athena while she is bathing, she is relatively kind to him, letting him live and giving him special powers to compensate for the loss of his eyesight. As Callimachus has her remark, when he tells the story of Tiresias, Actaeon's parents would have given Artemis many offerings to see him (merely) blinded (*Hymn to Athena* 5.107–9). At least she let Tiresias keep his voice and his identity as a human being. Ovid makes no comparisons but remarks: "Some thought that Diana's anger seemed too cruel; others praised it as deserved because she acted as a blameless virgin; each group had its reasons" (Ovid, *Metamorphoses* 3.253–55). But in the course of telling this story, and the stories of Daphne, Io, and Diana's nymph, his sympathy is not with the gods but with their victims.

When mortals behave foolishly, such as by boasting that they are better than the gods, it might be thought that they deserve to be punished. When Arachne brags that she is as good a weaver as the goddess Minerva herself, and then tries to prove it, Minerva destroys her exquisite work and turns her into a spider. Niobe should have taken warning from Arachne's fate. But she boasts at the very shrine of the goddess Latona (Leto), the mother of Apollo and Diana, that she ought to be worshiped as a goddess even though she is a mortal, because Latona has only two children whereas Niobe has seven boys and seven girls, and she will not feel the loss even of two. She drives the other women away from Latona's shrine.

When Latona goes to Delos to protest, Apollo interrupts her story, saying: "Enough! A protracted complaint delays the punishment" (6.215). The gods do not hesitate to take the lives of innocent people to avenge any slight to their honor. Apollo and Diana go to Niobe's palace in Thebes and, one by one, kill all her children. First Apollo's arrows strike the seven sons while they are exercising. The last son, seeing what has happened to the others, holds out his hands and asks the gods to spare him. "The god was moved, but it was too late to call back the arrow" (6.264–65). When Niobe hears what has happened "she is angry that

Artemis points her bow at Actaeon, who reaches up helplessly while
his hounds attack him. (Red-figure bell krater, ca. 470 B.C., by the Pan Painter.
© 2002 Museum of Fine Arts, Boston, James Fund and by Special Contribution, 10.185.)

the gods dared to do this, that they had so much power" (6.269–70). Her husband Amphion has already killed himself. Niobe tells Latona: "Feed on my sorrow, cruel Latona, saturate your heart with my grief" (6.280–81).

Yet Niobe still boasts that even with seven dead she has more children than
Latona. So once again the arrows fly, until only one child is left, which she shields
with her own body. She says: "'Leave me this one, my littlest; of many I ask only
for the littlest one.' And while she was asking, the one she was asking for fell"

While Artemis watches at left, deer's horns and ears appear on Actaeon's head
and his hounds attack him. (Red-figure Lucanian cup, 400–380 B.C.,
by the Dolon Painter. British Museum, London, no. F 176.)

(6.299–301). The gods were not quite so relentless in Sophocles' drama *Niobe*;
they let at least one daughter survive (frag. 444).[13] But in Ovid, Niobe loses all
her children and also (as always in such transformations) her humanity. As she
sits among the corpses, Niobe turns to stone, still weeping; a whirlwind carries
her away to a mountain in her homeland of Phrygia. This time no one fails to
understand the gods' message: "Then indeed everyone, woman and man, feared
the wrath displayed by the goddess, and all worshiped her with greater devotion
and worshiped the great divinities of her twin children" (Ovid, *Metamorphoses*
6.313–15).

Ovid's gods occasionally reward the pious, and some stories of change have a
happy ending, but the gods in most of his stories are angry and vindictive; they
come to punish rather than to rescue, as if they preferred to behave like Virgil's
Juno, rather than his Jupiter. Their actions seem even more selfish and frivolous
because they are not connected with some larger plan, as they are in epics with a
continuous narrative, as in the *Argonautica* or the *Aeneid*. In the *Metamorphoses*, one
can see only in retrospect why one story follows another, and the narrator moves
back and forth in time, from place to place, and from god to god, in rapid succession. Ovid does not leave his audience with the impression that there is a real

Artemis and Apollo shoot arrows at Niobe's children. (Red-figure krater, ca. 455–450 B.C., by the Niobid Painter. Réunion des Musées Nationaux/Art Resource, New York, G341.)

order in the world, and that in the end the will of Jupiter will be accomplished, except in one respect: the future of Rome. Ovid ends his epic with a description of how Julius Caesar became a god, and a prophecy that his adopted son Augustus Caesar, the present emperor, will someday join him. But in the final lines of the poem, Ovid himself defies the power even of the greatest of the gods, by claiming that he has written a work "that neither the wrath of Jupiter nor fire nor sword nor hungry old age can destroy" (15.871–72). That his prediction has proved to be right is in no small degree a result of his portrayal of the actions of the gods, which enabled his work to be readily accepted in Europe, long after people had stopped believing in the traditional deities.

If the gods exist simply to please themselves, and interfere in human life only to satiate their lust, do favors for their human lovers and children, and defend their honor, how can we avoid their unwanted attention and protect ourselves from offending them, even inadvertently? If Jupiter does not seem to care whether or not justice is done, what order is there in the universe, and how can we understand the workings of fate? One might live entirely for the day, and essentially forget about the gods, or one might turn to different gods and perhaps even abandon the old forms of worship. Once again, it is a story about a transformation of a human being into an animal that gave ancient writers an opportunity to explore the question of determination: Are there governing powers in the world, such as the traditional gods, who intervene in human life for particular purposes? Or do things just happen randomly, leaving human beings at the mercy of an unpredictable fate?

Chance or happenstance seems to determine most of what happens in Lucius, or the Ass, a work attributed to the second-century-A.D. writer Lucian of Samosata (a city on the Euphrates River). Lucius, the hero of the tale, happens to be going to Thessaly in Greece (the region that Jason came from), when he encounters some travelers who are on their way to the town where he has business. When he gets there, he stays with a man whose wife turns out to be a witch. Lucius watches his hostess change herself into a bird, and he asks Palaestra, a slave girl, to bring him the ointment that his hostess used. But when he smears it on, he changes into a jackass: the slave girl had brought him the wrong jar.

Lucius is a victim not of lustful or vindictive gods but of bad luck, magic, and human error. Nonetheless, the effects of the transformation are the same: "I looked all around and saw that I was a jackass, and I no longer had a human voice to scold Palaestra with"; "I was in all respects a jackass, except that in intelligence and mind I was that man called Lucius, but without a voice" (Lucius, or the Ass 13, 15). Palaestra tells him that he can get back his human form by eating roses; before he can find any, though, he has many adventures. At one point he is bought by eunuch priests of Cybele. When the priests turn out to be not celibate but particularly eager to avail themselves of the services of a strong young man from the neighborhood, Lucius, although he is an ass, tries to cry out, "Oh cruel Zeus," but succeeds only in braying (38).

In the end Lucius finds his roses only by chance, just in time to save him from having sexual intercourse with a condemned woman in an outdoor theater before a large audience. Once he has his voice and his human form back, he seeks out the foreign woman who had been paying to have intercourse with him while he was a jackass, but now that he is a man she rejects him. "You have come to me transformed from that beautiful and useful beast into a monkey," she says (56). When he returns home he offers sacrifices to the gods that saved him and puts up dedicatory offerings, even though he makes virtually no mention of the gods during the course of his narrative (56).

Surprisingly, the same basic story about Lucius and his transformation was turned by another writer into an account of a religious conversion. Apuleius of Madaura in North Africa lived at about the same time as Lucian of Samosata. The version of the story Apuleius told became known as *The Golden Ass*, but its original title was (like Ovid's poem) *Metamorphoses*. Apuleius may have drawn directly on *Lucius, or the Ass*, or both narratives may derive from a third source, now lost to us.[14] He tells the same basic story about the adventures of Lucius, including the slave girl with the wrong jar of ointment, the sexual escapades of the priests of Cybele, and the foreign woman's enjoyment of the jackass. But throughout his journey, both before and after he is transformed, the Lucius described by Apuleius happens to hear stories about changes in people's lives, about bad dreams that turn out to be reality, about sudden deaths, and about the work of poisoners. Sex is almost always the motive behind the crimes.

At the start of his narrative there appears to be little coherence in what Lucius sees and does. He runs into some travelers and hears about men who were turned into animals by witches, and about a man who was killed by witches; his informant says that he could not return home because of what he had seen and heard. Lucius goes to buy a fish for his supper at the market, only to have it confiscated by an old friend, who happens to be an official. He goes to a party at his aunt's house, where he sees in the entrance hall a marble statue of Diana. The goddess is surrounded by hounds, and behind her Actaeon is peering at her from behind some trees. Actaeon has not happened on her by chance, as he does in Ovid; he is waiting to see her take her bath, and his transformation into a stag is just beginning. Lucius's aunt says to him, "All that you see is yours" (Apuleius, *Metamorphoses* 2.5.1).[15] Her words prove to be prophetic: sex and curiosity both will lead him into trouble.

At another party Lucius hears a young man tell the story of how he discovered that witches had bitten off his ears and nose while he was guarding a corpse; the witches had turned themselves into weasels. On his way back home from the party, where he has had too much to drink, Lucius believes that he has killed three robbers. He is put on trial for their murders, and sentenced to be tortured and executed, only to discover that it is all a kind of joke: his victims were not robbers, they were wine bladders. A few days later he sees his hostess transform herself into an owl, and he asks for the same ointment. Again, as in *Lucius, or the Ass*, the slave girl brings the wrong jar, and the ointment turns him into a jackass; he is unable to speak, but he still retains his human intelligence (3.26.1). He understands that he can return to his human form by eating roses, but none of his attempts to find them succeeds. It seems that a hostile fortune is responsible for everything that happens to him. He gallops off to find what appear to be roses in the distance, "but this agile and brilliant effort could not prevail against the cruelty of my fortune," for when he comes near he discovers that the red flowers are laurel, which is poisonous to animals (4.2.7).

His transformation into a mute animal gives him an opportunity to hear many more stories. When he is captured by robbers and confined in a cave, he hears an old woman tell a young girl "some amusing stories and old wives' tales" (4.27.8).

But this characterization of the story she tells is deceptive. Lucius may not yet understand its meaning, but the old woman's story, the longest of the many "incidental" tales in Apuleius's narrative, predicts how he, too, will be rescued by the gods after long suffering.[16] Young Psyche (or "Soul") is so beautiful that people mistake her for the goddess Venus. Venus is furious at this insult and sends her son Cupid to make her fall in love with a man of the lowest rank, condemned by Fortune, the most miserable man in the world. After creating this problem for her mortal rival, Venus goes off across the sea in her chariot. Psyche's parents learn from an oracle that instead of being married, their daughter must be exposed on a rock, dressed for a "funeral wedding" to a winged immortal who exhausts the world and terrifies the other gods, even Jupiter (4.33.1). As usual, the mortals fail to understand the full meaning of the prophecy. Psyche is led by her parents to the rock, and she stands there prepared to die, but instead she is carried off by the mild west wind Zephyrus, who brings her to a beautiful palace.

Psyche never sees her husband, who comes to her only at night, although soon she becomes pregnant. She is happy but lonely, and asks him if she can see her two sisters. The sisters are jealous of Psyche, and her husband warns her not to listen to them, but the sisters persuade her to murder him. Psyche lights a lamp and approaches her husband with a dagger, only to discover that the terrible god described by the oracle is Cupid himself. She touches one of his arrows and falls in love with him, but as she rushes to kiss him, oil from her lamp spills on his shoulder and burns him. She tries to hold him back but he escapes and tells her that he will punish her by leaving her. Psyche throws herself into a river, but she is saved by the river god, who deposits her on his banks. The god Pan speaks to her kindly and advises her to pray to her husband, and to earn his favor by her love.

With the help of these gods, and others who will later manifest themselves, Psyche now starts on a long journey to try to recover what she has lost. At first she seems to have no clear plan of action. "She wandered around for some time in many directions, advancing with difficulty, until, without knowing it she approached on a certain path at the close of day a certain city, in which the husband of one of her sisters had his kingdom" (5.26.1). Once she realizes where she is, Psyche goes to her sister and tells her that her mysterious husband was Cupid, and that he now wants to replace her with her sister. The sister rushes off to the rock where Psyche was exposed, and throws herself off in the expectation that Zephyrus will rescue her, but instead she falls to her death. Psyche gets her revenge on her second sister in the same way. Meanwhile, Venus is so furious with her son Cupid that she rushes out to get the goddess Sobriety to punish him, but Ceres (Demeter) and Juno try to calm her down, because they want to stay in Cupid's good graces.

Psyche, still searching for Cupid, comes to a shrine of Ceres that has been left in some confusion by the harvesters. Psyche tries to set the shrine in order, "because she thought that she should not neglect the shrines or rituals of any god but that she should call upon them for their good will and sympathy" (6.1.5). When Ceres finds her at her task, Psyche prostrates herself before the goddess, but Ceres refuses to help her and tells her to leave, because she does not wish to offend Venus. Psyche then goes to Juno's temple, appeals to her, and is again rebuffed; the laws forbid Juno from helping a runaway slave. Venus asks Mercury to find Psyche and offers a reward for her return. Psyche comes to Venus voluntarily, only to be berated by her and savagely beaten.

The goddess demands that Psyche sort through a large pile of mixed seeds. Psyche does not know how to begin, but she is helped by ants, which come to her rescue and sort the seeds with great speed. Venus, still furious, now demands that she collect a tuft of golden fleece from wild sheep grazing beside a nearby river. Again Psyche despairs and wants to throw herself in the river, but a reed reassures her and tells her how to gather the fleece from the formidable and dangerous flock: all she needs to do is shake the fleece from the trees while the sheep are resting in the noonday heat. "So the simple, humane reed taught the miserable Psyche its plan for salvation" (6.13.1). Venus is still not appeased and sets her another task: she is to climb a mountain crag to fetch water from a cold spring. Psyche starts off undaunted only to discover that there is no way to climb the crag. The water warns her not to approach, and Psyche is paralyzed by despair; "but the sufferings of this innocent soul did not escape the solemn eyes of good Providence" (6.15.1). Jupiter's eagle comes, takes the urn Psyche had brought for the water, and flies it up to the top of the cliff to fill it.

Once again, Venus is not satisfied, so she sends Psyche on the most dangerous errand yet: to bring a box to Proserpina in the lower world and ask her to put some of her beauty into it. Psyche tries to throw herself off a tower, but the tower stops her, and then gives her directions to the underworld, along with detailed instructions about how to avoid all the traps that will be set for her there by Venus, how to get to Proserpina and come back again with the box. Psyche does everything the tower tells her to do. But when she is back in the light again, her mind is filled with "reckless curiosity" (6.20.5). She opens the box to take for herself a little bit of Proserpina's beauty, only to be overcome by an "infernal and Stygian sleep"— or is it death itself?[17] She is rescued, however, by Cupid, who wipes up the sleep and puts it back in the box. Psyche takes the box back to Venus, and Cupid asks Jupiter to permit him to marry Psyche and to make her immortal. Even Venus dances at the wedding, and in time a daughter is born who is called Pleasure (Voluptas).

Lucius remarks: "This is the tale that the crazy drunken old woman told to the captive girl, while I was standing nearby, miserable because I did not have tablets and a stylus so that I could write down such a pretty story" (6.25.1). These words warn us not to take everything Apuleius says literally, since in fact we know that he did write down the story we have just been reading. Apuleius now follows the outline of the plot of *Lucius, or the Ass*. Lucius tries to rescue the girl, but she is saved

Psyche embraces Cupid. (Terra-cotta statuette, first century B.C.–first century A.D., from Anatolia. The J. Paul Getty Museum, Malibu, California, no. 71.AD.136.)

Cupid caresses Psyche. (Bronze statuette, 340–320 B.C., from Epirus. Staatliche Museen, Berlin, Antikensammlung, no. Misc. 7806.)

instead by her fiancé. Lucius is sent out to grass as a reward, but he ends up instead being yoked to a millstone and persecuted by a boy. In the original story, the happy young couple is killed by a tidal wave, but in Apuleius their happiness is wrecked by sexual jealousy. The girl's husband is murdered by a friend who wants the girl for himself. The girl avenges his death by blinding his murderer, and then kills herself.

After more adventures and opportunities to hear more stories of jealousy and murder, Lucius (as in *Lucius, or the Ass*) becomes the lover of the foreign lady. His owners arrange for him to perform at a public show, and a condemned woman is found for him. Lucius tells the story of this woman, who had been inflicted by "savage Fortune" on a kind and generous husband (10.24.1). She murdered her husband's sister by thrusting a burning torch between her thighs, and then got a doctor to poison her husband. In addition, she tricked the doctor who prepared some of the potion into drinking some as well, and then poisoned the doctor's wife and her own small daughter. The doctor's wife lived just long enough to inform the authorities. Lucius is reluctant to be "married" to this creature, but he has no hands with which to take his own life. His only hope is that at the festival he will find roses to eat, which will turn him into Lucius again.

While he is waiting at the theater for the condemned woman to be brought in, he watches a ballet depicting the judgment of Paris. Mercury comes to tell the shepherd boy Paris to judge the contest. Then Minerva and Juno enter, followed by an almost naked Venus. She makes it clear when she dances before Paris that she will offer him the most beautiful woman in the world, and he hands her a golden apple to indicate that she has won the contest. As Lucius reflects on how easily judges can be corrupted, Juno and Minerva leave the stage in anger; Venus remains and a shower of wine mixed with saffron falls on the stage. But Lucius is no longer susceptible to the attractions of pure pleasure. He is ashamed of what he is about to do, and afraid of being attacked by a wild animal while he and the woman are on their bed. No one is watching him, so he runs off, all the way from ancient Corinth across the isthmus to the port of Cenchreae. He finds a sheltered place on the beach and falls asleep.

Nothing in the narrative so far has warned us of what happens next, although Apuleius has all along given hints that there are kindly forces in the world, such as the gods and animals who helped Psyche (or the Soul) on her journey, so that one need not be at the mercy of an aimless fortune. Lucius awakens at midnight to see the moon rising: "Having attained the silent secrecy of the black night, I was certain that the greatest goddess was strong in her decisive power and that human affairs were ruled by her providence; not only beasts and wild animals, but even lifeless things were nourished by the divine strength of her light and godhead" (11.1.2). He believes that Fate is now satisfied by his long suffering. He purifies himself in the sea, and, with tears in his eyes, he addresses a silent prayer to the goddess, "Queen of Heaven," who is known by various names—Ceres, Venus, Diana, Proserpina, Hecate. He asks her to restore him to his old form, or let him die, and then he falls asleep.

In a dream, Lucius sees the goddess before him: she has beautiful long hair, a diadem on her head with a disk, a viper, and ears of wheat; she is wearing a many-colored dress and an intricate black mantle. In her hands she holds a sistrum, an Egyptian musical rattling instrument, and she is carrying a special pitcher, with a handle in the form of an asp. On her feet she wears sandals made of the palm leaves awarded to victors, and she says to him: "I have come, Lucius, because I was moved by your prayers; I am the mother of the nature of things, the mistress of all the elements, the first-born of all the centuries, the highest of divinities, the queen of the shades, the first of the heavenly ones, the one face representing all

A Roman statue of the goddess Isis, with flowers in her hair; she holds an ankh in her left hand, and probably held a sistrum in her right hand. (Marble statue, first century A.D., from the Temple of Isis at Pompeii. Museo Nazionale, Naples, no. 976.)

the gods and goddesses" (11.5.1). She is known by different names to all the people in the world, but the Ethiopians and the Egyptians call her by her true name, Queen Isis. She continues: "I have come because I pity your misfortunes; I have come, bringing favor to you and good luck. Dry your tears; stop your lamenting, banish sorrow, for my providence is starting to bring to you the light of the day of your salvation. So therefore pay close attention to these my commands!" (11.5.4).

The goddess now gives Lucius specific directions: on this day her priests will dedicate and launch a special ship in honor of the beginning of a new season. Her priest will be holding a sistrum surrounded by roses. As soon as he takes a bite of the roses, he will immediately shed the skin "of that beast which is most detestable to me" (11.6.2). The crowd will welcome him, despite his sudden change of form. "But this you must remember clearly and always keep hidden in your repentant mind, that your life during its whole course until your last breath is devoted to me" (11.6.5). She will protect him, and see that he reaches the Elysian Fields; she can even prolong his life, if she chooses, beyond the boundaries of Fate. Then the goddess disappears, and Lucius awakes and bathes in the sea.

The storm is over, the day is fair, and Lucius is happy. He finds the procession the goddess has described, and the priest with a sistrum decorated with roses for the goddess, "and for me a victor's crown, yes, indeed a crown, because after I had endured so many struggles and survived so many dangers through the providence of the great goddess I had overcome the savage Fortune that had been my enemy" (11.12.2). After that he eats the roses and sheds his bestial form. The crowd is amazed, and the adherents of the goddess's cult bow down before this manifestation of her power. Now that Lucius has regained his power of speech, he is uncertain what to say, but the priest already knows his story, and someone gives him a cloak to wrap himself in.

The priest addresses him with a kind and more-than-human benevolence: "After enduring many and varied labors and great storms of Fortune and after being driven by the greatest winds you have come at last to the harbor of Quiet and the altar of Pity. Neither your birth nor your rank nor the learning in which you are so proficient were of any help to you, but in the debauchery of your green youth you fell into servile pleasures and carried off an unwelcome reward for your ill-omened curiosity. But nonetheless the blindness of Fortune, while she was torturing you with the most terrible dangers, with her unseeing malice has brought you to this religious happiness" (11.15.1–2). The priest urges him to serve the goddess, and through his service to gain a new freedom.

After visiting his old friends, Lucius slowly and with difficulty decides to become an initiate in the cult of Isis, even though serving as a priest of the goddess will require chastity and abstinence, and avoidance of all unholy foods, as well as great personal expense. His initiation enables him to descend to the underworld, and to see the sun shining at midnight; he sees the gods above and below face-to-face. Once he has celebrated his initiation and spent a few days in contemplation, he throws himself at the goddess's feet, promising that "I will contemplate your sacred face and divinity hidden in the secret places of my heart" (11.25.6).

A year later Lucius learns from a dream that he must be initiated again, this time into the service of the god Osiris, the Egyptian god of the underworld, the husband of Isis. The priest who is to initiate him also learns from a dream that he must teach the rites to a poor man from Madaurus (the hometown of Apuleius), "because Providence is preparing for that man literary renown and great remuneration" (11.27.9). Now we discover what the narrator Lucius had only hinted at before, when he said that a prophet had told him that he would have "a brilliant fame, and I would be the hero of a great history and incredible story in many books" (2.12.5). Lucius, at least to some extent, is Apuleius, and Apuleius wants his readers to know that he is talking about his own religious conversion.

The gods require a third initiation (and more expenditure) once Lucius, to support himself, becomes a successful lawyer. After the god Osiris appears to him in a dream, Lucius, with his head shaved like an Egyptian priest's, becomes a *pastophorus*, a priest who carries a replica of the shrine of Isis in the procession. Once again, he has undergone a metamorphosis.[18]

That the gods are responsible for the rescue of Lucius is not surprising; Aeneas could never have survived without his mother's help, and Achilles relies on his mother Thetis to make his withdrawal from battle have such deadly effectiveness. But unlike Achilles and Aeneas, Lucius does not have a divine parent. Unlike the resourceful Odysseus, he has no extraordinary talents that might attract the attention of such a powerful deity as Athena. Lucius is saved by Isis, even though she had no previous association with him, even though he has done nothing in the past to honor her, and has so far never even mentioned her name. Isis responds to his entreaty, even though he has been self-indulgent and greedy, and in spite of everything he has been and done. She rescues him even though he has been changed into the form of a beast that she particularly hates—the Egyptian god Seth could take the form of a donkey, and Seth was responsible for the death and dismemberment of Osiris. Nevertheless, Isis takes pity on Lucius when he appeals to her in his despair. The errant Psyche was rescued by her lover Cupid in the old woman's story, but the gods of traditional Greek mythology would probably have ignored her (and Lucius), and returned to their feasting.

Isis is unlike the Greek gods in other respects as well. She can be in two places at once, giving instructions simultaneously to Lucius in Cenchreae and to the priest in Corinth who will bring him the roses. "At this very moment, in which I am appearing to you," she says, "I am there also, and am instructing my priest while he sleeps what he must do next" (11.6.3). The goddess speaks to Lucius directly, without riddling oracles, and gives him precise instructions that he can easily follow. She and her husband Osiris do not come in disguise, but reveal themselves to him as themselves. In place of chaos, Isis offers Lucius certainty and hope, because she controls the universe. His existence is now ordered and secure, where before it had been lacking in purpose. She will protect him, now and in the life hereafter. In return, she asks not for honor but for devotion, which will require from him a lifetime commitment.

His religion takes Lucius from the confusion of the world into the special community of the faithful. He receives guidance from the priests who attend the goddess. He dresses differently from other men, and shaves his head like an Egyptian priest. He does not argue with the goddess or complain to her, as an ancient Greek might have done, but waits for his instructions. She offers him hope for the future and, in the present, a kind of peace and reassurance that was completely absent from his earlier life, where nothing was what it seemed to be, and no relationship was permanent. Within the restricted compass of his own world, Lucius has found security.[19]

The religion of Isis provides a ready answer to the uncertainty of the traditional religion. She is steadfast where the traditional gods appear to be whimsical. She can defend Lucius against hostile gods, like Fortune. Isis offers a kind of happiness that can come only from certainty, from knowing what is right and wrong, and from having been allowed to see what other people cannot see. Such happiness is a gift given only to those who have been specially chosen. Readers of Apuleius can understand what Lucius has experienced, but they cannot be what he has become without making a similar commitment to the worship of the goddess who saved him. But even if the reader were to become an adherent of Isis, and spend a fortune, as Lucius does, in the process, what guarantee is there that he or she would receive the same degree of favor? Has Isis really rescued Lucius, or has he just imagined that she, rather than chance, has saved him?[20]

For the rest of us, then, the peace that Isis offers may prove to be only an illusion, the hope that is left in Pandora's jar. The traditional religion offers a more accurate description of ordinary human life. At the beginning of the Aeneid, after the storm in which so many of his comrades appear to have been lost, Aeneas holds out the promise of such a peace when he tries to encourage his men: "Through our many misfortunes, through all the torments, we are heading to Latium, where the gods are showing us a peaceful settlement; there it is ordained that the kingdom of Troy will rise again" (Aeneid 1.204–6). But Virgil makes it clear that Aeneas does not believe in the "peaceful settlement" he talks about: "Thus he spoke, but sick with huge sorrows, he puts on a hopeful face and hides the deep sorrow in his heart" (1.208–9). At that point in the story neither Venus nor any other god has told Aeneas about the wars that he must fight in Latium. Aeneas, despite all the help he receives from the gods, would never have believed that the gods could offer him an existence without hardship and uncertainty, even though he is the son of a goddess.

CONCLUSION

The Gods in Our Lives

Do not be left behind in the house, maiden! You have lately seen terrible deaths, and many sufferings unprecedented, and none of these things is not Zeus. (Sophocles, *Women of Trachis* 1275–78)

When the chorus speaks these lines at the very end of the drama the *Women of Trachis*, the great hero Heracles is in agony.[1] His flesh is being eaten away by a gift that his wife sent him. She had intended it as a love gift, to win back his affection, and when she discovered that it was destroying him she hanged herself. Heracles has instructed his son Hyllus to see that he is burned alive on his funeral pyre, and he orders Hyllus to marry Iole, the woman he brought home with him to be his concubine, and whose presence indirectly has caused his death. He has destroyed a city and killed her father to capture her. Even though Zeus does not appear in person, or at the end of the drama as deus ex machina, the chorus holds him responsible for all the terrible things that have happened in the course of the drama. "None of these things is not Zeus."

Although the chorus is not aware of it, however, Zeus has not forgotten his son Heracles. He is responsible for his suffering. As the audience knows, he is also about to make his son Heracles immortal. Heracles believes that he must be placed on his funeral pyre because he is about to die. That is how he understands the prophecy given him by the Selli, the priests of Zeus's oracle at Dodona, that he would be released from his sufferings, because "the dead do not have to labor" (*Women of Trachis* 1173). In fact Heracles must be burned on the pyre while he is still alive because that is how gods make mortals immortal, by burning away their mortality.[2] As we have seen, the gods look out for their children, even at the expense of other people's lives and happiness. Heracles, because he is a mortal, cannot completely understand what his father has in store for him.

As the ending of the *Women of Trachis* illustrates, the myths, as the ancient authors relate them, do not offer hope so much as a means of understanding. They enable us as onlookers to place ourselves in the world, and to get a sense of what we may reasonably expect in the course of our lives. Suffering and hardship cannot be avoided; death is inevitable; virtue is not always rewarded. Justice may not be done in the short run, although eventually wrongs will be righted, even if many innocent people will suffer. There is no hope of universal redemption, no sense that in the future the victims of the terrible action of the drama will receive any recompense for their suffering.

Why should mortals worship gods who offer them so few benefits? Perhaps the most important reason is that they are powerful; they can change their shape in a moment; they can cover distances in seconds that would take men days or weeks. They live in comfort and health in a perfect climate, while mortals struggle with harsh conditions and constant change. Mortals need help from the gods if they hope to accomplish anything, but the gods need them only to give honor. They did not create humankind, and after the Trojan War they do not visit humans as often as they did in the age of the heroes. That is why mortals must look back at the age of the heroes, when the children of gods were still on earth, to appreciate the full potential of what the gods might be willing to do on our behalf.

Mortals also learn from the myths that they cannot control what happens to them. Certain events are determined by fate. Even Zeus, the greatest of the gods, cannot rescue his son Sarpedon from the battlefield at Troy when he wants to. Some mortals must work and fight to secure a future for their descendants. Aeneas must found Rome even though, as he says, it is not of his own free will that he seeks Italy (*Aeneid* 4.361). Other mortals are forced to suffer for a crime committed by an ancestor in the distant past. When Oedipus learned from the oracle that he would kill his father and marry his mother, he brought the dire prediction to fulfillment even as he was trying to prevent it. Gods persecute some mortals for deeds done by their ancestors or their relations. Because she is angry at Zeus for falling in love with Alcmena, Hera sees to it that Heracles does not become ruler over the Argives (*Iliad* 19.121–24). Only at the end of the *Aeneid* does Juno agree to stop persecuting Aeneas and the remaining Trojans.

But even within the confines of their fate, mortals still have choices. Hector might have prolonged his life by taking the advice of Poulydamas and retreating behind the walls of Troy. Odysseus did not need to steal food from the cave of the Cyclops. He did not need to tell the Cyclops his real name, and he did not need to put on his armor and challenge Scylla. Thus the myths encourage a deep piety, along with a determination to seek in any venture the acquiescence and support of the gods. Odysseus suffers when he pays insufficient attention to the warnings given him by the gods, but he is rewarded in the end because of his piety.

The myths teach us that mortals must struggle to appreciate and understand the advice the gods choose to give them. Odysseus, after he returns to Ithaca, realizes that he must always be on the alert for signals from Zeus and Athena so that he can do what they want him to do, when they want him to do it. The idea that one must be ever watchful and responsive to the wishes of the gods does not change over time. The fifth-century lyric poet Pindar asks Apollo "to look with kind intention upon all my goings according to a harmony" (Pythian Odes 8.67–69). Similar messages are conveyed in the narratives of Apollonius, Callimachus, and Virgil. Aeneas is terrified when Mercury comes to find him in Carthage and quickly prepares to carry out Jupiter's commands (Aeneid 4.279–82).

Ancient writers use myths as a means of reminding humans of the severe limitations imposed on them by the conditions of mortality, and the many dangers present in the world they inhabit. They use the myths to explain that living with gods like these requires patience, restraint, and forbearance. The last thing the Greek gods and their Roman counterparts seem to offer mortals is instant gratification, or the kind of response that would bring them a sense of lasting contentment. Ancient writers seem to be saying that life cannot be any easier for their audiences than it was for the greatest of heroes, who were the children of the gods themselves or their descendants.

As we have seen, some people in antiquity sought to reject the myths. The myths, they argued, required people to believe in fantastic animals and feats of strength that defied reason. Some objected strongly to the immorality of myths about gods committing what in the mortal world would be considered crimes. But in the end, I believe, what caused people to abandon the traditional mythology was not the many fantasies it contains, but rather its ultimate realism: the myths show a world full of evil forces, unpredictable change, difficult conditions, and inevitable death and defeat. By contrast, other religions offered security, and a promise of redemption and reward both in this life and after death.

Isis appears to come when Lucius calls on her. She claims that she is called by many different names: in Phrygia she is the Mother of the Gods, in Athens Minerva, in Cyprus Venus, and so on (Apuleius, Metamorphoses 11.5.2–3).[3] An ancient Egyptian would not be surprised if one god assumed the identity of another.[4] But to an ancient Greek or Roman, such a statement would be remarkable: by saying that she is in reality all the other goddesses, she removes much of the uncertainty presented by a world occupied by many competing divinities. She offers a control and security that the traditional religion, in all its diversity, simply could not provide. She has a plan, and oversees mortal existence; she communicates consistent instructions through her dreams and her priests. All Lucius needs to do is follow her orders, or those of her priests, and he will have a happy life in this world and be a king among the dead in the Elysian Fields (11.6.6).[5] Lucius appears to be satisfied with this new existence, which contrasts so vividly with the life he has led before his metamorphosis. But as Apuleius tells the story, we are left wondering if this security, this antidote to the traditional religion, is not itself an illusion.

In contrast with the structured existence described in the last book of Apuleius's *Metamorphoses*, the world portrayed in the traditional myths is full of uncertainties and surprises. It is assumed that no mortal can avoid suffering, that any human being is continually at the mercy of forces beyond his or her control, and that the dead (even the great heroes of the past) lead a shadowy existence in the underworld. The gods in the traditional myths can suddenly bring evil into human life, even if they have previously been favorably inclined. It may seem strange to those of us who have been raised in one of the great monotheistic traditions to have gods who can be both beneficent and hostile, and who can work at cross-purposes as well as in concert. But the ancient Greek understanding of divinity has the great advantage of allowing mortals to display their humanity: in the face of the implacable rage of Dionysus at the end of Euripides' *Bacchae*, Cadmus and his daughter Agave reach out and comfort each other; at the end of the *Iliad* Achilles tells Priam about the two jars on Zeus's threshold, from which men can draw either a mixture of good and evil, or all evil, in their lives. But a god that is all good, like Isis, takes away from humans the best qualities of their humanity, and arrogates them to herself: "I am here because I pity your sufferings; I am here bestowing favor, and with blessings" (11.5.4).

The traditional myths provide, with their combination of realism and fantasy, a way to understand why it is that disasters will strike, often when we are least expecting them, or that great prosperity cannot last, especially if it is acquired through dishonest means, or that we will not always see justice done in our lifetimes. This way of looking at the world made sense in the eighth century B.C. and the second century A.D. Despite the doubts about the gods expressed by the philosophers and by poets like Ovid, the old traditions continued to be observed. The Greeks and Romans used the myths as a means of understanding how the world worked, and the place of human beings in a universe that was created neither for nor by themselves. Homer was read everywhere in the Greek-speaking world and was still used as a guide for religious observance in the early centuries A.D.

When the second-century-A.D. writer Arrian of Nicomedia in Syria offered advice about the new hunting techniques made possible by the importation of Celtic greyhounds, he strongly advised hunters to observe the traditional pieties:

I declare that nothing turns out well for mankind without the gods. Indeed, all those who care about surviving begin with the gods when they embark on voyages, and when they do survive they offer sacrifices in thanks to the gods of the sea, Poseidon and Amphitrite and the Nereids. And all those who till the soil, begin with Demeter and her daughter and Dionysus, and all the craftsmen begin with Athena and Hephaestus; educators begin with the Muses and Apollo the leader of the Muses and Memory and Hermes, and those who are concerned with erotic matters begin with Aphrodite and Eros and Persuasion and the Graces. Thus all who are devoted to hunting must not neglect Artemis the huntress or Pan or the Nymphs or Hermes the god of the wayside and the guide, nor all the other gods of the mountains. If they neglect the gods, they must come away with their pursuits half-accomplished, and with their dogs injured, and their horses lame, and the human beings will hurt themselves. That is what Homer teaches in his poetry. (Arrian, *On Hunting* 35.1–36.1)

As Arrian describes it, each line of mortal endeavor has its own special patron god, and one neglects any of these many gods at one's peril. This same advice is embedded in many myths: Hippolytus learned that one must honor both Aphrodite and Artemis, because the support of one god does not necessarily cancel out the hatred of another. Even Zeus cannot prevent Hera from persecuting Heracles and Aeneas.

It is not surprising that ancient Greek religion was so retrospective; most religions derive their strength from a past that is remembered and shared. In Arrian's day, and for more than a century afterward, people went on learning about the gods from Homer and other traditional literature. Not only did Greeks and Romans learn from the ancient myths which gods might help them in particular endeavors. They learned what forms of attention were acceptable to these divinities. They made offerings before setting out on any undertaking. The most splendid form of tribute was the sacrifice of an animal, followed by a communal meal in which both mortals and gods participated. Other offerings included the pouring of libations of wine or other liquid foods; hand-woven robes or other favorite possessions might be left at sanctuaries. People might decorate the altars and temples of the gods with fragrant boughs of myrtle. They might sing hymns of praise, like the short anthem that Hippolytus and his hunters sing to Artemis when they return home with their slaughtered prey: "Mistress, mistress most holy, daughter of Zeus, hail, hail, Artemis daughter of Leto and Zeus, most beautiful by far of maidens, who live in the great sky in the house of your noble father, the golden home of Zeus; hail, fairest, fairest of all the Olympians!" (Euripides, *Hippolytus* 61–71). The hunters praise Artemis not for her power or prowess as a hunter, but for her beauty, for being a daughter of Zeus, and for living on Mount Olympus. Unlike them, she does not need to exhaust herself in the search for game, or feel tired or hungry at the end of a day. Nor does she need to fear the effects of passion, since as a goddess she can protect herself from Aphrodite; nor does she need to be concerned about illness, injury, or death.

In the drama by Euripides, Hippolytus was able to speak with Artemis: "For it is my privilege alone among mortals to be with you and converse with you, hearing your voice, but not seeing your face." Ordinary mortals, however, did not have conversations or close communication with the gods. They offered their prayers, and the gods answered them if and when they chose to. If anyone saw a god, it was in a dream, and then it was necessary to determine what the dream might have meant. In late antiquity people sought advice from special interpreters. In a dream handbook written by Artemidorus in the late second century A.D., the gods of Hesiod and Homer play their familiar roles. Of all the many gods, the Olympian gods were still the most powerful: to see Zeus or a statue of Zeus meant good fortune and wealth, and health for the sickly; Artemis can help a person who is afraid; Apollo is good for musicians and doctors; Athena is good for artisans (Artemidorus 2.35). Artemidorus adds advice about the gods that had been imported into the Greek and Roman world from Egypt. Seeing a god like Isis, he suggests, means upheaval and then unexpected rescue (2.39).

What advantages can this religion offer its adherents? Perhaps its main advantage is that it describes mortal life as it really is, fragile, threatened, uncertain, and never consistently happy. The myths portray a world where deities exist primarily to please themselves, not to please or serve humanity. They offer no hope that justice will be done to any individual or within the course of anyone's lifetime. They do not suggest that it is easy or always possible for a mortal to distinguish right from wrong; on the contrary, they show that it is almost inevitable that they will make serious mistakes, even when they have the best of intentions.

In practice, ancient worshipers paid tribute to the gods and did not expect to receive from them any direct communication or recompense. If mortals cannot look to the gods for comfort, they are compelled to seek consolation, so far as possible, from other mortals. They must turn to one another for support and affection, like Cadmus and Agave at the end of the *Bacchae* or Oedipus and his daughters at the end of the *Oedipus Tyrannus*. Because there is no orthodoxy and no one deity to depend on, the burden is left to the individual. It is a religion for adults, and it offers responsibilities rather than rewards. Yet despite its realism, and its clear differences from any of the religions we are now used to, these same stories can still offer a reliable guide to life in our own time. We still have much to learn from listening to what the ancient writers say, even if we are not prepared literally to believe in their theology.

NOTES

INTRODUCTION

1. On artists' attempts to convey the difference between anthropomorphic gods and mortals, see Steiner 2001, 90.

2. Lloyd-Jones 1990b, 78.

3. On Celsus, see Chadwick 1965, xxiv–xxix. Celsus's *True Doctrine* survives only in quotations cited by the Greek Christian Origen (A.D. 184–254) in his treatise *Against Celsus*.

4. Bulfinch 1898, 294, 318.

5. Hamilton 1940, 9, 295, 26.

6. Ibid., 318.

7. Graves 1957, 375.

8. Campbell 1968, 4, 24–29.

9. The earliest reference to the story about Tiresias having been both male and female comes from the lost epic *Melampodia* (frag. 275 M-W). On problems of the interpretation of the fragment, see Lefkowitz 1986, 10.

10. Campbell 1988, 134–35.

11. The phrase comes from Edgar Allan Poe, "To Helen," 9–10. The 1831 edition of the poem reads, "To the beauty of fair Greece / And the grandeur of old Rome."

CHAPTER 1. ORIGINS

1. The catalogue includes all the daughters of the sea god Nereus, the Harpies, Gorgons, Echidna, Hades' fifty-headed dog Cerberus, the Lernean Hydra, Echidna's children the Chimera, the Phix of Thebes, the Lion of Nemea, and the children of Cronus's siblings Tethys and Oceanus, such as the principal rivers of the world.

2. Apollo's sanctuary at Pytho is described in the Homeric Hymn to Apollo (*Homeric Hymns* 3.287–99).

3. In the drama *Prometheus Bound* of Aeschylus the chorus of Oceanids asks Prometheus, "What help is there from humankind?" (547). Prometheus is not mentioned as the creator of mankind before the fourth century B.C., but the myth may well be earlier; see Griffith 1983, 2n.6.

4. On the powers of the goddesses, see Lefkowitz 1989b.

5. On the cult of Hecate in Asia Minor, see West 1966, 278.

6. On the interpretation of this passage see Schwartz 1956, 51–55. It is usually assumed that the jar contains evils, which the woman scattered about the world, but then it is hard to explain what hope is doing in the jar. In fact, Hesiod does not say explicitly what is in the jar or what it is that the woman scattered. But there are jars of good and evil on Zeus's threshold, and before the woman came, man's life was good.

7. Hesiod can tell Perses about the best time for sailing (during the fifty days after the

summer solstice), even though the only ship he has been on is the ferryboat across the very narrow strait of the Euripus. He made the voyage to compete in a contest, won the prize, and dedicated it to the Muses of Helicon (*Works and Days* 650–59).

8. He should also wash his hands before crossing a river, because the gods are angry and give sorrows to the man who fails to do so (*Works and Days* 741). He should not say anything disparaging about a sacrifice that is still burning, "for a god is angry also at that" (755–56). He must avoid dreadful Rumor, because with her power to grow and her ability not to die "she too is also a god" (764).

CHAPTER 2. GODS AMONG MORTALS

1. The Nereids are listed in Hesiod, *Theogony* 240–64; rivers, 337–45; and Oceanids, 346–70. A similar list is that of the leaders of the Greek and Trojan armies (or "Catalogue of Ships") in Book 2 of the *Iliad*; this catalogue was memorized in some schools in the Hellenistic period (Cribiore 2001, 194–95).

2. Tyrtaeus, frag. 11.1 in Gerber 1999.

3. The god often grants a favor to the mortal he or she abducts: Poseidon gives Amymone a spring of water (Apollodorus, *Bibliotheca* 2.1.4); Apollo gives Cassandra the gift of prophecy (Aeschylus, *Agamemnon* 1210). Gods also give compensatory gifts to the mortal's parents: Zeus gives immortal horses to Ganymede's father, Tros (*Homeric Hymns* 5.210–11), and bestows an artifact made by Hephaestus on Europa's father, Phoenix (*Catalogue of Women* frag. 141.1–6).

4. Zeus also longs to protect Sarpedon in the *Iliad*, 12.402–4, 16.431–61.

5. On the Nephelim, see Scodel 1982, 42, and West 1997, 117.

6. *Cypria*, frag. 1 Bernabé.

7. As the poet Stesichorus told the story, Tyndareus forgot to sacrifice to Aphrodite, so she made his daughters "twice and thrice married and deserters of their husbands" (Stesichorus, frag. 223 Davies).

8. On this account of the destruction of mankind, see West 1985, 119–20.

9. Cytherea is one of Aphrodite's other names, for example in Hesiod, *Theogony* 198. On Aphrodite's appearance, see Steiner 2001, 97.

10. On the possible use of images of Eos and Memnon for consolation, see De Puma 1994, 187.

11. On the consequences for women of divine abduction, see Lefkowitz 1993.

12. On Demeter's incantations, see Faraone 2001.

13. On the authorship of the Homeric Hymn to Apollo, see Clay 1989, 18–19.

14. As the lyric poet Pindar tells the story, when Coronis was placed on her funeral pyre, Apollo "came with one step and took the child away" (*Pythian Odes* 3.43–44).

15. On the unusual chariot races at Onchestus, see Teffeteller 2001.

16. On the various accounts of Typhoeus's origin, see West 1966, 379–83.

CHAPTER 3. THE GODS IN THE ILIAD

1. More than a thousand papyri of Homeric texts survive, more than those of all other authors put together, ten times as many as those of Euripides, the next most popular author. The *Iliad* was much more popular than the *Odyssey*, and the first half of the *Iliad* more popular than the second; Cribiore 2001, 194–95.

2. On life and death in the *Iliad*, see esp. Griffin 1980b, 103–43; Macleod 1982, 1–8. *Atē* means delusion or folly, and also the damage that they cause.

3. Homer means "hostage"; it may well have been a nom de plume. Various stories

were told about him in antiquity, all made up long after the epics were composed. According to an ancient biography of Homer attributed to Aristotle (frag. 76 Rose) his original name was Melesigenes, and he came from Smyrna in Asia Minor; see Lefkowitz 1981, 12–24.

4. Just how the *Iliad* was originally divided is a question that cannot be answered decisively, though there have been many suggestions (see esp. Jensen et al. 1999, 5–35; Taplin 1992, 11–22, 285–93; Stanley 1993, 29–32). As it happens, the three sections in this chapter each amount roughly to a third of the total narrative: Books 1–7, Books 8–16 (if Book 10 is taken out of the calculation on the assumption that it is a later addition), and Books 17–24. This division corresponds to the divisions suggested (for different reasons) in Stanley 1993, 261–68. Taplin 1992, 16, not implausibly, divides the narrative by the days on which its action occurs, 1–9, 11–18.353, 18.354–end.

5. On the importance of the gods, see Griffin 1980b, 165–66. The term *Hellenes* came into use only in the fifth century B.C. The English term *Greek* is from the Latin *Graecus*, which in turn derives from the town Graia in Boeotia (*Iliad* 2.498).

6. On the role of Thetis, see esp. Redfield 1979, 106–7.

7. Zeus does not intervene directly in Homer, but the fifth-century poet Pindar describes how he appears to his son Polydeuces and offers him immortality, when his mortal twin brother Castor is dying; but because Polydeuces refuses to abandon Castor, Zeus allows them to live on alternate days in Olympus and in Hades (*Nemean Odes* 10.79–84).

8. A description of the aegis appears in the *Iliad* at 5.741–42. Although its name suggests that it was in origin the skin of a goat (*aix*, from the root *aig-*), the aegis when worn by Athena in art looks like a tasseled stole. By shaking it in battle she or another god can give one side advantage over the other; on its special powers see Griffin 1980b, 30–31. (Zeus lends it to Apollo at *Iliad* 15.229–30 and uses it himself at 17.593–96; Athena wraps Achilles in it at 18.203–6; Apollo uses it to protect Hector's body at 24.18–21.)

9. Achilles says that he and the other Greeks came to Troy to win requital for Agamemnon and Menelaus (*Iliad* 1.158–59). In the *Odyssey*, Agamemnon says that it took him a month to persuade Odysseus to join the expedition (*Odyssey* 24.118–19). According to the story in the *Catalogue of Women*, the other leaders came because along with Menelaus they had been suitors of Helen, and had sworn an oath that they would defend Menelaus if he ever was wronged by another man (*Catalogue* frag. 204.78–84).

10. On the numbers of ships and men, see Willcock 1970, 66.

11. When Paris tells Helen about the battle, he claims that "Menelaus has won with the help of Athena," since that provides a more honorable explanation of why Menelaus defeated him and was about to kill him. In fact both Athena and Hera had stayed in Olympus while Paris and Menelaus were fighting.

12. Homer represents Aphrodite as being the daughter of Zeus and Dione, but in Hesiod she is the motherless daughter of Heaven (*Theogony* 188–93).

13. Aphrodite is often referred to as the Cyprian (*Kypris*) because she came to Cyprus after she was born (Hesiod, *Theogony* 193, 199) and had an important temple at Paphos in Cyprus (*Homeric Hymns* 5.58–59).

14. The Gorgon's head on the aegis belonged to the one mortal Gorgon, Medusa, who was killed by the hero Perseus (Hesiod, *Theogony* 280). According to later sources (Apollodorus, *Bibliotheca* 2.4.2), Athena guided the hand of Perseus and advised him to strike while looking at Medusa's reflection in his shield, because any mortal who looked at her directly was turned to stone.

15. On vultures on the battlefield, see Kirk 1990, 239–40.

16. Homer may have forgotten that Zeus had forbidden her to intervene, or he may simply have intended to give the gods credit for the miraculous escape of Odysseus. See also Hainsworth 1993, 273.

17. In Book 2 the "lash" of Zeus meant the thunder he used to subdue the monster Typhon (Iliad 2.782). On the terms "lash" and "scourge," see Hainsworth 1993, 321, and Janko 1992, 145.

18. The Erinyes are divinities of retribution that work to restore the natural order of things. They avenge murders of kindred and protect oaths. In the Iliad they take away the voice of Achilles' immortal horse Xanthus (19.418) and see to it that men are deluded by Atē (19.86–92).

19. In Book 6 Hector says he knows that someday Troy must fall, yet at the same time he appears to believe that he may yet succeed in saving Troy, when he sees his son Astyanax, and prays to Zeus and the other gods to make him king of Troy and a better man than his father (6.476–81).

20. When Alcmena was about to give birth to Heracles, Zeus said that the descendant of his who would be born that day would rule over all those around him. But Hera deceived Zeus. She held back Alcmena's labor pains and caused Eurystheus to be born to his mother prematurely, so that Heracles, the later-born, would be subservient to Eurystheus (Iliad 19.114–26).

21. See esp. Smith 1981, 51–52. Nothing suggests that Homer or the author of the Homeric Hymn to Aphrodite knew of the legend that Aeneas and his followers went on to found a new kingdom in Italy, which is the subject of Virgil's Aeneid.

22. On Hermes' role, see Richardson 1993, 320.

CHAPTER 4. THE GODS IN THE ODYSSEY

1. On time in the Iliad, see Taplin 1992, 14–19.

2. Odusao is the first of several puns on the name of Odysseus (Odyssey 5.340, 5.423, 19.275); his grandfather Autolycus gave him the name because he was angry "at many people, men and women both, on the nourishing earth" (19.407–8; Russo, Fernández-Galiano, and Heubeck 1992, 97). There are many other such significant names in the Odyssey. Examples include the wise adviser Mentor, the hostile suitor Antinous ("with opposite intent"), the fair-minded suitor Amphinomus ("occupying both sides"), the Phaeacian Pontinous ("sea minded"), and King Alcinous ("strong minded").

3. The root men-/mon- in the names Mentes and Mentor means "think intensely"; the Greek (and English) word for remember also derives from it (Chantraine 1983, 685).

4. This gnawing hunger is what distinguishes mortals from gods, as the Muses say to Hesiod: "shepherds of the wilderness, evil disgraces, mere bellies" (Theogony 26).

5. According to Hesiod, the three Gorgons lived at the edge of the world, beyond the stream of Oceanus, toward the remote dwelling place of Night (Theogony 275–76). In the Odyssey the dead live on the boundaries of the stream of Oceanus, near the land of the Cimmerians, where "Night is stretched over them" (Odyssey 11.12–19). Odysseus is afraid because any mortal who looked at a Gorgon was turned to stone.

6. On time in the second half of the Odyssey, Taplin 1992, 19.

7. It seems impossible to identify Samos with any known island between Pylos and Ithaca; see Heubeck and Hoekstra 1989, 233.

8. The Phaeacians do not believe that Odysseus can be a god in disguise because the gods appear to them openly and dine with them, since the Phaeacians are "very near to them, like the Cyclopes or the savage tribes of the Giants" (Odyssey 7.205–6). Odysseus assures them that he is not a god, because he needs to eat.

9. "The dreams that come through the sawn ivory [*elephanti*], these do harm [*elephairontai*], since they convey words that will not be fulfilled, but those that come out through the gate of polished horn, these accomplish the truth, if a mortal sees them" (*Odyssey* 19.564–67). Homer does not say where the gates are, but Virgil locates them at the boundary of the underworld. On the interpretation of the *Odyssey* passage, see Russo, Fernández-Galiano, and Heubeck 1992, 103–4.

10. On the question of exactly how Homer imagined the axes to have been set up, see Russo, Fernández-Galiano, and Heubeck 1992, 143–47.

11. On the reasons why the Odyssey cannot end at this point, see ibid., 343–45.

12. On omens in the *Odyssey*, see Griffin 1980b, 164.

CHAPTER 5. THE GODS IN DRAMA I: APOLLO AND ORESTES

1. In the fourth century B.C. mechanical devices appear to have been used to raise the gods above the mortal characters, but in the fifth century gods may simply have appeared on top of the stage building; see Taplin 1978, 12, and for details, Barrett 1964, 305–6. Only later commentators use the phrase "god from the machine" (*theos ek mechanes*).

2. Translations of passages from the *Oresteia* (with a few minor changes) are by Hugh Lloyd-Jones (1993).

3. The ancients were reluctant to name the gods who dwell beneath the earth (*chthonioi*), but usually they included in their number Hades, Persephone, and the Erinyes.

4. In the *Oresteia* Clytemnestra appears to have used a sword to kill Agamemnon (*Agamemnon* 1262–63, 1525–28, *Choephoroe* 1010–13), but in Sophocles she and Aegisthus use an ax (*Electra* 99), and in Euripides Clytemnestra wields an ax and Aegisthus uses a sword (*Electra* 154). (That is also how they are depicted in the krater by the Dokimasia Painter shown here on pages 121 and 124; see Prag 1985, 23–26, and Cropp 1988, 110.)

5. Other euphemisms include Euxine ("friendly to visitors") for the notoriously rough Black Sea, and *aristera* (bester) for the notoriously unlucky left hand.

6. Some scholars have moved Orestes' first speech (85–87) to this place, but the order of speeches given in the transmitted text is much more effective dramatically, with Apollo's speech coming immediately after that of his priestess the Pythia.

7. Presumably the audience supposed that Orestes came to Athena's temple on the Acropolis. All buildings on the Acropolis were burned by the Persians in 479 B.C. Construction of the Parthenon began about a decade after the *Oresteia* was produced in 458 B.C.

8. On Apollo's special pleading, see Lefkowitz 1986, 25, 122.

9. Her action also explains the so-called "vote of Athena." This vote was a later custom on the court of the Areopagus, where murders were tried; it was always given on the side of mercy when the votes were equal.

10. It is possible that Sophocles' *Electra* was produced after Euripides' *Electra*; March 2001, 20–22.

11. Translations of passages from Sophocles' *Electra* (with a few minor changes) are by Hugh Lloyd-Jones (1994a).

12. Pelops wanted to marry Hippodameia, but her father, Oenomaus, insisted that her suitors compete with him in a chariot race. Pelops won because Myrtilus removed the linchpins that held the wheels of Oenomaus's chariot in place. But Myrtilus then tried to rape Hippodameia, and Pelops threw him into the sea.

13. Electra's anger toward her mother is implacable; *paison ei stheneis, diplen* has usu-

ally been translated as "strike a second blow, if you can," but *diplous* means "double," not "second"; see Lloyd-Jones and Wilson 1990, 74.

14. On the significance of Sophocles, Electra 1508–10, see March 2001, 19–20.

15. On the date of Euripides' Electra, see Cropp 1988, li.

16. Orestes never explains what Apollo has told him (Cropp 1988, 105), and the term "initiations" (*mysteriōn*) suggests secrecy (Denniston 1939, 62).

17. It is often assumed that Orestes brings Electra the severed head of Aegisthus, but in fact the Greek text says only that he "is bringing not a Gorgon's head but Aegisthus whom you hate" (Euripides, Electra 855–57; Kovacs 1987). Bodies are displayed with great dramatic effect at the end of Aeschylus's Agamemnon (1404–6) and of Sophocles' Electra (1458–80).

18. Castor's father, like Clytemnestra's, was Tyndareus, a mortal, but Polydeuces and Helen were the children of Zeus (Zeus's son Heracles and his twin brother Iphicles are another such divine-mortal pair). Twins were thought to have been conceived in separate acts of intercourse (the nine Muses are engendered by Zeus on nine consecutive nights in Hesiod, Theogony 96–97). Zeus offered to make Polydeuces immortal, but Polydeuces wished to share his immortality with his brother, so Zeus allowed the two to live on alternate days with the gods and spend the other days in Hades (Pindar, Nemean Odes 10.79–84).

19. The seventh-century poet Stesichorus seems to have invented the story that Helen never went to Troy and the war was fought over her image. Menelaus and Helen's escape from Egypt is the subject of Euripides' drama Helen. See Cropp 1988, 187.

20. The assignment of speakers in my discussion of this passage follows that of the original manuscript; see Kovacs 1985, 310–14.

21. Tantalus, grandfather of Atreus, was Zeus's son (Orestes 5); Pylades' mother was the sister of Atreus. But his father Strophius also was descended from Zeus's son Aeacus.

22. On the timing of Apollo's entrance, see West 1987, 290.

23. A small number of mortals become gods: other examples include Heracles, Dionysus's mother Semele, Phaethon (Hesiod, Theogony 988–91), and Psyche. But some attempts on the part of individual goddesses do not succeed: Thetis could not make Achilles immortal because she was interrupted by Peleus; for similar reasons Demeter failed to make Demophoön immortal (Homeric Hymns 2.231–74); Dawn succeeded in making Tithonus immortal but forgot to ask for eternal youth (Homeric Hymns 5.218–38); Calypso could not make Odysseus immortal because he preferred to return home (Odyssey 5.135–36).

24. The story that Zeus begot Helen in order to cause strife among mankind, also discussed in chap. 2 here, is from the seventh-century epic Cypria.

25. Many modern critics find this ending artificial and unsatisfactory; for example, Dunn 1996, 172, says Apollo's epiphany "confirms that the plot that careened out of control was indeed a joke and a contrivance"; cf. Knox 1985, 332.

26. See Kovacs 1985, 314: the Twin Gods "have come to console, not to condemn, their kinsman."

CHAPTER 6. THE GODS IN DRAMA II: APOLLO, ATHENA, AND OTHERS

1. Translations of passages from Oedipus Tyrannus and Antigone (with a few minor changes) are by Hugh Lloyd-Jones (1994b).

2. Laius, father of Oedipus, was the son of Labdacus. Laius had angered the gods by causing the death of Chrysippus, with whose care he had been entrusted. Because Laius

raped Chrysippus and the young man killed himself, the oracle advised Laius not to beget children. But Oedipus was born, and the cycle of deaths continued.

3. The oracle of the hero Trophonius was located near Lebadaea, on the way to Delphi from Athens. Xuthus is detained there because people who consult the oracle must remain for some time, offering sacrifices before they are allowed to descend into the chasm where the oracle is located (the procedure is described by the second-century-A.D. traveler Pausanias at 9.39.5–14).

4. Aphrodite is known as Cypris because she came to the island of Cyprus after she was born.

5. In Euripides' *Electra* the twin gods Castor and Polydeuces come to help because they are the uncles of Orestes and Electra (who was also Castor's former fiancée). In Euripides' *Helen* the twin gods help their sister Helen and her husband Menelaus escape from Egypt because they are "nobly born" (*eugeneis; Helen* 1678). Menelaus will dwell in the Elysian Fields because he is the son-in-law of Zeus (as in the *Odyssey*). And in Euripides' *Medea*, Helios sends his dragon chariot to take Medea away from Corinth to safety in Athens after she has murdered her children (*Medea* 1321).

6. Orestes was said to have brought the statue to Halai in Attica, and the myth of Iphigenia among the Taurians was commemorated in rituals at the temples of Halai and nearby Brauron; see Lloyd-Jones 1990a, 313–32.

7. *Rhesus* was included in a manuscript along with Euripides' dramas, but it was believed even in antiquity to have been written by another poet.

8. Translations of passages from *Ajax* are by Hugh Lloyd-Jones (1994a).

9. The chorus in *Agamemnon*, as it is about to describe the sacrifice of Iphigenia, also finds it hard to understand the will of Zeus. "Whoever Zeus may be, if this name is pleasing to him, by this name I address him. I can compare with him, measuring all things against him, none but Zeus, if from my mind the vain burden may be cast in all sincerity" (*Agamemnon* 160–66).

10. On the complicated question of whether this song is sung by one or two choral groups, see Halleran 1995, 243–45.

11. Artemis does not say why she is afraid of Zeus, but he is stronger than all the other gods, and he punished Hera by hanging her from the sky (*Iliad* 8.18–27, 15.18–23). Zeus punished Apollo for killing the Cyclops after Zeus killed Apollo's son Asclepius (Euripides, *Alcestis* 5–7); see also Halleran 1995, 261.

12. As Ovid tells the story in *Metamorphoses*, Hera, jealous of Semele's relationship with Zeus, appeared to her in disguise and persuaded her to ask Zeus to make love to her in the same way as to Hera. Semele then asked Zeus to grant her a favor, which she was entitled to do as his partner. Once she had made the request he could not refuse to grant it; she was destroyed when he appeared with his lightning: "Her mortal body could not endure the tumult of the heavens and was set on fire by the gifts of union" (Ovid, *Metamorphoses* 3.308–9).

13. The cult of Cybele originated in Phrygia in Asia Minor; it also had initiation rites and ecstatic rituals; Seaford 1996, 158–59, 161. Although the chorus of the *Bacchae* gives the impression that the cult of Cybele is strange and foreign, it had in fact been established in Athens since the sixth century B.C. (Camp 1986, 93).

14. On the birth of Dionysus, see Dodds 1960, 106–7.

15. Earlier in the play Amphitryon expresses similar doubts about divine justice, when he thinks that he, along with Heracles' wife and children, is about to be put to death (*Heracles* 339–47). Similar doubts are also expressed by the women after the fall of Troy.

16. On the inhumane behavior of the gods, see Yunis 1988, 143–44.

1. Homer mentions the *Argo* in *Odyssey* 12.70, and appears to have borrowed the story of the Clashing Rocks from this myth (Heubeck and Hoekstra 1989, 121).

2. Making a catalogue of all the rivers was an impossible task in the eighth century. "It is hard for a mortal man to know the names of all the rivers, but everyone knows the rivers in his vicinity" (Hesiod, *Theogony* 369–70).

3. Apollonius does not mention another matter that would have given Hera an even more serious reason to be angry with Pelias: he had violated her sanctuary. When he came to rescue his mother, Tyro, who was being persecuted by her stepmother, Sidero, Pelias killed Sidero at Hera's altar. The story of how Tyro was seduced by Poseidon is told in *Odyssey* 11.235–59; the story of her persecution and rescue was told in Sophocles' lost play *Tyro* (frags. 648–69 Radt).

4. Apollonius makes this demand by Pelias seem to be motivated by fear of Jason. As the poet Pindar tells the story, Apollo had told him that the Golden Fleece should be brought back to Greece (*Pythian Odes* 4.159–64).

5. On signs of favor from Cybele, see Hunter 1993, 82–83.

6. On Phineus, see Hunter 1993, 93–94.

7. Phineus had explained to Paraebius why he could not prosper: his father had cut down an oak that was a nymph's home. The story of Erysichthon provides another example of a goddess's concern for her tree.

8. The simile was inspired by *Iliad* 15.80–83, where the speed of Hera's ascent to Olympus is compared to the quickly shifting thoughts of a traveler, although Apollonius adds poignancy by having his traveler think of home. Since the simile is based on a Homeric model, it cannot have been meant to call special attention to the artificiality of divine intervention in the narrative (for a different view, see Feeney 1991, 73, and Hunter 1993, 86).

9. On the invocation to the muse Erato, see Lloyd-Jones 1990a, 247.

10. The ball may represent the sphere of the world over which Eros has dominion (Hunter 1989, 113; Feeney 1991, 82).

11. Here Apollonius uses medical language, *akēdeiēisi nooio*, or "acedia" (Hunter 1989, 131; Campbell 1994, 272–73).

12. On the simile comparing Medea to Artemis, see Nelis 2001, 254.

13. There was an ancient custom of calling on crows during weddings, because of the crow's monogamous habits (frag. 881 GLP; cf. Hunter 1989, 200). A raven (*korax*), as opposed to a crow (*korōnē*), would have been a bad omen, because the raven told Apollo that Coronis, who was pregnant with his son Asclepius, was sleeping with a mortal (*Catalogue of Women*, frag. 60 M-W; Callimachus, frag. 260Pf=74.18; Hollis 1990, 252).

14. Endymion was mentioned in the *Catalogue of Women* (frag. 245 M-W) and by the lyric poet Sappho (frag. 199 M-W). When the Moon offered to grant him a favor, he asked for eternal life. Then Endymion fell asleep, so that he could remain eternally young. It was not possible for him to become a god any more than it was for Tithonus (*Homeric Hymns* 5.217–38).

15. On the role of Hera in this passage, see Livrea 1973, 100; Vian 1981, 82n.4.

16. The location of the Hercynian Rock is uncertain, like the rest of the geography in this section of the *Argonautica*.

17. On Peleus in this passage, see Hunter 1993, 100.

18. According to Feeney 1991, 80, Apollonius calls attention to the remoteness and perversity of gods by having Triton change his form (cf. also Hunter 1993, 88–90). But gods change their forms in early epic also, appearing first in mortal form so as not to

frighten the mortals (such as Athena in the *Odyssey* and Aphrodite in the *Homeric Hymns*).

19. The story of how Medea rejuvenates Aeson and then tricks Pelias's daughters into murdering their father is told in Ovid, *Metamorphoses* 7.159–356.

20. Eros laughs and the Moon rejoices "eagerly" when they see Medea burning with love for Jason (*Argonautica* 3.286, 4.55–56).

21. Citations for the *Aetia* refer to book, fragment, and line number.

22. Like Callimachus, Apollonius also tells the story of how the god answers Jason's desperate prayer by appearing on the Melanteion rocks with his shining bow and makes Jason set up an altar to Apollo, the god of embarkation (*Argonautica* 4.1701–18, 1.359–62).

23. In Euripides' *Bacchae* (337–40), Cadmus reminds Pentheus of how Actaeon died for boasting that he was a better hunter than Artemis, not because he saw her bathing.

CHAPTER 8. THE GODS IN THE AENEID

1. On the *Aeneid* as a Latin Iliad, see Edwards 1991, 326.

2. On the Laocoön incident, see S. J. Harrison 1990, 52–53.

3. On the cloud surrounding mortal vision, see ibid., 48–49.

4. On the signs sent by Jupiter, see ibid., 56–58.

5. The Penates were gods of the inner household and probably included Vesta (Hestia), the goddess of the hearth; their being called "great" suggests a connection with the state cults of Rome (Williams 1962, 55).

6. On the function of the disclaimer, see Austin 1977, 92.

7. On the last lines of Book 6, see ibid., 274–76.

8. On the importance of sacred groves, cf. Callimachus, *Hymn* 6.40–41, where Demeter punishes Erysichthon cruelly for cutting down her trees.

9. Achilles seems to Priam like the Dog Star "who brings much fever to poor mortals" (*Iliad* 22.26–31). When Jason is on his way to Medea, he too resembles the Dog Star (*Argonautica* 3.958–59).

10. Creating the shade is similar to the strategy Apollo uses when he rescues the wounded Aeneas and leaves an effigy in his place for the Greeks to fight over (*Iliad* 5.449).

11. Hector tells his wife, Andromache, that he would be ashamed not to return to the fighting, even though he knows that Troy must fall (*Iliad* 6.441–49).

12. On the ease of Juno's concession, see Johnson 1976, 126, and Feeney 1991, 146–51.

13. On the increasing attention paid to the gods' deficiencies, see Feeney 1991, 94.

CHAPTER 9. CHANGES

1. Xenophanes of Colophon, 21 frags. B 11, 1 in Diels-Kranz 1956, 1:132, 128 = frag. 166 in Kirk, Raven, and Schofield 1983 and frag. 1 in Gerber 1999.

2. Ibid., 21 frags. B 23, 24, 14–16 in Diels-Kranz 1956, 1:135, 132–33 = frags. 170, 172, 167–68 in Kirk, Raven, and Schofield 1983.

3. Theagenes of Rhegium, 8 frag. A 2 in Diels-Kranz 1956, 1:52. When Pentheus says that if Tiresias were not an old man he would have put him in prison for introducing the rites of the new god, the chorus exclaims, "The impiety! Don't you respect the gods?" (Euripides, *Bacchae* 263).

4. Heraclitus of Ephesus, 22 frags. B 32, 41, 67, 57 in Diels-Kranz 1956, 1:159–60, 165, 163 = frags. 228, 227, 204 in Kirk, Raven, and Schofield 1983; cf. ibid., p. 189.

5. Protagoras of Abdera, 80 frag. B 1 in Diels-Kranz 1956, 2:263.

6. On Pseudo-Heraclitus, see Jaeger 1961, 127–28.

7. Cleanthes, frag. 1 in Powell 1925 (translation in Sandbach 1989, 110–11).

8. Vespasian himself was not prepared to fall for such flattery, but instead turned it into a joke. On his deathbed he is said to have remarked: "Alas, I think that I am turning into a god" (Suetonius 8.23.4).

9. Aeneas's helmsman Palinurus, who is killed by brigands when he swims ashore, is pleased that a stretch of the Italian coast is named after him (*Aeneid* 6.378–83).

10. In Aeschylus, *Supplices* 299–301, Hera turned Io into a cow, and Zeus then took the form of a bull. When Io appears as a character in *Prometheus Bound*, she is not a cow but a maiden with horns, pursued by the ghost of Argos in the form of a gadfly, who encounters Prometheus in the Caucasus. Both she and Prometheus represent themselves as victims of Zeus: she says she tried to resist the dreams that told her about Zeus's passion for her (*Prometheus Bound* 645–68).

11. An early example of Apollo as the sun god is Euripides, *Phaethon* 223–24; see Diggle 1970, 147. Such syncretism (combining of two or more different gods) was still a subject of debate in the third century B.C. (Hollis 1990, 201), but became increasingly generalized; in Apuleius, *Metamorphoses*, Isis claims that she is the same as Cybele, Minerva, Venus, and other goddesses.

12. Ovid does not call her by her name, Callisto, although he says she is the daughter of the wolfman Lycaon, even though supposedly Jupiter has already destroyed Lycaon and all humankind in the flood (Ovid, *Metamorphoses* 2.495–96, 1.209).

13. On Sophocles' *Niobe*, see Lloyd-Jones 1996, 227–28.

14. On the different versions of the story, see Mason 1999, 217–23.

15. Citations for Apuleius, *Metamorphoses*, refer to book, chapter, and section number.

16. On the function of the story of Psyche in the narrative, see Tatum 1999, 776–82; Kenney 1990, 12–28.

17. On the Stygian sleep, Kenney 1990, 217.

18. On Lucius's final transformation, see Witt 1997, 93, 297n.46; Tatum 1999, 193–94.

19. On the role of certainty in the religion of Isis, see Festugière 1954, 84.

20. On the question of the sincerity of the ending, see Kenney 1998, xxix–xxxi; S. J. Harrison 2000, 238–59.

CONCLUSION: THE GODS IN OUR LIVES

1. The translations of the lines from the *Trachiniae* are by Lloyd-Jones (1994b).

2. This burning away of mortality is the same procedure used by Thetis for Achilles (*Argonautica* 869–72) and by Demeter for Demophoön (*Homeric Hymns* 2.245–46).

3. The language of these lines in Apuleius associating Isis with other goddesses has close parallels in the hymns of Isidorus (second–first century B.C.); see Tatum 1979, 155–59, 183–84.

4. Morenz 1973, 139–41.

5. Being king in the Elysian Fields is a Greco-Roman version of the Egyptian belief that identifies the dead with the god Osiris; Gwyn Griffiths 1975, 164.

GLOSSARY

Achaeans. A term used by **Homer** for the Greeks in the Trojan War, but specifically the inhabitants of the region of Achaea in the northwestern Peloponnesus.

Achilles. Son of **Peleus** and **Thetis;** the greatest warrior of the Greek army during the Trojan War.

Actaeon. Grandson of **Cadmus,** first cousin of **Pentheus** and **Dionysus,** torn to pieces by his own dogs because he offended **Artemis.**

Aea. A city in Colchis ruled by Aeëtes, where the **Golden Fleece** hangs in a sacred grove.

Aeëtes. Son of **Helios,** father of **Medea,** and king of **Aea.**

Aegis. An invulnerable wrap (originally a goatskin?) belonging to **Zeus** but often worn by **Athena,** it is both terrible and powerful.

Aegisthus. Son of **Thyestes** and cousin of **Agamemnon.** He kills or helps to kill Agamemnon upon his return from Troy, and is then killed by **Orestes** in retribution.

Aeneas. The son of **Anchises** and **Aphrodite,** hero in the Trojan War; his descendants are destined to found Rome.

Aeolus. The god who controls the winds.

Aeschylus. Athenian tragic poet; 525–456 B.C.

Aeson. The father of **Jason,** and the half-brother of **Pelias.**

Agamemnon. Son of **Atreus,** cousin of **Aegisthus,** husband of **Clytemnestra.** He is king of **Argos** and leader of the Greek army in the Trojan War, but is killed by Aegisthus and Clytemnestra on his return from Troy.

Agave. Daughter of **Cadmus** and mother of **Pentheus;** she kills her son while in a Bacchic trance.

Ajax. A major hero of the Trojan War; the son of Telamon.

Ajax, son of Oileus. A Greek warrior who rapes **Cassandra** in **Athena**'s temple when the Greeks take **Troy;** the goddess punishes him and the rest of the Greeks for his crime.

Alcinous. The king of the Phaeacians, he grants **Odysseus** a safe escort home.

Alexander. Another name for **Paris.**

Alexandria. A Greek city in the Nile Delta in Egypt founded in the late fourth century B.C. by Alexander the Great, which became a center of scholarly and literary activity.

Allecto. One of the **Furies,** sent by **Juno** to stir up the people of **Latium** against **Aeneas** and his comrades.

Amata. Wife of **Latinus,** queen of **Latium,** and mother of **Lavinia.**

Ambrosia. The food of the gods.

Amphinomus. The most fair-minded suitor in the *Odyssey*, who nonetheless is killed by **Odysseus.**

Amphitrite. The wife of **Poseidon.**

Amphora. Two-handled vase used for storing provisions.

Anchises. Father of **Aeneas,** he is a member of the Trojan royal family.

Andromache. The wife of **Hector** and mother of **Astyanax.** After Hector's death she marries **Helenus.**

Antigone. Daughter of **Oedipus,** sister of **Eteocles, Polynices,** and **Ismene.** Sentenced to die by **Creon** because she gave her brother Polynices proper burial.

Antinous. The most powerful and malevolent suitor in the *Odyssey.*

Aphrodite. The goddess of love and desire, and mother of **Eros.** According to **Hesiod,** she was born from the foam of **Heaven**'s severed genitals.

Apollo. The powerful and important son of **Zeus** and **Leto,** twin brother of **Artemis;** the god of prophecy.

Apollonius of Rhodes. A third-century-B.C. poet who wrote the *Argonautica,* or *Voyage of the Argo.*

Apsyrtus. Brother of **Medea** and son of **Aeëtes;** he is killed by **Jason** while attempting to recover his sister.

Apuleius of Madaura. A second-century-A.D. writer and sophist; author of *Metamorphoses,* or *The Golden Ass.*

Areopagus. The Hill of Ares, site of the court in **Athens** where murders were tried; **Orestes** is tried here in the *Eumenides* of **Aeschylus.**

Ares. Son of **Zeus;** the god of war.

Arete. The wife of **Alcinous,** mother of **Nausicaa,** and queen of the Phaeacians.

Argives. A term used by **Homer** for the Greeks in the Trojan War.

Argo. The ship used by the **Argonauts** on their voyage to recover the **Golden Fleece.**

Argonauts. The heroes who sail with **Jason** to recover the **Golden Fleece.**

Argos. The homeland of **Agamemnon** in the Peloponnesus.

Artemis. The daughter of **Zeus** and **Leto,** twin sister of **Apollo;** protector of wild animals and goddess of the hunt.

Ascanius. Son of **Aeneas.**

Astyanax. Son of **Hector,** he is thrown from the walls of **Troy** when the city is taken by the Greeks.

Atē. Delusion, folly, and the destruction they cause.

Athena. Daughter of **Zeus** and one of the most important goddesses; patron of the Greeks in the Trojan War, particularly of **Odysseus.**

Athens. One of the most important cities of the ancient Greek world; **Athena** was its patron goddess.

Atreus. Son of **Pelops,** father of **Agamemnon** and **Menelaus.** After his brother **Thyestes** stole a golden lamb from his flocks and seduced Atreus's wife, he avenged himself by killing the children of Thyestes and serving them to their father at dinner.

Bacchant. A devotee of **Dionysus.**

Bacchus. Another name for **Dionysus.**

Black-figure. Technique of painting figures on vases with black glaze, used until ca. 530 B.C., when it was replaced by **red-figure.**

Boreas. The north wind.

Briseis. War prize of **Achilles,** claimed by **Agamemnon** when he has to send **Chryseis** back with her father.

Bromius. An epithet of **Dionysus.**

Cadmus. Founder of Thebes, father of **Semele** and **Agave,** grandfather of **Dionysus, Pentheus,** and **Actaeon.**

Calchas. The prophet of the Greek army during the Trojan War.

Callimachus. A third-century-B.C. poet, an associate of **Apollonius of Rhodes,** his most famous poem is the *Aetia,* or *Causes.*

Calliope. The **Muse** of epic poetry.

Calypso. A minor goddess who keeps **Odysseus** on her island for seven years during his long voyage home to Ithaca.

Carthage. City in Africa ruled by **Dido** where **Aeneas** and his comrades land; its patron goddess is **Juno.**

Cassandra. The daughter of **Hecuba** and **Priam,** she was given the gift of prophecy by **Apollo.** She is taken by **Agamemnon** as a war captive, and is killed by **Clytemnestra.**

Castor. Son of **Tyndareus** and Leda, brother of **Polydeuces,** one of the **Dioscuri.**

Celaeno. One of the **Harpies,** who prophesies to **Aeneas.**

Celsus. An educated pagan who wrote about Christianity around A.D. 178.

Centaur. A being that is half man, half horse; the centaur Chiron helps raise the infant **Achilles.**

Cerberus. A monstrous dog with three or more heads who guards the gates to **Hades.**

Ceres. The Roman counterpart of **Demeter.**

Chalciope. The half-sister of **Medea,** and wife of **Phrixus.**

Chariclo. The mother of **Tiresias,** and nymph favored by **Athena.**

Charybdis. See **Scylla and Charybdis.**

Chorus. A group of actors, representing either gods or mortals, which has a collective identity and plays the role of interested onlooker in a drama.

Chryseis. War captive of **Agamemnon** and the daughter of **Chryses.**

Chryses. A priest of **Apollo** who prays to the god when **Agamemnon** refuses to return his daughter **Chryseis,** thus bringing Apollo's wrath upon the Greeks.

Chrysothemis. Sister of **Electra.**

Cicero. Famous Roman statesman; 106–43 B.C.

Circe. A goddess who explains to **Odysseus** and his men how to get to the underworld; also the aunt of **Medea.**

Clytemnestra. The wife of **Agamemnon,** half-sister of **Helen,** mother of **Orestes, Electra,** and **Iphigenia;** she aids in the murder of Agamemnon.

Colchis. The region where the city of **Aea** is, to which the **Argonauts** sail.

Creon. The brother of **Jocasta,** uncle of **Eteocles, Polynices, Antigone,** and **Ismene.**

Creusa. (1) The daughter of **Erechtheus,** wife of **Xuthus,** mother of **Ion.** (2) The wife of **Aeneas** who is forced by the gods to stay behind in Troy.

Cronus. One of the **Titans,** father of **Hestia, Demeter, Hera, Hades, Poseidon,** and **Zeus;** he cuts off the genitals of his father, **Heaven,** and rules over the gods until he is deposed by his own son, Zeus.

Cupid. The Roman counterpart of **Eros.**

Cybele. A goddess whose worship originated in Asia Minor and included ecstatic rituals. Sometimes identified with **Rhea.**

Cyclopes. Monsters who have only one eye. **Odysseus** and his men encounter some in Sicily; others work on Mount Aetna at the forge of **Hephaestus.**

Cypris or the **Cyprian.** An epithet of **Aphrodite,** because she has a shrine on Cyprus.

Cytherea. An epithet of **Aphrodite.**

Danaans. A term used by **Homer** for the Greeks in the Trojan War.

Daphne. The daughter of the river god Peneus who flees from **Apollo** when he desires her; her father helps her by turning her into a laurel tree.

Delos. The birthplace of **Apollo.**

Delphi. The site of **Apollo**'s famous oracle.

Demeter. Daughter of **Cronus** and **Rhea**, sister of **Hestia, Hera, Hades, Poseidon,** and **Zeus,** mother of **Persephone;** goddess of grain and the harvest.

Demigods. Mortal children of gods and the heroes of myths.

Diana. The Roman counterpart of **Artemis.**

Dido. The queen of **Carthage** who falls in love with **Aeneas** and puts a curse on him and his descendants when he leaves her.

Diomedes. The son of Tydeus, and a Greek hero of the Trojan War.

Dionysus. The son of **Zeus** and **Semele,** cousin of **Pentheus** and **Actaeon;** god of wine and the theater.

Dioscuri. Castor and **Polydeuces,** the twin brothers of **Clytemnestra** and **Helen;** they were made gods by Zeus, and protect sailors.

Dirae. Roman name for the **Erinyes.**

Dis. The Roman counterpart of **Hades.**

Eileithyia. The daughter of **Hera** and goddess of childbirth.

Electra. Daughter of **Agamemnon** and **Clytemnestra,** sister of **Orestes.**

Elpenor. He dies just before **Odysseus** descends to the underworld, and is the first person Odysseus sees when he arrives there.

Elysian Fields. The part of the underworld where the blessed dead dwell.

Eos. The goddess of the dawn, who fell in love with Tithonus and asked **Zeus** to grant him immortality, but forgot to ask for eternal youth.

Epicaste. Homer's name for **Jocasta.**

Epicurus. Philosopher who believed that the gods exist but have no role in the world we live in; 361–270 B.C.

Epimetheus. Son of Iapetus, brother of **Prometheus,** who takes in the woman **Pandora.**

Erato. One of the **Muses,** the muse of love poetry.

Erechtheus. The king of **Athens,** father of **Creusa.**

Erinyes. Goddesses who avenge the shedding of kindred blood; called **Furies** by the Romans.

Eros. The son of **Aphrodite;** god of love and desire, known to the Romans as **Cupid.**

Erysichthon. A mortal who cuts down trees sacred to **Demeter;** she punishes him by sending him insatiable hunger.

Eteocles. Son of **Oedipus,** brother to **Polynices, Antigone,** and **Ismene;** he dies while defending **Thebes** against his brother.

Euhemerus of Messene. A philosopher who lived in the fourth century B.C., he believed that the gods were actually people, historical figures from the past.

Eumaeus. A swineherd loyal to **Odysseus** who aids him in reclaiming his home.

Euripides. Athenian tragedian; ca. 480–406 B.C.

Eurycleia. The nurse of **Odysseus** when he was young.

Evander. An ally of **Aeneas,** father of **Pallas.**

Fates. Named Clotho, Lachesis, and Atropos, they control men's fortunes and lives.

Faunus. The father of **Latinus.** He prophesies the arrival of a stranger, who turns out to be **Aeneas.**

Furies. Allecto, Megaera, and Tisiphone; the Roman name for the **Erinyes.**

Ganymede. A **Trojan** prince abducted and made immortal by **Zeus.**

Glaucus. Cousin of **Sarpedon,** and a leader of the **Trojans'** Lycian allies.

Golden Fleece. The fleece of a magical ram sent by **Zeus** to help **Phrixus** and his sister escape from their cruel stepmother.

Gorgon. Monsters that had snakes for hair; mortals would turn to stone if they looked at them. The head of one was depicted on the **aegis.**

Hades. Son of **Cronus** and **Rhea,** brother to **Hestia, Hera, Demeter, Zeus,** and **Poseidon;** god of the underworld.

Haemon. The son of **Creon,** who is in love with **Antigone** and kills himself when she dies.

Harpies. Monsters with the faces of women and bodies of birds.

Heaven (Ouranos). Son and husband of Earth.

Hecate. A maiden goddess honored by **Zeus** who has special connections with the underworld and to witches.

Hecatomb. A sacrifice of a hundred animals.

Hector. Son of **Priam** and **Hecuba,** brother to **Paris** and **Cassandra,** husband of **Andromache** and father of **Astyanax;** the greatest warrior of the Trojan army.

Hecuba. Queen of Troy, wife of **Priam,** mother of **Hector, Paris,** and **Cassandra.**

Helen. Daughter of **Zeus** by Leda; sister of **Clytemnestra** and wife of **Menelaus;** her abduction by **Paris** leads to the Trojan War.

Helenus. Son of **Priam,** prophet who gives **Aeneas** instructions on his journey to Italy.

Helios. The sun god, father of **Aeëtes, Circe,** and **Phaethon,** and grandfather of **Medea.**

Hephaestus. Son of **Hera,** god of fire, husband of **Aphrodite.**

Hera. Daughter of **Cronus** and **Rhea,** sister of **Hestia, Demeter, Hades, Poseidon,** and **Zeus,** wife of Zeus, mother of **Hephaestus** and **Eileithyia;** the goddess of marriage. She harbors special hatred for the **Trojans;** she is the patron goddess of **Carthage,** and shows particular favor to **Jason.**

Heracles. The strongest of all heroes, son of **Zeus** and Alcmena, who was made immortal by **Zeus.** He is called Hercules by the Romans.

Heraclitus. (1) Heraclitus of Ephesus, a philosopher who lived around 500 B.C. and described god as a unity or tension between opposites. (2) A writer of allegories of the late Hellenistic era who expressed skepticism about the existence of the gods.

Hermes. Son of **Zeus** and Maia, often sent by Zeus with messages to the other gods and to mortals; he also conducts the souls of the dead to the underworld.

Hermione. The daughter of **Helen** and **Menelaus.**

Hesiod. Epic poet, most likely from the late eighth–early seventh century B.C., author of *Theogony* and *Works and Days;* cheated out of part of his inheritance by his brother **Perses.**

Hestia. Daughter of **Cronus** and **Rhea,** sister of **Hera, Demeter, Hades, Poseidon,** and **Zeus;** goddess of the hearth.

Hippolytus. The son of **Theseus** and the Amazon Hippolyta. He refuses to honor **Aphrodite** but gives special honor to **Artemis;** Aphrodite punishes him by causing him to be killed by a curse from his father, **Theseus.**

Homer. A name meaning "hostage," ascribed in antiquity to the unknown author(s) of the *Iliad* and the *Odyssey.*

Hubris. Wanton violence, insolence.

Hydria. Large vase for carrying water.

Hyperion. One of the **Titans;** the sun god in the *Odyssey.*

Hypsipyle. The ruler of Lemnos, where the women have murdered all the men; she helps **Jason** on his voyage for the **Golden Fleece.**

Ichor. The "blood" of the immortals.

Idmon. The son of **Apollo,** a prophet who accompanies the **Argonauts.**

Io. The daughter of the river god Inachus, whom **Zeus** abducts but then changes into a cow to avoid the suspicions of **Hera**. She is eventually allowed to resume human form, and is worshiped as a goddess in Egypt; sometimes identified with **Isis**.

Iole. The woman whom **Heracles** carries off, causing his wife Deianeira to send him a love philter, which leads to his death.

Ion. The son of **Apollo** and **Creusa,** and founder of the Ionian race.

Iphigenia. Daughter of **Agamemnon** and **Clytemnestra** who is sacrificed to **Artemis** before the Trojan War so that the goddess will allow the ships to sail.

Iris. The goddess of the rainbow, often sent as a messenger by **Zeus** or **Hera**.

Isis. An Egyptian goddess, married to **Osiris**.

Ismene. Daughter of **Oedipus**, sister of **Antigone, Eteocles,** and **Polynices**.

Ithaca. A small island off the northwest coast of Greece; homeland of **Odysseus**.

Iulus. Another name for **Ascanius**.

Jason. Son of **Aeson,** he becomes the leader of the **Argonauts** when he is sent by his uncle **Pelias** on the quest for the **Golden Fleece**.

Jocasta. The wife of **Laius** and mother of **Oedipus,** who kills herself after she learns that unwittingly she has married her son.

Juno. The Roman counterpart of **Hera**.

Jupiter. The Roman counterpart of **Zeus**.

Juturna. The sister of **Turnus** who was made immortal by **Jupiter** in return for her virginity.

Krater. Large wide-mouthed ceramic vessel used for mixing wine and water, now often categorized by types: "bell," "calyx" (flower), "column" (with cylindrical handles), "volute" (with twisted handles).

Kylix. Drinking cup with a shallow bowl and two handles, often decorated on both the inside (tondo) and outside.

Laertes. Father of **Odysseus**.

Laius. Father of **Oedipus**, husband of **Jocasta**, he is killed by his son according to **Apollo**'s prophecy.

Latinus. The king of **Latium**, husband of **Amata**, father of **Lavinia**.

Latium. The region of Italy where **Aeneas** and his men settle.

Latona. The Roman counterpart of **Leto**.

Lavinia. The daughter of **Latinus**, originally betrothed to **Turnus** but then promised to **Aeneas** according to a prophecy that she would marry a stranger; she is the cause of the war over **Latium**.

Lekythos. One-handled jug for storing oil and unguent, often used as offering for the dead.

Leto. The mother of **Apollo** and **Artemis** by **Zeus**.

Loxias. An epithet of **Apollo**.

Lucian of Samosata. The second-century-A.D. writer of *Lucius, or the Ass*.

Lucius. Hero of **Lucian of Samosata**'s *Lucius* and **Apuleius of Madaura**'s *Metamorphoses* who is turned into an ass by a magic ointment.

Lucretius. A Roman poet of the first half of the first century B.C.; an Epicurean who thought that the gods were completely removed from the lives of mortals.

Lycean. An epithet of **Apollo**.

Maenads. Maddened devotees of **Bacchus**.

Mars. The Roman counterpart of **Ares**.

Medea. The daughter of **Aeëtes**, granddaughter of **Helios** the sun god, and niece of **Circe**; she helps **Jason** obtain the **Golden Fleece** and marries him.

Menelaus. The first husband of **Helen**, brother to **Agamemnon**, and ruler of **Sparta**.

Mentor. A friend of **Odysseus,** and a guise often used by **Athena** in the *Odyssey.*

Mercury. The Roman counterpart of **Hermes.**

Merope. The wife of **Polybus,** adoptive mother of **Oedipus.**

Minerva. The Roman counterpart of **Athena.**

Misenus. A comrade of **Aeneas** who dies and must receive proper burial before Aeneas descends to the underworld.

Mnemosyne. One of the **Titans,** the goddess of memory, and mother of the **Muses.**

Mopsus. A prophet of **Apollo** who accompanies **Jason** on his quest for the **Golden Fleece.**

Mount Olympus. The home of the gods.

Muses. The nine daughters of **Zeus** and **Mnemosyne** (Memory); patron goddesses of singers and poets.

Myrtilus. Charioteer murdered by **Pelops;** the murder brought down a curse on his descendants.

Nausicaa. The daughter of **Alcinous** and **Arete** who helps **Odysseus** upon his arrival in **Phaeacia.**

Nectar. The drink of the gods.

Neptune. The Roman counterpart of **Poseidon.**

Nereus. A sea god born of Earth, with no father; he has many daughters.

Nestor. An elderly and wise counselor of the Greeks.

Niobe. A mortal woman who boasts that she has more children than **Leto; Apollo** and **Artemis** punish her by killing all her children.

Oceanus. The river that surrounds the entire world.

Odysseus. Son of **Laertes,** a hero of the Trojan War known for being crafty and wily; especially favored by **Athena.**

Oedipus. The son of **Laius** and **Jocasta** who killed his father and married his mother, thus fulfilling **Apollo**'s prophecy.

Olympians. **Zeus** and his family, the gods who live on **Mount Olympus.**

Orestes. The son of **Agamemnon** and **Clytemnestra,** brother of **Electra,** who avenged his father's death by killing **Aegisthus** and his own mother.

Osiris. The Egyptian god of the dead, husband of **Isis.**

Ovid. Roman poet, author of the *Metamorphoses;* 43 B.C.–A.D. 17.

Palaephatus. A late-fourth-century-B.C. writer who argued that the poets had transformed normal events into the incredible elements of myth.

Palinurus. The helmsman of **Aeneas**'s ship, he drowns and is the first person Aeneas sees when he enters the underworld.

Pallas. (1) An epithet of **Athena.** (2) The son of **Evander,** who is killed by **Turnus** in the war at **Latium.**

Pandora. The woman created by all the gods on the orders of **Zeus** and sent to punish mankind.

Paris. Son of **Priam** and **Hecuba,** brother of **Hector;** he judged that **Aphrodite** was more beautiful than **Hera** or **Athena,** and was rewarded by being allowed to carry off **Helen** as a prize; her abduction led to the Trojan War.

Patroclus. A Greek hero, best friend of **Achilles;** killed by **Hector** during the Trojan War.

Peleus. The father of **Achilles.**

Pelias. Son of **Poseidon,** king of Thessaly, half-brother of **Aeson,** who sends **Jason** on a quest to recover the **Golden Fleece.**

Pelike. A type of **amphora.**

Peloponnesus. The "Island of Pelops," the name given to the large peninsula in Greece south of the Gulf of Corinth.

Pelops. The grandfather of **Agamemnon** who by killing his charioteer **Myrtilus** brought a curse upon his descendants.

Penates. Roman gods of the inner household.

Penelope. The wife of **Odysseus** who stays faithful to him during his twenty-year absence.

Pentheus. Son of **Agave,** first cousin of **Dionysus** and **Actaeon,** and ruler of **Thebes.**

Persephone. The daughter of **Zeus** and **Demeter,** goddess of the underworld and wife of **Hades.**

Perses. The brother of **Hesiod** who cheats him out of part of his inheritance.

Phaeacia. The land of the Phaeacians, who are close to the gods and grant **Odysseus** safe passage to **Ithaca.**

Phaedra. Wife of **Theseus,** who falls in love with her stepson **Hippolytus** and kills herself.

Phaethon. The mortal son of **Helios** who dies while driving his father's chariot.

Phineus. A prophet who did not show proper reverence toward **Zeus,** who punished him by blinding him and sending **Harpies** to snatch away and foul his food.

Phoebus. An epithet of **Apollo.**

Phrixus. Cousin of **Pelias; Zeus** sent a golden ram to rescue him and his sister from their stepmother. He sacrificed the ram and hung its **Golden Fleece** in a sacred grove.

Pindar. Theban lyric poet; 522 or 518–446 B.C.

Plato. Athenian philosopher who argued that the gods in the myths set bad examples, and wished to banish poets from his ideal state; 429–347 B.C.

Pliny the Elder. Roman author who suggested that mortals who do good things for other mortals should be honored as gods; A.D. 23–79.

Polybus. The king of Corinth and adoptive father of **Oedipus.**

Polydeuces. Son of **Zeus** and Leda, one of the **Dioscuri.**

Polynices. Son of **Oedipus,** brother of **Antigone, Ismene,** and **Eteocles;** he dies trying to regain the rule of **Thebes** from Eteocles, and **Creon** refuses to give his body proper burial.

Polyphemus. A Cyclops, the son of **Poseidon,** who is blinded by **Odysseus** and lays a curse on him.

Poseidon. Son of **Cronus** and **Rhea,** brother of **Hestia, Hera, Demeter, Zeus,** and **Hades;** god of the sea.

Priam. The king of **Troy,** husband of **Hecuba,** father of **Hector, Paris,** and **Cassandra.**

Prometheus. One of the **Titans,** the son of Iapetus, brother of **Epimetheus,** who according to some myths created mankind; he angers **Zeus** and is punished by being chained in the Caucasus Mountains, where his liver is eaten every day by Zeus's eagle.

Proserpina. The Roman counterpart of **Persephone.**

Protagoras of Abdera. A fifth-century-B.C. thinker who questioned the traditional religion.

Psyche (Soul). A mortal who is said to be as beautiful as **Aphrodite;** Aphrodite punishes her, but she later marries the goddess's son, **Cupid.**

Pylades. The son of the king of Phocis, and a friend of **Orestes.**

Pythia. The title of the priestess at **Apollo's** oracle at **Delphi.**

Pythian. An epithet of **Apollo.**

Red-figure. Technique (used after 530 B.C.) of showing figures on vases in the color of the clay by surrounding them with black glaze, in a process opposite to that of **black-figure.**

Rhea. One of the **Titans,** by **Cronus** the mother of **Hestia, Demeter, Hera, Hades, Poseidon,** and **Zeus.**

Rhesus. A Thracian prince who is killed by **Diomedes** during his raid with **Odysseus** on the **Trojan** camp.

Sarpedon. Son of **Zeus,** killed by **Patroclus** in the Trojan War while Zeus looks on and weeps.

Scamander. A river god of **Troy,** called **Xanthus** by the immortals.

Scylla and Charybdis. A sea monster and a whirlpool, respectively, who terrorize passing ships.

Semele. The mortal mother by **Zeus** of **Dionysus,** she was struck by lightning and died while giving birth.

Sibyl of Cumae. The priestess who leads **Aeneas** into the underworld.

Sophocles. Athenian tragic poet; ca. 496–406 B.C.

Sparta. Region in the southern **Peloponnesus** and the homeland of **Menelaus.**

Sphinx. A monster who kills all who fail to answer its riddle; **Oedipus** answers the riddle and then kills it.

Stamnos. Short-necked **amphora** used for wine.

Styx. A river goddess by whom the gods swear their most solemn oaths; a river in the underworld.

Tartarus. A place as far below the earth as heaven is above it, where the **Titans** are imprisoned by **Zeus.**

Telemachus. The son of **Odysseus** and **Penelope.**

Teucer. The ancestor of the **Trojan** royal family.

Theagenes of Rhegium. A late-sixth-century-B.C. writer who thought the gods represented forces of nature.

Thebes. Birthplace of **Dionysus,** ruled by his cousin **Pentheus;** homeland of **Oedipus.**

Theoclymenus. A suppliant and prophet who predicts the death of the suitors in the *Odyssey.*

Theseus. The son of **Poseidon,** husband of Hippolyta and then **Phaedra,** and father of **Hippolytus.**

Thetis. A sea goddess, and mother by **Peleus** of **Achilles.**

Thyestes. Brother of **Atreus,** father of **Aegisthus;** his other children are cut up by Atreus and served to him at a feast.

Thyrsus. A stalk of fennel crowned with ivy.

Tiresias. A mortal who is blinded by **Hera** or **Athena,** according to different stories, but in recompense is given the gift of prophecy.

Titans. The second generation of gods, born from **Heaven** and Earth, who include **Oceanus, Hyperion,** Iapetus, Theia, **Rhea,** Themis, **Mnemosyne,** Phoebe, Tethys, **Cronus,** and the **Cyclopes.**

Triton. A god of the sea, half god, half monster.

Trojan. A citizen of **Troy.**

Troy. The city ruled by **Priam,** on the coast of Asia Minor, taken by the Greeks in the Trojan War.

Turnus. A prince of the Rutulians who leads the fight over **Lavinia** against **Aeneas** and his comrades.

Tyndareus. Husband of Leda, father of **Clytemnestra** and **Castor.**

Typhoeus (also **Typhon** or **Typhaon**). (1) The son of Earth and **Tartarus,** a monster with a hundred fire-breathing snake-heads, defeated by Zeus. (2) A fatherless monster born to **Hera,** guarded by the snake that was killed by **Apollo** at Delphi.

Venus. The Roman counterpart of **Aphrodite.**

Virgil. Roman poet, author of the *Aeneid*; 70–19 B.C.

Vulcan. The Roman counterpart of **Hephaestus.**

White-figure. Technique of painting figures on a funerary **lekythos,** using soft colors on a white background.

Xanthus. Another name for the river **Scamander.**

Xenophanes of Colophon. A late-sixth-century-B.C. philosopher and poet who proposed that there was one single divinity.

Xuthus. The husband of **Creusa,** and through her ruler of **Athens.**

Zephyrus. The west wind.

Zeus. Son of **Cronus** and **Rhea,** brother of **Hestia, Hera, Demeter, Poseidon,** and **Hades,** and husband of Hera. He is the ruler of the gods and controls the thunder and lightning.

REFERENCES

Austin, R. G. 1977. *Virgil, Aeneid 6*. Oxford: Clarendon Press.

Barlow, Shirley A. 1986. *Euripides, Trojan Women*. Warminster: Aris and Phillips.

———. 1996. *Euripides, Heracles*. Warminster: Aris and Phillips.

Barrett, W. S. 1964. *Euripides, Hippolytus*. Oxford: Clarendon Press.

Blondell, Ruby. 2002. *Sophocles: The Theban Plays*. Newburyport, Mass.: Focus.

Bulfinch, Thomas. 1898. *The Age of Fable; or, the Beauties of Mythology*. Edited by J. Loughran Scott. Philadelphia: David McKay.

Bulloch, A. W. 1985. *Callimachus: The Fifth Hymn*. Cambridge: Cambridge University Press.

Burnett, Anne. 1970. *Ion: A Translation with Commentary*. Englewood Cliffs, N.J.: Prentice Hall.

Caldwell, Richard S. 1987. *Hesiod's Theogony*. Newburyport, Mass.: Focus.

Camp, John M. 1986. *The Athenian Agora*. New York: Thames and Hudson.

Campbell, Joseph. 1968. *The Hero with a Thousand Faces*, 2d ed. Bollingen Series, vol. 17. Princeton: Princeton University Press.

———. 1970. *The Masks of God*. New York: Penguin.

———. 1988. *The Power of Myth*. New York: Doubleday.

Campbell, Malcolm. 1994. *A Commentary on Apollonius Rhodius, Argonautica Book 3, 1–471*. Leiden: Brill.

Casson, Lionel. 1962. *Selected Satires of Lucian*. New York: Norton.

Chadwick, Henry. 1965. *Origen: Contra Celsum*. Cambridge: Cambridge University Press.

Chantraine, Pierre. 1983. *Dictionnaire étymologique de la langue grecque*. Paris: Klincksieck.

Clay, Jenny Strauss. 1989. *The Politics of Olympus: Form and Meaning in the Major Homeric Hymns*. Princeton: Princeton University Press.

Cribiore, Raffaela. 2001. *Gymnastics of the Mind: Greek Education in Hellenistic and Roman Egypt*. Princeton: Princeton University Press.

Cropp, Martin J. 1988. *Euripides, Electra*. Warminster: Aris and Phillips.

———. 2000. *Euripides, Iphigenia in Tauris*. Warminster: Aris and Phillips.

Davies, Malcolm. 1991. *Poetarum Melicorum Graecorum Fragmenta*. Oxford: Clarendon Press.

Denniston, J. D. 1939. *Euripides, Electra*. Oxford: Clarendon Press.

De Puma, Richard Daniel. 1994. Eos and Memnon in Etruscan Mirrors. In *Murlo and the Etruscans: Art and Society in Ancient Etruria*, edited by Richard Daniel De Puma and Jocelyn Penny Small, 180–89. Madison: University of Wisconsin Press.

Diels, Hermann. 1956. *Die Fragmente der Vorsokratiker*, ed. Walther Kranz. Berlin: Weidmann.

Diggle, J. 1970. *Euripides, Phaethon*. Cambridge: Cambridge University Press.

Dodds, E. R. 1960. *Euripides, Bacchae*. Oxford: Clarendon Press.

Dunn, Francis. 1996. *Tragedy's End: Closure and Innovation in Euripidean Drama*. New York: Oxford University Press.

Edwards, Mark. 1991. *The Iliad: Commentary*. Cambridge: Cambridge University Press.

Esposito, Stephen. 1998. *The Bacchae of Euripides*. Newburyport, Mass.: Focus.

Fagles, Robert, trans. 1975. *Aeschylus, The Oresteia*. New York: Viking.

———. 1982. *Sophocles, The Three Theban Plays*. New York: Viking.

———. 1990. *Homer, The Iliad*. New York: Viking.

———. 1996. *Homer, The Odyssey*. New York: Viking.

Faraone, Christopher. 1990. Aphrodite's Kestos and Apples for Atalanta: Aphrodisiacs in Early Greek Myth and Ritual. *Phoenix* 44, no. 3: 219–43.

———. 2001. The Undercutter, the Woodcutter, and Greek Demon Names Ending in -tomos (Homeric Hymn to Demeter 228–29). *American Journal of Philology*, 122 (Spring): 1–10.

Feeney, D. C. 1991. *The Gods in Epic: Poets and Critics of the Classical Tradition*. Oxford: Clarendon Press.

Festugière, Andre-Jean. 1954. *Personal Religion Among the Greeks*. Berkeley: University of California Press.

Galinsky, G. Karl. 1975. *Ovid's Metamorphoses*. Berkeley: University of California Press.

Gantz, Timothy. 1993. *Early Greek Myth: A Guide to the Literary and Artistic Sources*. Baltimore: Johns Hopkins University Press.

Gerber, Douglas E. 1999. *Greek Elegiac Poetry*. Cambridge: Harvard University Press.

Graf, Fritz. 1993. *Greek Mythology: An Introduction*. Translated by Thomas Marier. Baltimore: Johns Hopkins University Press.

Graves, Robert. 1957. *The Greek Myths*. New York: George Braziller.

Griffin, Jasper. 1980a. *Homer*. New York: Hill and Wang.

———. 1980b. *Homer on Life and Death*. Oxford: Clarendon Press.

———. 1986. *Virgil*. New York: Oxford University Press.

———. 1987. *Homer: The Odyssey*. Cambridge: Cambridge University Press.

Griffith, Mark. 1983. *Aeschylus: Prometheus Bound*. Cambridge: Cambridge University Press.

Grimal, Pierre. 1987. *Dictionary of Classical Mythology*. Translated by A. R. Maxwell-Hyslop. Oxford: Blackwell.

Gwyn Griffiths, J. 1975. *Apuleius of Madaurus, The Isis-Book*. Leiden: Brill.

Hainsworth, Bryan. 1993. *The Iliad: A Commentary, Books 9–12*. Cambridge: Cambridge University Press.

Halleran, Michael. 1995. *Euripides, Hippolytus*. Warminster: Aris and Phillips.

Hamilton, Edith. 1940. *Mythology*. Boston: Little, Brown.

Hammond, Martin. 1987. *Homer, The Iliad: A New Prose Translation*. Harmondsworth: Penguin.

———. 2000. *Homer: The Odyssey*. London: Duckworth.

Harris, Stephen L., and Gloria Platzner. 1995. *Classical Mythology*. Mountain View, Calif.: Mayfield.

Harrison, E. L. 1990. Divine Action in Aeneid Book 2. In *Oxford Readings in Vergil's Aeneid*, edited by S. J. Harrison, 46–59. Oxford: Oxford University Press.

Harrison, S. J. 1990. *Vergil, Aeneid 10*. Oxford: Clarendon Press.

———. 2000. *Apuleius: A Latin Sophist*. Oxford: Clarendon Press.

Heubeck, Alfred, and Arie Hoekstra. 1989. *A Commentary on Homer's Odyssey: Books 9–16*. Oxford: Clarendon Press.

Hollis, A. S. 1990. *Callimachus: Hecale*. Oxford: Clarendon Press.

Hopkinson, N. 1984. *Callimachus: Hymn to Demeter*. Cambridge: Cambridge University Press.

Hunter, Richard L. 1989. *Apollonius of Rhodes: Argonautica Book 3*. Cambridge: Cambridge University Press.

———. 1993. *The Argonautica of Apollonius: Literary Studies*. Cambridge: Cambridge University Press.

———. 1995. *Apollonius of Rhodes: Jason and the Golden Fleece*. Oxford: Oxford University Press.

Jaeger, Werner W. 1961. *Early Christianity and Greek Paideia*. Cambridge: Harvard University Press.

Janko, Richard. 1992. *The Iliad: A Commentary, Books 13–16*. Cambridge: Cambridge University Press.

Jensen, Minna Skafte, et al. 1999. SO Debate: Dividing Homer: When and How Were the Iliad and the *Odyssey* Divided into Songs? *Symbolae Osloenses* 74:5–91.

Johnson, W. R. 1976. *Darkness Visible: A Study of Vergil's Aeneid*. Berkeley: University of California Press.

Kenney, E. J. 1990. *Apuleius, Cupid and Psyche*. Cambridge: Cambridge University Press.

———. 1998. *Apuleius, The Golden Ass*. Harmondsworth: Penguin.

Kirk, G. S., J. E. Raven, and M. Schofield. 1983. *The Presocratic Philosophers*. 2d ed. Cambridge: Cambridge University Press.

Kirk, Geoffrey S. 1970. *The Bacchae. A Translation with Commentary*. Englewood Cliffs, N.J.: Prentice Hall.

———. 1974. *The Nature of Greek Myths*. New York: Penguin.

———. 1990. *The Iliad: A Commentary, Books 5–8*. Cambridge: Cambridge University Press.

Knox, Bernard. 1985. Euripides. In *Cambridge History of Classical Literature 1*, edited by P. E. Easterling and Bernard Knox, 316–38. Cambridge: Cambridge University Press.

———. 1990. Introduction. In Homer, *The Iliad*, translated by Robert Fagles, 3–64. New York: Viking.

———. 1996. Introduction. In Homer, *The Odyssey*, translated by Robert Fagles, 3–64. New York: Viking.

Kovacs, David. 1985. Castor in Euripides' Electra. *Classical Quarterly* 35, no. 2: 306–14.

———. 1987. Where Is Aegisthus' Head? *Classical Philology* 82:139–41.

———, ed. and trans. 1994. *Euripides: Cyclops, Alcestis, Medea*. Cambridge: Harvard University Press.

———. 1995. *Euripides 2: Children of Heracles, Hippolytus, Andromache, Hecuba*. Cambridge: Harvard University Press.

———. 1998. *Euripides 3: Suppliant Women, Electra, Heracles*. Cambridge: Harvard University Press.

———. 1999. *Euripides 4: Trojan Women, Iphigenia Among the Taurians, Ion*. Cambridge: Harvard University Press.

———. 2002a. *Euripides 5: Helen, Phoenician Women, Orestes*. Cambridge: Harvard University Press.

———. 2002b. *Euripides 6: Bacchae, Iphigenia at Aulis, Rhesus*. Cambridge: Harvard University Press.

Lattimore, Richmond. 1951. *The Iliad of Homer*. Chicago: University of Chicago Press.

Lee, K. H. 1997. *Euripides, Ion.* Warminster: Aris and Phillips.

Lefkowitz, Mary R. 1981. *The Lives of the Greek Poets.* Baltimore: Johns Hopkins University Press.

———. 1986. *Women in Greek Myth.* Baltimore: Johns Hopkins University Press.

———. 1989a. "Impiety" and "Atheism" in Euripides' Dramas. *Classical Quarterly* 39:70–82.

———. 1989b. The Powers of the Primeval Goddesses. *The American Scholar* 58:586–91.

———. 1993. Seduction and Rape in Greek Myth. In *Consent and Coercion to Sex and Marriage in Ancient and Medieval Societies,* 17–37. Cambridge: Harvard University Press.

Livrea, Enrico. 1973. *Apollonii Rhodii Argonauticon Liber 4.* Florence: La Nuova Italia.

Lloyd-Jones, Hugh. 1983. *The Justice of Zeus.* 2d ed. Sather Classical Lectures, vol. 41.

———. 1990a. *Academic Papers: Greek Comedy, Hellenistic Literature, Greek Religion, and Miscellanea.* Oxford: Clarendon Press.

———. 1990b. *Academic Papers: Greek Epic, Lyric, and Tragedy.* Oxford: Clarendon Press.

———. 1993. *Aeschylus, The Oresteia.* Berkeley: University of California Press.

———. 1994a. *Sophocles 1: Ajax, Electra, Oedipus Tyrannus.* Cambridge: Harvard University Press.

———. 1994b. *Sophocles 2: Antigone, The Women of Trachis, Philoctetes, Oedipus at Colonus.* Cambridge: Harvard University Press.

———. 1996. *Sophocles 3: Fragments.* Cambridge: Harvard University Press.

Lloyd-Jones, Hugh, and Nigel Wilson. 1990. *Sophoclea.* Oxford: Clarendon Press.

McKay, A. G. 1990. *Aeneid, Book 11.* Warminster: Aris and Phillips.

Macleod, Colin. 1982. *Homer, Iliad Book 24.* Cambridge: Cambridge University Press.

Mandelbaum, Allen. 1981. *The Aeneid of Virgil.* New York: Bantam.

March, Jenny. 1998. *Dictionary of Classical Mythology.* London: Cassell.

———. 2001. *Sophocles: Electra.* Warminster: Aris and Phillips.

Mason, H. J. 1999. Fabula Graecanica: Apuleius and His Greek Sources. In *Oxford Readings in the Roman Novel,* edited by S. J. Harrison, 217–36. Oxford: Oxford University Press.

Melville, A. D. 1986. *Ovid, Metamorphoses.* Oxford: Oxford University Press.

Merkelbach, R., and M. L. West. 1967. *Fragmenta Hesiodea.* Oxford: Clarendon Press.

Mikalson, Jon D. 1991. *Honor Thy Gods: Popular Religion in Greek Tragedy.* Chapel Hill: University of North Carolina Press.

Morenz, Siegfried. 1973 [1960]. *Egyptian Religion.* Translated by Ann E. Keep. Ithaca: Cornell University Press.

Morford, Mark P. O., and Robert J. Lenardon. 1991. *Classical Mythology.* New York: Longman.

Morwood, James. 1999. *Euripides, Iphigenia Among the Taurians, Bacchae, Iphigenia at Aulis, Rhesus.* Oxford: Oxford University Press.

———. 2000. *Euripides, Hecuba, Trojan Women, Andromache.* Oxford: Oxford University Press.

Nelis, Damien P. 2001. Apollonius and Virgil. In *A Companion to Apollonius Rhodius,* edited by Theodore D. Papanghelis and Antonius Rengakos, 237–59. Leiden: Brill.

Nisetich, Frank. 2001. *The Poems of Callimachus.* Oxford: Oxford University Press.

Nock, Arthur Darby. 1933. *Conversion.* Oxford: Clarendon Press.

———. 1972. Greek Religious Attitudes. In *Essays on Religion and the Ancient World,* edited by Zeph Stewart, 534–50. Oxford: Clarendon Press.

———. 1996. *Sallustius: Concerning the Gods and the Universe.* Chicago: Ares.

Podlecki, Anthony J. 1989. *Aeschylus, Eumenides*. Warminster: Aris and Phillips.

Powell, J. U. 1925. *Collectanea Alexandrina*. Oxford: Clarendon Press.

Prag, A. J. N. W. 1985. *The Oresteia*. Chicago: Bolchazy-Carducci.

Price, Simon. 1999. *Religions of the Ancient Greeks*. Cambridge: Cambridge University Press.

Redfield, James. 1979. The Proem of the Iliad: Homer's Art. *Classical Philology* 74:95–110.

Richardson, Nicholas. 1993. *The Iliad: A Commentary*, Books 21–24. Cambridge: Cambridge University Press.

Russo, Joseph, Manuel Fernández-Galiano, and Alfred Heubeck. 1992. *A Commentary on Homer's Odyssey: Books 17–24*. Oxford: Clarendon Press.

Sandbach, F. H. *The Stoics*. 1989. Indianapolis: Hackett.

Schwartz, Eduard. 1956. Prometheus bei Hesiod. In *Gesammlete Schriften*, vol. 2: 42–62. Berlin: Walter de Gruyter.

Scodel, Ruth. 1982. The Achaean Wall and the Myth of Destruction. *Harvard Studies in Classical Philology* 86.

Seaford, Richard. 1996. *Euripides, Bacchae*. Warminster: Aris and Phillips.

Segal, Robert A. 1990. *Joseph Campbell: An Introduction*. New York: Penguin.

———. 1999. *Theorizing About Myth*. Amherst: University of Massachusetts Press.

Shelmerdine, Susan C. 1995. *The Homeric Hymns*. Newburyport, Mass.: Focus.

Shewring, Walter. 1980. *The Odyssey*. New York: Oxford University Press.

Sissa, Giulia, and Marcel Detienne. 1989. *La vie quotidienne des dieux grecs*. Paris: Hachette.

Smith, Peter M. 1981. Aineiadai as Patrons of Iliad 20 and the Homeric Hymn to Aphrodite. *Harvard Studies in Classical Philology* 85:17–58.

Solodow, Joseph B. 1988. *The World of Ovid's Metamorphoses*. Chapel Hill: University of North Carolina Press.

Stanley, Keith. 1993. *The Shield of Homer: Narrative Structure in the Iliad*. Princeton: Princeton University Press.

Steiner, Deborah Tarn. 2001. *Images in Mind: Statues in Archaic and Classical Greek Literature and Thought*. Princeton: Princeton University Press.

Taplin, Oliver. 1978. *Greek Tragedy in Action*. Berkeley: University of California Press.

———. 1992. *Homeric Soundings: The Shaping of the Iliad*. Oxford: Oxford University Press.

Tatum, James. 1979. *Apuleius and The Golden Ass*. Ithaca: Cornell University Press.

———. 1999. The Tales in Apuleius' Metamorphoses. In *Oxford Readings in the Roman Novel*, edited by S. J. Harrison, 157–94. Oxford: Oxford University Press.

Teffeteller, Annette. 2001. The Chariot Rite at Onchestos: Homeric Hymn to Apollo 229–238. *Journal of Hellenic Studies* 121:159–66.

Tracy, Steven V. 1990. *The Story of the Odyssey*. Princeton: Princeton University Press.

Vian, Francis. 1981. *Apollonios de Rhodes, Argonautiques Chant 4*. Paris: Les Belles Lettres.

Walsh, P. G. 1994. *Apuleius, The Golden Ass*. Oxford: Oxford University Press.

West, David. 1991. *Virgil, The Aeneid: A New Prose Translation*. Harmondsworth: Penguin.

West, M. L. 1966. *Hesiod, Theogony*. Oxford: Clarendon Press.

———. 1978. *Hesiod: Works and Days*. Oxford: Clarendon Press.

———. 1985. *The Hesiodic Catalogue of Women*. Oxford: Clarendon Press.

———. 1987. *Euripides, Orestes*. Warminster: Aris and Phillips.

———. 1988. *Hesiod, Theogony, Works and Days: A New Translation*. New York: Oxford University Press.

———. 1989. *Iambi et Elegi Graeci ante Alexandrum Cantati*. 2d ed. Oxford: Clarendon Press.

———. 1997. *The East Face of Helicon: West Asiatic Elements in Greek Poetry and Myth.* Oxford: Clarendon Press.

———. 2003. *Homeric Hymns, Homeric Apocrypha, Lives of Homer.* Cambridge: Harvard University Press.

Willcock, M. M. 1970. *A Commentary on Homer's Iliad, Books 1–6.* London: Macmillan.

Williams, R. D. 1962. *Aeneid, Book 3.* Oxford: Clarendon Press.

Winnington-Ingram, R. P. 1980. *Sophocles: An Interpretation.* Cambridge: Cambridge University Press.

———. 1983. *Studies in Aeschylus.* Cambridge: Cambridge University Press.

Witt, R. E. 1997. *Isis in the Ancient World.* Baltimore: Johns Hopkins University Press.

Yunis, Harvey. 1988. *A New Creed: Fundamental Religious Beliefs in the Athenian Polis and Euripidean Drama.* Goettingen: Vandenhoeck and Ruprecht.

Zaidman, Louise Bruit, and Pauline Schmidt Pantel. 1992. *Religion in the Ancient Greek City.* Translated by Paul Cartledge. Cambridge: Cambridge University Press.

RECOMMENDATIONS FOR
FURTHER READING

CHAPTER 1

On Hesiod: Caldwell 1987 (with translation); West 1988 (translation)

CHAPTER 2

On the *Catalogue of Women*: West 1985
On the Homeric Hymns: Clay 1989; Shelmerdine 1995 (with translation)

CHAPTER 3

On the role of the gods: Lloyd-Jones 1983, 2–27; Griffin 1980b, 144–204
Introductions to the *Iliad*: Griffin 1980a, 16–45; Macleod 1982, 1–35; Knox 1990
Translations: Lattimore 1951 (verse); Hammond 1987 (prose); Fagles 1990 (verse)

CHAPTER 4

On the role of the gods: Lloyd-Jones 1983, 28–32
Introductions to the *Odyssey*: Griffin 1980a, 46–76; Griffin 1987; Tracy 1990; Knox 1996
Translations: Shewring 1980 (prose); Hammond 2000 (prose); Fagles 1996 (verse)

CHAPTER 5

On the gods in the *Oresteia*: Winnington-Ingram 1983, 132–74; Lloyd-Jones 1990b, 238–61
On the gods in Euripides: Lefkowitz 1989b

On plays discussed in this chapter

Oresteia: Winnington-Ingram 1983, 73–131; Lloyd-Jones 1993 (with translation); Podlecki 1989 (with translation); Winnington-Ingram 1980, 217–47
Sophocles, *Electra*: March 2001 (with translation); Lloyd-Jones 1994a (translation)
Euripides, *Electra*: Cropp 1988 (with translation)
Euripides, *Orestes*: West 1987 (with translation); Kovacs 1998 (translation); Kovacs 2002a (translation)

CHAPTER 6

On ancient Greek attitudes toward the gods: Mikalson 1991, esp. 203–36; Zaidman and Pantel 1992, 176–206; Price 1999, 11–46

Translations
Oedipus Tyrannus: Lloyd-Jones 1994a; Fagles 1982
Antigone: Fagles 1982; Lloyd-Jones 1994b; Blondell 2002
Ion: Burnett 1970; Lee 1997; Kovacs 1999
Helen: Kovacs 2002a
Medea: Kovacs 1994
Iphigenia Among the Taurians: Morwood 1999; Cropp 2000
Rhesus: Morwood 1999; Kovacs 2002b

Ajax: Lloyd-Jones, 1994a
Trojan Women: Barlow 1986; Kovacs 1999; Morwood 2000
Hippolytus: Kovacs 1995; Halleran 1995
Bacchae: Kirk 1970; Seaford 1996; Esposito 1998; Morwood 1999; Kovacs 2002b

CHAPTER 7

On the gods in Apollonius: Feeney 1991, 57–98; Hunter 1993, 75–100
Introduction to Apollonius: Hunter 1993
Introduction to Callimachus: Nisetich 2001

Translations

Of Apollonius: Hunter 1995
Of Callimachus, Hymn 5: Nisetich 2001; Bulloch 1985
Of Callimachus, Hymn 6: Hopkinson 1984

CHAPTER 8

On the gods in Virgil: Feeney 1991, 129–87
Introduction to Virgil: Griffin 1986
Translations: Mandelbaum 1981; D. West 1991; S. J. Harrison 1990 (Book 10); McKay
  1990 (Book 11)

CHAPTER 9

On the gods in Ovid: Galinsky 1975, 162–73; Solodow 1988, 89–96
On Cupid and Psyche in Apuleius: Kenney 1990, 12–28
On Isis in Apuleius: Nock 1933, 138–55; Festugière 1954, 68–84; Witt 1997, 158–84;
  Tatum 1979, 81–91

Translations

Ovid, *Metamorphoses:* Melville 1986
Lucian, *Lucius:* Casson 1962, 58–94
Apuleius, *Metamorphoses:* Walsh 1994; Kenney 1998

INDEX

Agamemnon
    and Aegisthus, 87, 89, 110, 115
    and Ajax, 153
    and Choephoroe, 123, 125, 130
    and Electra (Euripides), 133, 134, 135
    and Electra (Sophocles), 131, 132
    and Eumenides, 128
    and Iliad, 55–60, 63, 66, 67, 68–69,
        75, 85, 119
    illustrations of, 117, 118, 121
    and Iphigenia Among the Taurians, 152
    and Odyssey, 99, 110, 114–15
    and Orestes, 137
    and Trojan War, 116
    and Trojan Women, 154
Agamemnon (Aeschylus)
    chorus of, 116–17, 119, 120, 122, 163
    Electra (Sophocles) compared to, 131
    and role of gods, 114, 116–22, 247n9
Agave, 159, 161, 163, 166, 237, 239
Age of Fable, The (Bulfinch), 6–7
Agelaus, 108
Agenor, 78
Ahuramazda, 209
Ajax
    and Ajax, 153, 163
    and Iliad, 55, 60, 64, 65, 66, 67, 68, 69,
        70, 72–73, 80
    strength of, 54
Ajax (son of Oileus), 85, 154, 155, 156
Ajax (Sophocles), 153, 156, 163
Alcinous, 92, 93, 94–95, 111, 182–83,
    186
Alcmena, 31, 32, 69, 167, 235
Allecto, 200, 202, 207, 208
Allegories, 211–14
Amata, 200, 203, 204
Amphinomus, 105–6, 107, 108
Amphion, 220
Amphitrite, 183
Amphitryon, 167, 247n15
Amycus, 174
Ancaeus, 175
Anchises
    and Aeneid, 191, 192, 193, 195, 197, 199,
        206
    and Aphrodite, 36–40, 191
    illustration of, 194
    and Theogony, 31

Andromache, 72
Antigone
    and Antigone, 146–48
    and human suffering, 166
    and justice, 162
Antigone (Sophocles)
    and chorus, 146, 147, 148, 149
    and role of gods, 146–49
Antinous, 105, 108, 110, 111
Antony, 201
Aphrodite
    and Aeneas, 21, 62
    and Argonautica, 172, 174, 176, 177,
        178, 185, 186, 207
    and Bacchae, 161
    birth of, 16
    and Clytemnestra, 126
    and creation of women, 25
    Demeter compared to, 43, 44
    and Hera, 69
    and Hippolytus, 156, 157, 158, 161, 166
    Homeric Hymn to, 36, 50, 52, 191, 192
    and Iliad, 60–62, 76, 77, 80, 185, 192
    and Ion, 150
    and mortal men, 36–40
    and Odyssey, 106
    and Paris, 2, 3, 56, 57, 60
    and Rhesus, 152, 163
    and Trojan War, 53
    and Tyndareus's daughters, 35
    See also Venus
Apollo
    and Aeneid, 191, 193, 195, 198, 199, 201,
        202, 203
    and Aetia, 187
    and Agamemnon, 116, 120
    and Antigone, 149
    and Argonautica, 170, 172, 174, 175,
        184, 186
    and Bacchae, 164
    and Choephoroe, 122, 123–24, 125, 133
    and Electra (Euripides), 133, 135, 136,
        140
    and Electra (Sophocles), 131, 132–33,
        140
    and Eumenides, 126, 128, 139, 141, 143
    and Hestia, 36
    Homeric Hymn to, 46, 52, 214
    and humans, 35

Hermes
 and Aphrodite, 25, 37
 and *Argonautica*, 177, 179
 and *Choephoroe*, 122, 125
 and *Eumenides*, 126
 Homeric Hymn to, 141
 and *Iliad*, 76, 77–78, 80, 81–82, 84
 illustrations of, 57, 71, 81, 97, 160, 217
 and *Ion*, 149, 151
 and *Odyssey*, 86, 90, 95, 100, 110, 111, 115
 and *Oedipus Tyrannus*, 145
 and Persephone, 45
 and Zeus, 83
 See also Mercury
Hermione, 137, 138, 139
Hero with a Thousand Faces, The (Campbell), 8–9
Hesiod
 Apollonius compared to, 183
 and characterization of gods, 13, 209, 210, 211, 239
 and divinity, 210
 and Hecate, 22, 24
 and Muses, 13, 14–15
 and Perses, 24, 27, 28, 32
 and Prometheus, 3, 17–18
 and role of gods, 30
 Theogony, 13, 14–24, 28, 30, 31–32, 54, 183
 Works and Days, 13, 14, 18–19, 24–29, 30, 54, 167–68
Hesperids, 183
Hesperus, 183
Hestia, 36
Hippolyte, 156
Hippolytus
 and Artemis, 39
 and *Hippolytus*, 156–57, 158, 159, 166, 215
 and honoring gods, 238
Hippolytus (Euripides)
 Bacchae compared to, 161
 and honoring the gods, 156–57, 158, 159, 166, 238
 and memorials, 215
Homer
 and Aeneas, 191
 Aeschylus compared to, 116

authorship of, 54, 67, 86, 242–43n3
characterization of gods, 186, 207, 209, 210, 211, 213, 238, 239
and contrast between gods/human lives, 2
Cypria, 35
Euripides compared to, 133
Hesiod compared to, 13
and *Homeric Hymns*, 35–37, 42–43, 50–52, 141, 191, 192, 214
landscape of, 185
and patriarchy, 8
and power of gods, 206
and religious observance, 237, 238
and Zeus, 169
See also Iliad (Homer); *Odyssey* (Homer)
Homeric Hymns, 35–37, 42–43, 50–52, 141, 191, 192, 214
Hope, 25
Human condition, limitations of, 2, 209
Human gods, 7
Human suffering
 and *Aeneid*, 191, 192
 and *Antigone*, 147, 148
 and Apollo's prophecies, 143
 and *Argonautica*, 178
 and *Bacchae*, 166
 and Heracles, 167
 and *Iliad*, 55, 56, 62, 68, 73, 191
 and *Ion*, 151
 and *Oedipus Tyrannus*, 145–46
 and polytheism, 237
 reasons for, 189
 and resistance to gods' commands, 142
 unavoidability of, 235
Humans
 creation of, 3, 214
 limitations of, 4, 44, 49, 50–51, 54, 55, 58–59, 65, 66, 67, 83, 113, 142, 211, 236
 and prayer, 84
 ties of, 90–91
 understanding by, 83, 113, 116, 138, 146, 235–36
 work of, 14, 25, 28, 29
 See also Atē; Piety; Prayer; Sacrifice
Hylas, 174
Hyllus, 234

Orestes
    and Aegisthus, 87, 115, 116
    and Agamemnon, 114
    and *Agamemnon*, 122
    and *Choephoroe*, 122, 123, 124–25, 136
    and *Electra* (Euripides), 133–36, 139,
        246n17, 247n5
    and *Electra* (Sophocles), 130, 131–32,
        133
    and *Eumenides*, 126–28, 139–40, 143
    illustrations of, 124, 127, 129
    and *Iphigenia Among the Taurians*, 152
    Oedipus compared to, 145
    and *Oresteia*, 130
    and *Orestes*, 133, 137, 138, 139, 140, 143
Orestes (Euripides)
    Antigone compared to, 149
    and chorus, 137–38
    Eumenides compared to, 138–39
    and role of gods, 114, 133, 137–39,
        149, 151
Origen, 5
Orion, 90
Orpheus, 182
Osiris, 216, 232
Ovid
    Ars Amatoria, 214
    and doubts about gods, 237
    Metamorphoses, 214–17, 219–22

Palaephatus, 212
Palaestra, 223
Palinurus, 198, 208
Pallas, 200–201, 202, 206
Pan, 145, 225
Pandareus, 107
Pandarus, 61–62, 63, 64, 76, 202
Pandora
    and creation of women, 25
    and Hesiod, 19
    and Zeus, 32
Pandora's jar
    and hope, 233
    and scattering of good things, 25–26,
        241n3
Paraebius, 175, 248n7
Paris
    and *Aeneid*, 191–92, 198, 202
    and *Agamemnon*, 116, 119, 120

    and Aphrodite, 2, 3, 57, 62
    and Helen, 35, 85
    and *Iliad*, 60, 62, 64, 79, 191
    judgment of, 56, 60, 62, 73, 191–92,
        212, 229
    and *Rhesus*, 152–53, 163
    and *Trojan Women*, 154
Patriarchy, and Homer, 8
Patroclus
    and *Catalogue of Women*, 39
    and *Iliad*, 55, 56, 69, 70, 71–72, 73, 75,
        79, 80, 83
Peace, 20
Peiraeus, 104
Pelasgus, 32
Peleus
    and Achilles, 31, 72, 82, 246n23
    and *Argonautica*, 181–82, 183
    and Thetis, 81, 181–82, 246n23
Pelias, and *Argonautica*, 170, 172, 176,
        178, 179, 182, 184–85, 188, 191, 248n3
Pelops
    and *Catalogue of Women*, 32
    curse on family of, 132, 137
    and Myrtilus, 115, 131, 245n12
Penates, 195
Penelope
    and Odysseus, 7, 85, 90–91
    and *Odyssey*, 88, 89, 90–91, 104, 106–
        10, 111, 112
Peneus, 214, 215
Pentheus, 158–59, 161–63, 165, 166
Periclymenus, 34
Persephone, 43, 45, 46, 99–100, 123
    See also Proserpina
Perses, 24, 27, 28, 31, 32
Persians, 209
Persians (Aeschylus), 114
Persuasion, 25
Phaeacians, 91, 101–2, 105, 109, 111, 112,
        182, 244n8
Phaedra, 156, 157, 166
Phaenops, 72
Phaethon, 181, 216
Phemius, 109
Phineus, 174–75, 186, 195, 248n7
Phlegyas, 199
Phoebe, 125
Phoenix, 66, 72